Learn to Program Using C++ on the Raspberry Pi

An **easy** introduction to programming
for beginners using **Linux** and **GNU C++**

Phil Gardner

Revised Edition

Learn to Program Using C++ on the Raspberry Pi
An easy introduction to programming for beginners using Linux and GNU C++
by Phil Gardner

First published in the UK April 2017 - ISBN 978-0-9957918-0-0
Revised Edition published August 2017 - ISBN 978-0-9957918-1-7 - Catalogued in the UK by Nielsen.
Edited by Louise Carne.
Zero Index Technical Publishing - Uffculme, Devon, United Kingdom.
Enquiries: zero.index.publishing@gmail.com
Selected source-code downloads and further examples: https://program-using-gnu-cpp.blogspot.co.uk

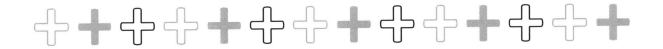

Chapters at a glance

Chapter 1:   **Getting things up and running**   15
Chapter 2:   **Writing some simple code**   39
Chapter 3:   **Data-types and values**   57
Chapter 4:   **Keyboard input and screen output**   87
Chapter 5:   **Using operators to process data**   129
Chapter 6:   **Making decisions**   173
Chapter 7:   **Repetition using loops**   211
Chapter 8:   **Characters and text strings**   241
Chapter 9:   **Arrays of data**   289
Chapter 10: **Functions**   321
Chapter 11: **Files of data**   389
Chapter 12: **Structures, pointers and memory**   435
Chapter 13: **Objects and classes**   481

Appendices: **Useful information**   517
             Answers to exercises   545

Index   571

Table of Contents

INTRODUCTION **11**

About this book 13
About the sample programs 13
Conventions used throughout the book 14
About the author 14

CHAPTER 1: GETTING THINGS UP AND RUNNING **15**

What is C++? 16
What do you need to get started? 18
The GNU g++ compiler 19
An example of some really simple C++ code and what it means 20
High-level and low-level code 20
Typing high-level C++ code into the Nano text editor 21
Compiling and running your first program 23
Using the Geany text editor instead of Nano 28
Finding out whether a program executes successfully 35
Reporting an error – returning a code other than 0 36
Summary of Chapter 1: Getting things up and running 37
Problems and exercises for you to try 38

CHAPTER 2: WRITING SOME SIMPLE CODE **39**

Programs and statements 40
Using a semi-colon ; to mark the end of a statement 41
Compound statements – groups of statements enclosed within { } curly braces 42
Putting comments in your code 43
Expressions 45
Operator symbols 47
How to set out your C++ program code 49
Adding spaces to make individual statements easier to read 51
Summary of Chapter 2: Writing some simple code 54
Problems and exercises for you to try 55

CHAPTER 3: DATA-TYPES AND VALUES **57**

Different types of data 58
Working with integer values: int 60
Working with a smaller range of integer values: short 61
Working with a larger range of integer values: long 61
Overflow – values that are too big for a particular data-type 62
Working with real numbers: float and double 65
Working with character symbols: char 67
Working with literal text: embedding text values in your code 69
Working with named sequences of characters: string 70
Named values: variables and constants 71
Declaring variables in a program 71
Declaring constants in a program 73
Using descriptive names for constants and variables 75
Rules for naming constants and variables 77
Namespaces: avoiding clashes between identifiers with the same name 79
Assigning a value to a constant or variable using = ... 79
Summary of Chapter 3: Data-types and values 85
Problems and exercises for you to try 86

CHAPTER 4: KEYBOARD INPUT AND SCREEN OUTPUT **87**

Output: displaying data on the screen using "channel-out": `cout` 88

Telling the computer to start a new line on the screen using `endl` 90

Using identifiers from a `namespace` in your code...91

Displaying several things at a time using the `<<` output redirection operator......................................92

Displaying the value of a stored variable on the screen 93

Special characters that are denoted by \ backslash...98

Controlling the cursor position on the screen when displaying values 108

Formatting values to change the way they are displayed...110

Input: getting a value into the computer from the keyboard using `cin` 115

Getting a whole line of text from the keyboard, including spaces 117

Clearing unwanted characters from `cin` 120

Validating numbers entered using the keyboard 123

Summary of Chapter 4: Keyboard input and screen output 127

Problems and exercises for you to try 128

CHAPTER 5: USING OPERATORS TO PROCESS DATA **129**

Changing the value of variables with the `++` increment and `--` decrement operators 130

Different ways to use `++` increment and `--` decrement 131

The `+=` "add amount" and `-=` "subtract amount" operators 132

Multiplying numbers using the `*` operator...134

Dividing numbers using the `/` operator..136

The problem of attempting to divide a number by zero 138

Mixing different data-types during division 139

The results of floating point division 140

Finding a remainder using the `%` modulus operator 142

Using random numbers to produce unpredictable behaviour in a program..143

Making the choices more random using a "seed" 144

Using `%` modulus to pick a random number within a certain range 145

Exponentiation: Raising a number to a power using the `pow()` function...147

Operator precedence – the order in which the computer carries out operations 148

Using `( )` brackets in an expression to change how expressions are evaluated 150

Finding the minimum or maximum of two values using `min()` and `max()` 151

Casts – converting between data-types 154

Using bit-wise operators to perform logical operations 157

The bit-wise `~` NOT operator...157

The bit-wise `|` OR operator..160

The bit-wise `&` AND operator...161

The bit-wise `^` XOR operator...162

Logical shifts that "slide" patterns of bits to the left or right..165

Summary of Chapter 5: Using operators to process data 170

Problems and exercises for you to try..171

CHAPTER 6: MAKING DECISIONS **173**

Making simple decisions using `if`..174

Simple decisions that use relational operators `<` `<=` `>` `>=` `==`..175

Determining whether two values are the same with the `==` equivalence operator 176

Comparing `string` values...177

Checking that all parts of an expression are `true` using the logical `and` operator 177

Determining whether two values are different using the `!=` non-equivalence operator......................181

More complex decisions 183

Checking that at least one part of an expression is `true` with the logical `or` operator 186

Setting Boolean variables using the result of a relational expression...193

Combining several `if` decisions together to deal with more than two outcomes..................................194

Finding the opposite of a value or expression using the `!` NOT operator..196

Adding extra `( )` brackets around parts of expressions to ensure the correct result............................197

Using a `switch` statement when there are many possible outcomes for a decision 200

Using the `?` conditional operator to decide between two possible values 206

Summary of Chapter 6: Making decisions..209

Problems and exercises for you to try..210

CHAPTER 7: REPETITION USING LOOPS **211**

A repetitive sequence of instructions... 212

Repeatedly executing the same code one or more times using a `do-while` loop......................... 213

Using a `do-while` loop to make choices from a menu of options... 215

Repeatedly executing some code `while` an expression/condition is true...................................... 216

A `for` loop that executes a statement several times 219

Increasing or decreasing the value of a controlling variable 221

Using the value of a `for` loop variable as part of a calculation 222

Working directly with a range of characters in a loop 225

Nesting: putting a loop within another loop 226

Adding extra { } curly braces to make your code more readable... 229

Creating and using variables that are not local to a `for` statement... 231

Global variables 232

Infinite loops – programs that go on forever without ever stopping 233

Forcing a loop to terminate using `break` 235

Counting things that happen... 236

Summary of Chapter 7: Repetition using loops 238

Problems and exercises for you to try.. 239

CHAPTER 8: CHARACTERS AND TEXT STRINGS **241**

Working with single characters.. 242

Converting between ASCII character codes and character symbols 243

Arithmetic operations on `char` values 244

Choosing character symbols at random 245

Examining and processing individual characters that are part of a `string` value.......................... 246

Finding whether a character is a numeric digit, letter of the alphabet, or other symbol 247

Finding the number of characters in a `string` value using the `length()` function........................ 249

Detecting different kinds of characters in a `string` value... 254

Replacing individual characters in a `string` value 258

Determining whether two `string` values are the same 259

Appending – joining `string` values together 261

Joining `string` values using the `append()` function... 267

Detecting a pattern of characters - finding whether a `string` contains a sub-string...................... 271

Finding more than one occurrence of a sub-string in a `string` value 273

Adding text characters inside a `string` value using the `insert()` function................................... 274

Manually copying characters from one `string` to another 275

Copying part of a `string` value using the `substr()` function 276

Erasing and replacing parts of a `string` value 278

Replacing part of a `string` using the `replace()` function.. 280

Finding characters in a `string` that are part of a certain set 282

Finding characters in a `string` that are not in a particular set 283

Splitting a `string` value into individual tokens 284

Swapping the values of two `string` variables around 285

Summary of Chapter 8: Characters and text strings 287

Problems and exercises for you to try.. 288

CHAPTER 9: ARRAYS OF DATA.. **289**

Working with several data values that have the same data-type 290

What is an array?.. 290

Creating a simple array of values 291

Using index numbers to refer to the values in an array 291

Accessing an individual value from an array... 292

Using a loop to efficiently access more than one value in an array 293

Going too far: attempting to use an index that is out-of-bounds 297

Recording raw data from user inputs using arrays 299

Categorising or counting up user inputs using arrays.. 301

Searching through an array of data values to find what you want: a linear search......................... 302

Searching through an array of data values to find a partial match 304

How to pick something at random from an array of values.. 306

Matching related items from more than one array 308

Inserting items of data into an array at a particular point 311

Multi-dimensional arrays 314
Creating and accessing a two-dimensional array 315
Summary of Chapter 9: Arrays of data 319
Problems and exercises for you to try 320

CHAPTER 10: FUNCTIONS **321**

What are functions? 322
Creating a function in C++ 323
Function names 324
Arguments – input values for a function 324
Functions that do not take any arguments as input 325
The body and return value of a function 325
Calling a function 327
How a call to a function affects the flow-of-execution within your program................... 328
Making use of a result that gets returned from a call to a function............................... 330
A function that accepts more than one argument as input 344
Functions that do not return any result 347
More about function arguments – copies of values 351
Functions that operate directly on their input data using & references to values 352
Passing an array as an input to a function.. 353
Deciding where to put functions in your code... 361
Declaring a function: telling the compiler that a function will exist later in your code 362
Creating your own re-usable library of useful functions... 364
Inline functions 366
Recursive functions: functions that call themselves 368
Summary of Chapter 10: Functions 386
Problems and exercises for you to try 387

CHAPTER 11: FILES OF DATA.. **389**

Why do we need to use files? 390
Using file streams to read and write data 390
Using an output stream to create a file of text.. 392
Appending data on to the end of an existing file 396
Detecting whether a file exists 398
Using an input stream to read text in from a file... 400
Processing data as it is read in from an input stream 403
Using an array to store and process the data from a file 409
Reading from files that contain columns of tab-delimited data 416
Reading from files that contain comma-separated data values 420
Choosing files: typing in the filename for the file that you want to use 423
Working with more than one file at the same time... 424
Converting between text and numeric values using `stringstream` 426
Summary of Chapter 11: Files of data 432
Problems and exercises for you to try 433

CHAPTER 12: STRUCTURES, POINTERS AND MEMORY **435**

Creating structures to group data values together... 436
Using a structure to create your own data-type... 437
Arrays of structures 437
Static and dynamic data.. 445
Memory locations and addresses 446
References: obtaining the memory address of a data value.. 448
Pointers 450
Accessing data from a pointer using the * de-reference operator................................... 451
Null pointers 454
Using pointers to create and access dynamic data stored on the heap........................... 455
Building your own data-structures.. 462
Recycling memory once you have finished using your dynamic data 470
Summary of Chapter 12: Structures, pointers and memory 478
Problems and exercises for you to try.. 479

CHAPTER 13: OBJECTS AND CLASSES **481**

Packaging up related data items 482
Packaging data and functions together in a class 484
Declaring the data and member functions that a class contains 485
The difference between `private` and `public` members of a class.. 486
Defining the body of a member function for a class... 488
Constructors: functions that are called when an instance of a class is created 488
The need for an empty constructor function 492
Creating objects dynamically on the heap.. 495
Overloading operators 501
Inheritance – creating new classes that are based on other existing classes 503
Declaring your classes using `.h` header files 510
Summary of Chapter 13: Objects and classes.. 514
Problems and exercises for you to try 515

USEFUL INFORMATION **517**

The ASCII character set and character codes... 518
C++ reserved words 519
Special symbols used in C++ and what they mean 520
Operators and their precedence 521
Data-types and ranges of values 522
Header files for C++ and C library functions that you can include in your programs.................... 523
Escape-sequences to control the colour of text on the screen 524
Finding and correcting common mistakes in your C++ source-code 525
Stages that g++ goes through when translating C++ source-code into an executable 530
Useful compiler options for g++ 531
Making it easier to run your executables at the command-line 532
Viewing assembly language that the compiler produces... 534
Viewing the machine code instructions of your executable 536
Useful Linux commands 538
Glossary of useful terms... 539
How to download the software that you need... 542
Useful web-links.. 543

ANSWERS TO EXERCISES **545**

Chapter 1: Getting things up and running 546
Chapter 2: Writing some simple code 546
Chapter 3: Data-types and values 546
Chapter 4: Keyboard input and screen output 546
Chapter 5: Using operators to process data 548
Chapter 6: Making decisions 549
Chapter 7: Repetition using loops 550
Chapter 8: Characters and text strings 552
Chapter 9: Arrays of data 554
Chapter 10: Functions... 556
Chapter 11: Files of data 558
Chapter 12: Structures, pointers and memory 561
Chapter 13: Objects and classes.. 562

INDEX.. **571**

Introduction

About this book

This book has been written for anyone that wants to try writing simple C++ programs on the Raspberry Pi™, including those that are completely new to computer programming. It covers many important parts of the C++ programming language so that you can gain enough confidence to write your own useful programs. It also introduces you to ideas and techniques that apply to writing programs in general, regardless of the languages that you choose to use in future.

Many people are already aware that the Pi can be used to create Scratch and Python programs, or that it can interface with electronic components. Relatively few people though realise that the Pi can be used to write programs using GNU C++, despite C++ being a widely-used and powerful programming language in the world of computing. There are many other C++ books available, but only a handful of them specifically cover GNU C++ for Linux®. It's also true to say that many programming books for the Pi aimed at beginners use Python instead.

Programming books can sometimes be a little difficult to wade through due to their sheer size and detailed nature. C++ in particular has a reputation for being rather technical, but don't let that put you off. Many books also attempt to cover every single part of the language and the many ways in which features can be used, including a lot of material that novices aren't ready to tackle. It can often be difficult to separate out what is relevant to the beginner and what is intended for more advanced programmers. This book concentrates on the most important and accessible C++ features that will let the beginner experiment with and create their own code. It does not attempt to cover the whole C++ language in minute detail.

Explanations are short and to the point, using plain English to make them accessible to all – you don't need to be a university student to understand what is going on. Standard terminology is introduced gradually to help you get into good habits. As you progress and grow in confidence, you should become ready to move on to more advanced topics that are outside the scope of this book.

I have included more than 200 programs for you to try, along with diagrams, explanations and some important computing theory. The source code for some of these programs can be downloaded from the accompanying blog:
https://program-using-gnu-cpp.blogspot.co.uk

You will also find useful technical information in the appendices at the back of the book that you can refer to when writing your own code.

Good luck and happy reading.
Phil Gardner - August 2017.

About the sample programs

Each one of the sample programs in this book has been tested to ensure that it compiles and executes without problems. You should find that the code is bug-free and easy to follow, with explanations to highlight the important ideas and techniques. Feel free to try out as many of the examples as you can on your own Pi. As you become more confident creating, compiling and testing programs, you can try making your own custom modifications and tweaks to them. Modifying other people's code is a good way to learn how things work. When you have mastered everything that we cover, you should be ready to move on to the more advanced features that C++ has to offer, or to transfer what you have learnt to other programming languages.

The programs have been tested on all of the different Raspberry Pi models available at the time of writing (specifically, these are the Model A, B, B+, A+, 2, 3 and Zero). Whilst the book has been specifically written for people that have a Raspberry Pi computer with Debian® or Raspbian® Linux as its operating system, the sample programs are written using a standard version of C++ (ANSI/ISO C++). This means that they can be used on many other computers and operating systems with either little or no modification to them. They have been tested on PC computers using the Debian and Ubuntu® Linux operating systems, as well on Apple Macintosh computers using various versions of MacOS®. When using GNU C++ on all of these setups, no modifications were necessary to the C++ programs – they all worked as they would on a Pi.

The only disadvantage that I have found when working with a PC is that many Linux varieties do not install the GNU Compiler Collection as standard. This means that it is up to you to install the compiler that lets you build your C++ programs, although this is very quick and easy to do. For Apple Macintosh users, Apple offer the LLVM compiler as part of the popular Xcode® software development kit. Alternatively, the GNU Compiler Collection can be downloaded for the Macintosh for free.

For instructions on how to install the GNU Compiler Collection (GCC) and the other simple tools that are used throughout the book, see the *"How to install software that you need"* section in the Appendices section.

Conventions used throughout the book

You will notice that program statements (the parts of the C++ program that do the work and that get executed by the computer) are written in bold type, using the fixed-width Courier New font:

```
score = time * 100;
```

Most programming languages allow programmers to include explanatory comments in their program code. All of the programs featured in this book contain comments that should be helpful in explaining what individual parts of the code do.

Comments and explanations throughout the book are presented using normal weight, rather than in bold:

```
// Calculate final score using the time left
```

As you type in the program code from each example, you are welcome to include or omit the comments as you see fit.

In a few places, statements are shown using normal weight with parts in bold or underlined:

```
int finalScore = flagsCollected + timeLeftOver;
```

These are to highlight the most important parts of a particular statement that might otherwise be missed by the reader.

Notice also that many items, including those that appear inside a pair of ( ) round-brackets, also feature some additional spacing:

```
int result = score + ( timeLeft * 10 ) - ( collisions * 50 ) + levelBonus;
```

...as opposed to:

```
int result=score+(timeLeft*10)-(collisions*50)+levelBonus;
```

This is to help the reader separate out the individual parts of a statement, rather than making the program code denser and potentially more difficult to understand for the beginner. More experienced programmers may well choose to leave out the extra spaces when typing in their program code.

About the author

Phil Gardner began programming in 1981 using BASIC on a Sinclair ZX81 microcomputer. This eventually led him to study Computer Science at the University of Exeter, where much of his programming work was carried out using the UNIX® operating-system. After graduating he went on to create analytical software for oil and gas exploration, crafting thousands of lines of C++ source-code. This software is now used worldwide by a large number of exploration companies and lives on through the efforts of a whole team of programmers. Following a move into teaching, Phil began using Raspberry Pi computers and GNU C++ in the classroom. He lives and works in Devon.

Chapter 1:

Getting things up and running

What is C++?

Modern electronic computers are extremely complex devices that can do amazing things, but every computer has something in common: they all need to follow a program - a sequence of very clear instructions that will tell them what to do. Unfortunately, even though the first electronic computers were invented in the 1940s and 1950s, they still can't understand the everyday language that we use when speaking, listening, reading and writing. Everyday "**natural languages**" that humans use are too awkward or ambiguous for most computers to work with when solving problems.

When we want to tell a computer to do something for us, we write instructions using a "**programming language**". These are simpler and more precise than the languages that humans use in their everyday lives. Many programming languages require you to write code that tells the computer **precisely** how to achieve something in a step-by-step manner. These are called "**procedural**" programming languages and C++ is one of the most popular among them. C++ lets you write programs that are very efficient and that will be executed **really** fast – ideal for writing complex software such as operating systems, video games or programs that use a graphical user interface. A lot of the well-known software that you use on your computer was created using C++ or similar languages.

Why learn C++?

Here are a few good reasons to try writing your programs in C++:

It's fast. Code written using C++ is often much faster than many other programming languages, such as Python or BASIC. This is partly because C++ programs only need to be "**compiled**" once to create machine code that the computer's processor can execute. The compiled program can then be executed as many times as you like. Unfortunately, programs written using "**interpreted**" languages undergo their translation into simpler code one piece at a time. For interpreted programs, this translation is carried out **every single time** that you execute them – a process that slows their execution down.

It's efficient. You can write very small, efficient programs to solve problems. You can often make them much shorter than programs written in other programming languages, especially once you start to use libraries of code that other people have previously written. Finished executable programs made using C++ can be very compact, taking up very little space in the computer's memory or on storage devices.

It's packed full of useful features. The C++ language includes many features that make it really easy to solve all kinds of problems. You can easily split large programs into smaller, more understandable parts and even re-use your code again in other programs. C++ also lets you work in some very clever ways, allowing you to solve problems using advanced ideas such as "**object-orientation**" and "**recursion**".

It's everywhere. C++ is widely used and you can write code on many different kinds of computers. Often, you can write a C++ program on one kind of computer, then compile and run the same program on another (we call this "**source-code portability**").

It's strangely familiar. C++ code often looks quite a bit like code written using other programming languages, such as C# or JavaScript. Once you have worked with one of these programming languages, learning to write code using others can be a lot easier. They share lots of the same words and symbols, using what we call "**C-like syntax**", which is derived from the older "C" programming language.

It's often free. Once upon a time, you would need to **buy** a C++ compiler, perhaps costing between £50 and £400. The GNU C++ compiler is absolutely free to obtain and use. Lots of other useful tools that help you create C++ programs are also free.

It's already on your Raspberry Pi computer. Most Pi owners don't realise that the C++ tools are already installed on their machine. If you work with the desktop GUI, you have probably seen icons for Scratch and Python, but there aren't any icons for C++. However, all you need is a text editor to type in your code, and a command-line prompt so that you can tell the computer to compile your program or to activate other tools. PC users running either Linux or Windows should also be able to download the GNU C++ tools from the Internet for free.

Different kinds of C++

Most different kinds of computer have their own C++ compiler. Some computers even have several to choose from. These C++ compilers tend to have their own custom features and differences - there is not just one kind of C++.

Years ago, as different varieties of C++ began to emerge, international standards for the language were drawn up. These C++ standards get updated from time to time, but only after much discussion about each possible improvement by some very knowledgeable people. This means that there is more than one version of the C++ standard that compilers can adhere to.

The original standard for C++ was produced by the American National Standards Institute (**ANSI**), and is known as "**ANSI C++**". More recently, the standards for C++ are set and agreed by the International Standards Organisation (**ISO**). Most versions of the C++ language attempt to conform to these standards as far as possible, although there are often slight differences between them. Whatever kind of computer you use and version of C++ you learn, the core features tend to be very similar - learn one version of C++ and you can understand many of the others. Most C++ compilers tend to comply broadly with these standards, and you can even choose which one you want your compiler to follow. At the time of writing, the most recently agreed update of the ISO standard is **ISO C++ 14** (which was finalised in 2014). Another emerging standard is C++ 17, although some of the details of this have not yet been finalized.

GNU C++ on the Raspberry Pi

Computers such as the Raspberry Pi, which use Linux as their operating system, depend on a lot of free software that was produced as part of the **GNU Open-Source project**. This project encourages the use of software that doesn't cost you anything to purchase and that can be used without many of the restrictions of commercially available software.

Linux computers can freely use the **GNU C++ compiler**. This lets you create standard ISO C++ programs for your computer. The most recent GNU C++ compiler (part of **GCC 6.3**, the **GNU Compiler Collection**, released December 2016) has support for **ISO C++ 14**, although many Raspberry Pi machines still use an older version of the GNU C++ compiler which by default (unless you tell it to do otherwise) will follow the **ISO C++ 98** standard.

By "freely use", I mean that anyone can download the GNU C++ compiler for free and use it in any way that they see fit (within reason and as long as they don't break any laws with the kind of programs that they write). There are fewer restrictions when using GNU software than with software that you might have otherwise paid for.

All of the sample programs in this book were written on a Raspberry Pi and tested using the GNU C++ compiler. By default, when Linux was installed on your Pi, this GNU compiler collection was also included, so you should find that you already have a C++ compiler on your Pi, ready to compile your first program. It shouldn't really matter how old or how new your Raspberry Pi is – whatever your Pi model and whatever the version of your GNU C++ compiler, the programs should all work without errors. Any differences between older and newer versions of the GNU C++ compiler should not affect the source-code included here as it only requires the core features of the C++ 98 standard, rather than newer features from later standards.

For more details about how GCC handles the different versions of C++ and the full list of terms and conditions for using it, go to **https://gcc.gnu.org/onlinedocs/libstdc++/index.html** on the web.

C++ on other computers

You may have heard of languages that have similar names to C++, such as Microsoft C#, C.net and Visual C++ for the PC, or Objective-C for the Apple Macintosh. Whilst there are differences between the standard C++ used in this book and other versions of C++, what you learn here should also give you a really good grounding for learning and working with these other languages and platforms because they all have quite a lot in common. Most people find that once they have learnt some C++, learning other programming languages becomes a lot easier. C# is actually based on the Java programming language, rather than C or C++, although there are still some similarities between C# and C++.

What do you need to get started?

The example programs in this book were made using a **Raspberry Pi** computer, but you can use other kinds of computer if you prefer, including a **PC** running a version of the Linux operating system, or an **Apple Macintosh** computer running MacOS.

There are several different Raspberry Pi models to choose from, but it doesn't matter which one you have. The programs in this book and the tools that you will need to make them should work on any Pi or any other kind of computer that can run Linux and GNU C++.

For Pi users, it is assumed that most people will have either **Debian** or **Raspbian** versions of the Linux operating system installed on their machine. This comes set up with the all of the basic tools that you need to create and work with C++ programs. Although some people have successfully used these tools with other operating systems on the Pi, such as **RISC OS**, there are a few differences that may make things a little more difficult for beginners. PC users should be able to run all of the programs under Ubuntu Linux.

It is possible to compile and run GNU C++ programs on a Windows PC using a compiler such as **MinGW**. Unfortunately, MinGW handles random number generation slightly differently and does not allow your programs to display text using different colours on the screen in the same way as the Pi. This means that you will find that some of the programs in the book do not work as on a Windows PC without a little modification to the code.

What you will need to type in C++ source-code

You will need a **text editor**. This is a program that lets you type in C++ source-code programs and save them as files. One of the most popular and easy to use text editors called **Nano** should already be installed on your Pi. Although it is fast and easy to use for very simple editing from the command line, Nano lacks many features that you might be used to, such as cut, copy, paste and undo. You can use a different editor if you prefer.

In particular, I recommend that you download and use the **Geany** text editor if you do not already have this installed on your Pi. Geany has a graphical user-interface and several helpful features that can make your coding easier.

What you will need to compile C++ source-code into executable programs

You also need a C++ **compiler**. This is a program that breaks your C++ source-code down into simple **machine-code instructions** that can be executed by the processor of your Raspberry Pi.

Debian Linux on the Raspberry Pi includes a set of several compilers called **GCC** - the **"GNU Compiler Collection"**. GCC includes the **GNU C++ compiler**, which is called **g++**.

All of this software is free to download and use on your computer, thanks to the **GNU Open Software Foundation**. You don't need to go out and buy these developer tools to start programming in C++.

The GNU g++ compiler

The compiler that we will be using is called the GNU **g++ compiler** and it is just one of the compilers on your Linux system.

Checking whether you have the GNU g++ compiler on your Pi

How do you know if you have the g++ compiler on your system? You can double-check by typing in the following command at the Linux command-prompt:

```
ls /usr/bin/g++
```

If you have the compiler collection installed, then you should see the following result on your screen:

```
/usr/bin/g++
```

But if you don't have it, you will see the following error:

```
ls: cannot access /usr/bin/g++: No such file or directory
```

You won't be able to compile your C++ code unless you have the g++ compiler. Look in the *"How to install software that you need"* section in the Appendices in the back of this book if you find that you haven't got the GNU compiler collection.

You will find out more about how g++ actually compiles a program in the following sections.

Checking whether the GNU g++ compiler on your Pi is up to date

If you really want to know, you can check which **version** of the g++ compiler you have by typing:

```
g++ -v
```

This will display quite a few lines of information about your compiler and the settings that it uses, but the last line should tell you the version of GCC that you have. Don't worry the numbers are slightly different on your machine.

For instance, on an older Raspberry Pi B+ model, you might see:

```
gcc version 4.6.3 (Debian 4.6.3-14+rpi1)
```

A newer Raspberry Pi 2 model with the newer Raspbian operating system might show something more like this:

```
gcc version 4.9.2 (Raspbian 4.9.2-10)
```

All or most of the programs in this book should still work for you, unless the compiler on your computer is really, and I mean **really,** old.

An example of some really simple C++ code and what it means

Let's take a look at a **very** simple C++ program. In fact, it is the smallest possible program that you can write using C++:

```
main()
{
    // Extremely simple C++ program
}
```

Nearly every C++ program ever written is bigger and more useful than the example above. This is the smallest possible C++ program that you can successfully compile and run. Nearly all C++ programs that you will ever write need to have a section called `main()` to show the computer where execution should begin.

The `( )` brackets are used to give the program any special information that it needs to start running, to control what it should do. Since this program does not need to be given anything special to work with, the `( )` brackets are empty for now. You will find out how to use them in other ways later on.

The special `{ }` *curly brackets* or *curly braces* mark the start and finish of the main **block** of C++ code. Inside these is where you put C++ instructions for the computer to carry out.

The line that begins with `//` is not actually an instruction for the computer to carry out – it is a **comment** for a human being to read. It tells us something about the program and helps us to understand how the code works. The computer always ignores comments and does not try to execute them. You'll find out more about comments in *"Chapter 2: Writing some simple code"*.

The computer will always execute any instructions that are inside the `{ }` curly braces of the `main()` section. In this program, there isn't anything in the `{ }` section apart from the ignorable `//` comment, so as soon as the program begins running, it finds it has nothing to do and finishes immediately.

High-level and low-level code

How do you actually make the computer **carry out** these program instructions? How do you get the computer to "**run-through**" or "**execute**" a program on your computer? They need to be **compiled** – broken down and translated into something much simpler for the computer's central processing unit (CPU) to execute.

The programs that we write in C++ are called **source-code** programs. Human programmers can often understand what C++ programs do and how they work just by reading them. A well-written program can sometimes even look a little bit like English, and you will learn to write high-level code that people can understand quite easily. We say that these kinds of programs are written in a **high-level language** – they can easily be understood by a human.

Unfortunately, a high-level C++ program is still too complicated for your computer's circuitry to execute straight away. Computers are not actually clever, they only do extremely simple things, but they do them very, very fast. Your program needs to be made into **really** simple instructions, called **low-level code**, for the processor to be able to carry it out.

Like other computers, the Raspberry Pi can only execute **machine code** instructions. They are the simplest possible instructions that the computer can work with. Each binary machine code instruction is composed of the symbols 0 and 1. The instruction usually contains two parts: an **operation code** or "op-code", as well as some data to operate on, or "**operand**" data. An op-code tells the computer's processor (the **CPU**) to activate a particular part of its electronic circuitry to make something useful happen, such as adding, subtracting, or comparing two data values to determine whether they are the same.

This means that something needs to be done to your C++ source-code before you can execute it on the Pi. It needs to be **changed** or "**translated**" from high-level code, into extremely simple low-level code. This is done by a special kind of computer program, the **compiler**. When we ask the compiler to change the high-level source-code into something simpler that the computer can run, this is called "**compilation**".

Typing high-level C++ code into the Nano text editor

Now let's try making our first C++ program on your Raspberry Pi. First of all, we will need to type the source-code into a **text editor**, such as **Nano**, to create a C++ file. As already mentioned, Nano is a popular and easy-to-use text editor that comes with many versions of Linux, including Debian and Raspbian on the Pi.

To start the Nano text editor, go to the command-line and type:

```
nano first.cpp
```

This makes a new empty file with the filename *"**first.cpp**"* in whatever directory you are currently working in. It is very unlikely, but if you find that Nano is not installed on your computer, you will see an error message. Take a look at *"**How to install software that you need**"* in the Appendices at the back of this book for simple instructions that tell you how to install Nano on your computer.

Assuming that everything worked, you should now have an empty Nano screen, ready for typing in some code:

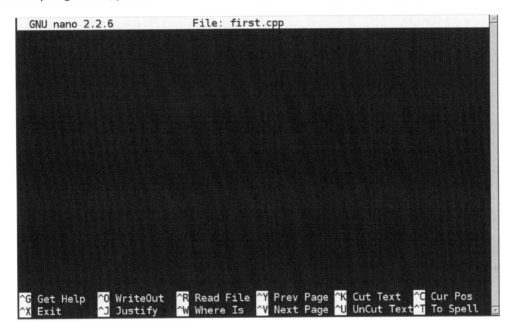

Type in the C++ code that you see in the white box below, exactly as you see it, but don't type in *"**Example 1.1 – first.cpp**"* or the suggested filename that you see in the black stripe. A word of warning, make sure that you type **"main"** using lower-case letters - **don't** use capitals. This matters in C++ as upper-case and lower-case letters are considered to be different things.

Example 1.1 – *first.cpp*

```
main()
{
  // Extremely simple C++ program
}
```

You can use the *tab* key on your keyboard or press the *space-bar* twice to **indent** a line of text, such the text between the { } braces. Indenting text can make your program code easier to read and to understand how the program works.

You should see that some parts of the code change colour. This is because Nano knows that you are writing a C++ program. You told it this when you chose to create a file with a name that ends in "*.cpp*". As you type, it looks for C++ words and symbols that it recognises. Note that Nano can also recognise lots of other programming languages, not just C++.

Here's what the same code looks like on my screen after I have typed it in:

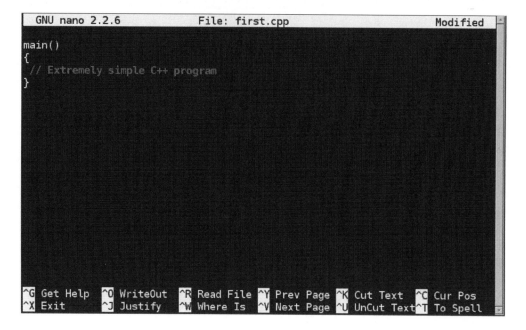

The title-bar of the Nano window tells you the name of the file that you are working on ("***first.cpp***") and warns you that you have made changes to the file that have not yet been saved (it displays "***Modified***" in the top-right corner).

Unlike the first program in the previous section, this program actually does something, although it is still very simple.

You now need to save your finished C++ code before you can try running it. If you are using Nano as your text editor, you can press ***Ctrl O*** to save the file. Then press ***Ctrl X*** to exit Nano. The Nano text editor will close and you should be returned to the command-line prompt. We are now ready to make the computer carry out your program instructions.

Some useful keys in the Nano text editor

How do you know which keys to press to make Nano do things? They are written at the bottom of the screen.

Most of the time, you only need to remember:

Ctrl O saves your text, it writes it <u>o</u>ut to your file.

Ctrl X e<u>x</u>its Nano

To fix mistakes or move lines of text around:

Ctrl K cuts the current line out of the text, remembering it for later use.

Ctrl U <u>u</u>n-cuts the line, placing it at the current cursor location. This is a bit like "paste" in other programs.

It's worth noting that Nano does not let you use the mouse to move around your text, even if you are working on the Linux desktop with Nano running in a "**terminal**" window. You will need to use the arrow and **PageUp/PageDown** keys to move around your program code. If you find Nano difficult to work with, you are welcome to try the Geany editor, which not only lets you use the mouse, but also allows you to cut, copy, paste and undo text. See the *"**How to install software that you need**"* section in the Appendices at the back of this book for details of how to install Geany.

Compiling and running your first program

Hopefully you didn't make any mistakes when you typed the program code in. Now we can try to get the computer to turn it into low-level code and then execute it.

Remember from earlier in this section that your Raspberry Pi will use a compiler to turn your C++ source-code into a machine code executable. The diagram below is a very simple illustration of what happens:

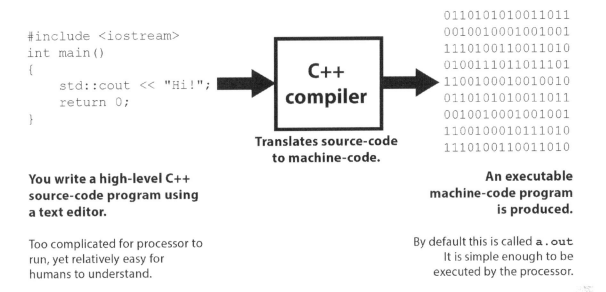

```
#include <iostream>
int main()
{
    std::cout << "Hi!";
    return 0;
}
```

C++ compiler

Translates source-code to machine-code.

```
0110101010011011
0010010001001001
1110100110011010
0100111011011101
1100100010010010
0110101010011011
0010010001001001
1100100010111010
1110100110011010
```

You write a high-level C++ source-code program using a text editor.

Too complicated for processor to run, yet relatively easy for humans to understand.

An executable machine-code program is produced.

By default this is called `a.out`
It is simple enough to be executed by the processor.

Compiling your C++ source-code

First of all we need to compile your high-level C++ program to create a low-level executable file. We will use the **GNU g++ compiler** to do this. All that you need to do is start the g++ compiler, telling it the name of the C++ source-code file that you want it to compile.

From the command-line prompt, compile your source-code program like this:

```
g++ first.cpp
```

Because you gave your program a filename that ends in "*.cpp*", the compiler knows that it is supposed to be working with a C++ program. It will use the **rules** of the C++ language, called the "**syntax**", to make sure that your program makes sense and that you have written it correctly.

Although you won't see anything while your program is being compiled, behind the scenes an awful lot is happening. Each part of your C++ source-code is being broken down into much simpler low-level code. Normally, the compiler does not tell you exactly what it is doing or how far it has got while it is busy, although as you'll see later, you can ask it to provide you with more information if you want it.

Once it has compiled successfully, a new executable program should exist on your computer, called "*a.out*". This program is made up of really simple low-level instructions, called **machine code**. Note that "*a.out*" is the standard name that a new executable program is given, unless you choose to give it a different name.

You can check that the new executable program has been created by typing the following command from the Linux command prompt:

```
ls -l a.out
```

You should see that the "*a.out*" file now exists in your current working directory, ready to be executed.

Below you can see a screenshot of what happened on my Raspberry Pi:

```
pi@eno ~ $ ls -l a.out
-rwxr-xr-x 1 pi pi 5096 Aug 25 12:17 a.out
pi@eno ~
```

Note that in the screenshot I am logged in as the user "**pi**" and that my machine has the host name "**eno**", thus "**pi@eno**" effectively means "*user **pi**, working on the computer called **eno***".

From the above results of the `ls` command we can see the following information about the file called "*a.out*":

It is an **executable** program. The "**x**" in "**-rwxr-xr-x**" part denotes this.

It has been created by user "**pi**" who has their own group of users, also called "**pi**".

The size of the program is **5096** bytes.

It was made at **12:17** on **August 25th**.

Running the executable program

To run the new executable program, type:

```
./a.out
```

This means:

*"in the current directory, run the program called **a.out**"*.

You should then be returned to the command prompt, as shown below:

```
pi@eno ~ $ ./a.out
pi@eno ~
```

When you run the finished ***a.out*** program, it does not actually appear to do anything! It is the smallest and simplest possible program that you can compile using C++. It does not display anything on the screen or ask you to type anything in. It simply starts and then stops almost immediately in a split-second. The next few programs that we create will be more useful than this.

When typing in C++ code for a program, it is very important not to make spelling mistakes. You must also use special symbols correctly, otherwise the compiler will not be able to break your code down into simple instructions that the computer can execute.

When you try to compile your program, the C++ compiler will check your code **very** carefully for such problems.

If the compiler finds something wrong with your program code, it will display one or more **error messages** on the screen. These are used to find what the problems are. You will learn to understand what they mean and how they can help your track down problems in your code.

Here's an example of a simple mistake in my code:

```
main()
{
    Extremely simple C++ program
}
```

In the above example, I have "accidentally" missed out the `//` at the start of the comment. When I try to compile this C++ code, the compiler will complain that it does not recognise the word "**Extremely**". It does not know what to do with it.

Below you can see the error message that the g++ compiler displays:

```
pi@eno ~ $ g++ first.cpp
first.cpp: In function 'int main()':
first.cpp:3:3: error: 'Extremely' was not declared in this scope
first.cpp:3:13: error: expected ';' before 'simple'
pi@eno ~
```

You would need to open the C++ source-code in a text editor, find where the problem is and edit the code. You would then need to save your changed code and try compiling it again using g++, looking out for any new error messages.

We can see from the information above that the problem is somewhere in the "**int main()**" section of our program. The error messages give us more specific information about where to start looking in our source-code.

The first error message says:

```
first.cpp:3:3: error: 'Extremely' was not declared in this scope
```

This tells us to look in the file "*first.cpp*", on line **3** of the program, **3** places along from the start of the line. This is the exact place where the problem has been detected.

All you need to do is put the missing "**//**" before the word "**Extremely**" to make it into a comment that the compiler will ignore. In fact, both error messages are caused by the same problem - there is only one change to make to the code to fix the errors.

You can now save and recompile your code, just as before. Notice that this time the program should compile without errors. Once it has compiled you should see the command prompt once again.

Now let's try making something slightly more useful. We will make a program to display a message on the screen.

Try creating a new program in Nano:

```
nano better.cpp
```

Type in the code that you see below, then save it:

Example 1.2 – *better.cpp*

```
#include <iostream>      // Program will display some text on the screen as output

main()
{
    // Display a simple message on the screen

    std::cout << "Hello from C++" << std::endl;

}
```

Once you have saved the code (by pressing **Ctrl O**), you can exit Nano (press **Ctrl X**) and then compile the program:

```
g++ better.cpp
```

A new "***a.out***" file will then be created, which you can run:

```
./a.out
```

You should see something like this on your screen:

```
pi@eno ~ $ g++ better.cpp
pi@eno ~ $ ./a.out
Hello from C++
pi@eno ~ $
```

Be aware that your previous "***a.out***" file has been overwritten by the new executable file. You will find out how to solve this problem in the next section.

Unless you tell the g++ compiler what you want the compiled low-level program to be called, it will always name the new executable file as "**a.out**". If you already have a file with this name in the directory that you are working in, this will get over-written by the new executable – you will lose your old file!

Luckily, you can tell the g++ compiler to use a different name for your executable instead. Indeed this is usually more helpful to you as it may be difficult to remember what a particular executable file actually does - the name "**a.out**" does not offer many clues.

When you type the **g++** command to run the compiler, you simply need to add a few extra details. The special **-o** option tells the compiler to **o**utput the new executable using a filename of your choice. You must also tell it what you want the executable to be called, such as "*sayhello*".

To re-compile the previous program and give it a better name than "*a.out*", you can type:

```
g++ -o sayhello better.cpp
```

g++	is the name of the GNU C++ compiler that you are using.
-o	means "call the new file something else instead of *a.out*".
sayhello	will be the name of the new executable that will be created.
better.cpp	is the file that holds the high-level C++ source-code that is to be compiled.

Assuming that your code did not contain any errors, you should now have a new executable file called "**sayhello**".

To run the new executable, type:

```
./sayhello
```

The executable file will only ever be created if your program compiles successfully without any errors. Imagine if you make a mistake when you are typing in your C++ source-code using Nano. The g++ compiler will examine your source-code really carefully when it starts compiling. If your program does not follow the strict rules of the C++ language, then it will display warnings or error messages to tell you that something is wrong. If the compiler encounters any errors then it will not make an executable file. An executable file can only be made if the C++ source-code can be compiled successfully, without any errors being found.

From this point onwards when we compile our programs we will tell the g++ compiler to call each new executable file something other than "*a.out*". The steps to do this may seem like a lot to remember at the moment, but you will get the hang of it very quickly with a little bit of practice.

Note: If you are used to using the Windows operating system on a PC, you are probably accustomed to executable programs having filenames that end in "*.exe*". Linux does not need to use any such file extension for an executable file. It uses a different way to tell whether a file is an executable program or not: "**file permissions**". Each file on a Linux system has a special setting that tells the computer whether the file can be executed or not.

Using the Geany text editor instead of Nano

Until now, you have carried out a lot of tasks manually by typing in commands at the Linux command-line prompt, with each command telling the computer what you want to do. It is easy to make mistakes when you type a command, especially if you are in a hurry. It can sometimes be difficult to remember which commands to type in order to do things.

The **Geany** text editor is a free piece of software that you can download to make it easier to write, compile and run C++ programs. You can even use it to work with other programming languages, as well as C++. As previously mentioned, you may need to take a look at the *"How to download the software that you need"* section in the Appendices in the back of this book for details of how to install Geany if you have do not already have it on your Pi.

Once you start using Geany, you won't need to type Linux commands to compile and run your programs – you can click on the toolbar buttons instead. Another good reason to use Geany is that it automatically names your new executable files using the name of your "*.cpp*" source-code files. If you write a program called "*jellyfish.cpp*", when Geany activates the g++ compiler it will automatically tell it to make an executable program called "*jellyfish*". Your executables will no longer be called "*a.out*".

You may also find it useful to know that Geany can automatically write very simple code to get you started when you are making a new program. When you create a new "*.cpp*" source file, Geany can generate simple code for the `main()` function to save you a little bit of typing.

Typing in a simple C++ program using Geany

On the Raspberry Pi, you can usually start Geany from the desktop by looking in the main menu of programs. From your desktop menu, look in "**Programming**" and choose the **Geany** icon. Alternatively, if you have a "*Bash shell*" or other kind of terminal window open on the desktop, you can type "**geany**".

Once started, Geany looks like a lot many other text editors that you may have seen or worked with before. On the left of the window is a drop-down list that you can use to inspect the parts that make up your C++ program, such as the names of functions and variables. On the right-hand side, the main part of the window is given over to the actual text editor for writing your code. The bottom of the window is used to display messages, particularly when compiling your programs.

You can immediately start typing your C++ code in the main window. Notice this is the code from *Example 1.2 – better.cpp*:

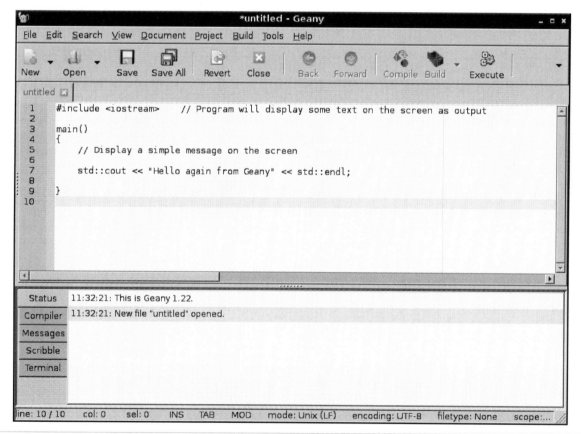

To begin with, all of the text appears plain until you save the code for the first time. This is because Geany does not yet know that you are working on a C++ program. (Remember that Geany can be used with many other programming languages, including Python, Java and JavaScript). It is not until you save your code for the first time with a filename that ends in ".*cpp*" that Geany will start to highlight parts of your C++ code in different colours. This is called "**syntax-highlighting**" and it can help you to spot typing errors and other mistakes in your code.

From the **File** menu choose "**Save as…**" and call your program "*again.cpp*". Notice that the appearance of your C++ code now changes in the main Geany editing window:

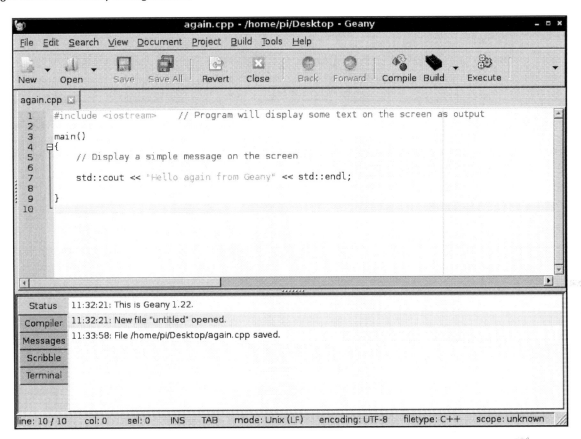

Remember that this is a *very* simple C++ program, in fact there are a few minor details that I have left out that a C++ programmer would normally put into their code. Geany is about to warn us about this when we try to compile the code.

Different versions of the Geany text editor

Once upon a time, it was necessary to download Geany on to the Pi yourself. It was not installed as part of the Debian Linux operating system. Now though, the latest version - Raspbian - comes with Geany already installed.

Whilst the latest version of Geany is very similar to previous versions, you may notice that the buttons on the toolbar are smaller than the originals and look a little different, especially the *Compile*, *Build* and *Execute* buttons:

Throughout the book, you will see that any screenshots of Geany feature the original buttons, which are still in use on many Raspberry Pi computers at the time of writing. If you are new to Geany, you may also find this handy since the original buttons show text descriptions to indicate what they do:

When you are ready to compile your C++ code, you should first make sure that you have saved it.

From the **Build** menu, choose the <u>**Build**</u> option:

For speed you can also use the keyboard shortcut *Alt B* to activate the **Build** menu, then press *B* to <u>**Build**</u>. Alternatively, you can click on the **Build button** (which looks like a larger version of the brick that you can see in the menu) or press the *F9* key:

Both methods will compile your source-code and, if successful, will then create an executable file that you can run. Once the executable has been made, you can run it again and again. It is not necessary to re-compile a program every single time that you want to run it. Usually, you only need to re-compile the program if you make changes to the source-code.

Why use "**Build**" and not "**Compile**"?

If you choose "<u>**Compile**</u>" from the **Build** menu, Geany will use the g++ compiler to translate your C++ source-code into low-level object code that can be executed directly by the processor of your Raspberry Pi. It will store this low-level code in what is called an "**object**" file. This object code cannot be used under Linux as a program that you can run from the command-line without first adding in some other essential low-level code from the Linux operating system. Once the extra code has been added or "**linked**" to your own object code, it makes a full executable program – an "**executable**" file. See *"Stages that g++ goes through when translating C++ source-code into an executable"* in the Appendices at the back of the book for more information about how C++ source-code is turned into an executable program.

When you choose "<u>**Build**</u>" from the **Build** menu, the g++ compiler not only compiles your C++ source-code into object-code, it also links in the extra code for you. The final product is usually an executable file that you can run, either from the Linux command-line again and again, or directly from the Geany window by clicking on the "**Execute**" button (shown above).

Geany compiles using the g++ compiler, using a special setting that we have not seen before: `-Wall`

> Status   g++ -Wall -o "again" "again.cpp" (in directory: /home/pi/Desktop)

When you choose **Build**, Geany activates the g++ compiler using the `-Wall` "**Warnings all**" option to display all **warning messages**, as well as the `-o` option to set a suitable name for the final executable file, instead of calling it "*a.out*".

If your program compiles without errors, you should see a success message in the **Compiler** section of the Geany window:

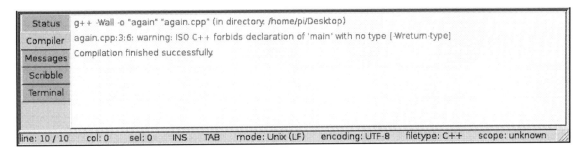

This is a little more user-friendly than typing **g++** yourself at the command line.

Your program has compiled successfully and is now ready to run. Unfortunately, you may have also noticed that there is a red warning message:

```
warning: ISO C++ forbids declaration of 'main' with no type
```

This is a little annoying, but it is not actually a major problem at this point – it will be explained later in this chapter.

Running your program from Geany

Once you have built the code and the executable file exists on your Pi, you may then run your new program. From the **Build** menu, choose "**Execute**" or press the **Execute button**.

A new "**LXTerminal**" window will appear showing any output that your program produces on the screen:

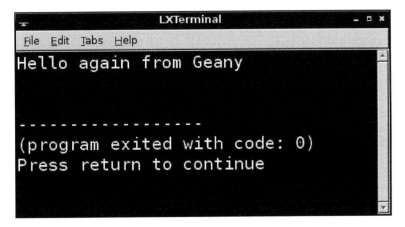

When the program has finished running you will be told that it has exited, along with the status or error-code that it returns. As you can see from the screenshot above, the code is 0 for our program, indicating that no errors were encountered during its execution.

The terminal window pauses to give you a chance to read its contents. Pressing *return* (or the *enter* key) will close the terminal window and reactivate the Geany window again.

If there is a problem with your C++ source-code when you try to build a program, the "**Compiler**" section of the Geany window should display details of the problem using one or more **error messages**:

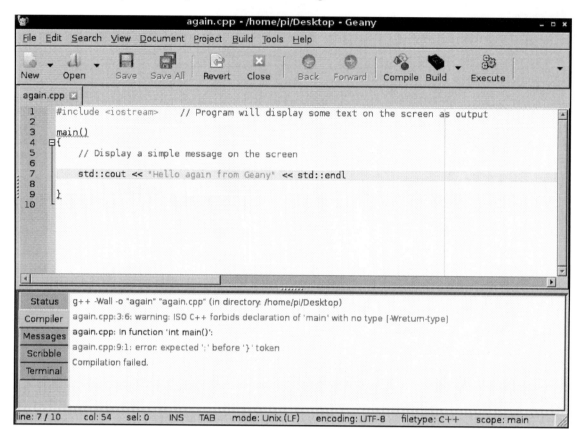

In the example above, you can see that g++ starts to compile the C++ program using the command:

```
g++ -Wall -o "again" "again.cpp"
```

The first line of text in the "**Compiler**" section tells us that it is working in the **/home/pi/Desktop** directory.

The last line tells the programmer that the program could not be compiled successfully:

```
Compilation failed.
```

Luckily, the compiler tells us *what* the problem is and *where* it was found in the source-code, so that you can find and correct the error. Geany helpfully makes these messages red.

First we are told which function the problem was found in: "`int main()`".

The compiler now tells us exactly **where** to start looking for the problem. It could not make any sense out of the code that it found on line **9, 1** character in from the beginning of the line.

The problem has been caused by accidentally forgetting to put a **;** semi-colon at the end of the seventh line of code. When the compiler examines the ninth line in the source-code, it does not expect to encounter a closing **}** curly-brace as the previous line of code has been left unfinished, thus the compilation process fails.

Whilst your program is compiling, if g++ finds a problem in your C++ code then it will display an **error message** on the screen (in Geany this is in the bottom pane of the window). If you have an error in your code, then the compiler will **not** be able to successfully translate it into lower-level code or make a new executable file from it.

We have already seen that the compiler can issue **warning messages** during compilation. If g++ finds a *potential* problem with your code that could cause unexpected results at run-time, or if it finds some code that defies conventional guidelines for good practice when writing C++ statements, then a **warning** message may be displayed. The compiler **will** still produce an executable file that should run, but you are being warned that you may experience problems once the executable is running.

There are different kinds of warnings - some are serious, some are more trivial. You can choose which kind of warnings you would like to see and some people even turn off some or all of the different kinds of warnings that the compiler generates. It is good practice however to tell the compiler that you want to see **all** kinds of warnings during compilation, including the most trivial, as these could have a negative effect on how your finished program operates during execution.

As mentioned previously, when Geany uses g++ to compile a program, you will notice that it uses the −**Wall** option. This tells the compiler to display all possible warnings, or "**Warnings all**".

We saw earlier what happens when your program does not follow the expected conventions for the **main()** function in ISO C++ programs:

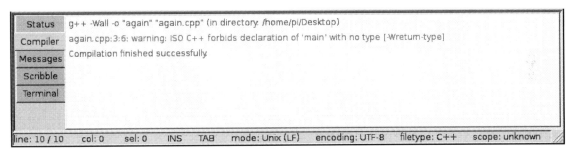

As we will find out in the next section, it is standard practice for a program to contain a little bit of extra code to indicate whether or not any errors occurred during execution. The code will pass a status code back to the Linux operating system.

Here is another example of a warning. This time it is from a program that does something unnecessary:

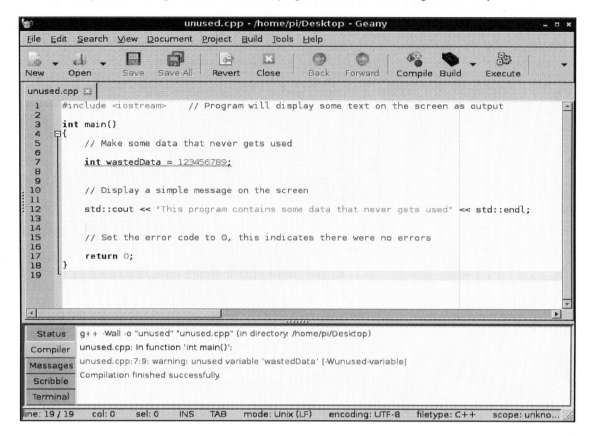

When compiling this program, a warning is generated to tell us about the unused data that has been included in the program on line number 7.

This particular warning is useful because the programmer might want to check whether they have forgotten a crucial line of code in their program. It also helps the programmer to identify inefficiencies in their program – the unused variable is a waste of time and space when the program executes!

Finding out whether a program executes successfully

As mentioned earlier, when we write a C++ program we can include an **error-code**. This is a special number that the program uses to indicate to the computer whether or not it encountered any errors or other problems while running.

A C++ program uses the `return` statement to give an error-code back to Linux once a program has finished running.

In general, a finished program returns an error code of 0 if no errors were encountered at all during execution. Any value other than 0 indicates that there was some kind of problem. As a programmer, you can choose the exact numbers that your program will use to indicate different kinds of errors.

Once your program has finished running, there is an easy way for you to check for any such errors from the Linux command-line prompt. We can ask it to tell us the error-code from the program that has finished execution.

To make a program return an error code, we usually add a few more details to our C++ source-code.

Let's try creating a better version of the program in Geany:

```
Example 1.3 – success.cpp

#include <iostream>      // Program will display some text on the screen as output

int main()
{
    // Display a simple message on the screen

    std::cout << "Hello from Geany" << std::endl;

    // Tell Linux the program finished OK without any problems

    return 0;
}
```

Save the code as **"success.cpp"**, then build it. As long as there are no errors in your typing, it should successfully compile:

| Status | g++ -Wall -o "success" "success.cpp" (in directory: /home/pi/Desktop) |
| Compiler | Compilation finished successfully |

Note that no **warning** messages are displayed. You should now be able to execute the new program.

After completing execution, the computer tells you the value of the exit code that was returned:

```
-------------------
(program exited with code: 0)
Press return to continue
```

In this case, the exit code is 0, which is the value that the `return` statement used in the program code.

Reporting an error – returning a code other than 0

A program does not always need to return the value **0** prior to finishing execution. You can choose any whole number value you like as long as it ranges between **0** and **255**. While they are running, programs can even make decisions about which value they should use for the error-code, depending on their circumstances.

Here is a simple example that returns an error-code of **13** rather than **0**:

Example 1.4 – *error_code.cpp*

```cpp
#include <iostream>      // Program will display some text on the screen as output

int main()
{
    // Display simple messages on the screen

    std::cout << "Hello again from Geany" << std::endl;

    std::cout << "This tells Linux something bad has happened." << std::endl;


    // Set the error-code to 13, this can be used to indicate a problem

    return 13;
}
```

Here is what you should see on the screen when the program executes:

```
Hello again from Geany
This tells Linux something bad happened.


------------------
(program exited with code: 13)
Press return to continue
```

Note the error code of **13** that is displayed at the bottom.

Here's what we have covered in this chapter:

C++ is a **high-level programming language**.

Programs written using the C++ language are called "**source-code**".

Most people use a **text editor** to type in C++ source-code, such as **Nano** or **Geany**.

A source-code file should usually be saved with a filename ending in "*.cpp*" to indicate that it holds C++ code.

Your C++ source-code can make use of **libraries** of code that other people have already written and shared, using `#include`. This makes writing programs an easier task as you can re-use existing code.

Before you can run a program written in C++, it must be **compiled** to break it down into simpler **machine-code instructions** that the central processing unit of your Raspberry Pi can execute directly.

The compiler used to translate C++ source-code into executable machine-code is called "**g++**", and it is part of the **GNU Compiler Collection (GCC)**.

If your program contains errors or other things that could potentially go wrong, the compiler will display **error messages** or **warnings** to help you find and fix your code, telling you roughly where to look for them.

After successfully compiling a C++ program, a new **executable file** is created that your Pi can run.

When compiling from the Linux command-line the default filename for a newly created executable file is "*a.out*".

You can use the `-o` compiler option to specify a different filename for the executable that will be produced.

You can compile and run programs either directly from the Linux command-line, or from within certain text editors, such as Geany.

A program can report an **error-code** after it finishes running. This code can tell you whether the program encountered any problems during execution.

1.	What is the difference between **"high-level"** and **"low-level"** code?
2.	Why does source-code need to be **compiled**?
3.	When writing a simple C++ program, what should the **filename** always **end with**?
4.	What is the name of the **executable file** that the g++ compiler will create if you don't tell it to use a particular name?
5.	What is the difference between an **"error"** and a **"warning"** during compilation?
6.	Why do C++ programs usually contain a `return` statement?

Chapter 2:
Writing some simple code

Programs and statements

Let's take a look at some of the basics of the C++ language, otherwise you will find that any code that you type in makes very little sense to you. With a little bit of background knowledge you will understand much more about the programs that we create.

We have seen an example of an extremely simple C++ program in the previous chapter, but what exactly are programs? How do we go about writing our own programs so that they make sense to the compiler?

> A program is a **precise sequence of instructions** that the computer carries out in order to make things happen.
>
> Computers **always** follow programs. Without them your computer would not know what to do.

Even when a computer appears to be doing something sophisticated, it is merely following a step-by-step sequence of instructions that tell it exactly how to behave.

Computers are not actually intelligent. Unlike a human, they don't even have any common sense. A computer will always faithfully attempt to follow the program of instructions that you give to it, even if those instructions tell it do something silly. You will see that unless you tell a computer how to cope with unexpected events they can do some really stupid things.

We say that a C++ program is made up of separate "**statements**". A statement is an **instruction** that tells the computer to **do something**. For example, a statement in a program could tell the computer to display a message, to calculate something, or to make a decision.

Simple one-line statements

Many statements in C++ are very short and take up only a single line of text.

Below are some examples - don't worry about what each statement means just yet, we will find out more in the next few chapters.

```
speed = 0;

cout << "Please type in your name:" << endl;

numCharsInSearchPattern = searchPattern.length();
```

Statements that are written using more than a single line of text

Some statements are made up of more than one line of text. Breaking a statement up in this way can make it easier to read.

Here is an example of a multi-line statement:

```
if ( speed <= 0 )
    cout << "Error! Please type a positive value." << endl;
else
    if ( speed > 70 )
        cout << "Warning! Speed limit is 70 mph." << endl;
```

(See *"Chapter 6: Making decisions"* for more information about `if` statements and how they work.)

Using a semi-colon ; to mark the end of a statement

How does the computer know where one statement finishes and another begins in a C++ program?

The end of each simple statement in a C++ program must be marked with a ; **semi-colon** symbol. It shows the compiler that a statement is complete. It is a little bit like the way that sentences in the English language usually end with a punctuation mark, such as a full-stop, a question-mark or an exclamation mark. With C++ though, the end-marker of a simple statement is always a ; semi-colon.

Here are several more examples of simple statements that can be written in a C++ program:

```
int player1Score, player2Score, player3Score;

gameOver = ( --time <= 0 ) ? true : false;

if ( forecast == "rain" ) displayCloud();
```

Notice the ; semi-colon symbol at the end of each simple statement above.

Often, even simple statements can be broken into more than one line of text. Breaking them up usually makes it easier for people to read and understand them. Just reaching the end of a line of text does not guarantee that it is the end of a C++ statement – it is the job of the ; semi-colon symbol to indicate this.

Here are the same examples again, but this time they have been written to span more than one single line on the screen:

```
int player1Score,
    player2Score,
    player3Score;

gameOver = ( --time <= 0 )
        ? true
        : false;

if ( forecast == "rain" )
    displayCloud();
```

Again, in the examples above, each simple statement always ends with the ; semi-colon symbol. This tells the compiler that the statement is now complete and the next piece of text encountered in the program will be the start of something else, such as a new program statement, a comment or a compiler directive.

You should always be really careful not to put a semi-colon in the middle of a statement when you don't actually need one as unwanted extra semi-colons can cause errors. Your program code might **look** to you as though it should work, but it will actually do something that you didn't expect it to.

```
if ( forecast == "rain" );
    displayCloud();
```

In the above statement, putting an unnecessary ; semi-colon halfway through the statement effectively cuts it in half. It turns the original statement into two separate simple statements which behave very differently when executed. See the *"Finding and correcting common mistakes in your C++ source-code"* section in the Appendices at the end of this book for advice on how to spot simple errors such as this in your program code.

Compound statements – groups of statements enclosed within { } curly braces

It is often useful to take several simple statements and group them together. We call this a **"block"** of statements. The program can then use the block of statements as though they were one single thing.

Take a look at this code, which makes three different things happen when the user chooses a certain option:

```
if ( cancelOptionChosen )
    displayMessage();

if ( cancelOptionChosen )
    playWarningSound();

if ( cancelOptionChosen )
    deleteTemporaryFile();
```

Instead of three separate program statements that all make the same decision and then execute a single statement if found to be true, we could make the decision only once and decide whether to execute a whole block of several statements. We call this a **"compound statement"**:

```
if ( cancelOptionChosen )
{
    displayMessage();
    playWarningSound();
    deleteTemporaryFile();
}
```

The code above uses { and } *curly braces* to group the statements together into a single block.

Note that the end of the compound statement is marked by the } curly brace symbol. It does not require a ; semi-colon after the curly brace.

Putting comments in your code

Comments are lines of text in your C++ source-code that serve as **explanations** for a human. They help us to understand how a program works.

Because comments are not instructions to the computer, they are not compiled. The compiler does not attempt to translate comments into low-level code. Instead, it completely ignores them when compiling the source-code for your program.

Single-line comments using //

A simple, short comment in C++ usually begins with two *forward-slashes*:

```
//
```

Everything on a line of text that appears after // will be ignored, such as in these examples below:

```
// Display message to the user
// about their password
cout << "Your password has been changed.";    // Display confirmation message
```

Notice that single-line comments don't need to end with a semi-colon as they are not actually program statements. Once the compiler encounters the // symbol that marks the beginning of a single-line comment, it ignores the rest of the line and begins searching for the next program statement on the next line of source-code text.

Multi-line comments using /* and */

Longer comments may take up more than one single line of text in your code. Although you could start each line with // every time, you can instead create a whole block of comments using the symbols /* and */ to enclose one or more lines of text.

After the /* symbol, anything you type will be regarded as a **multi-line comment** and will be ignored by the compiler. To mark the end of the comment, tell the compiler that you have finished it using the */ symbol.

Here is an example of a multi-line comment:

```
/*
This program searches for keywords in a page of text.
It will highlight all places where the keywords have been found.
You can choose an option to ignore capital letters or not.
*/
```

As in the above example, you may find that using /* and */ is easier than preceding every one of your comment lines with //.

Here is a program that does very little! The **main ()** block contains only comments and a simple **return** statement:

Example 2.1 – comments.cpp

```cpp
int main()
{
    // This program does very little.

    // Feel free to compile it and run it yourself.

    /* All it does
       is return an error code
       that tells the operating system
       that everything went fine. */

    // The return statement makes this happen...
    return 0;    // 0 means there weren't any problems
}
```

"Commenting out" parts of your program code

Not only are comments brilliant for explaining what your code does, they can also be used to temporarily **de-activate** or **"comment-out"** parts of your code. You can temporarily turn parts of your code into comments so that the computer does not compile and execute them. This is really handy when you are trying to find and correct errors in your programs.

To de-activate a single-line program statement, add **//** to the beginning of that line of code. This turns it into a comment.

In the example below, you can see that the call to the function called **playWarningSound** has been commented-out:

```cpp
    if ( cancelOptionChosen )
    {
        displayMessage();
        // playWarningSound();
        deleteTemporaryFile();
    }
```

To de-activate a whole chunk of your program, simply enclose it between **/*** and ***/** markers, turning it into a multi-line comment block:

```cpp
    if ( cancelOptionChosen )
    {
        /* displayMessage();
        playWarningSound();
        deleteTemporaryFile(); */
    }
```

Expressions

Now things start to get a little more technical. Many program statements contain "**expressions**", such as those that perform calculations or decide whether or not to carry out a certain action.

Expressions are mixtures of "**literal values**", "**named values**", "**returned values**" and "**operators**".

Expressions can be **evaluated** or "worked out" to produce a **result** or **value**.

Let's consider a few examples of each of these things...

Literal values

A **literal value** is a data value that is "embedded" or built into a statement in your program code.

It is data that is ready to use immediately in a statement.

All of the examples below are **literal values**:

the literal whole number value **32**, which could be used in a calculation;

the literal decimal value **0.5**;

the literal text value **"Thank you"**;

the literal character value **'Q'**;

the literal Boolean values **true** or **false**.

Below are some statements that use literal values. Notice that you can see exactly what these values are as they are embedded within the code and are easy to pick out:

```
cout << 1000;     // Display the number 1000 on the screen


cout << "Thank you";    // Display the message "Thank you" on the screen


// Repeatedly execute a block of statements to display messages on the screen
while ( true )
{
    cout << "This code never stops executing!";
    cout << '*';
}
```

Note: You will learn more about **cout** and how to display things later on in *"Chapter 4: Keyboard input and screen output"*, whilst *"Chapter 7: Repetition using loops"* covers how to repeatedly execute parts of your code.

Named values

A **named value** is a data value that has been given a **name**, such as `highScore`, or `weeksInOneYear`.

The computer uses the name to find the data value again once it has been stored in memory.

The name itself (what you choose to call the data value) is up to you. Programmers often choose names that mean something to them, perhaps describing what the data value is for or how it will be used by their program. This helps them to write code that is easy to understand and stops things from getting too confusing.

In the above examples, the computer might use the name `highScore` to refer to the value `10350` which has been stored in the computer's memory.

The computer could use the name `weeksInOneYear` to refer to the value `52`, which is also stored in memory.

You don't need to worry about **where** in memory the values are stored, all you need to remember is **what you called them**.

Here are some statements that use named values. Each name refers to a data-value that is stored somewhere in the computer's memory:

```
cout << myScore;      // Display the number of points that I have at the moment

cout << VALUE_OF_PI;      // Display the constant (unchanging) value of Pi
```

Values returned from functions

We can also obtain values by executing other parts of program code, called **"functions"**. A function is a chunk of code that has been given a name.

Many functions produce some kind of result when they are executed – they produce a **"return value"**.

Such a returned value can be used as part of an expression, in the same way as any other literal or named value.

Here is an example of a statement that calls a function and then does something with the resulting returned value:

```
cout << random();  // Display the result of calling the function named "random"
```

Operators

An **operator** is a special **symbol** that tells the computer to **process** or perform an **operation** on some data.

For instance, the * symbol tells the computer to multiply two numbers together.

Operator symbols

Some of the most common operators that can be used in expressions are shown below:

+	Tells the computer to **add up** a pair of numbers, producing a result that is also a number. It can also be used to tell the computer to **join** two text values together, producing a new text value.
–	Tells the computer to **subtract** one number from another.
*	Tells the computer to **multiply** two numbers together.
/	Tells the computer to **divide** one number by another number.
%	The **"modulus"** operator. Tells the computer to divide one number by another to find the **remainder**.
>	Tests whether one value is **greater than** another value.
>=	Tests whether one value **is greater than or equal to** another.
<	Tests whether one value **is less than** another.
<=	Tests whether one value **is less than or equal to** another.
=	The **"assignment"** operator. **Sets** or **"assigns"** a value to a variable or a constant.
==	The **"equivalence"** operator. Tests whether two values are **equivalent** i.e. **the same**. Produces either a `true` or a `false` Boolean value as a result. It will produce `true` if the values are equivalent (the same) or `false` if the values are different.
!=	The **"non-equivalence"** (**not equal**) operator. Tests whether two values are **different** i.e. **non-equivalent**. Produces either a `true` or a `false` Boolean value as a result. It will produce `true` if the values are different or `false` if the values are the same.
not_eq	Another way to write the **non-equivalence** operator. This can help to make your code easier to read instead of using the `!=` symbol.
!	The **"negation"** or **"NOT"** operator. Tells the computer to find the **opposite** of a value or expression. The opposite of the value `true` is `false`, and vice-versa.
not	Another way to write the **negation** operator instead of using the `!` symbol. This can help to make your code easier to read.
&&	The **"logical AND"** operator. Tests whether **all parts** of an expression are `true` at the same time. It produces either a `true` or a `false` Boolean value as a result.
and	Another way to write the **logical AND** operator instead of using the `&&` symbol. This can help to make your code easier to read.
||	The **"logical OR"** operator. Tests whether **at least one part** of an expression is `true`. It produces either a `true` or a `false` Boolean value as a result.
or	Another way to write the **logical OR** operator instead of using the `||` symbol. This can help to make your code easier to read.

C++ includes several other operators that are not covered here, including **"bit-wise operators"** for more advanced programs. See the *"Using bit-wise operators to perform logical operations"* section in *"Chapter 5: Using operators to process data"* for further details.

Different kinds of expressions

Here are some examples of how we can **combine** different literal values, named values and operators together as expressions:

Arithmetic expressions

Arithmetic expressions are **evaluated** by the computer to give you a **numeric result** (a **number**).
They can use a combination of literal values, named values and arithmetic operators:

```
+    -    *    /    %    (    )
```

```
3 + 5     // Add up the numbers 3 and 5

currentScore + 100     // Add 100 to the value of variable currentScore

pi * radius * radius     // Multiply value of pi times the radius squared

15000 / numWeeksInOneYear     // Divide 15000 by value of numWeeksInOneYear

numberOfBiscuits % peopleInRoom     // Find remainder after dividing
                                    // numberOfBiscuits by peopleInRoom

( widthOfRectangle + heightOfRectangle ) * 2     // Add width and height,
                                                 // then multiply result by 2
```

Relational expressions

Relational expressions are evaluated by the computer to give you a **Boolean** result that is either **true** or **false**.
They can use a combination of literal values, named values and relational operators:

```
<    <=    >    >=    ==    !=    not_eq
```

```
playerScore > 10000     // Is the value of playerScore greater than 10000?

typedIn == password     // Is value of typedIn the same as value of password?

today != "Tuesday"      // Is value of today different to "Tuesday"?
today not_eq "Tuesday"  // Another way to write the same comparison
```

Logical expressions

As with relational expressions, **logical expressions** are evaluated to give you a **Boolean true** or **false** result.
They can use a combination of the literal values **true** or **false**, named values and Boolean operators:

```
!    &&    ||    not    and    or
```

```
!tooHot     // Produce the opposite of the value of the variable called tooHot

isRaining && sunIsShining     // Produce a true value if isRaining is true
                              // AND also sunIsShining is currently true

isPayDay or justWonLottery     // Produce true value if EITHER isPayDay is
                               // true OR justWonLottery is true, OR BOTH true
```

How to set out your C++ program code

Before we try writing any more programs, there are several things that can be done to make the C++ source-code easier to read and to help people to understand how it works. You may not think that this is necessary, but with larger programs you can sometimes lose track of what the parts of your code are supposed to do, however good you are at programming. It becomes even more important if you want other people to understand your code, such as when you work together in a team to create a piece of software.

The first thing that you can do is **line things up neatly** or "**indent**" your code. Most programmers either press the *tab* key to move a line of code over to the right, or they press the *space* key several times.

You can also press the *enter* or *return* key to put in extra **blank lines**. Blank lines separate one part of your code from another. If your program does three different things, you can use blank lines to split it into three clear blocks of code.

Below is a C++ program that is quite difficult to read. In the next few chapters, we will quickly learn what each part of this program means.

Don't worry! For the moment we will just consider how it **looks**:

Example 2.2 – messy_pizza.cpp

```cpp
#include <iostream>
using namespace std;
int main()
{
const float VALUE_OF_PI=3.14159;
int radius;
cin >> radius;
if (radius>0)
{
float area=VALUE_OF_PI*radius*radius;
cout << "Pizza area: " << area << " sq in." << endl;
return 0;
}
else
{
cout << "Radius too small for your pizza to exist!" << endl;
return 1;
}
}
```

The program above is organised in one single chunk, without any blank lines or indentation.

If you showed it to an experienced programmer, regardless of the programming language that they like to use, they would probably look at it and then tell you how awful it looks.

The code is difficult to read quickly. The reader needs to concentrate harder than usual because the parts of the program are all crammed together in one single chunk of text. Consequently, it is not easy to understand what the program actually does or whether it contains any errors.

Now look at the way that the program has been set out below after indenting some of the statements, moving them along using the **tab** key and adding a few blank lines to separate out the main parts of the code using the **return** key:

Example 2.3 – indented_pizza.cpp

```cpp
#include <iostream>

using namespace std;

int main()
{
    const float VALUE_OF_PI=3.14159;

    int radius;
    cin >> radius;

    if (radius>0)
    {
        float area=VALUE_OF_PI*radius*radius;
        cout << "Pizza area: " << area << " sq in." << endl;
        return 0;
    }
    else
    {
        cout << "Radius too small for your pizza to exist!" << endl;
        return 1;
    }

}
```

Many people would find this version easier to read. It is easier to pick out the different parts of what the program does once you have indented the code and organised it into smaller chunks or **"blocks"**. The actual words and symbols are the same in both versions of the code.

Most people find it easier to read a program that has been grouped into such chunks. Your eyes can skim through the different parts quicker. It becomes easier to pick out blocks or groups of statements and to work out what each one does. You are not trying to make sense of the entire program all at once.

Adding spaces to make individual statements easier to read

It can sometimes be difficult to distinguish between the different words and symbols that make up a line of program code.

You may have noticed that the examples so far contain spaces between individual words and symbols. We have seen that adding extra space makes it easier for most people to read and understand statements. Any extra spaces that you type in-between whole words and symbols don't matter to the computer, they will simply be ignored when your C++ program gets compiled.

Watch out though – you can't type extra spaces in the **middle** of a special C++ "**reserved word**" or any other names that your program uses. You can only add extra spaces **between** complete words, numbers or other symbols.

A program statement such as:

```
    const float AREA=VALUE_OF_PI*radius*radius;
```

...could be made clearer by adding spaces **between** the individual words and operators that it is made of:

```
    const float AREA = VALUE_OF_PI * radius * radius;
```

However, the following examples are not allowed and the compiler will display an error if you use them in your program:

```
    const float A R E A = VALUE OF PI * r a d i u s * r a d i u s;

    const fl oat AREA = VALUE_OF_PI * radius * radius;
```

Both examples have spaces smack-bang in the middle of words, and this is not allowed.

Similarly, you cannot put spaces in the middle of numbers that you type, even though in real life some people often write really big numbers on paper that contain spaces to make them easier to read:

```
    int grainsOfRice = 50 000 000;
```

The compiler would consider that this line of code contains three different numbers:

50

000

000

...rather than the single number **50000000**.

As already mentioned, lines of program code often include **"expressions"**, which are mixtures of **symbols** such as **mathematical operators**, **logical operators** and **identifiers** (names for things).

The line below is quite dense. It is difficult to pick out the individual parts of this particular expression:

```
(score<5000) and (time>0)
```

You can add extra spaces between each part of the expression to make it easier to read and understand:

```
( score < 5000 ) and ( time > 0 )
```

You will find out more about identifiers and expressions throughout the rest of the book.

What happens to white-space when C++ code gets compiled?

Why don't extra spaces and blank lines matter when compiling? One of the first things that the compiler does to a C++ program at the start of the compilation process is remove all of the **"white-space"**. It takes out all of the spaces, blank lines and invisible *tab* indentations, leaving only the letters, numeric digits and operator symbols.

Here's what the pizza program would look like after the compiler has removed all of the unnecessary white-space:

```
using namespace std;int main(){const VALUE_OF_PI=3.14159;int radius;cin>>radius;if
(radius>0){float area=VALUE_OF_PI*radius*radius;cout<<"Pizza area is "<<area<<"sq
in."<<endl;return 0;}else{cout<<"This radius is too small for your pizza to
exist!"<<endl;return 1;}}
```

You'll probably agree that this code is a complete nightmare if you try to read through it. It is much more difficult to read and to understand without the white-space.

Technical Note: I have cheated a little in the example above...

I have deliberately left out the first line `#include <iostream>` as this is a special kind of instruction to the C++ compiler, called a **"directive"**. It is not actually C++ code – it tells the compiler how to behave during the compilation of your program.

The `#include` directive instructs the compiler to use some extra code from a different file, which in this case is in the standard `iostream` file. In the compacted example above, I have only shown the code from our program, not the additional code from `iostream`.

For more detailed information about what actually happens when you run the compiler, see the Appendix: *"Stages that g++ goes through when translating C++ source-code into an executable"*.

Here's the pizza program again, but this time it contains indentation, additional line spacing and comments to help us understand what each part of the code is for.

I have also added a message that will appear on the screen once the program begins execution, telling the user that they need to type something in:

Example 2.4 – *comments_pizza.cpp*

```cpp
#include <iostream>      // Program will be displaying some text on the screen

using namespace std;      // Will be using standard identifiers cin, cout, endl

int main()
{
    // Define approximate value for "pi" that we will use to calculate area
    const float VALUE_OF_PI = 3.14159;

    // Ask user to type in radius of pizza
    cout << "Please type in the radius of your pizza..." << endl;

    // User types in a number (the radius of a circle)
    int radius;
    cin >> radius;

    // Decide whether radius is acceptable and calculate the area
    if ( radius > 0 )
    {
        // Radius is larger than zero, so calculate the area
        float area = VALUE_OF_PI * radius * radius;
        cout << "Pizza area: " << area << " sq in." << endl;
        return 0;
    }
    else
    {
        // Radius zero or negative, so display error message
        cout << "Radius too small for your pizza to exist!" << endl;
        return 1;
    }   // end of the else block of statements

}
```

Here's what happens if you compile and run the program, first with a sensible radius, then with a negative radius:

```
Please type in the radius of your pizza...
7
Pizza area: 153.938 sq in.
```

```
Please type in the radius of your pizza...
-7
Radius too small for your pizza to exist!
```

Here's what we have covered in this chapter:

A C++ program is made up of **statements**. A statement is an instruction that tells the computer to do something.

A ; semi-colon is used to mark the end of a statement.

One or more statements can be grouped together by putting them inside a pair of { } curly braces. This is known as a **block** of statements.

Adding blank lines between sections of your code and spaces between parts of statements can make it easier to read C++ code quickly.

Putting comments in your C++ code can make it easier for a person to understand what the code does and how it works.

A single-line comment begins with //

A multi-line comment begins with /* and ends with */

Any blank lines, extra spaces or comments are ignored by the compiler when translating your source-code into an executable.

A **literal-value** is a data-value that is embedded in your program code, such as a number, a character or some text.

A **named-value** is a data-value that has been given a name. This name can be used elsewhere in your program code to refer to the value.

An **operator** is a symbol (or group of symbols) that tells the computer what kind of operation to carry out on some data.

An **operand** is an item of data that is used by an operation.

An **expression** is a mixtures of literal values, named values and operators that can be **evaluated** (or "worked out") to produce a result or value.

Adding extra pairs of ( ) brackets in an expression can make it easier to understand. The ( ) brackets can affect the **order** in which operations within the expression are carried out.

Problems and exercises for you to try

1.	What would be the result of evaluating the following expression? `99 % 33`

2.	Why would the following statements produce an error if you tried to compile them in a program?
	
	    `int numberOfPeople = 12`
	
	    `int numberOfKayaks = 7`

3.	Which of these assignment statements is correct?
	
	    `string myName = 'CAPTAIN SENSIBLE';`
	
	    `string myName = "CAPTAIN SENSIBLE";`

4.	In the following expression, which parts are "**operands**" and which parts are "**operators**"? `( heightA + heightB + heightC ) / 3`

5.	What is wrong with this simple program?
	
	    `main`
	    `{`
	        `Return 0;`
	    `}`

Chapter 3:
Data-types and values

Different types of data

As we have seen so far, most programs use **"data values"**. These are things that the computer can process while a program is running. Values can be numbers, text, or other kinds of data.

To make it easier to work with values and to refer to them from our program code, we can give each data value a **name** (these names are sometimes called **"identifiers"** as they are used to identify where to find a value in the computer's memory).

The name that you choose to give your data value usually describes what it is for or how it is going to be used. For instance, we might want to use the data value **4**, giving it a name to describe what it means: `numberOfWheels`.

We might have another data value, **"green"**, giving it the name `colourOfCar`.

C++ can work with many different **kinds** of data (called **"data-types"**) although you must first tell the computer **which** kind you want to use. The kind of data that you choose for a value affects what the computer can do with it.

Integer values: `int`, `short` and `long`

Many programs use numbers in some way. As humans, we frequently use **whole** numbers. We often only make use of the **positive** whole numbers, such as when counting things. Sometimes we also need to use **negative** whole numbers as well, such as when working with co-ordinates to describe a location.

An **"integer"** is a whole-number. C++ can work with different kinds of whole numbers using the `int` data-type. Your program can work with very small values, very large values, positive values or negative values.

Examples of integer values include **32**, **0**, **−100** and **10000**.

The `short` data-type allows a smaller range of integers (which uses less of the computer's memory to store and represent each number). The `long` data-type may be used for a larger range of integers, using more memory for each **value**.

Decimal values: `float` and `double`

These are **"real"** or **"decimal"** numbers – numbers that contain a decimal point. They are stored in a special way using **"floating-point"** representation.

They can be used to store values such as **2.99**, **3.14**, **−0.5**, **0.0125**.

In many cases, the `float` data-type is used to work with everyday real values, although the `double` data-type can be used to allow a larger range of real values.

Boolean values: `bool`

These are values that can be used to represent one of two possible alternatives. Boolean values are particularly useful in programs when making decisions, as you will see in later chapters.

The `bool` data-type stores either a `true` or `false` value.

Single characters: `char`

This is a single **"character"** or symbol, such as those that can be typed on a keyboard or displayed on a screen.

The `char` data-type can be used to store values such as **'A'**, **'/'**, **'g'**, **'6'**, **'~'**.

It can also be used to store special "invisible" characters, often called the **"non-printable"** characters. These will be described later.

Strings of characters: `string`

A sequence of characters is often called a "**text string**".

C++ supports an optional data-type called `string` which you can use in your programs.

The `string` data-type can be used to store values such as:

> `"Hi!"`
>
> `"Raspberry Pi"`
>
> `"http://www.gnu.org"`.

Despite being extremely useful, the `string` data-type is not actually built into the core of the C++ language. Before you can use it, your program must include extra-code from the `<string>` library:

```
#include <string>
```

This library also includes useful functions that you can use to process values, such as to extract parts or individual characters from a `string` value.

Because `string` is not a special "**reserved**" word that forms part of the C++ language, it is defined elsewhere in the standard namespace, `std`. To create variables and constants that use the `string` data-type, you can declare that you are going to be using this namespace in your code:

```
using namespace std;
```

Other types of data

As you learn more about C++ you will find there are also other more specialist types of data. It is also possible to **modify** several of the numeric data-types described so far, changing the **range** of values that they can represent. When working with numbers, you can choose **whether** you want to work with small, or large values. You can also choose whether to work with **signed** values or **unsigned** (positive) values. The prime number program *Example 10.9 - primes_in_range.cpp* in *"Chapter 10: Functions"* demonstrates how to work with really large positive numbers, as large as 54 billion.

Working with integer values: `int`

The most common way to use a whole number in C++ is to use the `int` data-type.

For example:

```
int numberOfPeopleEatingLunch = 12;
```

The above statement makes a whole-number variable, setting its value to **12**.

```
const int DAYS_IN_THE_WEEK = 7;
```

This second example makes a "**constant**" (a fixed value that cannot be changed while the program is running), setting its value to **7**.

Positive and negative integer values: `int`

Normally, when working with integers, the largest possible `int` value that GNU C++ on the Pi can use is **2147483647** and the smallest `int` value is **−2147483648**. Many problems can be solved by working within this range of numbers.

Unless you tell it otherwise, the compiler assumes that you want to use both positive and negative numbers when you make an `int` variable or constant.

If you are sure that you only want to deal with positive numbers for a particular variable, you can tell the compiler using the "**unsigned**" prefix:

```
unsigned int numberOfPeopleEatingLunch = 12;
```

This means...

"make an unsigned (positive) integer variable called **numberOfPeopleEatingLunch**, *giving it the value* **12** *".*

Positive only integer values: `unsigned int`

Making the above variable **unsigned** is common sense. The number of people eating lunch cannot be negative in real life. It must always be **0** or above.

There is also a practical advantage in using **unsigned** values. When you choose a data-type that allows only positive values, such as **unsigned int**, the computer can store and process larger numbers than if you had chosen the usual signed alternative as it no longer needs to store and represent any negative values.

Obviously, an **unsigned** integer value cannot be negative, so the smallest **unsigned int** value that can be represented on the Pi is **0**. The largest **unsigned int** value that can be represented is **4294967295**.

Working with a smaller range of integer values: `short`

If you definitely know that you only need to store small values, you can use the **short** data-type. This uses less storage space for each value than **int**, allowing a smaller range between **−32768** and **32767**:

```
short daysWorkedThisWeek = 0;
```

Although your computer has plenty of storage space for data, the savings from using **short** values can mount up, especially if your program stores and processes thousands or millions of numbers.

Again, you can prefix the variable or constant definition with "**unsigned**" if you do not intend to use negative values:

```
unsigned short daysWorkedThisWeek = 0;
```

Working with a larger range of integer values: `long`

If you want to work with a larger range of whole numbers than **int** allows, beyond the range of **−2147483648** to **2147483647**, you can use **long**. This kind of data-type makes use of more storage space for each whole number that you create, allowing the computer to store and process a much larger range of values.

```
long reallyBigPrimeNumber;
```

By choosing not to use any negative values, an **unsigned long** value allows even larger numbers - all the way up to **4294967295**:

```
unsigned long reallyBigPrimeNumber;
```

Values that use the **long long** data-type can be anywhere within the range of **−9223372036854775808** to **9223372036854775807**:

```
long long reallyBigPrimeNumber;
```

Finally, GNU C++ allows an even larger range of values with the modified type **unsigned long long**. This can represent really large numbers up to **18446744073709551615** - over 18 million-trillion!

If you really need to use such very large numbers in your programs, you can declare your variable like this:

```
unsigned long long reallyMassivePrimeNumber;
```

Overflow – values that are too big for a particular data-type

What happens if you try to use a value that is too large for a particular data-type to hold? For instance, what if you try to store an `int` value that is larger than **2147483647** (the largest value that your Pi will allow when using this data-type)?

If you attempt to use a value larger than the range of acceptable values that a data-type can handle, the value will **"wrap-around"** back to the beginning of the number-line again.

With `short` values, trying to go beyond the number **32767** will send you back to the smallest possible `short` value that can be represented, which is **−32768**.

In the case of `int` values, trying to go beyond the number **2147483647** will send you back to the smallest possible `int` value, which is **−2147483648**.

Try this example to see what happens if you try to add **1** on to the maximum possible `short` value:

Example 3.1 – short_max.cpp

```
#include <iostream>      // Program will be displaying some text on the screen

using namespace std;     // Will be using standard identifiers cout and endl

int main()
{
    short myVal = 32767;      // Set the starting value for myVal to the max for short

    cout << "The value of myVal is " << myVal << endl;

    myVal++;      // Increase the value of myVal by 1, pushing it past the maximum

    cout << "After adding 1 to myVal, the new value is " << myVal << endl;

    return 0;
}
```

Here's what you will see if you compile and execute the above program:

```
The value of myVal is 32767
After adding 1 to myVal, the new value is -32768
```

It shows you that when adding **1** to the value **32767**, the result is too large to be stored using the `short` data-type. What actually gets stored is **−32768**, the **smallest** possible `short` value. The value has **"wrapped around"** the number-line. After exceeding the maximum possible value, the computer jumps back to **minimum** possible value for `short` data, which is **−32768**. This is also known as **"overflow"**.

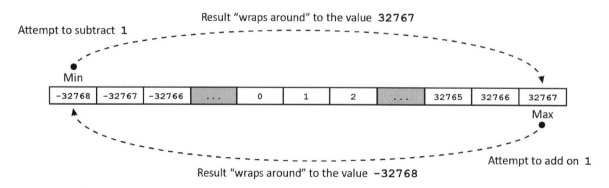

When using a particular data-type, how do you know what the largest or smallest values are that your program is allowed to use? We have already seen on the previous page that overflow can lead to problems at run-time, producing unexpected results.

Luckily, the **<climits>** library defines several useful constant identifiers that tell us the largest and smallest acceptable values that can be represented by each of the numeric data-types.

To make use of these identifiers, your program will need a directive to include the **<climits>** library:

```
#include <climits>
```

Constant identifiers are defined for the maximum allowable value of each data-type. In the case of signed data-types, which can represent both positive and negative values, constant identifiers are also defined for each minimum allowable value.

Below is a program that uses these constant identifiers to display the range of values for several simple data-types:

Example 3.2 – int_range.cpp

```cpp
#include <iostream>     // Program will be displaying some text on the screen
#include <climits>      // Program uses min and max constants for integer values

using namespace std;    // Will be using standard identifiers cout and endl

int main()
{
    cout << "char ranges from " << CHAR_MIN;    // char can be used for 8-bit values
    cout << " up to " << CHAR_MAX;

    cout << endl << endl;

    cout << "short ranges from " << SHRT_MIN;
    cout << " up to " << SHRT_MAX;

    cout << endl << endl;

    cout << "unsigned short ranges up to " << USHRT_MAX;

    cout << endl << endl;

    cout << "int ranges from " << INT_MIN;
    cout << " up to " << INT_MAX;

    cout << endl << endl;

    // Note there is no identifier for UINT_MIN as smallest possible value is 0
    cout << "unsigned int ranges up to " << UINT_MAX;

    cout << endl << endl;
```

continues on next page...

continued...

```
    cout << "long int ranges from " << LONG_MIN;
    cout << " up to " << LONG_MAX;

    cout << endl << endl;

    // Note there is no identifier for ULONG_MIN as smallest possible value is 0
    cout << "unsigned long int ranges up to " << ULONG_MAX;

    cout << endl << endl;

    cout << "long long int ranges from " << LLONG_MIN;
    cout << " up to " << LLONG_MAX;

    cout << endl << endl;

    // Note there is no identifier for ULLONG_MIN as smallest possible value is 0
    cout << "unsigned long long int ranges up to " << ULLONG_MAX << endl;


    return 0;
}
```

Here is what you will see when *Example 3.2 - int_range.cpp* executes:

```
char ranges from -128 up to 127

short ranges from -32768 up to 32767

unsigned short ranges up to 65535

int ranges from -2147483648 up to 2147483647

unsigned int ranges up to 4294967295

long int ranges from -2147483648 up to 2147483647

unsigned long int ranges up to 4294967295

long long int ranges from -9223372036854775808 up to 9223372036854775807

unsigned long long int ranges up to 18446744073709551615
```

Working with real numbers: `float` and `double`

As already mentioned, if you want to use a real number that contains a decimal point, rather than a whole number, the simplest data-type to use is "**`float`**". This is short for "**floating-point number**".

Below are some examples of variables that can store real values:

```
float weightOfSuitcase = 7.3;
float weigthOfBackPack = 1.25;
float weightOfBook = 1;
float totalWeight = weightOfSuitcase + weightOfBackPack + weightOfBook;
```

In the above example, notice that **weightOfBook** is a floating point variable, but the value for this has been typed in as the whole number **1**. The decimal point and places have been omitted to save some key strokes. The computer would actually store the value **1** as **1.0000000**. Because the variable **weightOfBook** has data-type **`float`**, it has the **potential** to use decimal places, even when they are not typed in.

The **`double`** data-type allows a larger range of floating-point values. It can be used where you need to work with a much larger positive value or much smaller negative value than the ordinary **`float`** data-type allows.

As with integers, you can tell the compiler that you only want to work with positive values only, but not negatives:

```
unsigned float weightOfSuitcase = 7.3;
```

I have used **unsigned** here as you can't have a weight that is negative. As with integers, when we chose to work with only positive numbers we can use a larger range of values by creating an **unsigned float** value.

The smallest and largest floating-point values that your Pi can work with using C++ can be displayed on the screen using the special constants **FLT_MIN**, **FLT_MAX**, **DBL_MIN** and **DBL_MAX**. These are defined in the **`<cfloat>`** library.

The program below displays the minimum and maximum values for **`float`** and **`double`** on the screen.

Example 3.3 – float_range.cpp

```cpp
#include <iostream>    // Program will be displaying some text on the screen
#include <cfloat>      // Program uses min and max constants for floating point values

using namespace std;   // Will be using standard identifiers cout and endl

int main()
{
    cout << "float ranges from " << FLT_MIN;
    cout << " up to " << FLT_MAX << endl;

    cout << endl << endl;

    cout << "double ranges from " << DBL_MIN;
    cout << " up to " << DBL_MAX << endl;

    return 0;
}
```

Here is what you will see when *Example 3.3 - float_range.cpp* executes:

```
float ranges from 1.17549e-38 to 3.40282e+38

double ranges from 2.22507e-308 to 1.79769e+308
```

The minimum values are so small and the maximum values are so large that they are written in a different way to the numbers that we have seen so far. This way of writing numbers is often called "**e-notation**". It often allows the computer to display very large or very small numbers in a much more compact way using fewer numeric digits.

In the above screenshot, `1.17549e-38` means 1.17549 *times* 10^{-38}

This is the same as:

1.17549 *times* $0.000000000000000000000000000000000000001$

...which is another way of writing the value:

$0.0000000000000000000000000000000000000117549$

Similarly, `3.40282e+38` means 3.40282 *times* 10^{+38}

This is the same as:

3.40282 *times* $100000000000000000000000000000000000000$

...which is another way of writing the value:

$340282000000000000000000000000000000000$

The accuracy and range of floating point numbers

Although they can work to a large number of decimal places, floating-point values in computers can sometimes be slightly inaccurate. The computer may not be able to store the *exact* number that you want using a floating-point value. In practice, these inaccuracies do not usually have any major effect on the results of your programs, but in theory they can lead to problems.

Imagine that you type in `4.0` and the computer stores it using data-type `float`. It is possible that inside the computer's memory, the actual value that gets stored might be `4.00000000000000000001`. Although this is very close to the actual number that you wanted to store, it is not *exactly* the same – it is an *approximation*.

Working with character symbols: `char`

Surprisingly when digital computers solve problems for us, all they are doing is following a program of instructions that tells them how to manipulate symbols.

A "**character**" is a single **symbol** that can be stored and processed by the computer.

We work with characters all the time, and there are several different kinds:

> **A B C X Y Z a b c** etc. are all **alphabetic characters**.
> These are the letters of the Roman alphabet; the symbols that are used by the English language.
>
> **0 1 2 3 4 5 6 7 8 9** are all **numeric digits**.
> These are the symbols used to represent numbers.
>
> **! @ £ $ % ^ & * ( ) [ ] { } < ?** etc. are all **symbols**.

All of the above examples are the kind of characters that can be typed on a keyboard, displayed on a screen or printed on a page. We can see them and we are familiar with what they look like. Together, they are called the "**printable characters**".

There are also other characters that you cannot normally see. These character values can be used to **control** what the computer does, hence they are called "**control characters**" or "**non-printable characters**". One of the most obvious control characters are the symbol that tells the computer to start a new line of text characters on the screen, called the *return* character. There is also a character that indents a line of text, moving it along to the right, called the *tab* character (which is short for "**tabulate**"), as well as characters for *backspace*, *delete* and for moving the cursor around on the screen.

Because everything that a digital computer stores and processes is represented as numbers, characters are actually stored in the computer using numeric "**character codes**". Each different kind of character symbol that a computer can work with has a corresponding numeric character code. For example, the letter "**A**" has the character code **65**. Whenever a key is pressed on the keyboard, it actually generates a character code for the symbol that we require. For instance, if you press the **!** key, the character code **33** is given to the computer.

Nearly all computers use **standard** codes – they use the **same** numeric codes for each common character. This means data and files can be swapped easily from one computer to another without problems. A "**character set**" is the whole collection of different symbols, digits and letters that a computer can store, process and display. The character set defines all of the allowable control characters and printable characters that the computer device can work with.

One of the most common sets of characters codes is **ASCII** – the **American Standard Code for Information Interchange**. It originally defined 128 standard characters that computers could use along with the standard numeric codes that go with them, using 7-bits to store each character code. ASCII was later improved to allow 256 different characters and this standard is referred to as **Extended ASCII**. Extended ASCII uses 8-bits (or **1-byte**) to store each numeric character code. This allows character codes between **0** and **255**.

Although Extended ASCII includes enough symbols for the English language and many other European languages, it still does not contain all of the characters that are needed for many other languages used around the world, such as Japanese, Russian or Mandarin. A more advanced character set is **UNICODE** which allows many more symbols than ASCII. UNICODE can cope with all of these different languages and the characters that they use.

C++ allows you to work with both ASCII and UNICODE characters, although to keep things simple, nearly all of the programs in this book use ASCII. UNICODE characters may require more than one byte of storage, thus they are called "**wide characters**" in C++. Note however that the first 127 characters of both the ASCII and UNICODE character sets are actually the same. For instance, the capital letter "**C**" has the code **67** in both ASCII and UNICODE. UNICODE can use up to 32 bits (or 4 bytes) to store each character code, allowing codes between **0** and **4294967295**, thus it is able to cope with every known symbol for all international languages that are used today, as well as emojis and other useful symbols.

To work with wide characters, your C++ programs can use the **`wchar_t`** data-type. This represents characters using two bytes, rather than as single byte **`char`** data values. This can get quite technical, especially for beginners, so to avoid confusion **`wchar_t`** is not covered here in this book. If you want to know more, further reading elsewhere is recommended.

To work with simple ASCII characters in C++, you can use the `char` data-type.
Here is how you can create a character variable:

```
char firstInitial = 'B';
```

Notice that you put a single quotation mark `'` before and after the character value that you want to use. You should not enclose a `char` value in a pair of `"` double quotes.

Instead of setting the value of a character variable to a particular symbol, you can use the numeric character code:

```
char firstInitial = 66;
```

In the above example, the character code used is **66**. This is the ASCII code for a capital letter **'B'**. Notice that the character code is not enclosed between any quotation marks. Both examples do the same thing, setting the variable called `firstInitial` to 'B'.

The largest character code in the original ASCII character set is **127**, which corresponds to the *delete* character. In general, the printable characters that can be displayed on the screen range between **32** (the code for the *space* character) and **126** (the code for the ~ *tilde* character) inclusive. Character **127** is said to be a **"control character"** and is not displayed in the same way as other printable characters on the screen.

A list of the printable ASCII characters is shown in the Appendix at the back of this book: *"The ASCII character set and character codes"*.

Special ASCII characters

Some characters cannot be typed in directly into a literal text value using the keyboard, most notably the *tab* and *return* characters. To use a *tab* or a *return* character in your program code, you must type a special sequence of keys. In the examples below, `'\t'` means *"tab"* and `'\n'` means *"new-line"*:

```
char tabSymbol = '\t';
char newLineSymbol = '\n';
```

Thus, many special characters are denoted by the `\` *backslash* character. It tells the computer *"here comes something special"* when you are working within a pair of `'` single quotes.

Another special character is the `'` **apostrophe** symbol. You cannot directly place an apostrophe between a pair of single quotes and expect it to work in the same way as other characters that you type from the keyboard:

```
char apostropheSymbol = '''; // This is NOT allowed in C++
```

Thus, some characters need to be preceded by a `\` *backslash* character when you want to use them:

```
char apostropheSymbol = '\''; // This *is* allowed in C++
```

Working with literal text: embedding text values in your code

Many computer programs make use of text – either a lot of it, or small amounts of it. But what actually is text? What we call text is a collection of character symbols, whether they are letters of the alphabet, numerals or other symbols.
In programming, we call a sequence of character symbols a "**string**".

When you want to use a literal text value in a C++ program, it must be enclosed by " double quotation marks. There must a be a " double quotation mark to denote the start of the text value and another to indicate the end. Note the use of " double quotation marks when working with literal text, rather than ' single quotation marks for single characters.

A literal text value could be a word, or a phrase:

```
"dinosaur"
"The Ace of Spades"
```

A really long literal text value could be a whole paragraph:

```
"Once upon a time there was an Ug, who lived at the top of a really big hill.
 Every morning, to get to work, the Ug would get in his car and walk to the train
 station. Then he would catch the bus to the airport and cycle up the stairs to his
 office, before immediately returning to his home on Mars."
```

A really short literal text value might hold one single character symbol:

```
"!"
```

It is even possible to have an **empty** text value that contains no characters at all, denoted by a pair of " quotation mark symbols next to each other with nothing between them (known as an "**empty string**"):

```
""
```

Many programs use literal text values such as those shown above without ever giving them a name, simply embedding them in their code. These are called "**literal strings**".

The statement below makes use of two literal strings, both of which are enclosed within " double quotation marks to show where they begin and where they end:

```
if ( password == "hello" )
    cout << "You have chosen the world's most obvious password.";
```

In the above statement, **"hello"** is a literal string value.

Similarly, the message that gets displayed on the screen is also a literal value:

```
"You have chosen the world's most obvious password."
```

Working with named sequences of characters: `string`

The **string** data-type allows text values to be given a name and to be re-used throughout your C++ program.

Here is how you could create a **string** variable:

```
string greeting = "Good morning! How are you today?";
```

The statement above creates a variable called **greeting** that has the data-type **string**.

The value that **greeting** holds is "Good morning! How are you today?"

Notice how you should put a " double quotation mark before and after the text value that you want to give your **string**.

If a program needs to repeatedly use the text "Good morning! How are you today?" in several places, it can re-use the literal text value by referring to **greeting**, which is the name that the **string** has been given.

As with literal text values, a **string** value can be short, long, or even "empty" (if it does not contain any characters at all):

```
// A short string value
string emoji = ":-)";

// A longer string value
string story = "Once upon a time there was an Ug, who lived at the top of a
really big hill. Every morning, to get to work, the Ug would get in his car
and walk to the train station. Then he would catch the bus to the airport
and cycle up the stairs to his office, before immediately returning to his
home on Mars."

// An empty string
string emptyTextValue = "";
```

Once a **string** variable has been created, its value can be changed or modified while your program is running:

```
string story = story + " " + emoji;
```

The statement above would add the emoji characters on to the end of the story text with a single space between them to aid legibility:

```
Once upon a time there was an Ug, who lived at the top of a really big
hill. Every morning, to get to work, the Ug would get in his car and walk
to the train station. Then he would catch the bus to the airport and cycle
up the stairs to his office, before immediately returning to his home on
Mars. :-)
```

Named values: variables and constants

As we saw at the start of this chapter, data values are often so important to our program code that we give them a **name**. The C++ statements in our code can refer to these names. They tell the computer where to find the values in the computer's memory. When we give a name to a value, we call it a **"named value"**. You will see that some of these values can **change** as the program is executed, or alternatively they can **stay the same**.

Named values that can **change** while a program is running are called **"variables"**.

Conversely, values that **cannot be changed** while a program is running and that **always stay the same** are called **"constants"**.

Remember:

> A **"variable"** is a data value that has a **name**, and this data value can **change** during the program's execution (while the program is running). The name of a variable is often written using **lower-case**.

> A **"constant"** is a useful data value in your program that is given a **name**, but its value **cannot ever change** while the program is running. The name of a constant is often written using **upper-case** (capital letters).

Another word for the name of a constant or variable, is an **"identifier"** – an **alias** that identifies an item of data. There are strict rules that must follow when you create identifiers for constants and variables. For now though, just make sure your names always begin with a letter rather than a number and that they do not have any spaces or punctuation marks in them.

The exception is the _ *underscore* character. Many programmers use _ *underscore* in their identifiers as a substitute for a space, for example `high_score`, and these are allowed in C++ as part of an identifying name. Using underscores in this way can make it easier to read identifiers that are made up of more than one separate word.

Declaring variables in a program

When we want to create a variable or a constant in a C++ program we need to tell the compiler what **kind** of data that it should use. This is called a **"declaration"**. We **declare** (or **"tell"**) the program that we are making a new variable or constant, and that it has a certain name. We also tell the program what kind of data it is going to store, which affects how the value can be processed.

When you make a variable or constant in your program, you must **always** tell the compiler what kind of data it will be storing: its **data-type**. You cannot leave the type of data undecided - the compiler will not let you do this.

The declaration:

```
int myAge;
```

...is a bit like saying:

> I want an *integer* variable, called *"myAge"*. I am not giving it a value yet.

Note that your age is usually changing as you get older and older, so `myAge` will be a **variable** rather than a **constant**.

As we have seen in the previous example, although you must say what kind of data each variable will use, you don't actually need to give it a value straight away. A variable that is **declared** (created) in this way without being given a starting value is called an "**uninitialized variable**".

You can declare more than one variable at the same time in a single line of code, but only if all of the variables concerned have exactly the same type.

Supposing your program is going to use lots of different `int` variables. You could declare them all at once:

```
int daysWorked, daysHolidayEarned, sickDaysTaken;
```

This is slightly shorter than a separate line of code for each variable that you want to declare:

```
int daysWorked;
int daysHolidayEarned;
int sickDaysTaken;
```

Notice though that all of these variables are **uninitialized** – none of them have been given a starting value yet.

Remember that if you don't explicitly set the value for a numeric variable (such as **short**, **int**, **long**, **float**, or **double**) then it will usually hold an unpredictable value. You should not **assume** that an `int` variable will begin with the value **0**.

Why will the value be unpredictable? Because the variable uses a small part of the computer's memory to store its value. Unless you give the new variable a starting value, then that memory will probably still contain some other data value that has previously been used by Linux or another program that has been running on your Pi.

Declaring constants in a program

Some data values cannot be changed while a program is running. This kind of data is called **constant** data. You can tell the computer that a named value is a constant and that it is not variable by adding the word "**const**" before the data-type:

```
const int EGGS_IN_A_BOX = 6;
```

The statement above would make a constant integer called "**EGGS_IN_A_BOX** ". This constant would have the value **6**.

The program would be able to use this name **EGGS_IN_A_BOX**, which would always refer to the constant value **6**.

Notice that when you are declaring a constant, you must **always** give the constant a **value**. Setting the value of the constant cannot be put off until later in your program. The place in your program code where you declare that you are going to use a constant is the **only** opportunity that you get to set the value for it. After the constant has been created in the program, it cannot be changed by any other program statements later on in your code.

Not all constant values are numbers. The statements below define several named **string** constants:

```
const string EYE_COLOUR = "Blue";
const string FIRST_DAY = "Monday";
const string HELP_LINE = "0117-4960111";
const string WEB_ADDRESS = "http://www.raspberrypi.org";
const string SMILEY = ":^)";
```

The first statement makes a constant called "**EYE_COLOUR**". The type of data for the constant is **string** i.e. text. The constant has the value "**Blue**", and this value cannot be changed by the computer while the program is running.

The values for **EYE_COLOUR, FIRST_DAY, HELP_LINE, WEB_ADDRESS** and **SMILEY** would remain constant throughout the execution of the program - they would never change.

Note that you will need to include the **<string>** library and use the **std** standard namespace if you want to use the **string** type for your constants:

```
#include <string>

using namespace std;
```

The statements below create two named **char** constants called **HASH_SYMBOL** and **TAB**:

```
const char HASH_SYMBOL = '#';
const char TAB = '\t';
```

In the code above, note that both character values are enclosed by ' *single-quotes*. Remember that **\t** is the special sequence for a single *tab* character, a handy constant that we might want to use in our program.

During execution of a program, it would not be possible for the constant values of **HASH_SYMBOL** or **TAB** to change. Their values would always stay the same.

Constants are well worth using as they can make your program much easier to understand. They also save you time and effort if you need to make changes to your code in the future. If you use a named constant in more than one place, you won't need to edit every line of code that makes use of it. You will only need to change one single line of code in your program, where the named constant is assigned a value.

In the example below, **DAYS_IN_WEEK** , **DAILY_RATE** and **DAYS_IN_WEEK** are the **names** for three **different constant values**, whilst **discount** is the name of a **variable**:

```
const int DAYS_IN_WEEK = 7;
const float DAILY_RATE = 124.99;
const float ADMIN_FEE = 24.50;
float discount = 35.00;
```

Remember that the word **"const"** at the start of a declaration tells C++ that a value cannot be changed. It tells the compiler that the value will not be a variable and that its value is fixed throughout the entire lifetime of the program's execution.

You can use this constant **DAYS_IN_WEEK** in your code. Whenever the computer finds **DAYS_IN_WEEK**, it knows that you want to use the value **7**. By choosing a descriptive name for the constant, it becomes much easier to tell what the code does:

```
float weeklyCharge = DAYS_IN_WEEK * DAILY_RATE + ADMIN_FEE - discount;
```

Without named constants, the purpose of each number in the calculation may not be so obvious:

```
float weeklyCharge = 7 * 124.99 + 24.50 - 35.00;
```

Remember that once you have made constants in this way, other statements in your program code will not be allowed to change their values while the program is running. You can think of the constant values as being "locked" or "read-only".

Using constants to save you typing specific values again and again

Here's another constant:

```
const PI = 3.141592653589793;
```

If you want to use pi several times in your program code, it is easier to type the **name PI** than to keep typing the **literal value 3.141592653589793** again and again.

By typing the name of the constant, rather than the sequence of digits that make up the value, you are less likely to make a mistake somewhere or introduce **inconsistencies** in your program. All you need to do is use the **name** of the value in your program statement:

```
area = PI * radius * radius;
```

Creating text constants can make your code easier to read. This is especially true when such text values are lengthy. Using simple identifiers can make statements in your code shorter, as the example on the next page shows.

```
const int DANGER_LEVEL = 600;
const string ALERT_MSG = "Warning! Problem detected with hyper-drive engines!";
const string NORMAL_MSG = "Hyper-drive engine operating normally.";

if ( temperature < DANGER_LEVEL )
    cout << NORMAL_MSG << endl;
else
    cout << ALERT_MSG << endl;
```

Using descriptive names for constants and variables

You should always try to think of variable names that mean something. It is easy to guess what the variable called "highScore" is used for in a game, but a variable that is just called "h" would be much more mysterious, since "h" could stand for many different things. Unless you have a very good reason for not doing so, such as trying to make your source-code as short as possible, it is highly recommended that you get into the habit of using descriptive names.

As we have already seen, each variable and constant that your program declares has both a **data-type** and a **name**. The data-type tells the computer what kind of data you are storing and what can be done with it. The name allows your program to refer to the variable or constant elsewhere in your code.

Many C++ programmers use **capital letters** for the names of **constants** and **lower-case letters** for the names of **variables**. This convention helps you to distinguish whether a particular name represents a constant or a variable very quickly:

```
speed = speed + ACCELERATION;   // speed is a variable, ACCELERATION is a constant
```

The program below declares several variables, each one with a different data-type.
It should be obvious what each variable is for as they have all been given meaningful names that describe their purpose.

Example 3.4 – declare_variables.cpp

```
#include <string>      // Program uses variable of type string

using namespace std;    // Will be using standard identifier string

int main()
{
    int myAge;

    float myWeight;

    string nearestAirport;

    bool gotACold;

    char bulletPoint;

    return 0;
}
```

Running the previous program would not display any results on the screen. All of the action occurs in the memory of the computer, you wouldn't actually see anything happening.

Similarly, the next program declares several constants with different data-types, assigning a value to each one:

Example 3.5 – declare_constants.cpp

```
#include <string>      // Program uses constant of type string

using namespace std;      // Will be using the standard identifier string

int main()
{
    const int MONTHS_IN_YEAR = 12;

    const float GRAVITY = 9.8;

    const char AT_SYMBOL = '@';

    const string EYE_COLOUR = "Blue";

    const char BULLET_POINT = '*';


    return 0;
}
```

Again, you wouldn't expect to see much happen when running the above program. It merely creates several constants, placing values in special places in the computer's memory, giving each one a data-type and a name. You wouldn't see anything displayed on the screen.

Remember that when working with values of the **char** data-type, you must use single ' quotation marks around any character value that you want to define, such as the '@' value for the constant **AT_SYMBOL**. When working with **string** values however, you must use double " quotation marks, such as the value **"Blue"** for the constant **EYE_COLOUR**.

Using named constants can help you to avoid silly mistakes in your code, such as trying to change the value of a constant accidentally.

The following error would be quite easy to spot:

```
        const int MAX_SPEED = 70;
    MAX_SPEED += 10;     // Attempt to increase value of the constant by 10
```

Because the identifier **MAX_SPEED** is written in capitals, you should instantly be able to see that it is a constant and that you cannot possibly change the value that it refers to. It makes no sense to increase the value of a constant by **10** while the program is running. Many programmers would quickly spot such a problem when working on a piece of source-code.

Rules for naming constants and variables

Let's consider in a little more detail how to create suitable names for constants and variables.

When you give a name (or **identifier**) to a new variable or constant, you must follow strict rules to make sure that the compiler can make sense of it and that you can successfully use it in your program code.

Spaces in identifiers are not allowed

Spaces are not allowed in a constant or variable name. You cannot put a space anywhere in an identifier:

```
    string first person to visit;   // ERROR! This is not allowed in C++
```

In the above example, the compiler would think that you are trying to use four different variable names, called **first**, **person**, **to** and **visit**.

The compiler would display the following message:

```
    error: expected initializer before 'person'
```

To make this into an acceptable name you would need to remove all of the spaces:

```
    string firstpersontovisit;   // This IS allowed as a variable name
```

Without spaces, long variable names that are made out of several words can difficult to read, so the start of each subsequent word usually begins with a capital letter to help it stand out:

```
    string firstPersonToVisit;   // Extra capital letters used at start of words
```

Another widely used convention is to use an **_ underscore** character anywhere in the identifier where you would normally expect to see a space, such as between words:

```
    first_person_to_visit
```

Thus, underscores are also widely used by programmers to make their identifier names more readable.

Do capital letters matter?

It is important to understand that names for constants and variables are **case sensitive**. It really matters whether you type **upper-case letters** (capitals) or **lower-case letters**. This means that mistakes in your typing can cause problems when you try to compile your C++ code.

The compiler would consider `highscore`, `HighScore` and `Highscore` as three completely different variables - they are not the same! A human being has common sense and would probably guess that they are actually meant to refer to the same thing. Unfortunately, your computer does not have any common sense and you will find that it is extremely fussy.

Using digits in identifiers

Another rule is that identifiers are not allowed to begin with a **numeric digit**. The name of your variable or constant should begin with a letter of the alphabet; it cannot begin with a number.

`2ndPersonToVisit`   is **not** a valid name as it begins with a numeric digit.

`secondPersonToVisit`   **is** acceptable to the compiler as it begins with a letter of the alphabet.

Avoid using special C++ reserved words

When choosing a name, you are not allowed to use the special "**reserved words**" that are part of the C++ language itself. For instance, you cannot make a variable called "`return`" as this word is already in use by C++ to mean something else.

If you ever try to compile a program that attempts to use a reserved word as an identifier name, you will see an error message.

Imagine that I try to use the reserved word `return` as an identifier name in the following statement:

```
int return = 13;
```

Attempting to compile the program would give me the following error message:

```
error: expected unqualified-id before = 'return'
```

This message tells me that the compiler expected to use the word `return` in a different way. It cannot be used as an identifier for a variable and should not be preceded by a data-type, such as `int`.

See *"C++ reserved words"* section in the Appendices at the back of this book for a list of the special words that you need to avoid when thinking of identifier names.

Namespaces: avoiding clashes between identifiers with the same name

Nearly all C++ programs include libraries of code that have been written by other programmers. When you use `#include` to make use of someone else's code, a part of the C++ compiler called the **"pre-processor"** finds the other person's code that you want to use and adds a copy of it to your own code. The complete source-code is then translated by the compiler.

Stop for a moment and think about the other person's source-code. Their code probably contains various variables and constants. What happens if they have chosen the same identifier names in their code as you have in yours? When two people use the same identifiers in different pieces of code, how does the compiler know which name refers to which value?

To solve this problem, we can group all of the constant and variable names together that we have used in the code we have written. Such a collection of identifier names is called a **"namespace"**.

Several of the programs in this book so far have made use of the **"standard"** namespace, which is called **"std"** for short. You have already seen that they contain this line of code:

```
using namespace std;
```

Assigning a value to a constant or variable using =

This program declares several variables, as in the previous program *Example 3.4 - declare_variables.cpp*, assigning a value to each variable that is created:

Example 3.6 – assign_values.cpp

```cpp
#include <string>      // Program will be using variable that has string data-type

using namespace std;     // Will be using the standard identifier string

int main()
{
    // Create some variables and set a starting value for each one
    int myAge = 44;
    float myWeight = 10.5;
    string nearestAirport = "Exeter";
    char bulletPoint = '*';
    bool gotACold = false;


    // Change the values of the variables to something else
    myAge = 45;
    myWeight = 11.2;
    nearestAirport = "Bristol";
    bulletPoint = '>';
    gotACold = true;


    return 0;
}
```

In the program on the previous page, the following statement:

```
int myAge = 44;
```

...means:

*I want to make an **integer** variable, called "**myAge**". Set its value to **44**.*

Any of these **variable** values can **change** (or **vary**) while the program is being executed by the computer. All you need to do is tell the computer which variable you want to change (using the name of the variable) and what you want to happen to it.

The value of **nearestAirport** gets changed from "**Exeter**" to "**Bristol**". The Boolean variable called **gotACold** has been set to **true**. I have also got a year older and have got heavier from eating birthday cake, so the values of both **myAge** and **myWeight** have now increased.

We can see the effect of such a change in this next example. The program creates a **string** variable called **airport**, setting its original value to **Exeter** before displaying this on the screen. The value of **airport** is then changed to **Bristol** and redisplayed.

Example 3.7 – display_string_vals.cpp

```cpp
#include <iostream>     // Program will be displaying some text on the screen

using namespace std;    // Will be using standard identifiers string, cout and endl

int main()
{
    // Create the original string
    string airport = "Exeter";

    // Display the original string value
    cout << "Originally you were flying from... ";

    cout << airport << endl;

    // Update the string value
    airport = "Bristol";

    // Display the updated string

    cout << "You are now flying from... ";

    cout << airport << endl;


    return 0;
}
```

This is what happens when the program runs:

```
Originally you were flying from... Exeter
You are now flying from... Bristol
```

You can see that the value of the **string** variable **airport** changes from **Exeter** to **Bristol**.

Using assignment to swap the contents of two variables – a common problem

Here is an old programming problem that involves changing the values of two different variables. What happens if you try to swap two **string** values around using the following code?

Example 3.8 – swap_values_problem.cpp

```cpp
#include <iostream>     // Program will be displaying some text on the screen

using namespace std;    // Will be using standard identifiers string, cout and endl

int main()
{
    // This program tries to swap two string values around.
    // It tries to exchange the values stored in two different string variables.
    // Can you see why it does not work correctly?

    string firstValue = "Albatross";
    string secondValue = "Zebra";

    // Display the strings before attempting to swap values over
    cout << "The first value is... " << firstValue << endl;
    cout << "The second value is... " << secondValue << endl;

    cout << endl;

    // Attempt to swap the string values around
    firstValue = secondValue;
    secondValue = firstValue;

    // Display the strings after attempting to swap values over
    cout << "The first value is... " << firstValue << endl;
    cout << "The second value is... " << secondValue << endl;

    return 0;
}
```

When the contents of **firstValue** are updated to hold the value of the variable **secondValue** (**"Zebra"**), the program overwrites the original value (**"Albatross"**). This original value is then lost forever.

The original contents of **firstValue** no longer exist anywhere in the computer's memory. They have been wiped out and there is no way of getting them back.

The solution is to use an extra variable as a temporary place to store the original value:

```
    // Attempt to swap the string values around

    string temporaryCopyOfFirstValue = firstValue;

    firstValue = secondValue;

    secondValue = temporaryCopyOfFirstValue;
```

This technique is used in the program below:

Example 3.9 – swap_values_correctly.cpp

```cpp
#include <iostream>     // Program will be displaying some text on the screen

using namespace std;    // Will be using standard identifiers string, cout and endl

int main()
{
    string bobsPrize = "a toaster";
    string janesPrize = "a gold speedboat full of money";

    cout << "Bob has currently won " << bobsPrize << endl;
    cout << "Jane has won " << janesPrize << endl;


    cout << endl << "SWAP THEIR PRIZES!!!" << endl << endl;

    string bobsOriginalPrize = bobsPrize;  // Remembers what Bob had originally won
    bobsPrize = janesPrize;  // Give Bob what Jane has won
    janesPrize = bobsOriginalPrize;  // Give Jane what Bob had originally won


    cout << "Now Bob has won " << bobsPrize << endl;
    cout << "Jane has won " << janesPrize << endl;

    return 0;
}
```

As you can see below, this time the values are swapped correctly:

```
Bob has currently won a toaster
Jane has won a gold speedboat full of money

SWAP THEIR PRIZES!!!

Now Bob has won a gold speedboat full of money
Jane has won a toaster
```

We'll use swapping later in *"Chapter 10: Functions"* to create a program that sorts several data values using the well-known **"bubble-sort"** technique.

Many computers often give uninitialized numeric variables a starting value of zero, and uninitialized strings are set to empty i.e. `""`, but you should not take this for granted. Be very careful not to rely on this happening when your program runs. Not all C++ compilers follow exactly the same rules for uninitialized variables, so the same C++ source-code program could actually behave differently depending on the type of computer that compiles and runs it!

Using what we have learnt so far, we could write a program to take a look at what happens on your Pi when you declare a variable without giving it a starting value:

Example 3.10 – unassigned_variables.cpp

```cpp
#include <iostream>     // Program will be displaying some text on the screen

using namespace std;    // Will be using standard identifiers string, cout and endl

int main()
{
    // Create two variables but don't set any values for them
    int myAge;
    string myName;

    // Display the values of the unassigned variables - what will be displayed?
    cout << "The value of myAge starts as... " << myAge << endl;
    cout << "The value of myName starts as... " << myName << endl;

    // Assign (or set) values to the variables
    myAge = 68;
    myName = "Florence";

    // Display the updated values of the variables
    cout << "Now myAge is... " << myAge << endl;
    cout << "Now myName is... " << myName << endl;

    return 0;
}
```

The program above displays messages on the screen and contains a few unfamiliar lines of code to achieve this. Don't worry - these will be explained fully in *"Chapter 4: Keyboard input and screen output"*.

Often, it is more convenient to set a value for each variable straight away, as soon as it is declared. Just remember that if you ever forget to assign a value to a variable, then your program might behave in unexpected and unpredictable ways.

If you use the `-Wall` option with the g++ compiler, such as when compiling your program from within Geany, you will normally see a warning during compilation if your code attempts to use a variable that has not yet been assigned a value:

```
warning: 'myAge' is used uninitialized in this function
```

Although the compiler generates this warning message, it **will** still create a new executable file for you to run, as long as there are no errors that would stop it doing so.

Remember that a "warning" message from the compiler is not the same as an "error". (The `-Wall` compiler option was introduced earlier in *"Chapter 1: Getting things up and running"*.)

Note also that **34796** is what I see for the value of **myAge** on my Pi. When you run the same program on your own Pi, you may see a different value, depending upon the particular memory location that is chosen by your computer to store the value of **myAge** and the value that was previously stored there.

```
The value of myAge starts as... 34796
The value of myName starts as...
Now myAge is... 68
Now myName is... Florence
```

Summary of Chapter 3: Data-types and values

Here's what we have covered in this chapter:

You must **declare** any constant or variable values that your program code will need to use before your code tries to use them.

When declaring a **constant** or a **variable**, you must say what **type** of data it will use.

The **name** of a **constant** is often written using **capital letters**, to distinguish it from the name of a variable.

The **name** of a constant or a variable is not allowed to contain **spaces**. You can use an **underscore** instead of a space, or begin each new word in the variable name with a capital letter to make it easier to read.

The **value** of a **constant cannot be changed** once your program is running.

The **value** of a **variable can be changed** once your program is running.

Whole numbers can be stored and processed using the `int`, `short`, `long` or `long long` data-types. The range of values that these data-types can handle can be modified using the `signed` or `unsigned` prefixes.

Real numbers can be stored and processed using the `float` or `double` data-types. The range of values that these data-types can handle can be modified using the `signed` and `unsigned` prefixes.

If a numeric value exceeds the maximum allowable value that can be represented by a particular data-type then we say that an **overflow error** has occurred.

Boolean `true` or `false` values can be represented using the `bool` data-type.

A single ASCII character symbol can be represented using the `char` data-type.

By including the `<string>` library, your program-code can use the `string` data-type to represent and work with sequences of characters.

A **namespace** is a collection of identifier names that you can use in your code to avoid clashes between names.

The **standard namespace**, `std`, defines the commonly used identifier names `cout`, `cin` and `endl`.

When declaring a new constant or variable, you can give it a value using the `=` **assignment** operator.

Problems and exercises for you to try

1.	What value would be stored in the variable **myVal** after executing the following expression? `int myVal = -32768 - 3;`

2.	Why would each one of the following variable names be unacceptable to the compiler?
	
	    `1stPersonToGuessCorrectly`
	    `D.O.B.`
	    `weight Of Kyak`
	    `phoneNumber@Work`

3.	Which of these statements correctly assigns a value to the Boolean variable **onHoliday**?
	
	    `bool onHoliday = 'True';`
	    `bool onHoliday = True;`
	    `bool onHoliday = true;`
	    `bool onHoliday = TRUE;`

4.	Write a program that defines an integer constant called **NEVER_CHANGING_INT**. Try to increase the value of **NEVER_CHANGING_INT** by one using the **++** increment operator. What actually happens when you try to compile the program?
5.	Decide which data-type you would use for each of these facts: Gender of a person. Number of people in a room. Telephone number. Weight of a person in kilograms.

Chapter 4:

Keyboard input and screen output

Output: displaying data on the screen

Often, we need to be able to see what the computer is doing while a program is running, but it is not always easy to tell exactly what your Pi is up to. We can tell the computer to display messages or data on the screen to show us what is going on.

You may have noticed the word `cout` in some of our programs so far. This is used to display things on the screen. Let's take a closer look at how `cout` works and different ways to write program statements that will display text and data values.

Before your program can display anything on the screen, you must first tell it to include one of the standard libraries of code:

```
#include <iostream>
```

Strictly speaking, this is not actually a C++ statement. Any line of code that begins with the `#` sign is an instruction to the **compiler** to do something special, called a "**directive**". This particular `#include` directive tells the compiler to go and find a library of code that has been written by someone else that will allow your program to interact with the screen and keyboard. The compiler will search for it in a special directory which was automatically created during the installation of Linux on your Pi.

"`iostream`" actually stands for "**input-output stream**". Streams are **pathways** along which data values can flow.

If you didn't use the `<iostream>` library, you would need to write your own low-level code to place each individual letter or symbol in the correct place on the screen. You would probably need to learn to program using **assembly-language**. This would be a very tricky and time-consuming task, so it makes sense to use the existing code instead. Many programs that display writing on the screen, or that let you type things in using the keyboard, also use the same `<iostream>` code.

Using "channel-out": `cout`

You can think of displaying things as "pushing" them from your program towards the screen. The data flows from your program to the screen along a pathway called a "**channel**". When displaying data, the values are always flowing along the channel from your computer program, out towards the screen. The data travels in one direction only. Data never flows back from your screen into your program.

The name of the channel that leads out of your program to the screen is "***channel-out***". For convenience, programs abbreviate "***channel-out***" to `cout`. Note though that `cout` is not one of the special reserved words that make up the C++ language. It is actually defined within the standard namespace, `std`. This means that the full, official name for the screen is `std::cout`.

To instruct the computer to display something on the screen, you can push or direct values towards `cout`:

```
std::cout << "Hello";    // Displays some literal text on the screen
std::cout << myScore;    // Displays the value of a variable
```

You can think of the examples above as telling data to move towards the screen. Note that the `<<` operator symbol that you see in the statements above is called the "**output redirector**" – it tells values where to go.

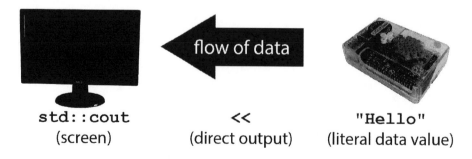

| std::cout | << | "Hello" |
| (screen) | (direct output) | (literal data value) |

Below is a very simple program that will display some text on the screen and then finish with a message to the Linux operating-system, telling it that everything went OK:

```
#include <iostream>      // Program will be displaying some text on the screen

int main()
{
    std::cout << "Hello GNU!";

    std::cout << "How are you?";


    return 0;
}
```

What the code in *Example 4.1 – cout.cpp* means - a step by step explanation...

The first line is the **#include** directive which tells the compiler that our program will be using the **<iostream>** library of screen and keyboard code.

Inside the **main()** section, between the **{ }** braces, there are three program statements.

The first statement displays the "**Hello GNU!**" text on the screen. It directs the text to **std::cout**, which is the channel that leads to the screen.

As we saw previously in *"Chapter 3: Data-types and values"*, **std** is the name of the **standard namespace**, a collection of useful names for things that we can make use of in our programs.

The **::** symbol is called the "**scope-resolution operator**". This is used in a program to show that a name **belongs to** or **is part of** some other thing.

cout means "*channel-out*" (which on the Pi is the screen). It is one of the names that is defined in the standard namespace.

Consequently, **std::cout** literally means "*channel-out, which belongs to the standard namespace*".

<< is the "**output redirector**". It sends text and data from the computer to an output stream. In this case, the output stream that we are using is the screen.

The **;** semi-colon at the end of each line marks the end of each individual program **statement** (each single instruction).

Thus the first two statements in the **main()** section display the text "**Hello GNU!**" and "**How are you?**".

The final statement, **return 0**, tells Linux that the program did not encounter any errors and that everything is OK.

When you run the program, your screen should display the following:

```
Hello GNU!How are you?

------------------
(program exited with code: 0)
Press return to continue
```

You can probably see that the computer has not left a space in-between the two different messages "**Hello GNU!**" and "**How are you?**" - they appear as one long message. Unless you specifically tell the computer not to do this, it will display each message immediately after the previous message on the screen without any regard for presentation or readability. It is up to you to tell the computer how to present things neatly!

Telling the computer to start a new line on the screen using `endl`

Whenever your program displays something on the screen, it is your responsibility to tell the computer when each line of text is finished. To move on to the next line, or to break up the text, you need to tell the program that it is the end of the text line using a special character called "**end-of-line**", or **endl** for short.

Here is the same program from the previous page, but with an **end-of-line** character added after each message is pushed on to the screen:

Example 4.2 – end_of_line.cpp

```cpp
#include <iostream>      // Program will be displaying some text on the screen

int main()
{
    std::cout << "Hello GNU!";

    std::cout << std::endl;    // Tell the computer it is the end of the line

    std::cout << "How are you?";

    std::cout << std::endl;    // Tell the computer it is the end of the line


    return 0;
}
```

So the program above tells the computer to do the following:

> *Display the message* `"Hello GNU!"` *on the screen.*
>
> *Move on to the next line on the screen.*
>
> *Display the message* `"How are you?"` *on the screen.*
>
> *Move on to the next line on the screen (so that the Linux command-prompt will start on a line of its own).*
>
> *Return a status code of* **0** *to tell Linux that everything is fine.*

This time, if you compile and run the executable program, you should see:

```
Hello GNU!
How are you?


------------------
(program exited with code: 0)
Press return to continue
```

This time, each message is given its own line on the screen, making the text easier to read.

Using identifiers from a `namespace` in your code

Both "**cout**" and "**endl**" are **identifiers** – they are **names** for things that have already been made by another programmer and are defined in a special place called the "**standard namespace**". Remember that a namespace is a list of identifier names that have been made by another programmer in some other program code that your computer uses.

Namespaces are great for programming projects where the code is written by more than one person. To avoid different people using the same identifiers or names for different things, they can say who or what the identifiers belong to. They are a really good way to avoid clashes between the code that **you** write and the code that has been written by other people which you are including and using in your program.

The standard namespace will make our code easier to read and will also save us a little bit of typing. To avoid having to type **std::** every time you want to use **cout** and **endl**, all you need to do is put an extra line of code at the top of your program to tell the compiler that the program uses names from someone else's namespace. It will then recognise these identifiers in the code.

To tell the program below that we will be using the identifiers "**cout**" and "**endl**" from the **std** standard C++ namespace, we add the line:

```
using namespace std;
```

When we try to use **cout** and **endl** from now on in our program, the compiler will recognise them without us needing to add the **std::** prefix. However, if we didn't tell the compiler about the namespace that they are from, it would cause an error each time we try to compile our program – the compiler would not know what they are.

Example 4.3 – *namespace.cpp*

```cpp
#include <iostream>     // Program will be displaying some text on the screen

using namespace std;    // Will be using standard identifiers cout and endl

int main()
{
    cout << "Hello GNU!";

    cout << endl;     // Tell the computer it is the end of the line

    cout << "How are you?";

    cout << endl;     // Tell the computer it is the end of the line


    return 0;
}
```

Notice that in the program above, most of the statements inside **main()** are now shorter and the code looks a little simpler than the previous *Example 4.2 - end_of_line.cpp* example. You don't need to tell the compiler where **cout** and **endl** are from because it will look in the **std** namespace.

It is also worth knowing that professional programmers often avoid adding whole namespaces to their code via **using**. By deliberately prefixing every identifier with the namespace and the scope-resolution operator, they can make it absolutely clear which namespace each identifier belongs to, avoiding any potential confusion. For the beginner though, **using** certainly makes writing simple programs a little easier, particularly since we are only using the **std** namespace.

Displaying several things at a time using the << output redirection operator

The previous program is still quite long for such a small amount of text to be written on the screen. To make the program shorter, you can push more than one thing on to the screen at a time using only a single statement.

You can imagine a line of things being pushed towards the screen. If you push from the back of the line then they all move, pushing into each other. Think of the end of the statement as pushing all of the the data towards **cout** (the screen).

Example 4.4 – display_several.cpp

```
#include <iostream>      // Program will be displaying some text on the screen

using namespace std;     // Will be using standard identifiers cout and endl

int main()
{

    cout << "Hello GNU!" << endl << "How are you?" << endl << endl;


    cout << "I'm off now," << endl << "to feed the cow..." << endl << endl;


    return 0;
}
```

Compiling and running this program should display the following text:

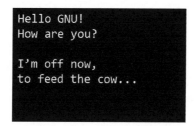

Note that the effect of the two **endl** *end-of-line* characters (shown below in bold) will create a blank line in-between the lines of text that are displayed:

```
    cout << "Hello GNU!" << endl << "How are you?" << endl << endl;
```

Displaying the value of a stored variable on the screen

The program below uses a **variable** called `score`. It is an **integer** – a **whole number**. These ideas were introduced earlier in *"Chapter 3: Data-types and values"*.

When `score` is first created, it has the value **0** (zero). Once the program is running, the **value** of the `score` variable will change several times.

What happens if you use `cout` to display a variable? What will it actually display on the screen?

The statement...

```
cout << score << endl;
```

...displays the **value** of the variable called `score` on the screen. This value is **100**.

It does **not** display the **name** of the variable, when the program runs you will not see the word `score` displayed on the screen.

The `endl` *end-of-line* character then tells the computer it is the end of this line and that it needs to move on to the start of the next line on the screen.

Example 4.5 – display_variable.cpp

```cpp
#include <iostream>      // Program will be displaying some text on the screen

using namespace std;     // Will be using standard identifiers cout and endl

int main()
{
    // The variable score starts off as zero.
    // Then it CHANGES during the program.
    int score = 0;  // score starts as zero

    cout << "My score is ";
    cout << score << endl;

    score = 100;  // Changes the value of score to something different

    cout << "Now my score is ";
    cout << score << endl;

    return 0;
}
```

The finished program should display:

```
My score is 0
Now my score is 100
```

...showing the original and final values stored in the `score` variable.

Here is a program that performs some simple calculations using literal integer values and the `*` multiplication operator. It tells you how many bytes there are in 1 kilobyte, 1 megabyte, 1 gigabyte and so on:

Example 4.6 – display_overflow.cpp

```cpp
#include <iostream>     // Program will be displaying some text on the screen

using namespace std;    // Will be using standard identifiers cout and endl

int main()
{
    cout << "In 1 kilobyte there are 1000 bytes" << endl;

    cout << "In 1 megabyte there are ";
    cout << 1000 * 1000 << " bytes" << endl;

    cout << "In 1 gigabyte there are ";
    cout << 1000 * 1000 * 1000 << " bytes" << endl;

    cout << "In 1 terabyte there are ";
    cout << 1000 * 1000 * 1000 * 1000 << " bytes" << endl;

    cout << "In 1 exabyte there are ";
    cout << 1000 * 1000 * 1000 * 1000 * 1000 << " bytes" << endl;

    return 0;
}
```

The program should compile successfully and allow you to run the executable file that is produced, but you may notice that the compiler displays two **warning messages**, referring to the calculations for a terabyte and an exabyte:

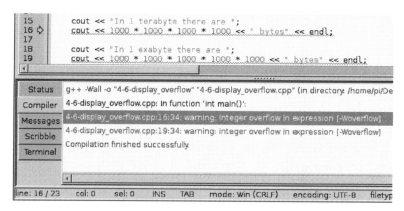

This is because **cout** does normally expect to work with such large values. The results of the calculations for 1 terabyte and 1 exabyte are too large to display. On running the program, you should see the following:

```
In 1 kilobyte there are 1000 bytes
In 1 megabyte there are 1000000 bytes
In 1 gigabyte there are 1000000000 bytes
In 1 terabyte there are -727379968 bytes
In 1 exabyte there are -1530494976 bytes
```

In the second line displayed on the screen, the **expression 1000 * 1000** has been **evaluated** and the **result 1000000** is displayed. Similarly, the third line shown has been evaluated and displayed correctly.

Unfortunately, the last two lines displayed on the screen appear to incorrectly show how many bytes there are in a terabyte and an exabyte. This is because the results are too large to be displayed as an ordinary `int` value, causing them to overflow.

To overcome the problem of displaying unexpectedly large numbers, we can use a variable that has a data-type capable of storing larger values than when using the `int` data-type.

When we attempt to display the value of the **numBytes** variable using **cout**, the program will succeed in displaying it on screen because we have given it an indication as to the possible size of the number – your Pi has an idea of what to expect.

When **cout** encounters the **unsigned long long** variable **numBytes**, it behaves differently as it is prepared for a much larger value than usual:

Example 4.7 – display_large_values.cpp

```
#include <iostream>      // Program will be displaying some text on the screen

using namespace std;     // Will be using standard identifiers cout and endl

int main()
{
    // Store the result of each calculation in a very large variable
    // cout will know that it needs to work with extremely large numbers
    unsigned long long numBytes = 1000;

    cout << "In 1 kilobyte there are ";
    cout << numBytes << " bytes" << endl;

    cout << "In 1 megabyte there are ";
    numBytes *= 1000;
    cout << numBytes << " bytes" << endl;

    cout << "In 1 gigabyte there are ";
    numBytes *= 1000;
    cout << numBytes << " bytes" << endl;

    cout << "In 1 terabyte there are ";
    numBytes *= 1000;
    cout << numBytes << " bytes" << endl;

    cout << "In 1 exabyte there are ";
    numBytes *= 1000;
    cout << numBytes << " bytes" << endl;

    return 0;
}
```

This time, the program compiles without warnings. On execution, the results are now correct:

```
In 1 kilobyte there are 1000 bytes
In 1 megabyte there are 1000000 bytes
In 1 gigabyte there are 1000000000 bytes
In 1 terabyte there are 1000000000000 bytes
In 1 exabyte there are 1000000000000000 bytes
```

This program uses **cout** to display several items of text on the screen, all on the same line.

Because it uses variables that have the data-type **string**, the program contains the following line at the beginning:

```
#include <string>
```

Strictly speaking, because the **<string>** library is also used by the **<iostream>** library - it is not essential to include it in the program below. The second **#include** line is actually unnecessary. By including the **<iostream>** code, our program will also bring in the **<string>** library code. Adding this unnecessary line of code can however make it a little bit clearer which libraries our program uses, helping other programmers to understand how it works. In all subsequent programs throughout the book the extra **#include** directive will be omitted, helping to make the code as short as possible.

Example 4.8 – display_strings.cpp

```cpp
#include <iostream>    // Program will be displaying some text on the screen
#include <string>      // Program will be using string variables

using namespace std;    // Will be using standard identifiers string, cout and endl

int main()
{
    // Store some data in two different string variables

    string greeting = "Hello there";

    string name = "Stupid-Trousers";

    // Display the values stored in the variables
    // with a space in between them

    cout << greeting;

    cout << " ";

    cout << name;

    cout << endl;


    return 0;
}
```

The finished program should display:

```
Hello there Stupid-Trousers
```

Note that it does NOT display:

```
greeting name
```

(It displays the **values** of the variables, not the **names** of the variables.)

This next program displays several lines of text to draw an alien on the screen. Each part of the alien is followed by the **endl** *end-of-line* character, which tells the computer that it is time to start a brand new line on the screen before displaying the next line of text.

Example 4.9 – *display_picture.cpp*

```cpp
#include <iostream>    // Program will be displaying some text on the screen

using namespace std;    // Will be using standard identifiers cout and endl

int main()
{
    cout << endl << endl;  // Display two blank lines

    cout << "   #       #  " << endl;
    cout << "    #    #    " << endl;
    cout << "  #########  " << endl;
    cout << " ##  ###  ## " << endl;
    cout << "#############" << endl;
    cout << "# ######### #" << endl;
    cout << "# #       # #" << endl;
    cout << "   ##   ##   " << endl;

    cout << endl << endl;  // Display two more blank lines



    return 0;
}
```

The code uses **#** symbols to draw out the picture of the alien. The whole picture is composed of spaces and **#** symbols, with invisible **endl** *end-of-line* markers that tell the computer when it is time to start each new line on the screen.

Here's what you should see when you run the program:

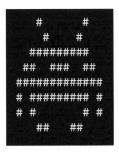

Note the statements at the beginning and the end of the code in **main()** produce a blank line before and after the alien:

```cpp
    cout << endl << endl;
```

Special characters that are denoted by \ backslash

Some symbols that you can type on the keyboard are treated a little differently when displaying things on the screen. One such symbol is the **\ backslash** character, which is used in C++ to indicate that something special is about to follow.

The **backslash** character tells the computer that you want to display or use a special character, either on its own or as part of another string value.

Whenever you see a **\ backslash** somewhere in a text or character value, it's like saying:

"The next character is a special character…"

Here are some of the most important characters that can be used with the **backslash** symbol:

\n   means "***new-line***". It tells the computer to start a fresh line on the screen, in exactly the same way as **endl**.

\t   means "***tab***" (or "**tabulate**"). It tells the computer to move along the current line of the screen to the right. Tab is useful for arranging text into columns, helping you to space it out neatly for legibility.

\v   means "***vertical tab***". It tells the computer to move downwards to the next line on the screen. It does not affect the current horizontal position on the screen, it only changes the vertical position.

\e   marks the start of an "***escape-sequence***". An escape-sequence is a sequence of special codes. These tell the screen to change the way it display characters, such as using colour, bold or other formatting.

\b   means "***backspace***". This character instructs the cursor to move back one place to the left on the screen, erasing the previous character.

\r   means "***carriage return***". This character instructs the cursor to move horizontally all the way to the beginning of the current line on the screen without changing vertical position. The cursor stays on the same row on the screen.

\0   means "***null***". This character is often used to mark the endpoint of a text value or a file, especially in older C-style program code.

The \n new-line character

Instead of using **endl**, you could actually use the **\n new-line** character. Both have exactly the same effect when displaying text, but using **endl** makes your program code easier to read.

Which of the following two lines of code do you think is easier to read and understand?

The first statement below makes use of **<< endl**:

```
cout << "# ######### #" << endl;
```

The second statement embeds a **\n new-line** character inside the text between the pair of **"** quotation marks:

```
cout << "# ######### #\n";
```

Many people might consider that the first line of code is easier to read, as you see exactly what will be displayed. With the second line of code though, you need to pick out the **\n** character visually to see which printable characters will actually be displayed on the screen - this is not always easy to do.

The **\t** *tab* character creates a horizontal gap, moving along towards the right before displaying any further characters on the screen. (Remember: the term "*tab*" is short for "tabulate", meaning "to make into a table".)

Example 4.10 – tab_char.cpp

```cpp
#include <iostream>     // Program will be displaying some text on the screen
#include <unistd.h>     // Uses the sleep() function to pause 1 second

using namespace std;    // Will be using standard identifiers cout and endl

int main()
{
    cout << "3..." << flush;
    sleep( 1 );

    cout << "\t2..." << flush;
    sleep( 1 );

    cout << "\t1..." << flush;
    sleep( 1 );

    cout << "\tGO!" << endl;

    return 0;
}
```

The **\v** vertical-tab character

The **\v** *vertical-tab* character moves vertically down one line, but stays in the horizontal position before displaying any further characters on the screen:

Example 4.11 – vertical_tab.cpp

```cpp
#include <iostream>     // Program will be displaying some text on the screen

using namespace std;    // Will be using standard identifiers cout and endl

int main()
{
    cout << "H\vE\vL\vP\v!" << endl;

    return 0;
}
```

Below you can see the effect of using the vertical tab character after displaying each letter:

Here is an example that uses the **** *double backslash* character when displaying several literal text values:

Example 4.12 – backslash_char.cpp

```cpp
#include <iostream>    // Program will be displaying some text on the screen

using namespace std;    // Will be using standard identifiers cout and endl

int main()
{
    cout << endl << endl << endl;  // Display 3 blank lines

    cout << "(    )" << endl;
    cout << "/> <\\" << endl;
    cout << "|    |" << endl;
    cout << "\\_._/" << endl;
    cout << "  moooOOOOOOooooo!";

    cout << endl << endl << endl;  // Display 3 more blank lines

    return 0;
}
```

When you run the program, you should see this picture:

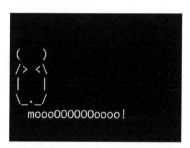

To produce the picture of the cow, two of the lines of code use a **** *double-backslash* to make a single **** *backslash* character appear on the screen:

```cpp
cout << "/> <\\" << endl;

cout << "\\_._/" << endl;
```

It's like saying:

"Here's a special character to display, it's a backslash."

Note that one single backslash on its own would not be displayed as such, it would instead be an indication that a further special character was to be expected. You would not see a backslash symbol displayed on the screen.

The program below changes the colour of different lines of text using **\e escape-sequences**. The **\e** character tells the screen that it is about to display something using a special sequence of codes to alter the appearance of any further text.

For example:

```
cout << "\e[31m TOMATO" << endl;
```

The above line would display the word **TOMATO** on the screen using red text, rather than in the usual colour for your terminal. This is because the literal text value contains an escape-sequence at the start.

\e marks the start of a new escape-sequence. The **[** symbol tells the display to change the colour. The code **31m** is for the foreground colour **red**, which will be used for each subsequent letter that gets displayed on the screen.

Example 4.13 – display_colours.cpp

```
#include <iostream>     // Program will be displaying some text on the screen

using namespace std;    // Will be using standard identifiers cout and endl

int main()
{
    // Different foreground colours
    cout << "\e[31m RED" << endl;
    cout << "\e[32m GREEN" << endl;
    cout << "\e[33m MELLOW YELLOW (urrgh!)" << endl;   // Looks more like brown?!
    cout << "\e[34m BLUE" << endl;
    cout << "\e[35m MAGENTA (purple)" << endl;
    cout << "\e[0m YOUR DEFAULT (USUAL) TEXT COLOUR" << endl;

    // Different background colours
    cout << "\e[41m White on red" << endl;
    cout << "\e[42m White on green" << endl;

    // Normal and bold weight
    cout << "\e[0m Normal weight text." << endl;
    cout << "\e[1m BOLD TEXT - super chunky!" << endl;

    // Reset everything back to normal - otherwise the terminal will
    // continue with the settings once the program has finished execution
    cout << endl << "\e[0m Back to how things were again." << endl;

    return 0;
}
```

Unfortunately the escape code for yellow often looks more like brown on the Pi. A brighter yellow can be obtained using a slightly longer escape-sequence, allowing a wider range of colours:

```
cout << "\e[38;5;226m BRIGHT YELLOW!" << endl;
```

See the *"Escape-sequences to control the colour text on the screen"* section in the Appendices for more colour codes.

Example 4.14 – sleep.cpp

```cpp
#include <iostream>     // Program will be displaying some text on the screen
#include <unistd.h>     // Uses the sleep() function to pause during execution

using namespace std;    // Will be using standard identifiers string, cout and endl

int main()
{
    string message = "   mmMMMoooOOOOOOooooo!!!";

    cout << endl << endl << endl;    // Display 3 blank lines

    // Display the cow
    cout << "(    )" << endl;
    cout << "/> <\\" << endl;
    cout << "|    |" << endl;
    cout << "\\_._/" << endl;

    // Escape-sequence to turn on bold formatting
    cout << "\e[1m";

    // Display the message, one letter at a time with 1 second delay
    for ( unsigned int position = 0;  position < message.length();  position++ )
    {
        cout << message.at( position ) << flush;
        sleep( 1 );
    }  // end of for loop

    // Escape-sequence to return to normal formatting
    cout << "\e[0m";

    cout << endl << endl << endl;    // Display 3 blank lines

    return 0;
}
```

The code above introduces several new tricks. Firstly, it uses the **at()** function to extract a single character from the message at a certain place. It also uses a **for** loop to control which of the characters to extract from the message, using the **position** variable. The loop starts at the very first character in the message, working towards the final character, one position at a time.

After extracting each character, the program displays it on the screen:

```cpp
cout << message.at( position ) << flush;
```

Note that the characters in a **string** value are individually numbered beginning at position zero, so the first character in the message is actually at position **0**, rather than position **1**. This is why the **for** loop begins at the value **0**. We say that the **string** value is "**zero-indexed**".

The statement above also makes use of a special character, called **flush**, which will be explained later on the next page.

After displaying each character from the message, the program calls the `sleep()` function:

```
sleep( 1 );
```

The `sleep()` function causes the computer to pause for a given time, measured in seconds. Thus `sleep( 1 )` makes the computer pause for 1 second after displaying each letter in the message **mmMMMoooOOOOOOOoooo!!!**

In order to use the `sleep()` function in your program, you will need to make use of an additional library of code:

```
#include <unistd.h>
```

This is the "**UNIX standard library**" which allows you to call or activate several special operating system functions.

There is a problem however. Telling the computer to display each individual character and then pause for one second sounds fine in theory, but in practice you would find that the Pi displays the entire line of text after a delay of several seconds, all in one go.

This is because the computer tries to improve the efficiency of the program by grouping different things together that have been sent to channel-out. It displays them all as a finished line of text on the screen in one single operation when it reaches the `endl` character.

Clearing channel-out using the `flush` character

We can force the Pi to immediately display individual characters instantly by "**flushing**" the contents of channel-out (the pathway to the screen). This clears out any data that is waiting to be displayed, putting it straight on to the screen without any further delay.

Sending a special character, called the `flush` character (which is defined in the `std` namespace) to channel-out tells the screen to instantly display anything that is currently waiting. The computer will not wait for any other display statements - it will go ahead and update the screen right away.

Thus the previous program tells the computer to immediately display the single character using `flush`:

```
cout << message.at( position ) << flush;
```

Each single character in the message from the cow is now displayed on the screen one at a time, followed by a one second pause, rather than all at once.

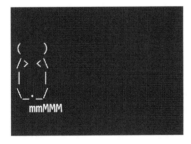 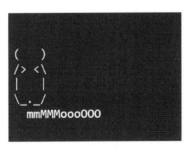 

For more details about working with text and characters, see *"Chapter 8: Characters and text strings"*.

This final example of special characters uses **\b** *backspace* to adjust the position along a line of text:

Example 4.15 – backspace_char.cpp

```cpp
#include <iostream>    // Program will be displaying some text on the screen
#include <unistd.h>    // Uses the sleep() function to pause during execution

using namespace std;    // Will be using standard identifiers cout and flush

int main()
{
    // Display original message
    cout << "Ready in... 3" << flush;
    sleep( 1 );

    // Use backspace character to move left one place and display "2"
    cout << "\b2" << flush;
    sleep( 1 );

    // Use backspace character to move left one place and display "1"
    cout << "\b1" << flush;
    sleep( 1 );

    // Move back to beginning of line using carriage-return character
    cout << "\rAll systems GO!" << endl;
    sleep( 1 );

    return 0;
}
```

After displaying the first message **"Ready in... 3"**, the program calls **sleep()** to pause for **1** second.

Several of the **cout** statements use the **\b** *backspace* and **flush** characters to tell the screen to overwrite and redisplay its contents straight away. For example, the **cout** statement below uses the **\b** backspace character to move one character to the left on the same line of the screen, before displaying **"2"** in place of the original **"3"**:

```cpp
    cout << "\b2" << flush;
```

Again, the statement uses the **flush** character to immediately update the display during the countdown:

```
Ready in... 1
```

The final statement uses a **\r** *carriage-return* character to move back to the beginning of the line, before displaying the text:

```cpp
    cout << "\rAll systems GO!" << endl;
```

This returns to the start of the current line on the screen, ready to display the final message:

```
All systems GO!
```

Here is another simple program that repeatedly displays a message across the screen using different colours, pausing for a second after displaying each of them:

Example 4.16 – *flush.cpp*

```cpp
#include <iostream>      // Program will be displaying some text on the screen
#include <unistd.h>      // Uses the sleep() function to pause during execution

using namespace std;     // Will be using standard identifiers string, cout and endl

int main()
{
    const string COLOUR_RED = "\e[31m";

    const string COLOUR_GREEN = "\e[32m";

    const string COLOUR_NORMAL = "\e[0m";

    string message = "GNU/Linux";  // The message to be displayed

    // Infinite loop that will display message repeatedly across the screen
    while ( true )
    {
        cout << COLOUR_RED << message << flush;
        sleep( 1 );

        cout << COLOUR_GREEN << message << flush;
        sleep( 1 );

        cout << COLOUR_NORMAL << message << flush;
        sleep( 1 );

    }  // end of the infinite while loop

    return 0;
}
```

As you can see from the code above, this program uses the constant identifiers **COLOUR_RED**, **COLOUR_GREEN** and **COLOUR_NORMAL** to make it clearer what each statement does. This is a handy because the identifiers can serve as a short-hand to save you remembering the actual codes for each colour.

It is easier to understand the following line of code that uses a constant identifier for a particular colour:

```cpp
cout << COLOUR_GREEN << message << flush;
```

...than the equivalent statement that directly contains the escape-sequence for that colour:

```cpp
cout << "\e[32m" << message << flush;
```

Note that the **while** loop is explained fully in *"Chapter 7: Repetition using loops"*.

Rather than creating the same code repeatedly in every single C++ program that you write it is possible to re-use handy pieces of code by storing them in separate files. Programs that you write can make use of these files and the code they contain.

First of all, let's make a file that contains some useful code that our other programs can make use of. This file will contain several useful **string** constants that will allow us to use colours when displaying text on the screen, without having to remember the ANSI escape-sequences for each colour.

The *colours.h* file below is called a "**header file**". It simply contains declarations for the **string** constants, assigning values to each one. Header files should always be saved ending in ".*h*". The programs that you write can then include the contents of header files along with their own code.

You can include your new header file in any program that you create in the future. Your program code can then make use of the constants from the header file as though they were part of the main program itself.

Example 4.17a – *colours.h*

```
// This file can be included in your programs. They will be able to use the names
// RED, AMBER, GREEN and NORMAL instead of using escape-sequences to change the
// colour of text that is displayed on the screen.

using namespace std;    // Will be using the string standard identifier

const string RED = "\e[41m";      // Red background
const string AMBER = "\e[43m";    // Amber background
const string GREEN = "\e[42m";    // Green background
const string NORMAL = "\e[0m";    // Normal terminal settings
```

You can make use of the header file in your programs by adding an **#include** directive. Note that there is no need for you to compile or build the actual *colours.h* header file - it will simply be "absorbed" into the main program that you create.

Example 4.17b – *traffic_lights.cpp*

```
#include <iostream>      // Program will be displaying some text on the screen
#include <unistd.h>      // Uses the sleep() function to pause during execution

#include "colours.h"     // Header file defines names for useful escape-sequences

using namespace std;     // Will be using standard identifiers cout and endl

int main()
{
    cout << RED << "Stop!    " << endl;
    sleep( 3 );

    cout << AMBER << "Ready..." << endl;
    sleep( 3 );

    cout << GREEN << "Go!      " << endl;

    cout << NORMAL;

    return 0;
}
```

Note that the filename of the included file is enclosed in a pair of " double quotation marks, rather than < > angle-braces.

```
#include "colours.h"
```

This tells the compiler to look for the file in the same directory as the source-code for your program file. Angle braces are used however when including a file from the **standard** Linux directory of library files. On the Pi, the standard library files are usually stored in a particular directory (which can vary, depending on the version of GCC that you have installed) such as:

```
/usr/include/c++/4.9
```

A potential problem when including files: declaring constants and variables more than once

When including a file, it is important to make sure that your code does not attempt to declare the same constants, variables or functions more than once as this would lead to a compilation error.

Your header file can contain additional directives that check to see whether the header file has already been included by your program or by any other file that your program uses. The header file below contains the same code as before, but sandwiches it in-between some extra directives that check whether the identifier **_myColours** has previously been created.

The first time that any program code includes the header file below, two things happen. Firstly, the identifier **_myColours** gets defined. This will be used by the g++ pre-processor when checking any subsequent attempts to include the header file.

If **_myColours** is found to have been defined already, then this means that the header file has already been included and the code should not been included a second time. If **_myColours** has **not** already been defined though, the rest of the code in the header file gets brought into your program by the pre-processor. This ensures that the code is included once only.

Modified Example 4.17a – *colours.h*

```
// This file can be included in your programs. They will be able to use the names
// RED, AMBER, GREEN and NORMAL instead of using escape-sequences to change the
// colour of text that is displayed on the screen.

// It determines whether or not this file has already been included already in your
// program - it can only be included once! Any code that tries to include it will
// cause _myColours identifier to be defined.

#ifndef _myColours
#define _myColours

// This block of code will only be included if _myColours has not previously been
// defined and is now being defined for the first time.

using namespace std;     // Will be using the string standard identifier

const string RED = "\e[41m";     // Red background
const string AMBER = "\e[43m";    // Amber background
const string GREEN = "\e[42m";    // Green background
const string NORMAL = "\e[0m";    // Normal terminal settings

#endif
```

Controlling the cursor position on the screen when displaying values

When displaying values on the screen it is possible to change the cursor position using an escape-sequence.

You can specify the row number and the column number for the cursor to move to, prior to displaying any values. This will ensure that they are placed exactly where you want them.

On the Raspberry Pi using an LXTerminal window, the default size of the window is 24 rows tall and 80 columns wide.

To place a message roughly in the middle of such a terminal window you could use the following code:

```
// Move to 13th row, 37th column, then display message
cout << "\e[12;36H" << "Hola!";

// Move the cursor towards bottom of screen, ready for prompt to appear
cout << "\e[20;0H";
```

In each of the escape-sequences above, the first part is the **row number**, followed by a **;** **semi-colon**, then the **column number**, followed by **H** to mark the end of the escape-sequence.

Note that the row and column numbers begin at zero, so the 40th column is number **39**. As mentioned earlier, this is called **"zero-indexing"**. I have moved the cursor a little to the left of the middle column as the message is five characters long, starting at the 37th column to account for approximately half of the width of the text.

This technique is simple when you know exactly where you want your text to be positioned. But what about when you want to determine the position of some text while the program is running, perhaps using a calculation, a random number or iteration?

It is not possible to substitute a variable name or an expression inside the escape-sequence - it won't work at run-time!

What is needed is a way to convert any expression or variable to a simple sequence of characters. The program below repeatedly uses random numbers to choose the row and column number for the cursor. It then converts each random number that has been chosen to a sequence of characters, building it into an escape-sequence to control the cursor position.

Example 4.18 – *digital_snowstorm.cpp*

```cpp
#include <iostream>  // Program will be using screen
#include <cstdlib>   // Program uses the random() function
#include <unistd.h>  // To slow things down using usleep() function
#include <sstream>   // To convert between numbers and strings

using namespace std;  // Will be using standard identifier cout

int main()
{
    // Will count number of flakes
    // This is used to determine which colour to display
    int snowflake = 0;

    // Do this code again and again forever...
    while ( true )
    {
```

continues on next page...

```
        // Pick a random column number for the screen
        int column = random() % 80;

        // Pick a random row number
        int row = random() % 25;

        // Convert the column number to a string of characters
        stringstream columnConverter;
        columnConverter << column;
        string columnString;
        columnConverter >> columnString;

        // Convert the row number to a string of characters
        stringstream rowConverter;
        rowConverter << row;
        string rowString;
        rowConverter >> rowString;

        // Position the cursor on screen at particular row and column
        cout << "\e[" + rowString + ";" + columnString + "H";

        // Decide what colour to use to display snowflake
        switch ( snowflake % 3 )
        {
            case 0:   cout << "\e[38;5;226m";   break;   // Yellow
            case 1:   cout << "\e[31m";         break;   // Red
            case 2:   cout << "\e[37m";         break;   // White
        }   // end of switch statement

        // Increase snowflake counter
        snowflake++;

        // Display 1 or 0 symbol
        // (obtained by modulo 2 remainder on the number of snowflakes)
        cout << snowflake % 2;

        // Update screen immediately to show new snowflake
        cout << flush;

        // Pause for part of a second
        usleep( 10000 );

    }   // end of while loop

    return 0;
}
```

When executed, you should see your screen fill with mutli-coloured **0** and **1** symbols at random places.

Note that the program uses several new ideas that will be introduced in subsequent chapters, most notably **stringstream** conversions between integers and character strings, which are explained fully in *"Chapter 11: Files of data"*. It also uses the **usleep()** function, which is similar to the **sleep()** function, but which can pause for part of a second. Pausing for only a split-second means that the snowstorm is not too slow when the program runs.

Formatting values to change the way they are displayed

C++ allows your program to modify or "format" the way that values are displayed on the screen. Often you might want to display extra spaces alongside a value to ensure that it has exactly the correct width. Alternatively, you might want to change the way in **float** or **bool** values get displayed.

It is possible to send special instructions called "**stream manipulators**" to a stream, telling the stream how to behave. To use the screen and keyboard stream manipulators, your code must include the **<iomanip>** library:

```
#include <iomanip>
```

Controlling the display width of a value

To instruct channel-out to display a data-value using a particular width, you can use the **setw()** "**set width**" manipulator before submitting the value itself to the channel:

```
cout << setw( 10 ) << "2.5";
```

Normally, displaying the value **2.5** would occupy only three characters on the screen, but the **setw()** manipulator above tells the Pi to use a width of **10** characters when displaying the value. To ensure that the value is wide enough, the Pi adds seven extra spaces prior to displaying the digits of the number.

Note that **setw()** is defined in the **std** standard namespace, just like **cout, cin** and **endl**. Declaring the **std** standard namespace in your code avoids the need for you to type **std::setw()** instead of **setw()**.

The program below shows the effects of padding out a value with varying amounts of space on the screen:

Example 4.19 – set_width.cpp

```
#include <iostream>     // Program will be using screen and keyboard
#include <iomanip>      // Program will be formatting values that are displayed

using namespace std;    // Will be using standard identifiers cout, endl and setw

int main()
{
    const int NUM = 13;     // Value has only 2 digits

    // Show how the value would normally be displayed without any formatting
    cout << "Without any formatting:" << endl;
    cout << "[" << NUM << "]" << endl;
    cout << endl << endl;     // Display blank line

    // Show what the value would look on the screen with some formatting
    cout << "With formatting:" << endl;

    // Repeatedly display the value on the screen, padding it with extra spaces
    for ( int width = 12;  width >= 1;  width-- )
        cout << "[" << setw( width ) << NUM << "]" << endl;

    return 0;
}
```

How does the previous program work? It creates a named constant called **NUM** which has the value **13**.

It then displays the value of **NUM** using an ordinary `cout` statement, enclosing it within **[ ]** braces. You should see that there is no white-space between the **[** brace and the first digit **1**. Similarly, there is no white-space between the **]** brace and the final digit **3**. This demonstrates that under ordinary circumstances, when displaying a numeric value using `cout`, no white-space is displayed before or after the digits of the value.

The next part of the program uses a `for` loop to repeatedly display the value of **NUM** with decreasing amounts of padded white-space appearing before the first digit. To begin with, `setw()` is used to set the display width of the value of **NUM** to **12**. There are only two digits that make up the value **13**, thus **10** spaces will be added in front of the value when it is displayed.

Each iteration of the loop decreases the display width that will be used by **1**, leading to fewer and fewer spaces being used to pad out the value. Eventually, no spaces are required at all as the number of digits that make up the value matches the required width.

As with the unformatted value, the **[ ]** braces around each value displayed within the loop allow you to see the number of additional spaces that have been added as padding each time around.

```
Without any formatting:
[13]


With formatting:
[          13]
[         13]
[        13]
[       13]
[      13]
[     13]
[    13]
[   13]
[  13]
[ 13]
[13]
[13]
```

If ever your code attempts to set the width to a number that is smaller than the number of characters that make up the value, then the full value is displayed - it is not truncated. For instance, if a value is normally displayed using **5** characters, but the width is set to **2**, the Pi would go ahead and display all of the **5** characters that make up the value.

You can see this in the final lines that are displayed in the screenshot above. In this case, the `setw()` instruction will appear to have no effect on the way that the value is displayed on screen. The number **13** requires **2** digits to be displayed in full. Once `setw()` attempts to set the display width to only **1** as part of the `for` loop, your Pi ignores the suggested width and instead uses the minimum number of characters that will allow the number to be displayed in its entirety.

When displaying numeric values, such as those that use the **float** or **double** data-types, your program can specify how many decimal places to show after the decimal point.

The first-step is to instruct the stream to format any real numbers using fixed point notation, as opposed to floating-point:

```
cout << fixed;      // Display numeric value using fixed point notation
```

The next step is to tell the computer how many decimal places you would like to see after each decimal point:

```
cout << setprecision( 5 );      // Set the number of decimal places to display
```

Any numeric values that you subsequently choose to display on the screen will be shown to five decimal places.

These steps can be combined, as shown in the example below:

```
cout << fixed << setprecision( 3 ) << 0.62525;   // Display to 3 dec places
```

The program below uses a simple **for** loop to display the same numeric value using successively fewer decimal places:

Example 4.20 – set_precision.cpp

```cpp
#include <iostream>      // Program will be using screen and keyboard
#include <iomanip>       // Program will be formatting values that are displayed

using namespace std;     // Will be using standard identifiers cout, endl and setw

int main()
{
    const float NUM = 0.66666;      // Actual value, uses 5 decimal places

    // Show how the value would normally be displayed without any formatting
    cout << "Without any formatting:" << endl;
    cout << NUM << endl;
    cout << endl << endl;      // Display blank line

    // Show what the value would look on the screen with some formatting
    cout << "With formatting:" << endl;

    // Force the computer to display numbers using fixed point notation
    cout << fixed;

    // Repeatedly display the value on screen using fewer and fewer decimal places
    for ( int places = 5;  places >= 0;  places-- )
        cout << setprecision( places ) << NUM << " to " << places << " dp" << endl;

    return 0;
}
```

The screenshot below shows how value of **NUM** is displayed each time around the `for` loop:

```
Without any formatting:
0.66666


With formatting:
0.66666 to 5 dp
0.6667 to 4 dp
0.667 to 3 dp
0.67 to 2 dp
0.7 to 1 dp
1 to 0 dp
```

Note that attempting to display a real value to zero decimal places will result in it appearing to be rounded to the nearest whole number.

Controlling the way that `bool` values are displayed

By default, if you try to display a **bool** value by directing it to `cout`, your Pi will display it using the numbers **1** or **0**.

Using the **boolalpha** stream-manipulator though, it is possible to tell `cout` (or any other stream) to display the words **true** or **false** instead:

```cpp
cout << boolalpha;    // Display bool values as true or false
```

The stream manipulator **noboolalpha** tells the screen to revert to display **bool** values as **1** or **0** again:

```cpp
cout << noboolalpha;    // Display bool values as 1 or 0
```

The program below makes use of both the **boolalpha** and **noboolalpha** manipulators to change the way two different **bool** variables are displayed:

Example 4.21 – display_true_false.cpp

```cpp
#include <iostream>    // Program will be using screen and keyboard
#include <iomanip>     // Program will be formatting values that are displayed

using namespace std;    // Will be using standard identifiers cout, endl etc

int main()
{
    bool happy = true;
    bool sad = false;

    // To begin with, the screen will display bool values as 1 or 0

    cout << "I am happy... " << happy << endl;
    cout << "I am sad... " << sad << endl;
```

continues on next page...

```cpp
    cout << endl;

    // Tell the screen to start displaying bool values as true or false

    cout << boolalpha;     // Display bool values as true or false

    cout << "I am happy... " << happy << endl;
    cout << "I am sad... " << sad << endl;

    cout << endl;

    // Tell the screen to go back to displaying bool values as 1 or 0 again

    cout << noboolalpha;     // Display bool values as 1 or 0

    cout << "I am happy... " << happy << endl;
    cout << "I am sad... " << sad << endl;


    return 0;
}
```

Here is what the program displays on the screen:

```
I am happy... 1
I am sad... 0

I am happy... true
I am sad... false

I am happy... 1
I am sad... 0
```

Input: getting a value into the computer from the keyboard using `cin`

So far, the only data that we have given the computer has been included as part of the actual program code itself. Messages that we have displayed on the screen have been built in or embedded within individual C++ statements.

Most programs allow you to communicate with the computer while the program is running. You can supply your own data values using the keyboard or give the computer some data using some other kind of device. This is called **input**. Data flows **into** the computer for storage and processing.

The simple code for transferring data from the keyboard into the computer has already been written for you. You can include it in your own programs as part of the **<iostream>** library:

```
#include <iostream>
```

Now your code can go ahead and work with the keyboard using a stream called "***channel-in***", or `cin` for short.

Again, as with `cout` (***"channel-out"***) in our previous programs, we can avoid having to type `std::` before `cin` by including the standard namespace, `std`:

```
using namespace std;
```

When someone types something into the computer, our program will need to **store** what they typed so that their data can be used by other statements in the program. We store the data that was typed in as a **variable** – a value in the memory of the computer with an identifying name that will help us find it again when we want to use it.

To get data from the keyboard and put it into a variable, we can use the following code:

```
cin >> myVariable;
```

When the computer executes the statement above, it allows the user to type in a single value. As soon as they press the ***return*** or ***enter*** key, the data they typed in will be transferred into the variable and stored for later use by the rest of the program code.

> `cin` means "***channel-in***", the way into the computer, which is the keyboard.

> The `>>` symbol is called the "***input redirector***". It shows the data which direction in which to flow.

> The data will flow from the keyboard into the variable called **myVariable**.

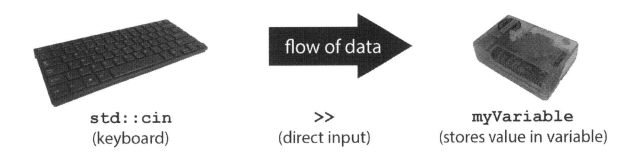

| std::cin | >> | myVariable |
| (keyboard) | (direct input) | (stores value in variable) |

Example 4.22 – simple_input.cpp

```
#include <iostream>      // Program will be using screen and keyboard

using namespace std;     // Will be using standard identifiers string, cin, cout, endl

int main()
{
    // Get user to type in their name
    string myName;
    cout << "Enter your name please..." << endl;
    cin >> myName;

    cout << "Hello " << myName << endl;

    return 0;
}
```

Here's an example of what happens when you run the above program:

```
Enter your name please...
Egghead
Hello Egghead
```

The program is able to "remember" and make use of whatever you type in.

Failing to enter a value - typing in a blank input

We have just seen that programs can use `cin` to read in a value from the keyboard. But what happens if the user doesn't type anything in, such as when they just press the *return* or *enter* key and enter a blank value?

In the examples in this chapter, you will notice that a blank value will not be accepted if you fail to type any digits or characters.

When pressing *enter* on your keyboard, the computer repeatedly expects you to try again until it is given a non-blank value.

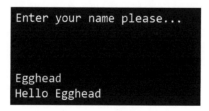

```
Enter your name please...



Egghead
Hello Egghead
```

Getting a whole line of text from the keyboard, including spaces

Staying with **Example 4.22 - simple_input.cpp**, what happens if there is a space in the name that you type in, such as between a person's first-name and a surname?

Try typing in the name `"Emperor Tomato Ketchup"` and you will see that only the first word gets stored in the variable. The computer stops reading characters from the keyboard as soon as it reaches the first space, so the actual value stored for `myName` is `"Emperor"`. The rest of the text that has been typed in (`"Tomato Ketchup"`) appears to have been ignored.

```
Enter your name please...
Emperor Tomato Ketchup
Hello Emperor
```

Solving the problem of spaces in keyboard input

We can use a different method to allow keyboard input. Try changing the line that says...

```
cin >> myName;
```

to...

```
getline( cin, myName );
```

What does the above `getline()` statement mean?

> `getline` is a function that will read in a whole line of text from the keyboard until reaching a certain special character (which is usually the `'\n'` *new-line* character).
>
> `cin` tells the function to get characters from *channel-in*, which is the input stream from the **keyboard**.
>
> `myName` is the name of a **string** variable that will store the characters once they have been typed in.

Most of the time, `getline()` is used by programmers to take in text characters until reaching the `'\n'` character, indicating that the user has pressed the *enter* or *return* key on the keyboard. You can actually give `getline()` a third argument if you want to change the kind of character at which it should stop reading:

```
getline( cin, myName, '\n' );    // Stops reading characters when reaching "new-line"
getline( cin, myName, '\t' );    // Stops reading characters when reaching "tab"
getline( cin, myName, ',' );     // Stops reading characters when reaching a comma
```

If you compile and run the program again after adding the `getline()` statement to your code, you will be able to enter text that contains spaces and more than one word. The computer will no longer stop when it reaches a space. The entire text will be stored in the `myName` variable and will be displayed on the screen:

```
Enter your name please...
Emperor Tomato Ketchup
Hello Emperor Tomato Ketchup
```

You may have seen by now that it is possible to enter unnecessary characters when being prompted for a number, a character or text. Your Pi usually ignores these unwanted excess characters. Sometimes however, you need to clean out the characters to make sure that they do not interfere with other keyboard inputs later on in your program, otherwise your code may display some very strange behaviour when it executes. This is especially true when typing letters of the alphabet whilst your Pi is expecting you to type in an integer value.

Try this program, which asks for a range of different values using several different data-types:

Example 4.23 – inputs_no_clear.cpp

```cpp
#include <iostream>      // Program will be using screen and keyboard

using namespace std;     // Will be using standard identifiers string, cin, cout, endl

int main()
{
    // Get user to type in floating-point value
    float myFloat;
    cout << "Enter a float..." << endl;
    cin >> myFloat;
    cout << "Stored as " << myFloat << endl;

    // Get user to type in floating-point value
    float anotherFloat;
    cout << "Enter another float..." << endl;
    cin >> anotherFloat;
    cout << "Stored as " << anotherFloat << endl;

    // Get user to type in a single word - no spaces allowed
    string myString;
    cout << "Enter a string using cin..." << endl;
    cin >> myString;
    cout << "Stored as " << myString << endl;

    // Get user to type in a single character
    char myChar;
    cout << "Enter a char..." << endl;
    cin >> myChar;
    cout << "Stored as " << myChar << endl;

    // Get user to type in a whole number
    int anotherInt;
    cout << "Enter another integer..." << endl;
    cin >> anotherInt;
    cout << "Stored as " << anotherInt << endl;

    // Get user to type in a string of text - spaces allowed
    string anotherString;
    cout << "Enter another string using getline..." << endl;
    getline( cin, anotherString );
    cout << "Stored as " << anotherString << endl;
```

continues on next page...

continued...

```
    // Get user to type in a string of text - spaces allowed
    string oneMoreString;
    cout << "Enter one more string using getline..." << endl;
    getline( cin, oneMoreString );
    cout << "Stored as " << oneMoreString << endl;

    return 0;
}
```

When running the above program, you can easily type in values that will cause a problem.

For instance, try more than one word for the value of **myString**. If you type **"Many words together!"** the computer will only use the first word: **"Many"**. As we have seen with **cin**, the computer stops reading characters when it encounters the first space in the sentence, storing only the first word in the **myString** variable.

The rest of the string that has been typed in (**"words together!"**) is kept by the computer and is immediately used for the very next input, **myChar**. The computer then behaves as though it is operating on auto-pilot. Instead of waiting for you to type in the next value, it automatically starts to use the characters that were left over. This means that it takes the **"w"** from **"words"** as the next character, instead of letting you type a character in yourself.

Why does the computer hold on to the extra characters? They have been temporarily stored in a small amount of memory called the **"keyboard buffer"** and are kept just in case your program wants to make use of them in the future, as is the case with some programs.

Whenever you type anything in on a keyboard, the characters make their way into the computer via the keyboard buffer. It is a holding place, just in case the keyboard supplies characters faster than the computer can actually process them. It helps to make sure that no typed character is ever "missed" by the computer because the processor was not ready to receive and process it in time.

How do you stop the computer from using the unwanted characters from the keyboard buffer? The answer is to clear them out from *channel-in*, telling the computer to ignore any of the left-over data.

```
Enter a float...
1.25
Stored as 1.25
Enter another float...
2.75
Stored as 2.75
Enter a string using cin...
Many words together!
Stored as Many
Enter a char...
Stored as w
Enter another integer...
Stored as 0
Enter another string using getline...
Stored as
Enter one more string using getline...
Stored as


------------------
(program exited with code: 0)
Press return to continue
```

Clearing unwanted characters from `cin`

This updated version of the program clears out any characters from the keyboard buffer after each `cin` input:

Example 4.24 – clear_cin.cpp

```cpp
#include <iostream>      // Program will be screen and keyboard
#include <climits>       // Program needs to use the largest allowable integer INT_MAX

using namespace std;     // Will be using standard identifiers string, cin, cout, endl

int main()
{
    // Get user to type in floating-point value
    float myFloat;
    cout << "Enter a float..." << endl;
    cin >> myFloat;
    cout << "Stored as " << myFloat << endl;

    // After using cin >> need to throw away any unwanted text, just in case
    cin.clear();
    cin.ignore( INT_MAX, '\n' );

    // Get user to type in floating-point value
    float anotherFloat;
    cout << "Enter another float..." << endl;
    cin >> anotherFloat;
    cout << "Stored as " << anotherFloat << endl;

    // Throw away any unwanted text again
    cin.clear();
    cin.ignore( INT_MAX, '\n' );

    // Get user to type in a single word - no spaces allowed
    string myString;
    cout << "Enter a string using cin..." << endl;
    cin >> myString;
    cout << "Stored as " << myString << endl;

    // Throw away any unwanted text again
    cin.clear();
    cin.ignore( INT_MAX, '\n' );

    // Get user to type in a single character
    char myChar;
    cout << "Enter a char..." << endl;
    cin >> myChar;
    cout << "Stored as " << myChar << endl;

    // Throw away any unwanted text again
    cin.clear();
    cin.ignore( INT_MAX, '\n' );
```

continues on next page...

continued...

```
    // Get user to type in a whole number
    int anotherInt;
    cout << "Enter another integer..." << endl;
    cin >> anotherInt;
    cout << "Stored as " << anotherInt << endl;

    // Clear out any unused characters from channel-in before next input
    cin.clear();
    cin.ignore( INT_MAX, '\n' );

    // Get user to type in a string of text - spaces allowed
    string anotherString;
    cout << "Enter another string using getline..." << endl;
    getline( cin, anotherString );
    cout << "Stored as " << anotherString << endl;

    // Get user to type in a string of text - spaces allowed
    string oneMoreString;
    cout << "Enter one more string using getline..." << endl;
    getline( cin, oneMoreString );
    cout << "Stored as " << oneMoreString << endl;

    return 0;
}
```

After each value is typed in by the user, the program uses the following statements to clear out the keyboard buffer:

```
    cin.clear();
    cin.ignore( INT_MAX, '\n' );
```

The **clear()** function resets any error indicators that may have been set as a result of invalid characters. The **ignore()** function tells the Pi to skip any **\n** *new-line* characters that are currently waiting in the **cin** *channel-in* stream.

INT_MAX tells the computer what the largest acceptable integer value is. This allows our program to clear out as many characters from the input channel as possible, just in case someone has typed in an awful lot of unwanted data while the program is running.

As explained earlier in *"Chapter 3: Data-types and values"*, **INT_MAX** is a special constant value that is defined in the **<climits>** library, so an additional directive is needed at the start of the program:

```
    #include <climits>
```

On running the program, it doesn't matter if you type more than a single word as an input, even if the code uses **cin**. Any excess characters will be ignored and discarded, ready for your Pi to accept the next data value that you type. You can see the results on the next page.

```
Enter a float...
1.25
Stored as 1.25
Enter another float...
2.75
Stored as 2.75
Enter a string using cin...
More than one word!
Stored as More
Enter a char...
@
Stored as @
Enter another integer...
32
Stored as 32
Enter another string using getline...
Many words on one line.
Stored as Many words on one line.
Enter one more string using getline...
Many more words, all on one line.
Stored as Many more words, all on one line.
```

A simple program: take in some data as input, process it, and display the results

We can illustrate the importance of valid data by attempting to process some invalid inputs.

This next program allows you to type in two separate integer values which are then added up and displayed on the screen:

Example 4.25 – value_of_inputs.cpp

```cpp
#include <iostream>      // Program will be using screen and keyboard

using namespace std;     // Will be using standard identifiers cin, cout, endl

int main()
{
    int firstInt, secondInt, sum;

    // Get user to type in the first whole number
    cout << "Enter 1st integer... ";
    cin >> firstInt;

    // Get user to type in the second whole number
    cout << "Enter 2nd integer... ";
    cin >> secondInt;

    // Add the two integers together and store the result
    sum = firstInt + secondInt;

    // Display the result on the screen
    cout << "The sum of the integers is " << sum << endl;

    return 0;
}
```

The values that you type using the keyboard get stored in two different variables: **firstInt** and **secondInt**. These are added up by the computer and the result is stored in a new integer variable, called **sum**. The value of **sum** is then displayed on the screen. (We'll assume you don't accidentally type in some text instead of a whole number.)

Try running the program and typing in two sensible whole numbers - you should see that the correct sum is displayed. But if instead you try supplying the program with some text, such as the value "**tomato**", you will see a clue as to how the computer treats the invalid data.

Here's what happens on my Pi:

```
Enter 1st integer... 27
Enter 2nd integer... tomato
The sum of the integers is 27
```

It does not make any sense to attempt to add up the data if the user entered invalid values for one or both of the inputs. The text value "**tomato**" that has been entered instead of a number has been interpreted by the Pi as the value **0**.

Validating numbers entered using the keyboard

When your program expects the user to type in a number, how do you ensure that no letters of the alphabet or other symbols have been entered? How can we check that the value that is typed in is actually a **valid** number?

Once a value has been typed in using **cin**, we can check the status of the value using the **good()** member function:

```cpp
int myInt;
cin >> myInt;

if ( cin.good() )
    cout << "This was a valid integer" << endl;
else
    cout << "This was NOT a valid integer" << endl;
```

After checking the contents of **cin** for invalid characters using **good()** your program can decide whether to process the value sensibly, or to abandon the characters that were typed in, as the flow-chart below shows:

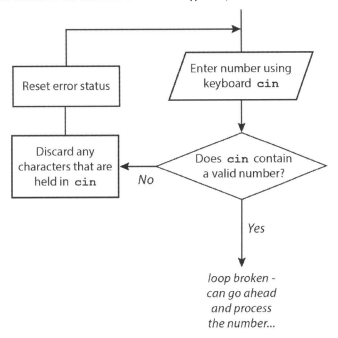

The program below puts this idea into practice, asking for an integer value and then checking for invalid characters:

Example 4.26 – *validate_int.cpp*

```cpp
#include <iostream>      // Program will be using screen and keyboard
#include <climits>       // Program needs to use the largest allowable integer INT_MAX

using namespace std;     // Will be using standard identifiers cin, cout, endl

int main()
{
    int myInt;

    // Repeatedly ask user to type in a number and check it is valid
    bool needValue = true;
    do
    {
        // Get the value and store it as an integer
        cout << "Enter a number..." << endl;
        cin >> myInt;

        // Check whether value is an acceptable number
        if ( cin.good() )
            needValue = false;
        else
        {
            cout << "Aaaargh! Not a number!" << endl;
            // Clear out any unused characters from channel-in before next input
            cin.clear();
            cin.ignore( INT_MAX, '\n' );
        }   // end if

    } while ( needValue );

    // Now have an acceptable number
    cout << "Thank-you." << endl;
    cout << "This was stored as " << myInt << endl;

    return 0;
}
```

This time, if you type "**tomato**" instead of a whole number, you will now see an error message:

```
Enter a number...
tomato
Aaaargh! Not a number!
Enter a number...
5
Thank-you.
This was stored as 5
```

Here's an improved version of the earlier program **Example 4.25 - value_of_inputs.cpp** that uses the **good()** member function to stop any text values getting through when the computer expects to be given whole numbers:

Example 4.27 – validate_two_numbers.cpp

```cpp
#include <iostream>     // Program will be using screen and keyboard

using namespace std;     // Will be using standard identifiers cin, cout, endl

int main()
{
    int errorCode = 0;  // Indicates no errors encountered at all

    int firstInt, secondInt, sum;

    // Get user to type in the first whole number
    cout << "Enter 1st integer... ";
    cin >> firstInt;

    // Check the first whole number was acceptable
    if ( cin.good() )
    {

        // Get user to type in the second whole number
        cout << "Enter 2nd integer... ";
        cin >> secondInt;

        // Check the second whole number was acceptable
        if ( cin.good() )
        {
            // Both inputs were accepted - go ahead and process the data.

            // Add the two integers together and store the result
            sum = firstInt + secondInt;

            // Display the result on the screen
            cout << "The sum of the integers is " << sum << endl;
        }
        else
        {
            cout << "Sorry. The second input was not a number." << endl;
            errorCode = 2;  // Indicates the second number was the problem
        }  // Finished checking second input
    }
    else
    {
        cout << "Sorry. The first input was not a number." << endl;
        errorCode = 1;  // Indicates the first number was the problem
    }  // Finished checking first input

    return errorCode;  // Let Linux know whether the data was valid
}
```

How does the program work? After the first input is typed in, the value is checked using a call to the `cin.good()` function. This determines whether the first value was an acceptable number or not.

If the first value was valid, the program proceeds to prompt the user for a second value. Again, it calls `cin.good()` to check that this second value is a valid number.

If the second value was also found to be a valid number then both numbers are added together and the result is displayed on the screen.

However, if either of the numbers is found to be invalid, a value for the `errorCode` variable is set. This will tell Linux which of the values that the user typed in was found to have caused a problem.

Notice that the program uses **"nested"** `if` statements - one of the `if` statements is embedded **inside** the other. The program only bothers to check the second input if the first input has been found to be valid.

Below you can see the result when both inputs are valid numbers:

```
Enter 1st integer... 45
Enter 2nd integer... 13
The sum of the integers is 58
```

Here, you can see that spelling out a number using letters does not get interpreted as a valid integer, even though a human being might well have understood what the user was trying to enter. Unfortunately the computer has no common sense:

```
Enter 1st integer... forty
Sorry. The first input was not a number.
```

Finally, here is what happens when an arbitrary, random text value is entered:

```
Enter 1st integer... alphabet
Sorry. The first input was not a number.
```

Here's what we have covered in this chapter:

`cout` *channel-out* takes a value from the computer and displays it on the screen.

The `endl` *end-of-line* character marks the end of the current line of text. Any further text that is to be displayed will begin at the start of a new line on the screen.

A special sequence of characters, called an **escape-sequence** can be used to control the way the characters are displayed on the screen, including their **colour**, **position** and **weight**.

Your program can also change the **position of the cursor** on the screen using an escape-sequence, specifying the position using row and column numbers.

The `sleep()` function can control the speed that text is displayed, causing your program to pause for a specified number of seconds. The `usleep()` function can pause your program for a fraction of a second.

The `flush` character clears out buffered characters from channel-out, sending any text that it contains immediately to the screen to be displayed, rather than waiting until the whole line is finished and ready for display.

The `setw()` stream-manipulator allows you to control the width of a value when it gets displayed on the screen or sent to any other stream. The value is padded-out with spaces if necessary.

The `fixed` stream-manipulator forces a stream to treat real values as fixed-width, rather than floating-point numbers.

The `setprecision()` stream-manipulator allows you to specify how many decimal places should be included after the decimal point when displaying fixed-width values.

The `boolalpha` stream-manipulator allows you to change how `bool` values are displayed, displaying them as `true` or `false`, rather than `1` or `0`.

The `noboolalpha` stream manipulator reverts to displaying `bool` values using `1` or `0` again.

`cin` takes a single value (such as a word or a number) from the keyboard and stores it in a variable.

The `>>` *input-redirector* symbol shows data the direction in which to flow from a channel to a variable.

Data that has been typed in using `cin` can be validated using the `good()` member function if you need to check that it forms a valid number.

Unlike `cin`, the `getline()` function can be used to enter a whole line of text, including spaces.

The `clear()` and `ignore()` functions can be used to get rid of unwanted characters from previous inputs that are stored in the `cin` keyboard buffer.

Problems and exercises for you to try

1.	Write a program that lets you type in a whole number. Display the number three times, using `setw()` to change the width of the number to **1**, **5** and **10** characters.
2.	Write a program that asks you to type in a sentence. Display the sentence three times, each time using a different colour.
3.	Write a program that asks you to type in a whole number. Make the program wait for this number of seconds before finishing execution.
4.	Write a program that asks you to type in three numbers, one at a time. Make it display the sum total of the three numbers.

Chapter 5:
Using operators to process data

Changing the value of variables with the ++ increment and −− decrement operators

We have previously seen how to set the value of a variable to store a **literal** value using the = *assignment operator*.

There are also other ways to set the value of a numeric variable, including those that are integers and those that are floating-point numbers. Instead of setting a variable to a certain specific value, you can **change** the value of the variable **relative** to what its value is at the moment. You can assign the result of an **expression** to the value of a variable, such as below:

```
livesLeft = livesLeft + 1;
```

The statement above means:

"make the new value of the livesLeft *variable equal to whatever the value of* livesLeft *is at the moment, with an extra* 1 *added on".*

Note that livesLeft + 1 is a simple **expression**, combining a named value livesLeft, the + operator and the literal value 1.

Adding 1 on to a value with the ++ increment operator

C++ has another easy way to **add one on to the value of a variable**, called the *increment operator*: ++

Instead of writing:

```
livesLeft = livesLeft + 1;
```

...you can use the increment operator to increase the value of the livesLeft variable by one:

```
livesLeft++;
```

Subtracting 1 from a value with the −− decrement operator

C++ also has an operator to **subtract one** from the value of a variable, called the *decrement operator*: −−

Instead of writing:

```
livesLeft = livesLeft - 1;
```

...you can use the decrement operator to decrease the value of the livesLeft variable by one:

```
livesLeft--;
```

Different ways to use ++ increment and -- decrement

Both the ++ increment and -- decrement operators can work in different ways, depending on **where** you put them in relation to the name of the variable that they operate on. You can choose to put the operator either **before** or **after** the name of the variable.

Increment as a simple statement on its own

Remember that the ++ operator increments the value of a variable by **1**. Here it is being used as a simple statement to increment the value of the variable called `people`:

```
int people = 5;
people++;
cout << people << endl;
```

The first line of this code creates an integer variable called `people` with the value **5**. It then increments the value of `people`, changing it from **5** to **6**. Once incremented, the final line of code displays the value of the variable, showing a **6**.

Pre-increment, as part of another statement

In the example below, the increment operator has been embedded in the statement that is used to display the value of the variable, resulting in one less line of code:

```
int people = 5;
cout << ++people << endl;
```

The first line of code creates the variable called `people`, just as in the first example. The next line of code will display the value of the variable on the screen, **but before it uses the variable, the ++ operator increases its value by 1**. It then proceeds to use the **changed** value, displaying a **6** on the screen.

When you place the ++ increment operator **before** the variable name, it is called the *pre-increment* operator. The value of the variable will be increased by **1 before** it gets used.

Post-increment, as part of another statement

```
int people = 5;
cout << people++ << endl;
```

The effect of this code would be to create an integer variable with the value **5**. It would display the variable, showing the value **5** on the screen. Once the variable has been used, it would then increment the value, changing it from **5** to **6**.

When you place the ++ increment operator **after** the variable name, it is called the *post-increment* operator. The value of the variable will only be increased by **1 after** it gets used.

Pre-decrement and post-decrement as part of another statement

As with the ++ increment operator, you can place the -- decrement operator either **before** or **after** the name of the variable that it operates on. These are called *pre-decrement* and *post-decrement* operations.

The += "add amount" and -= "subtract amount" operators

The ++ **increment** operator adds one on to the value of a variable, whilst the -- **decrement** operator subtracts one. But how can you add or subtract different numbers **other than one**?

You could write a statement such as this:

```
    playerScore = playerScore + 100;
```

...which tells the computer to set a new value for the variable **playerScore**, making it equal to the old value of **playerScore** with an extra **100** added on.

Alternatively, you could use the += *add-amount* operator to add a specific number on to the current value of the variable, or the -= *subtract-amount* operator to subtract a specific number:

```
    playerScore += 100;
    timeLeft -= 30;
```

You can also add on or take away the value of another variable or constant instead of a literal numeric value. Here, the value of a variable called **bonusAmount** is added on to the value of **playerScore**:

```
    playerScore += bonusAmount;   // Same as playerScore = playerScore + bonusAmount
```

Similarly, you can subtract the value of a variable or constant:

```
    time -= penalty;   // Same effect as time = time - penalty
```

The following program demonstrates how both ++ and += can be used to change the value of a variable:

Example 5.1 – *increase_int.cpp*

```cpp
#include <iostream>      // Program will be displaying some text on the screen

using namespace std;     // Will be using standard identifiers cout and endl

int main()
{
    int score = 0;   // score starts as zero

    cout << "My score starts as ";

    cout << score << endl;
```

continues on next page...

continued...

```
    score++;   // Increases the value of score by 1

    cout << "It increases by 1 and is now ";

    cout << score << endl;

    // Increase the value of score by 3
    score++;
    score++;
    score++;

    cout << "It increases by 3 more to ";

    cout << score << endl;

    // Increase the value of score by 10 using one single statement
    score += 10;   // adds 10 to score

    cout << "After adding 10, my final score is ";

    cout << score << endl;


    return 0;
}
```

In the above program, the simple statement:

```
    score++;
```

...adds **1** to the current value of the integer variable called **score**.

The following statement:

```
    score += 10;   // adds 10 to score
```

...adds an extra **10** on to the value of **score**.

You should see the following results when you run the program:

```
My score starts as 0
It increases by 1 and is now 1
It increases by 3 more to 4
After adding 10, my final score is 14
```

Multiplying numbers using the * operator

Values can be multiplied together using the * *multiply* operator.

For instance, each one of these statements sets the value of a variable to be equal to the result of a simple multiplication:

```
bonus = timeLeft * 10;
areaOfRectangle = width * height;
areaOfCircle = pi * radius * radius;
```

The * (asterisk) symbol is used instead of the **x** cross symbol that people usually use for multiplication on paper to avoid confusion with the letter **"x"**.

You can multiply values together that have the same data-type, such as multiplying two integers together:

```
int hoursInOneWeek = 7 * 24;
```

You can also multiply values together that have **different** data-types, such as multiplying a `float` value by an `int` value:

```
float dailyPay = 8.25 * 6;
```

In the above example, the floating-point value `8.25` is multiplied by the integer value `6`. Because one of the values being multiplied together is a value that makes use of a decimal point, the compiler will assume that the result will also need a decimal point - hence the result will also be a floating-point value rather than an integer. For this reason, the variable `dailyPay` has been declared using the `float` data-type.

We have already learnt that **constants** are named items of data that **cannot possibly change** while the program is running.

The program below uses three different integer constants: **DAYS**, **HOURS** and **MINUTES**. Remember that the names of constants are typed using capital letters to distinguish them from variables.

Example 5.2 – multiply.cpp

```cpp
#include <iostream>      // Program will be displaying some text on the screen

using namespace std;     // Will be using standard identifiers cout and endl

int main()
{
    // This program calculates how many hours there are in a week.
    // These constants can never be changed while the program running.

    // Create the constants and set their values
    const int DAYS = 7;
    const int HOURS = 24;
    const int MINUTES = 60;
```

continues on next page...

```cpp
    // Perform calculations using them and display the results

    cout << "There are ";

    cout << DAYS * HOURS;

    cout << " hours in a week." << endl;


    cout << "There are ";

    cout << HOURS * MINUTES;

    cout << " minutes in a day." << endl;


    return 0;
}
```

In the above code, the value of the constant **DAYS** is **7** and the value of the constant **HOURS** is **24**.

The statement:

```cpp
    cout << DAYS * HOURS;
```

...displays the result of **7** times **24**, which is **168** hours.

Similarly, the value of the constant **MINUTES** is **60**, so the statement:

```cpp
    cout << HOURS * MINUTES;
```

...displays the result of **24** times **60**, which is **1440** minutes.

```
There are 168 hours in a week.
There are 1440 minutes in a day.
```

Dividing numbers using the / operator

You can divide one numeric value by another using the **/** *divide* operator.

Example 5.3 – divide.cpp

```cpp
#include <iostream>     // Program will be using screen and keyboard

using namespace std;    // Will be using standard identifiers cin, cout, endl

int main()
{
    cout << "What is the top part of the fraction?" << endl;
    int top;
    cin >> top;

    // ------

    cout << "What is the bottom part of the fraction?" << endl;
    int bottom;
    cin >> bottom;

    // ------

    cout << "As a decimal value, your fraction is: ";

    float asDecimalValue = top / bottom;

    cout << asDecimalValue;

    cout << endl << endl;


    return 0;
}
```

Running this program may produce some rather unexpected results. **10 / 5** gives the answer **2**, which is correct, but you may notice that **1 / 2** gives an answer of **0**, rather than **0.5**. This is because the computer has ignored the digits after the decimal point as it thinks it is dealing purely with integers.

Casts - converting values to different data-types

The solution is to the problem above is to tell the computer to treat both the top and bottom values as though they are of type **float** before performing the division. This kind of conversion between **different** data-types is called a "**cast**".

```cpp
        float asDecimalValue = (float) top / (float) bottom;
```

In the statement above, **(float)** forces the computer to treat the **top** and **bottom** variables as **float** values instead of **int** values, and consequently the computer does not discard the decimal places.

Casts are covered in more detail later in this chapter, indeed you will see that it is best practice to use the **static_cast** keyword when converting from one data-type to another.

Here's an example that makes use of many of the points covered during this chapter. It examines the time on your Pi to determine how many seconds have elapsed since the beginning of "UNIX time" (which is defined as January 1st 1970).

Example 5.4 – *calc_age.cpp*

```cpp
#include <iostream>     // Program will be displaying some text on the screen
#include <ctime>       // Program uses the time() function as the random seed

using namespace std;     // Will be using standard identifiers cout and endl

int main()
{
    const float DAYS_IN_YR = 365.25;
    const int HRS_IN_DAY = 24;
    const int MINS_IN_HR = 60;
    const int SECS_IN_MIN = 60;

    // Work out how many seconds there are in 1 year...
    const float SECS_IN_YEAR = SECS_IN_MIN * MINS_IN_HR * HRS_IN_DAY * DAYS_IN_YR;

    // Find out the age of UNIX (answer is given in seconds)
    int ageOfUnixInSeconds = time( 0 );

    // Divide this age by the number of seconds in one year,
    // this will be the age of UNIX in years, rather than seconds...
    cout << "Unix is " << ageOfUnixInSeconds / SECS_IN_YEAR;
    cout << " years old." << endl;

    return 0;
}
```

When the program runs, you should see something like this:

```
Unix is 47.214 years old.
```

Calculating this age relies on the current system date being correct on your Raspberry Pi. Unlike most PCs, the Raspberry Pi does not have a battery-powered circuit to "remember" the date when the computer is switched off. The Pi usually refreshes the system date when it connects to the Internet via a Wi-Fi link or Ethernet cable.

You can check the current system date from the Linux command-line using the **date** command:

```
pi@eno ~ $ date
Sat Feb 18 11:46:42 GMT 2017
```

When the program above calls the **time()** function, the system determines the number of seconds that have elapsed since January 1st 1970 (the date that UNIX time officially begins). To find out how old UNIX is in years, the program divides this number of seconds by the total number of seconds in 1 year, using the constant value **SECS_IN_YEAR**.

Note that to use the **time()** function, your program needs to include the **<ctime>** library of code:

```cpp
#include <ctime>
```

The problem of attempting to divide a number by zero

Computers cannot divide a number by zero. If your code tries to do this, although the program will compile and run, it will trigger a **run-time error** when your Pi attempts to execute that particular part of your code.

```
int biscuitsPerPerson = biscuitsInPacket / 0;
```

As in the example above, the error would be easy to spot where a statement divides something by the literal value zero. Indeed, the compiler should warn you if your code **explicitly** contains a division by zero. If you don't spot such a division, the compiler will! Unfortunately, it is much more likely that a program which attempts to divide the value of one variable by the value of another variable may cause a division by zero error at run-time. This is not always so easy to spot in your code.

For example:

```
int biscuitsPerPerson = biscuitsInPacket / peopleInRoom;
```

If the value of **peopleInRoom** is ever set to **0**, the above statement would trigger an error at run-time:

```
What is the top part of the fraction?
12
What is the bottom part of the fraction?
0
Floating point exception
```

Similarly, in the previous *Example 5.3 - divide.cpp* program, if you type **0** as the value for the bottom of the fraction then the program should also display the same **Floating point exception** error. The same message will be displayed even when you are dividing one integer by another integer and trying to store the result in an integer variable, even though the **float** data-type is not being used.

Try it for yourself...

Example 5.5 – *div_by_zero.cpp*

```cpp
#include <iostream>     // Program will be using screen and keyboard

using namespace std;    // Will be using standard identifiers cout and endl

int main()
{
    int totalBiscuits = 12;
    int people = 0;

    int biscuitsEach = totalBiscuits / people;     // Divides by zero!!!

    cout << "They will get " << biscuitsEach << " biscuits each" << endl;

    return 1;    // Let Linux know this program produces an error
}
```

To avoid a division-by-zero error, a programmer will often write extra program code to check that the data about to be used is sensible. As we have seen, this is called "**validation**". The next chapter shows you how to use **if-else** decisions to make such checks when dividing.

Mixing different data-types during division

Remember that when you are dividing one integer number by another integer, C++ will always produce another integer as a result.

The program below uses the example from the previous page:

Example 5.6 – *int_by_int.cpp*

```cpp
#include <iostream>      // Program will be displaying some text on the screen

using namespace std;     // Will be using standard identifiers cout and endl

int main()
{

    int biscuits = 36;
    int people = 5;

    cout << biscuits;

    cout << " divided between ";

    cout << people;

    cout << " people means they each get ";

    cout << biscuits / people;   // Gives whole number result ignoring decimal places

    cout << endl;

    return 0;
}
```

The program will display this result:

```
36 divided between 5 people means they each get 7
```

This is not an exact answer. If we were using only whole numbers, the answer would be **7 remainder 1**. Consequently, the computer chooses to ignore the decimal part of the answer, **0.2**, displaying only the whole-number part of the answer: **7**.

Whilst it is true that there are **7** lots of **5** in **36**, we may not always be happy that the computer has thrown away the decimal part of our answer. It may have been useful!

In many cases we would prefer to see the decimal places. We might prefer the computer to display the answer **7.2** instead.

Indeed, with this program we might be interested in seeing the result if it involves half a biscuit, such as any answer that ends in **0.5**.

The results of floating point division

Now what happens when you try to divide an integer by a real number, such as the **float** value **0.5** ?

Example 5.7 – *int_by_float.cpp*

```cpp
#include <iostream>      // Program will be displaying some text on the screen

using namespace std;     // Will be using standard identifiers cout and endl

int main()
{
    int distance = 10;
    float half = 0.5;

    cout << "How many times does " << half;
    cout << " go into " << distance;
    cout << " ? ";

    cout << distance / half;
    cout << endl << endl;


    float third = 0.333333;

    cout << "How many times does " << third;
    cout << " go into " << distance;
    cout << " ? ";

    cout << distance / third;
    cout << endl << endl;


    return 0;
}
```

This time, the result is displayed as:

```
How many times does 0.5 go into 10 ? 20

How many times does 0.333333 go into 10 ? 30
```

The computer does not display any decimal places in either of the results on the screen. If you try the latter example using a pocket calculator, you may actually see the result **30.00003** (or something very similar, depending upon the accuracy of your calculator).

Finally, this program illustrates what happens when one real number is divided by another:

Example 5.8 – float_by_float.cpp

```cpp
#include <iostream>      // Program will be displaying some text on the screen

using namespace std;     // Will be using standard identifiers cout and endl

int main()
{
    float myNumber = 2.5;
    float half = 0.5;

    cout << "How many times does " << half;
    cout << " go into " << myNumber;
    cout << " ? ";

    cout << myNumber / half;
    cout << endl << endl;


    float threeQuarters = 0.75;

    cout << "How many times does " << threeQuarters;
    cout << " go into " << myNumber;
    cout << " ? ";

    cout << myNumber / threeQuarters;
    cout << endl << endl;


    return 0;
}
```

The results displayed on the screen are shown below:

```
How many times does 0.5 go into 2.5 ? 5

How many times does 0.75 go into 2.5 ? 3.33333
```

Because $2.5 / 0.5$ gives an answer that is an exact whole number, any unnecessary zeroes are not shown after the decimal point. Decimal places are only shown if they are actually needed, such as in the second division in the screenshot above that results in the answer 3.33333 recurring.

Finding a remainder using the % modulus operator

As we have seen earlier, when dividing integers using the / divide operator, the computer gives the number of times that one value goes into another completely (called the "**quotient**"). Anything that is left-over (the "**remainder**") gets conveniently ignored. However, sometimes we want to know what this remainder is because it can be very useful.

For instance, we know that the result of 16 / 3 is 5, because the number of times that 3 goes into 16 is 5, **leaving a remainder of 1 left-over**.

To find a remainder we can use the % *modulus* operator.

---

16 % 3 means *"find the **remainder** when 16 is divided by 3"*.

The result is 1, because 16 divided by 3 is 5 **with a remainder of 1**.

Example 5.9 – modulus_leftover.cpp

```cpp
#include <iostream>    // Program will be using screen and keyboard

using namespace std;    // Will be using standard identifiers cin, cout, endl

int main()
{
    cout << "Number of chocolates in the box?" << endl;
    int numChocs;
    cin >> numChocs;

    // ------

    cout << "How many people are there?" << endl;
    int numPeople;
    cin >> numPeople;

    // ------

    // Calculate the number of chocolates left-over after sharing
    // them fairly between everybody
    int leftOver = numChocs % numPeople;

    cout << "Chocolates leftover: " << leftOver;

    cout << endl << endl;

    return 0;
}
```

Here is what happens at run-time:

```
Number of chocolates in the box?
16
How many people are there?
3
Chocolates leftover: 1
```

Using random numbers to produce unpredictable behaviour in a program

Like all computers, the Raspberry Pi follows a program that tells it exactly what to do. But how do you get a computer to do something unexpected? How can it surprise you when you are the one that is telling it, step-by-step, exactly what to do next?

Many programs use **random numbers**. The computer uses a special method (an **"algorithm"**) to choose a number from a sequence of values that it generates. The sequence itself is predictable though as the algorithm will always generate the same values, so this in itself is not random. We can use the `random()` function to select one of the values from the sequence. This `random()` function is part of the older C standard library of code, called `<cstdlib>`.

The program below chooses three numbers at random using this approach:

Example 5.10 – random.cpp

```
#include <iostream>      // Program will be displaying some text on the screen
#include <cstdlib>       // Program uses the random() function

using namespace std;     // Will be using standard identifiers cout and endl

int main()
{
    // Picks and displays a sequence of three apparently random numbers

    cout << "I picked the number ";
    cout << random();
    cout << endl;

    cout << "Then I picked ";
    cout << random();
    cout << endl;

    cout << "Finally, I picked ";
    cout << random();
    cout << endl;

    return 0;
}
```

The first time that you run the program, you might think that the numbers have been chosen at random and that there is no connection between them. Unfortunately, if you run the program repeatedly, you should notice that it always picks the same numbers from the sequence that the algorithm generates. It will actually behave predictably, rather than randomly!

Here are the results from the first time that I ran the program:

```
I picked the number 1804289383
The I picked 846930886
Finally, I picked 1681692777
```

Now here are the results from the second time that I ran it:

```
I picked the number 1804289383
The I picked 846930886
Finally, I picked 1681692777
```

Do you notice that the results are actually the same? What is needed is a way to make a program behave **more** randomly.

Making the choices more random using a "seed"

To introduce more of a random element into the choice of numbers, the algorithm must also use something that is relatively unpredictable, such as the current time. Your Pi measures this to a tiny fraction of a second.

This starting element is called the **"seed"** of the random number process. It makes sure that if you run a program again and again and again, the algorithm will not always keep choosing the same random numbers each time that it executes. Each time the program starts, the algorithm looks at the current time (the seed) and uses this to help decide which number to pick from the sequence of values. A program can call the **srandom()** function to do this, supplying it with the result returned from calling the **time()** function as the unpredictable seed.

This still means that the chosen numbers won't be completely random. If two computers ran the same program at exactly the same time - they **might** produce the same results. We therefore say that they are **"pseudo-random"** (or "nearly" random).

This next program uses the time to make sure that the program chooses different numbers each time that it executes:

Example 5.11 – seed_random.cpp

```cpp
#include <iostream>    // Program will be displaying some text on the screen
#include <cstdlib>     // Program uses the random() and srandom() functions
#include <ctime>       // Program uses the time() function as the random seed

using namespace std;    // Will be using standard identifiers cout and endl

int main()
{
    // Seed random number generator
    // Sets it up so that does not always select the same numbers

    srandom( time( 0 ) );

    // Pick and display a sequence of three random numbers

    cout << "I picked the number ";
    cout << random();
    cout << endl;

    cout << "Then I picked ";
    cout << random();
    cout << endl;

    cout << "Finally, I picked ";
    cout << random();
    cout << endl;

    return 0;
}
```

There are two other things that you might notice about these random numbers. Firstly, the smallest possible number that the computer can choose is **0**. Secondly, the computer can choose numbers that are very large. For example, my Raspberry Pi chose the numbers **1504404952**, **1116713186** and **1781026634**.

We often want a random number from a different range of possibilities, not just between **0** and some massive number. For example, when you roll a normal die, it is only possible to get a number between **1** and **6** inclusive.

Using % modulus to pick a random number within a certain range

This next example chooses three different random numbers, each one within a different range. To do this, after each random number is chosen (which is potentially a very large value) the program uses % *modulus* to divide the random number by another amount to obtain a remainder. Depending on the divisor that % modulus uses for the division, the random number can be controlled within a certain range. How do you know what number to use with % modulus? Just use the number of different possible choices (or "outcomes") that you would like.

Example 5.12 – random_range.cpp

```cpp
#include <iostream>     // Program will be displaying some text on the screen
#include <cstdlib>      // Program uses the random() and srandom() functions
#include <ctime>        // Program uses the time() function as the random seed

using namespace std;    // Will be using standard identifiers cout and endl

int main()
{
    // Seed random number generator so that does not always select the same numbers
    srandom( time( 0 ) );

    // Pick and display a sequence of three random numbers

    cout << "I picked a number between 0 and 99. It was... ";
    cout << random() % 100;     // 100 possible outcomes
    cout << endl;

    cout << "Then I picked a number between 0 and 5... ";
    cout << random() % 6;       // 6 possible outcomes
    cout << endl;

    cout << "Finally, I picked a number that is either 0 or 1... ";
    cout << random() % 2;       // 2 possible outcomes
    cout << endl;

    return 0;
}
```

Here are the numbers that my Pi picked – don't expect the same values to be picked by your computer:

```
I picked a number between 0 and 99. It was... 61
Then I picked a number between 0 and 5... 2
Finally, I picked a number that is either 0 or 1... 0
```

How would you choose a number from a range that does not begin at zero? As already mentioned, the sides of a die are numbered from **1** to **6** inclusive. The solution is to add on an extra **1** to the random number:

```cpp
int side = ( random() % 6 ) + 1;
```

In the statement above, `random() % 6` always gives a value between **0** and **5** inclusive. By adding an extra **1** to this value, the smallest possible outcome (which is **0**) becomes **1**, and the largest possible outcome (which is **5**) becomes **6**.

The random results will always be within the required range of outcomes for a die.

Another way to write the statement without brackets is:

```
        int side = 1 + random() % 6;
```

Notice that the % operation is carried out before the + operation because % has a higher "**operator precedence**". C++ considers % to be "more important" than + in an expression.

Here is an example that simulates the rolling of two separate dice. Their scores are added together to give a total between **1** and **12** inclusive:

Example 5.13 – *random_dice.cpp*

```cpp
#include <iostream>    // Program will be displaying some text on the screen
#include <cstdlib>     // Program uses the random() and srandom() functions
#include <ctime>       // Program uses the time() function as the random seed

using namespace std;    // Will be using standard identifiers cout and endl

int main()
{
    // Seed random number generator so does not always select the same numbers
    srandom( time( 0 ) );

    // Chooses a random number for each of the dice, divides it by 6
    // and obtains the remainder (which will be between 0 and 5), then adds 1
    // The result will be a number somewhere between 1 and 6

    int firstRoll = ( random() % 6 ) + 1;

    int secondRoll = ( random() % 6 ) + 1;

    // Display the first number that was rolled
    cout << "First I rolled " << firstRoll << endl;

    // Display the second number that was rolled
    cout << "Then I rolled " << secondRoll << endl;

    // Display the total score from both dice
    cout << "My total score was " <<  firstRoll + secondRoll  << endl;

    return 0;
}
```

These were the results when I ran the program for the first time:

```
First I rolled 6
Then I rolled 1
My total score was 7
```

Notice that the second time the program runs, the results will **probably** be different:

```
First I rolled 2
Then I rolled 4
My total score was 6
```

Exponentiation: Raising a number to a power using the pow() function

C++ can calculate the power of a number in various ways. In **Example 4.6 - display_overflow.cpp** we saw that C++ can perform **repeated multiplication**, which is fine for lower powers, such as a single number times itself.

Alternatively, you could use the **pow()** function, which **raises a number to a certain power**. This is called "**exponentiation**" and is usually more convenient for higher powers.

In the program below, the statement:

```
cout << pow( width, 3 );
```

...tells the computer to display the value of the variable called **width**, raised to the power of **3**. In mathematics, we might normally write this as w^3, where **w** is the width of the cube.

To use this function though, you must include code from the standard C++ mathematical library at the start of your program:

```
#include <cmath>
```

Here is an example that uses the **pow()** function to calculate the volume of a cube:

Example 5.14 – power_of.cpp

```cpp
#include <iostream>    // Program will be using keyboard and screen
#include <cmath>     // Program uses the pow() function

using namespace std;     // Will be using standard identifiers cin, cout, endl

int main()
{
    // Type in the width of the cube in cm
    cout << "Type in the width of the cube in whole cm" << endl;
    int width;
    cin >> width;

    // Calculate and display the volume of the cube
    cout << "The volume of the cube is ";

    // pow is a function - raises value of width to power 3, i.e. cubes it
    cout << pow( width, 3 );

    cout << " cubic cm" << endl;

    return 0;
}
```

Below is an example of what happens when the program is executed:

```
Type in the width of the cube in whole cm
3
The volume of the cube is 27 cubic cm
```

Operator precedence – the order in which the computer carries out operations

Different operator symbols in C++ expressions are treated according to their importance. This is called "**operator-precedence**". If you have ever used the **BIDMAS** (**B**rackets, **I**ndex, **D**ivide, **M**ultiply, **A**dd, **S**ubtract) rule in mathematics then you should be able to understand how C++ carries out operations. For instance, multiplication has a higher precedence than addition.

The order of precedence in C++ is:

( )	Brackets
function call	Call to a function, such as **pow()** *"power-of"*
/	Divide
*	Multiply
+	Add
–	Subtract

As an example, consider the area of a triangle:

```
base * height / 2
```

Of the two operators in the expression, **/** has a higher precedence than ***** so the computer first divides the value of **height** by **2** before multiplying the result by the value of **base**.

Where an expression contains several operators that have the **same** precedence (such as an expression that contains many addition operations), these operations get evaluated from left to right, relative to the start of the expression.

Example 5.15 – calc_area_circle.cpp

```cpp
#include <iostream>     // Program will be displaying some text on the screen

using namespace std;    // Will be using standard identifiers cin, cout, endl

int main()
{
    const float PI = 3.14159;

    // Type in the radius of a circle in cm
    cout << "Type in the radius in cm" << endl;
    float radius;
    cin >> radius;

    // Calculate and display the area of the circle
    cout << "The area of the circle is ";

    // "radius times radius" is the same as "radius squared"
    cout << PI * radius * radius;

    cout << " square cm" << endl;

    return 0;
}
```

Note also that in the previous program, the following expression:

```
PI * radius * radius
```

...could instead be written as:

```
PI * pow( radius, 2 )
```

The call to the **pow()** function means:

"*The value of* **radius** *raised to the power of* **2**".

Here is the code for you to try:

Example 5.15 modified – *calc_area_circle_pow.cpp*

```cpp
#include <iostream>     // Program will be displaying some text on the screen
#include <cmath>     // Program will be using the pow() function

using namespace std;     // Will be using standard identifiers cin, cout, endl

int main()
{
    const float PI = 3.14159;

    // Type in the radius of a circle in cm
    cout << "Type in the radius in cm" << endl;
    float radius;
    cin >> radius;

    // Calculate and display the area of the circle
    cout << "The area of the circle is ";

    // "radius times radius" is the same as "radius squared"
    cout << PI * pow( radius, 2 );

    cout << " square cm" << endl;

    return 0;
}
```

```
Type in the radius in cm
15
The area of the circle is 706.858 square cm
```

Both versions of the program produce the same results on the screen, despite using different methods to produce them. Note that the modified program now also includes the **<cmath>** library, which allows it to use the **pow()** function:

```
#include <cmath>
```

Using ( ) brackets in an expression to change how expressions are evaluated

By enclosing parts of an expression within ( ) brackets, you can change the order in which the computer carries out the operations that it contains.

For instance, / division operations are normally carried out before + addition operations in an expression. This is because / has a higher operator precedence than +.

Imagine if we wanted to calculate an average of several values. To do this we might want to add the different values together to produce a sum total, then divide the total by the number of values that we started with.

The following code would produce an incorrect result:

```
// Calculate mean of 3 values
float meanAverage = 122 + 107 + 124 / 3;
```

This is because the computer would carry out **124 / 3** first. It would then proceed to carry out the addition operations. The answer given would not be correct.

To correctly calculate the average of the three values, a pair of brackets needs to be added around the addition operations:

```
// Calculate mean of 3 values
float meanAverage = ( 122 + 107 + 124 ) / 3;
```

This forces all of the addition operations to be carried out first, prior to the division operation.
The resulting sum is then divided by **3** to produce the correct result.

As already described, when operators in an expression have the **same** precedence, such as the two + addition operators within these brackets, the operations are carried out in order from **left-to-right**.

This means that:

```
122 + 107 + 124
```

...will be calculated firstly by performing **122 + 107**, to obtain the result **229**, then adding on **124** to give the final result **353**.

Finding the minimum or maximum of two values using `min()` and `max()`

C++ includes an easy way to help you find the **minimum** or the **maximum** of two values.

Firstly, you can use the `min()` function. Given two values, this will find the **smallest** of the two:

```
int smallestValue = min( firstValue, SecondValue );
```

Similarly, you can use the `max()` to find the **largest** of two values:

```
int largestValue = max( firstValue, SecondValue );
```

This is more compact that writing your own code using an `if` decision:

```
int smallestValue;

if ( firstValue < SecondValue )
    smallestValue = firstValue;
else
    smallestValue = secondValue;
```

These functions can be used with any numeric value or even with individual characters.

When asked to find the minimum of two characters, the `min()` function will choose the character that has the lowest ASCII character-code.

When asked to find the maximum of two characters, the `max()` function will choose the character that has the highest ASCII character-code.

The following program makes use of the **min()** and **max()** functions to calculate the mid-point of a straight-line:

Example 5.16 – calc_mid_point.cpp

```cpp
#include <iostream>      // Program will be using keyboard and screen

using namespace std;     // Will be using standard identifiers cin, cout, endl

int main()
{
    float xBegin, yBegin, xEnd, yEnd;

    // User types in the co-ordinates of start of the line
    cout << "Type in x co-ordinate of where the line begins: " << endl;
    cin >> xBegin;
    cout << "Type in y co-ordinate of where the line begins: " << endl;
    cin >> yBegin;

    // User types in the co-ordinates of end of the line
    cout << "Type in x co-ordinate of where the line ends: " << endl;
    cin >> xEnd;
    cout << "Type in y co-ordinate of where the line ends: " << endl;
    cin >> yEnd;

    // Determine which are the smallest and largest x co-ordinates
    float xSmallest = min( xBegin, xEnd );
    float xLargest = max( xBegin, xEnd );

    // Determine which are the smallest and largest y co-ordinates
    float ySmallest = min( yBegin, yEnd );
    float yLargest = max( yBegin, yEnd );

    // Calculate x co-ordinate of mid-point
    float xMid = xSmallest + ( xLargest - xSmallest ) / 2;

    // Calculate y co-ordinate of mid-point
    float yMid = ySmallest + ( yLargest - ySmallest ) / 2;


    // Display the mid-point of the straight line

    cout << "The mid-point of the line is ";

    cout << "(" << xMid << ", " << yMid << ")" << endl;

    return 0;
}
```

Here is what happens when the program runs:

```
Type in x co-ordinate of where the line begins:
5
Type in y co-ordinate of where the line begins:
2
Type in x co-ordinate of where the line ends:
9
Type in y co-ordinate of where the line ends:
3
The mid-point of the line is (7, 2.5)
```

For the straight line with end-points `(5, 2)` and `(9, 3)` the program calculates the mid-point as `(7, 2.5)`.

`7` is half-way between `5` and `9`.
`2.5` is half-way between `2` and `3`.

To calculate the x co-ordinate of the mid-point, the program first determines the smallest and largest values out of the different x co-ordinates using the `min()` and `max()` functions: `5` and `9`.

```
// Determine which are the smallest and largest x co-ordinates
float xSmallest = min( xBegin, xEnd );
float xLargest = max( xBegin, xEnd );
```

The program then uses subtraction to calculate the difference between them, taking the smallest value away from the largest, then dividing this difference by `2` and adding the result to the smallest x co-ordinate:

```
// Calculate x co-ordinate of mid-point
float xMid = xSmallest + ( xLargest - xSmallest ) / 2;
```

To obtain the y co-ordinate of the mid-point, the same process is carried out using the y co-ordinates of the end-points.

Again, the smallest and largest y values are determined:

```
// Determine which are the smallest and largest y co-ordinates
float ySmallest = min( yBegin, yEnd );
float yLargest = max( yBegin, yEnd );
```

The y co-ordinate is then calculated from these values:

```
// Calculate y co-ordinate of mid-point
float yMid = ySmallest + ( yLargest - ySmallest ) / 2;
```

This has now given us both the x and y co-ordinates of the mid-point for the straight line between the co-ordinates that the user has typed in.

Casts – converting between data-types

Sometimes, we may want to use data values of a particular type which are different from the data-types that we have given to the variables and constants in our program.

For instance, we may want to compare two variables to see whether their values are the same or perform some sort of calculation on them. But what if the two variables have different data-types? One might be a `float` value and the other might be a `char` value. These different data-types may cause the operations to behave in different ways.

As we have seen earlier in this chapter, in C++, you can **force** a data-value to behave like a particular data-type that you want to use.

Consider this example:

> Take the whole-number value **65**, which has the data-type `int`.
>
> You could force the value **65** to behave like a real number, such as the `float` value `65.000000`.
>
> Alternatively, you could force the value **65** to behave like the `char` value that has the ASCII code **65**, namely the character **A**.

This conversion is called a **"cast"**. You can imagine a data-value being made of metal, having a particular shape. The metal data can be melted down and then poured into a mould (or a "cast") to make it into a new, different shape.

Casts are useful when setting values for variables which need to use a particular kind of data, but which actually have values that are of a different type. They can help you get around the problem of functions and operations that require a particular kind of data-type. You cast the data into an arrangement or "shape" that the function or operation expects to work with.

All you need to do in order to force the value into behaving like a different data-type is to tell the computer **which** data-type you want it to behave as. The easiest way to do this is to prefix the data-value, variable or constant with name of the data-type that you want to use, enclosing it in a pair of **( )** brackets. This is called a simple cast.

For example we can take the result of a division, which would normally display decimal places, and force it to display as a whole number without them:

```
float distance = 12.5;
float steps = 0.5;

// Display the number of steps taken to cover the distance as a
// whole number without a decimal point or decimal places
cout << (int) ( distance / steps );
```

Although this is the **simplest** way to perform a cast - it is not actually the **preferred** way in C++. We will consider an alternative way to perform casts on the next page.

The previous example used a simple cast to convert a **float** value to an **int** value. Similarly, you can convert integers to floating-point numbers.

Example 5.17 – cast_numbers.cpp

```cpp
#include <iostream>      // Program will be using keyboard and screen

using namespace std;     // Will be using standard identifiers cin, cout, endl

int main()
{
    // Get user to type in a float
    cout << "Please type in a decimal number:" << endl;
    float decimalNum;
    cin >> decimalNum;

    // Cast the float as an integer
    cout << "As an int, this gets displayed as: ";
    cout << (int) decimalNum;

    cout << endl << endl;



    // Get user to type in an integer
    cout << "Please type in a whole number:" << endl;
    int wholeNum;
    cin >> wholeNum;

    // Cast the integer into a floating-point number
    cout << "As a float, this gets displayed as: ";
    cout << (float) wholeNum;

    cout << endl << endl;

    return 0;
}
```

Here is what you should see if you try to type in the numbers **7.5** and **8.25**:

```
Please type in a decimal number:
7.5
As an int, this gets displayed as: 7

Please type in a whole number:
8.25
As a float, this gets displayed as: 8
```

When the **float** value **7.5** is cast as an **int** and displayed it becomes the value **7**. No attempt has been made to round the value up or down to nearest whole number, the decimal places have simply been discarded.

Similarly, when **8.25** is typed in and stored as an **int** value, the decimal places are again discarded. Beware though - casting to a **float** again does not bring them back, the discarded decimal places have been lost forever!

To change the way that a value behaves in the original C language, casts were performed in the same way that we saw in *Example 5.17 - cast_numbers.cpp*.

Consider the statement below, which casts an `int` value called **wholeNum** to a **float**:

```
cout << (float) wholeNum;
```

Although many programmers still use the above simple method in their programs, the preferred "official" method in C++ is to use a slightly different style to make it easier to spot where casts are used in your program code.

To ensure that it is **really** obvious when and where casts are used in a program, C++ allows a special keyword to be used:

```
static_cast
```

To make casts even more obvious to spot, a new convention was also introduced to enclose the data-type that you are casting into in **< >** angle braces, rather than **( )** parentheses.

Thus, our example has been rewritten below using the preferred style of cast that you should use:

```
cout << static_cast <float> ( wholeNum );
```

The **< >** angle braces make it easier to spot where casts are taking place when reading through code - they stand out more than the conventional **( )** parentheses that are used in expressions. This style will be used throughout the rest of the book wherever casts are performed.

There are other more advanced kinds of casts that C++ can perform, including **"dynamic casts"**. I don't attempt to cover them here as they are beyond the scope of this book or what beginners might typically expect to find useful.

Using bit-wise operators to perform logical operations

All of the operators discussed so far work with data values. This data is stored in your Pi **digitally**, which means that it is composed of numbers. More specifically, all of the data values are stored and processed as **binary** numbers - patterns of 0s and 1s. If you didn't already know, "**bit**" is short for "**binary-digit**", meaning a single 0 or a 1.

It is also possible in C++ to work with **parts** of a data value rather than whole values. Your code can manipulate individual binary digits or bits within a data-value. To do this, we use the **bit-wise** operators to carry out Boolean or "**logical**" operations on patterns of bits.

C++ offers the following bit-wise operators that you can use:

~	compl	Bit-wise NOT (complement)
|	bitor	Bit-wise OR
&	bitand	Bit-wise AND
^	xor	Bit-wise XOR (exclusive-OR)

How do they work? Each bit-wise operator takes one or two numbers as operands (values to work with). Inside the Pi, each operand is represented as a sequence of binary digits. These sequences of binary digits are then transformed using the rules for each particular operator to produce a new pattern of binary digits. These rules are shown in the tables below.

The bit-wise operators can be used on any simple data-type, such as `int`, since all data is always represented as a pattern of bits. In the following examples I have chosen to use `unsigned short` values to keep the patterns and calculations relatively simple, since these values use relatively few bits. You may otherwise find working with negative values or with a larger range of values from some other data-types to be a little trickier.

The bit-wise ~ NOT operator

This takes a single operand (or value) and **toggles** the pattern of binary digits that is used to represent it. Each 1 in the original bit pattern is changed to a 0. Each 0 in the original bit pattern is changed to a 1.

Each binary digit from the operand		
0	gets changed to	1
1	gets changed to	0

With a bit-wise NOT operation, the resulting binary pattern will always be the **opposite** of the original pattern that was used to represent a value.

For instance, take the `unsigned short` value **13**. This is represented inside your Pi as the following 16-bit binary pattern:

`0000000000001101`

Performing a logical NOT on the bits in this pattern would produce the following result:

`1111111111110010`

Notice that any 0 in the original bit-pattern has now become a 1. Any 1 in the original bit-pattern has now become a 0.

Original value: **13**

Place-values (base-2 column-headings)

32768	16384	8192	4096	2048	1024	512	256	128	64	32	16	8	4	2	1

Pattern of binary digits that are used to represent the data value 13

0	0	0	0	0	0	0	0	0	0	0	0	1	1	0	1

Equivalent values of each binary digit in base 10

0	0	0	0	0	0	0	0	0	0	0	0	8	4	0	1

Base 10 Total = **13**

Bit-wise **NOT** operation on the value **13**

Place-values (base-2 column-headings)

32768	16384	8192	4096	2048	1024	512	256	128	64	32	16	8	4	2	1

Original pattern of binary digits for the value 13 before the NOT operation

0	0	0	0	0	0	0	0	0	0	0	0	1	1	0	1

New pattern of binary digits after the NOT operation has been carried out

1	1	1	1	1	1	1	1	1	1	1	1	0	0	1	0

Equivalent values of each binary digit in base 10

32768	16384	8192	4096	2048	1024	512	256	128	64	32	16	0	0	2	0

Base 10 Total = **65522**

Converting the resulting bit-pattern to base 10 again would give us the number **65522**.
Thus bit-wise **NOT** 13 is **65522**.

Similarly, consider the value **0**, which is the smallest allowable **unsigned short** value and is represented by the bit pattern **0000000000000000**.

NOT **0** results in a pattern of **1111111111111111**, which is **65535**, the maximum allowable **unsigned short** value.

As with the previous examples, the program below allows you to type in a whole number which gets stored as an **unsigned short** (using a pattern of 16 binary digits, allowing positive values between **0** and **65535**). It then performs a bit-wise **NOT** operation on the 16-bit pattern that your Pi uses to represent that number and displays the base-10 result.

Example 5.18 – bitwise_not.cpp

```cpp
#include <iostream>      // Program will be using keyboard and screen

using namespace std;     // Will be using standard identifiers cin, cout, endl

int main()
{
    unsigned short originalNumber, resultAfterNOT;

    // Allow user to type in value
    cout << "Type in a whole number: " << endl;
    cin >> originalNumber;

    // Perform a logical NOT on the bit pattern
    resultAfterNOT = ~ originalNumber;

    // Display the result
    cout << "After the NOT operation, the result is " << resultAfterNOT << endl;

    return 0;
}
```

Here are a few examples of the program in action:

```
Type in a whole number:
138
After the NOT operation, the result is 65397
```

```
Type in a whole number:
65397
After the NOT operation, the result is 138
```

```
Type in a whole number:
0
After the NOT operation, the result is 65535
```

```
Type in a whole number:
65535
After the NOT operation, the result is 0
```

```
Type in a whole number:
65534
After the NOT operation, the result is 1
```

```
Type in a whole number:
1
After the NOT operation, the result is 65534
```

Instead of using the ~ symbol, your code may use the **compl** synonym. In computer science, the negation or "opposite" of a pattern of bits is often called the **ones' complement**, thus **compl** is short for "**complement**".

The following statement:

```
// Perform a logical NOT on the bit pattern
resultAfterNOT = ~ originalNumber;
```

...can also be written as:

```
// Perform a logical NOT on the bit pattern
resultAfterNOT = compl originalNumber;
```

Both of the statements above produce exactly the same result.

The bit-wise | OR operator

This operates on a pair of operands, each being represented as a sequence of binary-digits. Each bit in the first operand is compared with its corresponding bit in the other operand, using the table below to give a result:

A pair of binary digits from the operands			
0	0	gives the result	0
0	1	gives the result	1
1	0	gives the result	1
1	1	gives the result	1

With Boolean OR, the result will always be a **1** if any of the pair of bits is **1**, including when **both** bits are **1**.

Note also that the synonym for the | bitwise OR operator is `bitor`.

An example of bit-wise OR in use

What would be the result of **99 `bitor` 586** ?

First value: **99**

Place-values (base-2 column-headings)

32768	16384	8192	4096	2048	1024	512	256	128	64	32	16	8	4	2	1

Pattern of binary digits that are used to represent the data value **99**

0	0	0	0	0	0	0	0	0	1	1	0	0	0	1	1

Equivalent values of each binary digit in base 10

0	0	0	0	0	0	0	0	0	64	32	0	0	0	2	1

Base 10 Total = **99**

Second value: **586**

Place-values (base-2 column-headings)

32768	16384	8192	4096	2048	1024	512	256	128	64	32	16	8	4	2	1

Pattern of binary digits that are used to represent the data value **586**

0	0	0	0	0	0	1	0	0	1	0	0	1	0	1	0

Equivalent values of each binary digit in base 10

0	0	0	0	0	0	512	0	0	64	0	0	8	0	2	0

Base 10 Total = **586**

99 `bitor` 586

Place-values (base-2 column-headings)

32768	16384	8192	4096	2048	1024	512	256	128	64	32	16	8	4	2	1

Pattern of binary digits for first value **99**

0	0	0	0	0	0	0	0	0	1	1	0	0	0	1	1

Pattern of binary digits for second value **586**

0	0	0	0	0	0	1	0	0	1	0	0	1	0	1	0

Combined pattern of binary digits **after** performing the OR operation

0	0	0	0	0	0	1	0	0	1	1	0	1	0	1	1

Equivalent values of each binary digit in base 10

0	0	0	0	0	0	512	0	0	64	32	0	8	0	2	1

Base 10 Total = **619**

Converting the resulting bit-pattern to base 10 again would give us the number **619**.

Thus **99 `bitor` 586** is **619**.

The bit-wise & AND operator

A pair of binary digits from the operands			
0	0	gives the result	0
0	1	gives the result	0
1	0	gives the result	0
1	1	gives the result	1

With Boolean AND, the result will **only** ever be a **1** when **both** of the pair of bits is **1**.

Note also that the synonym for the **&** bitwise AND operator is **bitand**.

An example of bit-wise AND in use

What would be the result of **99 bitand 46** ?

First value: **99**

Place-values (base-2 column-headings)

32768	16384	8192	4096	2048	1024	512	256	128	64	32	16	8	4	2	1

Pattern of binary digits that are used to represent the data value **99**

0	0	0	0	0	0	0	0	0	1	1	0	0	0	1	1

Equivalent values of each binary digit in base 10

0	0	0	0	0	0	0	0	0	64	32	0	0	0	2	1

Base 10 Total = **99**

Second value: **46**

Place-values (base-2 column-headings)

32768	16384	8192	4096	2048	1024	512	256	128	64	32	16	8	4	2	1

Pattern of binary digits that are used to represent the data value **46**

0	0	0	0	0	0	0	0	0	0	1	0	1	1	1	0

Equivalent values of each binary digit in base 10

0	0	0	0	0	0	0	0	0	0	32	0	8	4	2	0

Base 10 Total = **586**

99 bitand 46

Place-values (base-2 column-headings)

32768	16384	8192	4096	2048	1024	512	256	128	64	32	16	8	4	2	1

Pattern of binary digits for first value **99**

0	0	0	0	0	0	0	0	0	1	1	0	0	0	1	1

Pattern of binary digits for second value **46**

0	0	0	0	0	0	0	0	0	0	1	0	1	1	1	0

Combined pattern of binary digits **after** performing the AND operation

0	0	0	0	0	0	0	0	0	0	1	0	0	0	1	0

Equivalent values of each binary digit in base 10

0	0	0	0	0	0	0	0	0	0	32	0	0	0	2	0

Base 10 Total = **34**

Converting the resulting bit-pattern to base 10 again would give us the number **34**.

Thus **99 bitand 46** is **34**.

The bit-wise ^ XOR operator

The Boolean **XOR** "**exclusive-OR**" operation produces similar results to the OR operation, but with one difference: When **both** inputs are 1, XOR produces 0 as a result, rather than the value 1 which would be produced by an OR operation.

A pair of binary digits from the operands			
0	0	gives the result	0
0	1	gives the result	1
1	0	gives the result	1
1	1	gives the result	0

With Boolean XOR, the result will only ever be a 1 when **both** of the pair of bits is **different** from each other.

In C++, your programs can use the ^ operator to perform a bit-wise XOR operation on two values. Alternatively, you can use the `xor` synonym.

An example of bit-wise XOR in use

What would be the result of **99 xor 46** ?

First value: 99

Place-values (base-2 column-headings)

32768	16384	8192	4096	2048	1024	512	256	128	64	32	16	8	4	2	1

Pattern of binary digits that are used to represent the data value 99

0	0	0	0	0	0	0	0	0	1	1	0	0	0	1	1

Equivalent values of each binary digit in base 10

0	0	0	0	0	0	0	0	0	64	32	0	0	0	2	1

Base 10 Total = 99

Second value: 46

Place-values (base-2 column-headings)

32768	16384	8192	4096	2048	1024	512	256	128	64	32	16	8	4	2	1

Pattern of binary digits that are used to represent the data value 46

0	0	0	0	0	0	0	0	0	0	1	0	1	1	1	0

Equivalent values of each binary digit in base 10

0	0	0	0	0	0	0	0	0	0	32	0	8	4	2	0

Base 10 Total = 586

99 xor 46

Place-values (base-2 column-headings)

32768	16384	8192	4096	2048	1024	512	256	128	64	32	16	8	4	2	1

Pattern of binary digits for first value 99

0	0	0	0	0	0	0	0	0	1	1	0	0	0	1	1

Pattern of binary digits for second value 46

0	0	0	0	0	0	0	0	0	0	1	0	1	1	1	0

Combined pattern of binary digits **after** performing the XOR operation

0	0	0	0	0	0	0	0	0	1	0	0	1	1	0	1

Equivalent values of each binary digit in base 10

0	0	0	0	0	0	0	0	0	64	0	0	8	4	0	1

Base 10 Total = 77

Converting the resulting bit-pattern to base 10 again would give us the number 77.

Thus **99 xor 46** is 77.

The program below allows you to experiment with the bit-wise AND, OR and XOR operations:

Example 5.19 – *bitwise_and_or_xor.cpp*

```cpp
#include <iostream>     // Program will be using keyboard and screen

using namespace std;     // Will be using standard identifiers cin, cout, endl

int main()
{
    unsigned short firstNumber, secondNumber, result;
    char operation;

    // Allow user to type in values and choose kind of operation to perform

    cout << "Type in first whole number: " << endl;
    cin >> firstNumber;

    cout << "Type in second whole number: " << endl;
    cin >> secondNumber;

    cout << "Choose which operation to perform:" << endl;
    cout << "a for AND, o for OR, x for XOR" << endl;
    cin >> operation;

    // Determine what to do to the value
    switch ( operation )
    {
        // Perform AND operation
        case 'a': case 'A':
        {
            result = firstNumber & secondNumber;
            cout << "After performing AND, the result is " << result << endl;
        }
        break;

        // Perform OR operation
        case 'o': case 'O':
        {
            result = firstNumber | secondNumber;
            cout << "After performing OR, the result is " << result << endl;
        }
        break;

        // Perform XOR operation
        case 'x': case 'X':
        {
            result = firstNumber ^ secondNumber;
            cout << "After performing XOR, the result is " << result << endl;
        }
        break;
```

continues on next page...

```
        // Made a bad choice - neither left nor right
        default:
            cout << "Error - must either choose and/or/xor" << endl;
        break;

    }  // end of switch statement


    return 0;
}
```

Note that this program uses a **switch** statement to decide what to do with the character value that the user types in. This kind of statement can be more convenient than using several separate **if** decisions and will be explained in *"Chapter 6: Making decisions"*.

Below you can see the results of several bit-wise operations that have been carried out:

Bit-wise AND: **65535 & 15**

```
Type in first whole number:
65535
Type in second whole number:
15
Choose which operation to perform:
a for AND, o for OR, x for XOR
a
After performing AND, the result is 15
```

Bit-wise OR: **21 | 10**

```
Type in first whole number:
21
Type in second whole number:
10
Choose which operation to perform:
a for AND, o for OR, x for XOR
o
After performing OR, the result is 31
```

Bit-wise XOR: **255 ^ 252**

```
Type in first whole number:
255
Type in second whole number:
252
Choose which operation to perform:
a for AND, o for OR, x for XOR
x
After performing XOR, the result is 3
```

Logical shifts that "slide" patterns of bits to the left or right

C++ includes operators that allow you to **shift** a pattern of binary digits to the left or to the right by a certain number of places:

> `<<` **Shift a pattern of bits to the left**
>
> `>>` **Shift a pattern of bits to the right**

Notice that the bitwise logical operators use the same symbols as when directing inputs and outputs to streams such as `cin` and `cout`, although they do very different things.

Shifting towards the left

```
newValue = originalValue << 3;
```

The above statement would take the pattern of binary digits that represents the value of `originalValue` and then move each bit three places towards the left. Any binary digits that "move past" the left-most column would be lost. Any "empty" places on the right-hand side of the pattern would be filled with the digit **0**. The result would then be stored in `newValue`.

If `originalValue` was an **unsigned short** variable with the value **13**, this might be represented as the bit pattern:

> `0000000000001101`

When the pattern is shifted three places to the left, any new "empty" columns on the right are filled with **0**:

> `0000000001101`000   (The three left-most binary digits are also lost, whatever they were originally.)

The resulting pattern of bits represents the base-10 value gives **104** (which is **64 + 32 + 8**).

Shifting towards the right

```
newValue = originalValue >> 2;
```

The above statement would take the pattern of binary digits that represents the value of `originalValue` and then move each bit two places towards the right. Any binary digits that "move past" the right-most column would be lost. Any "empty" places on the left-hand side of the pattern would be filled with the digit **0**. The result is then stored in `newValue`.

If `originalValue` was an **unsigned short** variable with the value **81**, represented as the bit-pattern:

> `000000001010001`   (81 is represented as **64 + 16 + 1**)

As the pattern is shifted, "empty" columns on the left are filled with **0**:

> 00`0000000010100`   (the right-most pair of binary digits from the original value `01` are lost)

This gives the result **20** (which is **16 + 4**).

The following program allows you to try out some left and right bit-wise shifts for yourself:

Example 5.20 – bitwise_shifts.cpp

```cpp
#include <iostream>       // Program will be using keyboard and screen

using namespace std;      // Will be using standard identifiers cin, cout, endl

int main()
{
    unsigned short originalNumber, placesToShiftBy, shiftedResult;
    char direction;

    // Allow user to type in value, choose kind of shift and how many places to shift

    cout << "Type in a whole number: " << endl;
    cin >> originalNumber;

    cout << "Shift by how many places? " << endl;
    cin >> placesToShiftBy;

    cout << "Shift to the left or to the right? l or r: " << endl;
    cin >> direction;

    // Determine what to do to the value
    switch ( direction )
    {
        // Shift value to the left
        case 'l': case 'L':
        {
            shiftedResult = originalNumber << placesToShiftBy;
            cout << "After shifting, the result is " << shiftedResult << endl;
        }
        break;

        // Shift value to the right
        case 'r': case 'R':
        {
            shiftedResult = originalNumber >> placesToShiftBy;
            cout << "After shifting, the result is " << shiftedResult << endl;
        }
        break;

        // Made a bad choice - neither left nor right
        default:
            cout << "Error - must either shift left or right" << endl;
        break;

    }  // end of switch statement


    return 0;
}
```

Shifting the bit-pattern for the value **64** to the right by **2** places results in the new value **16**.

Here's an example of what happens when the program executes:

```
Type in a whole number:
64
Shift by how many places?
2
Shift to the left or to the right? l or r:
r
After shifting, the result is 16
```

Remember that this is because the first shift to the right effectively **halves** the value to make **32**, then the second shift to the right halves the value again to make **16**.

Thus, shifting the value **64** to the right by **3** places would result in the new value **8** as the original value will be halved, then halved again, and then finally halved again:

```
Type in a whole number:
64
Shift by how many places?
3
Shift to the left or to the right? l or r:
r
After shifting, the result is 8
```

Here is another example, this time shifting a bit-pattern to the left:

```
Type in a whole number:
5
Shift by how many places?
3
Shift to the left or to the right? l or r:
l
After shifting, the result is 40
```

Shifting the bit-pattern for the value **5** by each place to the left results in the value **doubling with each movement**.

This means that shifting it by **3** places to the left will first double the value to make **10**, then double it again to make **20**, then double it a third and final time to make the value **40**.

Shifting the value **5** by **4** places to the left will double the value to make **10**, then again to make **20**, a third time to make the value **40**, then a final time to give **80**:

```
Type in a whole number:
5
Shift by how many places?
4
Shift to the left or to the right? l or r:
l
After shifting, the result is 80
```

In *"Chapter 4: Keyboard input and screen output"* we saw that you can redirect the keyboard input to a character variable. You could use this to let someone choose an option from a menu, allowing them type in a single letter for the choice that they want to make:

Example – *typing a single character*

```
cout << "Please type in a letter for your choice:" << endl;
char letter;
cin >> letter;
```

The problem is that once they have typed a letter, it might be either upper-case or lower-case – you don't know which the person has used. This is important because the computer does not treat upper-case and lower-case letters as the same when making decisions or processing data. It is often inconvenient to write a lot of code in a program to handle both possibilities. You may find it simpler to convert characters to a particular case before trying to do anything useful with them.

We can force a letter to become a lower-case character by "turning on" one of the binary digits in its ASCII character code. If you look at the ASCII codes for lower-case letters as binary numbers, they have almost the same the codes as the upper-case versions of the same letters, but in addition they also have bit **32** set to **1**. The statement below will take whatever the value this bit has from the character code and combine it with the value **32**, meaning that bit **32** is guaranteed to become set to **1**. As we have seen previously in this chapter, such an operation is called a "**logical OR**".

The `if` statement below performs a `|=` bit-wise OR operation:

```
if ( letter >= 'A' and letter <= 'Z' )
    letter |= 32;  // OR ensures case-bit set to 1 (lower-case)
```

Similarly we can force a letter to become an upper-case character by "turning off" one of the binary digits in its ASCII character code. If you look at the ASCII codes for upper-case letters as binary numbers, they all have bit **32** set to **0**.

The `if` statement below shows the `^=` bit-wise XOR operator in use:

```
if ( letter >= 'A' and letter <= 'Z' )
    letter ^= 32;  // XOR ensures case-bit set to 0 (forces char to upper-case)
```

The statement takes the value of bit **32** from the character code and performs an exclusive OR operation to check that it is different to **1**, meaning it is guaranteed to become set to **0**.

It is worth noting that C++ offers two simpler ways to convert the case of a letter, namely the `toupper()` and `tolower()` character functions. These are covered later in *"Chapter 8: Characters and text strings"*.

The program below swaps the case of each letter of the alphabet by reversing the binary digit in each character code that determines whether a letter is upper-case or lower-case. As we saw in the previous example, this is bit **32**.

If bit **32** is currently a **1** then it gets changed to a **0**. Alternatively, if it is currently a **0** then it gets changed to **1**. Consequently, all lower-case letters are changed to upper-case and all upper-case letters are changed to lower-case. This is called "**toggling**" the case of the letters.

Example 5.21 – xor_toggle_case.cpp

```cpp
#include <iostream>      // Program will be using keyboard and screen

using namespace std;     // Will be using standard identifiers string, cin, cout, endl

int main()
{
    // Get user to type in a line of text
    cout << "Please type in a line of text:" << endl;
    string text;
    getline( cin, text );

    // Find out how many characters are in the text
    unsigned int len = text.length();

    // Change upper-case to lower-case and vice versa
    // then display them on the screen
    cout << "Toggled case: ";

    // Examine each character in the text
    // If it a letter of the alphabet then swap its case
    char current;
    for ( unsigned int pos = 0;  pos < len;  pos++ )
    {
        current = text.at( pos );

        if ( ( current >='a' and current <= 'z' )
        or ( current >= 'A' and current <= 'Z' ) )
            current ^= 32;    // Exclusive-OR of bit 32

        cout << current;

    }  // end of for loop


    cout << endl;



    return 0;
}
```

As you can see, the case for each letter has been swapped:

```
Please type in a line of text:
"GNU is not UNIX!"
Toggled case: "gnu IS NOT unix!"
```

Here's what we have covered in this chapter:

The `++` **increment operator** increases the value of a variable by **1**.

The `--` **decrement operator** decreases the value of a variable by **1**.

Expressions can make use of the standard **arithmetic operators** `+` `-` `*` `/` to **add**, **subtract**, **multiply** and **divide**. Care must be taken not to divide a value by zero.

The value of a variable can be changed using the `+=` `-=` `*=` `/=` `%=` operators, leading to shorter program statements.

The `%` **modulus operator** finds the **remainder** when one value is divided by another.

C++ can make **pseudo-random choices** using the `random()` function.

To make the choices less predictable, the random number generator needs to be **seeded** using the `srandom()` function. The function is usually given the current **system time** as the "seed" by calling the `time()` function.

An expression can include values that have different data-types. The data-types do not always need to be the same.

When evaluating an expression, the order of operations normally follows the **BIDMAS** rule.

Operations that have the **same** precedence in an expression are carried out in order from **left-to-right**.

Parts of an expression can be enclosed in `()` brackets to change the order in which operations are performed.

The `pow()` function **raises a value to a particular power**.

The `min()` and `max()` functions find the **smallest** and **largest** values from a pair of operands.

A **cast** operation forces a value that has a certain data-type to behave as though it has a different data-type.

It is best to use the `<static_cast>` operator when performing a cast to improve the readability of your code.

The **bit-wise** `~` **operator** performs a **logical NOT** on a single value.

The **bit-wise** `|` **operator** performs a **logical OR** on a pair of values.

The **bit-wise** `&` **operator** performs a **logical AND** on a pair of values.

The **bit-wise** `^` **operator** performs a **logical XOR (exclusive-OR)** on a pair of values.

The **bit-wise** `<<` and `>>` **operators** allow you to perform a **logical shift** on a pattern of binary digits, moving them **left** or **right** by a certain number of places.

1.	Write a program that chooses six different random numbers for a lottery ticket.
	Each one of the numbers should be a value between **1** and **60**.
	If you run the program several times, it should not choose the same values each time.
2.	Write a program that allows you to type in two different whole numbers.
	It should display the first number raised to the power of the second number.
3.	Write a program that creates an integer variable called **power**.
	The starting value of **power** should be **0**.
	Use the **--** decrement operator to decrease the value of the power variable four times.
	After decreasing the value of **power** each time, display the value **10** raised to the value of **power**.
4.	Write a program that chooses two different random numbers.
	Use the **max()** function to display only the largest of the two numbers.

Chapter 6:

Making decisions

Making simple decisions using `if`

C++ allows you to make a very simple decision by examining whether a **condition** (or an **"expression"**) results in a `true` or a `false` value. The outcome is used to decide whether or not to execute a particular piece of code. Your program can decide whether to execute a single statement, or even a whole block of statements, depending on what happens when the computer **evaluates** the condition.

All simple `if` statements use an expression within `( )` brackets to make a decision. The expression will be **evaluated** and if it is found to be `true`, then the body of the statement will be executed. If the expression is found to be `false`, then the body of the statement will be ignored.

Here is an example of a simple `if` statement that displays a message when the value of the variable `timeLeft` falls below `10` seconds:

```
if ( timeLeft < 10 )
    cout << "Time's running out!" << endl;
```

In the above example, when the program reaches the `if` statement, it evaluates the contents of the `( )` brackets. If the result of the evaluation is found to be `true`, then the computer will execute the next statement. So if it is `true` that the value of `timeLeft` is less than `10`, then the next statement gets executed, displaying the message `"Time's running out!"`

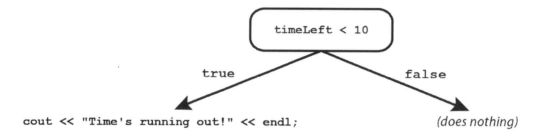

If you want more than one thing to happen when the result of the condition is `true`, you must use `{ }` braces to bind several statements together into a single block (called a **"compound statement"**) that you would like to be executed:

Example – a block of statements that are executed when a simple `if` decision evaluates to `true`

```
if ( timeLeft < 10 )
{
    cout << "Time's running out!" << endl;
    cout << "You only have ";
    cout << timeLeft << " seconds left..." << endl;
}
```

```
    {
        cout << "Time's running out!" << endl;
        cout << "You only have ";
        cout << timeLeft << " seconds left..." << endl;
    }
```

timeLeft < 10

true   false

(does nothing)

Simple decisions that use relational operators < <= > >= ==

This program makes decisions using two simple **if** statements.

In the first **if** statement, the expression **waterTemp <= 0** is evaluated, giving either a **true** or **false** value.

If the result is **true** (i.e. the value of the variable **waterTemp** is less than or equal to the value zero) then the following statement is executed:

```
cout << "Frozen." << endl;
```

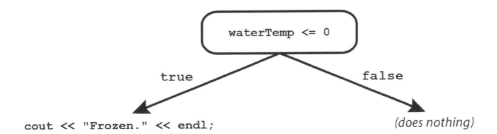

Similarly, in the second **if** statement, **waterTemp >= 100** is evaluated, giving either a **true** or **false** value.

If the result is **true** (i.e. the value of the variable **waterTemp** is greater than or equal to the value **100**) then the next statement after the condition is executed:

```
cout << "Boiling." << endl;
```

Example 6.1 – if_decision.cpp

```cpp
#include <iostream>      // Program will be using keyboard and screen

using namespace std;     // Will be using standard identifiers cin, cout, endl

int main()
{
    // Type in a temperature value
    cout << "Enter the water temperature: ";
    float waterTemp;
    cin >> waterTemp;

    // Decide if the value is less than zero - ice
    if ( waterTemp <= 0 )
        cout << "Frozen." << endl;

    // Decide if the value is 100 or above - boiling
    if ( waterTemp >= 100 )
        cout << "Boiling." << endl;

    return 0;
}
```

Determining whether two values are the same with the == equivalence operator

To compare two values or expressions to see whether they are the same, use the == *equivalence operator*.

This will result in either a **true** or a **false** value: **true** when both things are the same, **false** when they are not.

For instance, the value of the variable **timeLeft** can be compared with the value of **0** (zero):

```
timeLeft == 0
```

The program below uses the equivalence operator as part of an **if** decision to decide whether a value that the user types in is exactly zero:

Example 6.2 – if_compare_value.cpp

```cpp
#include <iostream>     // Program will be using keyboard and screen

using namespace std;    // Will be using standard identifiers cin, cout, endl

int main()
{
    cout << "Type in a number..." << endl;
    int num;
    cin >> num;

    // Decide whether the number was exactly zero
    if ( num == 0 )
        cout << "It was exactly zero" << endl;

    return 0;
}
```

Warning! Be very careful not to confuse the == *equivalence* operator with the = *assignment* operator. If you accidentally try to use = to make a comparison, your program may well produce some every strange results at run-time.

Consider this code which is supposed to compare the value of the variable **num** with zero:

```cpp
    // WHOA! DELIBERATE ERROR IN NEXT LINE!!!
    if ( num = 0 )
        cout << "It was exactly zero" << endl;
```

What the above code actually does is to **set** the value of the variable **num** to zero, instead of **comparing** it with zero. This assignment succeeds and thus the expression within the **( )** brackets then gets evaluated to produce the result **true**, whatever the original value of **num**.

The effect is that the **if** decision shown above will **always** execute the body of statements unconditionally. Note that many C++ compilers will produce a warning message to alert you to such a problem. This is another reason why you should not ignore warnings during compilation.

Comparing `string` values

The previous program made use of the `==` equivalence operator to test whether two numeric values are the same. The equivalence operator can also be used with other data-types in a similar manner.

Note however that for two **string** values to be considered as exactly the same, they must be exactly the same length as each other and any letters of the alphabet must be the same case (upper or lower) in both values.

The following **string** values would **not** be considered equal to each other:

```
"Custard"      // Mixed-case
"CUSTARD"      // Entirely upper-case
"custard"      // Entirely lower-case
"custArd"      // Mixed-case
" Custard"     // Different length, preceded by a space character
```

For further details about comparing and working with **string** values, see *"Chapter 8: Characters and text strings"*.

Checking all parts of an expression are `true` using the logical `and` operator

Some expressions are used to make more complicated decisions. The `&&` AND operator tests whether **every single part** of an expression evaluates to **true**.

For instance, given the values of these variables:

```
bool shopIsOpen = true;
bool soldOut = false;
float priceOfIceCream = 1.50;
float moneyInPocket = 23.20;
```

We can use an expression to work out whether or not you can buy an ice-cream. You can only buy an ice-cream if **all** parts of the expression evaluate to **true**:

```
bool canBuyIceCream = ( shopIsOpen == true )
                && ( soldOut == false )
                && (  moneyInPocket >= priceOfIceCream )
```

If one or more parts of the expression are **false**, then the value of the overall result will be **false** for the whole expression. Consequently the value of the variable **canBuyIceCream** will be set to **false** as a result.

The expression can be rewritten to use the reserved word **and** instead of the `&&` operator, making it slightly easier to read:

```
bool canBuyIceCream =  ( shopIsOpen == true )
                and ( soldOut == false )
                and (  moneyInPocket >= priceOfIceCream )
```

Here is another example that uses `==` to check that several values are the same. This program asks the user to type in three whole numbers. It then tests whether any two of them, or all three of them, are the same.

Example 6.3 – *if_compare_variables.cpp*

```cpp
#include <iostream>      // Program will be using screen and keyboard

using namespace std;     // Will be using standard identifiers cin, cout, endl

int main()
{
    cout << "Please type in 3 whole numbers:" << endl;

    int num1, num2, num3;

    cin >> num1;
    cin >> num2;
    cin >> num3;


    // Check whether the first pair of numbers is the same
    if ( num1 == num2 )
        cout << "First and second numbers are the same" << endl;
    else
        cout << "First and second numbers are different" << endl;


    // Check whether the first and last numbers are the same
    if ( num1 == num3 )
        cout << "First and third numbers are the same" << endl;
    else
        cout << "First and third numbers are different" << endl;


    // Check whether the second and third numbers are the same
    if ( num2 == num3 )
        cout << "Second and third numbers are the same" << endl;
    else
        cout << "Second and third numbers are different" << endl;


    // Check whether all three numbers are the same
    if ( ( num1 == num2 ) and ( num1 == num3 ) )
        cout << "All three numbers are the same" << endl;
    else
        cout << "The three numbers are not all the same" << endl;


    return 0;
}
```

Here's what happens on entering two numbers that are different:

```
Please type in 3 whole numbers:
4
2
4
First and second numbers are different
First and third numbers are the same
Second and third numbers are different
The three numbers are not all the same
```

```
Please type in 3 whole numbers:
8
8
2
First and second numbers are the same
First and third numbers are different
Second and third numbers are different
The three numbers are not all the same
```

But when all three numbers are the same you should see the following:

```
Please type in 3 whole numbers:
9
9
9
First and second numbers are the same
First and third numbers are the same
Second and third numbers are the same
All three numbers are the same
```

Using % and == to produce predictable patterns

The % *modulus* operator is often used to switch between a fixed number of alternatives to produce simple, regular patterns of behaviour.

This next example displays text one letter-at a time, alternating between two different colours:

Example 6.4 – *alternating_sequence.cpp*

```cpp
#include <iostream>      // Program will be displaying some text on the screen
#include <unistd.h>      // Uses the sleep() function to pause during execution

using namespace std;     // Will be using standard identifiers string, cout and endl

int main()
{
    const string MESSAGE = "GREETINGS!";

    const string GREEN = "\e[32m";
    const string RED = "\e[31m";
    const string NORMAL = "\e[0m";

    string colourToUse;
```

continues on next page...

continues on next page...

```
    // Display the message, one letter at a time with 1 second delay
    for ( unsigned int pos = 0;  pos < MESSAGE.length();  pos++ )
    {
        if ( ( pos % 2 ) == 1 )
            colourToUse = GREEN;   // Odd number - set colour to green
        else
            colourToUse = RED;   // Even number - set colour to red

        // Display singleletter from the message, then pause for 1 second
        cout << colourToUse << MESSAGE.at( pos ) << flush;
        sleep( 1 );

    }  // end of for loop

    // Escape-sequence to return to normal formatting
    cout << NORMAL << endl << endl;

    return 0;
}
```

The code uses the **pos** variable to keep track of the current position in the text to be displayed. Before displaying each letter, the program uses **%** to determine whether the remainder of dividing **pos** by 2 is an odd or an even number.

Odd numbers always give a remainder of **1** when divided by **2**, whereas even numbers always give a remainder of **0**, because they are exactly divisible by **2**. The outcome of this decision is used to set the colour of the individual letter that is displayed. If **pos** is odd, then the program sets the text colour to green, otherwise it sets the colour to red.

This effect is achieved by the **if** statement shown below:

```
    if ( ( pos % 2 ) == 1 )
        colourToUse = GREEN;   // Odd number - set colour to green
    else
        colourToUse = RED;   // Even number - set colour to red
```

Alternatively, we could use the **?** *conditional operator* as a more compact way to make the decision about whether the colour should be green or red, instead of using an **if** statement:

```
    colourToUse = ( pos % 2 ) ? GREEN : RED;
```

When the program runs, you should see that the colour of the letters alternates between green and red:

Determining whether two values are different using the != non-equivalence operator

Sometimes a program needs to check whether two values or expressions are **not** the same.

A simple way to do this is to use the **!=** *non-equivalence* operator. When making comparisons between two values or expressions, **!=** will only return a **true** value if they are **not** the same. Alternatively, if they **are** the same, it will return a **false** value.

You may also use the **not_eq** synonym instead of the **!=** operator. They mean the same thing, but some people find **not_eq** easier to understand when reading program code.

Example 6.5 – if_different.cpp

```cpp
#include <iostream>      // Program will be using keyboard and screen

using namespace std;     // Will be using standard identifiers string, cin, cout, endl

int main()
{
    cout << "Please type in new password TWICE!" << endl;

    // Get the user to type in the password
    string password1;
    cin >> password1;

    // Get the user to type it in again
    string password2;
    cin >> password2;

    // Check whether passwords were not the same
    if ( password1 != password2 )
        cout << "They were DIFFERENT!" << endl;
    else
        cout << "Cool. That worked." << endl;

    return 0;
}
```

The program decides whether both password strings are exactly the same, including their case:

```
Please type in new password TWICE!
xyl0ph0ne
xyl0ph0ne
Cool. That worked.
```

In the example below, the passwords are clearly different lengths, as though I had made a spelling mistake:

```
Please type in new password TWICE!
xl0ph0ne
xyl0ph0ne
They were DIFFERENT!
```

In this final example, I have forgotten to type '0' (zero) for one of the letter 'o' characters in the first password:

```
Please type in new password TWICE!
xyloph0ne
xyl0ph0ne
They were DIFFERENT!
```

As already mentioned, the following **if-else** statement:

```cpp
if ( password1 != password2 )
    cout << "They were DIFFERENT!" << endl;
else
    cout << "Cool. That worked." << endl;
```

...could instead be written as:

```cpp
if ( password1 not_eq password2 )
    cout << "They were DIFFERENT!" << endl;
else
    cout << "Cool. That worked." << endl;
```

...or even:

```cpp
cout << ( password1 not_eq password2 ) ? "They were DIFFERENT!"
                                       : "Cool. That worked.";

cout << endl;
```

All three statements are forms of the same decision:

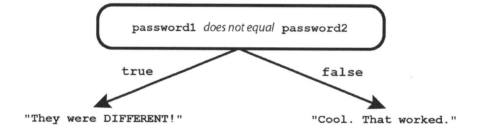

More complex decisions

Many programs make use of simple `if` decisions. Several simple decisions can often be combined together into a single statement using a **logical operator**, such as `&&` the *logical AND operator*.

Below is an example that checks whether a person's age is within certain limits. It checks that the value of variable **age** is greater than or exactly equal to **4**, **and** also at the same time that the value of **age** is less than **18**:

Example 6.6 – if_value_in_range.cpp

```cpp
#include <iostream>      // Program will be using keyboard and screen

using namespace std;      // Will be using standard identifiers cin, cout, endl

int main()
{
    // User types in a number
    cout << "Type in your age in years..." << endl;
    int age;
    cin >> age;

    // Check number is not less than zero
    if ( age < 0 )
        cout << "Impossible!" << endl;

    // Check number is between 4 and 18 (inclusive)
    if ( age >= 4  and  age < 18 )
        cout << "Must be in education" << endl;
    else
        cout << "Don't need to be in education" << endl;

    return 0;
}
```

Consider the statement below:

```cpp
if ( age >= 4  and  age < 18 )
    cout << "Must be in education" << endl;
else
    cout << "Don't need to be in education" << endl;
```

It contains two separate tests, each one results in a **true** or **false** value:

```cpp
age >= 4
age < 18
```

Once both tests have been carried out, the **and** operator combines their results to produce a single Boolean value, which is either **true** or **false**. This final value will only ever be set to **true** if **all** parts of the expression are **true**. If one or more parts of the expression are **false**, then the overall final result will also be **false**.

Thus, the result of the expression is only ever **true** if both **age** `>= 4` is **true** and **age** `< 18` is also **true**.

We can use a similar technique for the previous water example. Here is an updated version of *Example 6.1 – if_decision.cpp*. It uses the **and** operator to check whether the water temperature is greater than 0 **AND** at the same time less than 100:

Example 6.7 – *if_temp_range.cpp*

```cpp
#include <iostream>      // Program will be using keyboard and screen

using namespace std;     // Will be using standard identifiers cin, cout, endl

int main()
{
    // User types in a value from the keyboard
    cout << "Enter the water temperature: ";
    float waterTemp;
    cin >> waterTemp;


    // Decide if the value is 0 or below
    if ( waterTemp <= 0 )
        cout << "Frozen." << endl;


    // Decide if the value is 100 or above
    if ( waterTemp >= 100 )
        cout << "Boiling." << endl;


    // Decide if the value is above 0
    // and also lower than 100 (liquid water)
    if ( waterTemp > 0  and  waterTemp < 100 )
        cout << "Liquid state." << endl;

    return 0;
}
```

The statement:

```cpp
if ( waterTemp > 0  and  waterTemp < 100 )
    cout << "Liquid state." << endl;
```

...means:

"if the value of variable **waterTemp** is greater than 0

AND at the same time

the value of **waterTemp** is less than 100

then

the computer will display **"Liquid State"** on the screen"

This program allows you to type in exam marks, making use of several `if` decisions to determine their corresponding grades:

Example 6.8 – if_exam_grades.cpp

```cpp
#include <iostream>     // Program will use keyboard input and screen output

using namespace std;    // Will be using standard identifiers cin, cout, endl

int main()
{
    int mark;
    while ( true )
    {
        cout << "Type in a mark " << endl;
        cin >> mark;

        if ( mark >= 0  and  mark < 31 )
            cout << "UNGRADED!" << endl;

        if ( mark >= 31  and  mark < 38 )
            cout << "Grade E" << endl;

        if ( mark >= 38  and  mark < 45 )
            cout << "Grade D" << endl;

        if ( mark >= 45  and  mark < 53 )
            cout << "Grade C" << endl;

        if ( mark >= 53  and  mark < 61 )
            cout << "Grade B" << endl;

        if ( mark >= 61  and  mark <= 100 )
            cout << "Grade A" << endl;

        cout << endl;  // Display blank line

    }  // end of while loop

    return 0;
}
```

Below, you can see what happens when several exam marks are entered:

```
Type in a mark
42
Grade D

Type in a mark
76
Grade A

Type in a mark
19
UNGRADED!
```

Checking that at least one part of an expression is `true` with the logical `or` operator

The `||` *logical OR operator* tests whether **at least one part** of an expression evaluates to `true`.

We could use this to add a final check to the previous program to determine whether the user has typed in an exam mark that is not valid. If a person types in a mark that is less than `0` (zero) **or** more than `100` (the maximum mark in the exam) then they must have made a mistake, as you can't possibly score such a mark.

```
// Check for a value that is out of the possible range of marks
if ( mark < 0  ||  mark > 100 )
    cout << "ERROR!!!" << endl;
```

Note the use of the `||` logical OR operator in the expression to trigger the error message if an invalid mark is typed in. If one of the parts of the expression in the above `if` statement is `true` then the error message will be displayed.

Instead of using the `||` symbol, your code can use the `or` synonym. This has the same effect, but may make your code easier for people to read and understand:

```
// Check for a value that is out of the possible range of marks
if ( mark < 0  or  mark > 100 )
    cout << "ERROR!!!" << endl;
```

Adding either of these `if` decisions allows marks that are below zero or above one hundred to be flagged as invalid:

```
Type in a mark
-5
ERROR!!!

Type in a mark
0
UNGRADED!

Type in a mark
100
Grade A

Type in a mark
120
ERROR!!!
```

One of the advantages of using the logical **or** operator is that it is often used to reduce the number of simple **if** statements in a program, because it allows several of them to be combined together.

Consider these statements:

```
// Set up what the weather is like at the moment
bool itIsWindy = false;
bool itIsRaining = true;
bool itIsSnowing = false;

// Decide whether we have bad weather: windy OR raining OR snowing
bool badWeather = false;  // Initial value - assumes it is not bad weather

if ( itIsWindy )
    badWeather = true;  // If it is windy then we have bad weather

if ( itIsRaining )
    badWeather = true;  // If it is raining then we have bad weather

if ( itIsSnowing )
    badWeather = true;  // If it is snowing then we have bad weather
```

In the above code, we begin by assuming that we don't have bad weather at the moment, setting the Boolean variable **badWeather** to **false**.

The program then uses three separate **if** decisions to examine whether the weather is bad. First it checks if it is windy, then it checks if it is raining, finally it checks if it is snowing. After executing all three **if** statements, **badWeather** will either be **true** or **false**, depending on the values of the variables **itIsWindy**, **itIsRaining** and **itIsSnowing**.

An alternative approach would be to **combine** the three **if** statement together into one single decision, testing whether it is windy **or** raining **or** snowing, all in one go:

```
// Decide whether we have bad weather: windy OR raining OR snowing
bool badWeather = false;  // Initial value - assumes it is not bad weather

if ( itIsWindy or itIsRaining or itIsSnowing )
    badWeather = true;  // If it is windy, raining or snowing then weather is bad
```

Even this code can be streamlined further. We can directly set the value of the Boolean **badWeather** variable to be the result of the expression, since this result will also be a **bool** value (it will either be **true** or **false**).

Here is the simplified code as a single statement:

```
bool badWeather = itIsWindy or itIsRaining or itIsSnowing;
```

If one or more of three Boolean variables **itIsWindy**, **itIsRaining** or **itIsSnowing** has the value **true**, then the result of the expression will also be **true**.

Note also that in the above examples, the **||** operator could have been used instead of the **or** synonym.

Here's the full program, making use of only a single `if-else` decision:

Example 6.9 – if_weather.cpp

```cpp
#include <iostream>     // Program will be displaying some text on the screen

using namespace std;     // Will be using standard identifiers cout and endl

int main()
{
    // Set up what the weather is like at the moment
    bool itIsWindy = false;
    bool itIsRaining = true;
    bool itIsSnowing = false;

    // Decide whether we have bad weather: windy OR raining OR snowing
    bool badWeather = itIsWindy or itIsRaining or itIsSnowing;

    // Decide which message to display
    if ( badWeather )
        cout << "The weather is bad.";
    else
        cout << "The weather is good.";

    cout << endl;



    return 0;
}
```

As we can see, the program uses an `if` statement to decide which literal text message should be displayed at run-time, based on the value of the **badWeather** variable:

```cpp
    // Decide which message to display
    if ( badWeather )
        cout << "The weather is bad.";
    else
        cout << "The weather is good.";
```

When executed, the program produces this simple output:

```
The weather is bad.
```

This next example examines individual characters from a **string** value. It uses the **at()** function, which belongs to the **string** data-type. Note that characters and strings are covered in detail in *"Chapter 8: Characters and text-strings"*.

The program below makes decisions about each character in the **myWord** variable, deciding whether it is a particular lower-case or upper-case vowel. To do this it uses the logical **or** operator.

Example 6.10 – if_vowels.cpp

```cpp
#include <iostream>      // Program will be using keyboard and screen

using namespace std;     // Will be using standard identifiers string, cin, cout, endl

int main()
{
    // User types in a word
    cout << "Type in a word:" << endl;
    string myWord;
    cin >> myWord;

    unsigned int numChars = myWord.length();  // Find num chars are in the word

    // Variables to count which vowels have been found in the word
    bool haveA = false;
    bool haveE = false;
    bool haveI = false;
    bool haveO = false;
    bool haveU = false;

    // Start at beginning of word, then examine each symbol
    char symbol;
    for ( unsigned int position = 0;  position < numChars;  position++ )
    {
        // Extract single character from the word
        symbol = myWord.at( position );

        // Decide whether have letter A (or a)
        if ( ( symbol == 'A' ) or ( symbol == 'a' ) )
            haveA = true;

        // Decide whether have letter E (or e)
        if ( ( symbol == 'E' ) or ( symbol == 'e' ) )
            haveE = true;

        // Decide whether have letter I (or i)
        if ( ( symbol == 'I' ) or ( symbol == 'i' ) )
            haveI = true;

        // Decide whether have letter O (or o)
        if ( ( symbol == 'O' ) or ( symbol == 'o' ) )
            haveO = true;
```

continues on next page...

```cpp
        // Decide whether have letter U (or u)
        if ( ( symbol == 'U' ) or ( symbol == 'u' ) )
            haveU = true;

    }   // end of for loop


    // Decide whether have found at least one vowel or not
    if ( haveA or haveE or haveI or haveO or haveU )
        cout << "Contains at least one vowel." << endl;
    else
        cout << "No vowels in this word." << endl;


    // Display WHICH vowels were found in the word

    if ( haveA )
        cout << "Contains letter a/A" << endl;

    if ( haveE )
        cout << "Contains letter e/E" << endl;

    if ( haveI )
        cout << "Contains letter i/I" << endl;

    if ( haveO )
        cout << "Contains letter o/O" << endl;

    if ( haveU )
        cout << "Contains letter u/U" << endl;

    return 0;
}
```

When the program executes, it displays a summary of the vowels that are contained in the word that the user types:

```
Type in a word:
toucan
Contains at least one vowel.
Contains letter a/A
Contains letter o/O
Contains letter u/U
```

It does not matter whether the vowel is in upper-case or lower-case, both cases are detected:

```
Type in a word:
Avocet
Contains at least one vowel.
Contains letter a/A
Contains letter o/O
Contains letter u/U
```

Suppose that your program needs to examine combinations of characters to determine whether they conform to a simple set of rules.

This program asks the user to type in symbols to make a "smiley", such as any of the following examples:

```
    :-)          :o)         ;-)         :o]
```

The rules for what constitutes a smiley or not are encoded in the program as **if** decisions.
These rules make use of the **or** operator and the **and** operator.

The eyes for the smiley are allowed to be either **:** or **;**

The nose for the smiley is allowed to be either **-** or **o**

The mouth for the smiley is allowed to be either **)** or **]**

The symbols form a smiley if the eyes are acceptable **and** the nose is acceptable **and** the mouth is acceptable.

Example 6.11 – *validate_smiley.cpp*

```cpp
#include <iostream>     // Program will be using keyboard and screen

using namespace std;    // Will be using standard identifiers cin, cout, endl

int main()
{
    // Get user to type in eyes.
    cout << "Type in eyes..." << endl;
    char eyes;
    cin >> eyes;

    // Check what kind of symbol they typed.
    bool validEyes =  eyes == ':'  or  eyes == ';';

    // -----------------

    // Get user to type in nose.
    cout << "Type in nose..." << endl;
    char nose;
    cin >> nose;

    // Check what symbol they typed.
    bool validNose =  nose == '-'  or  nose == 'o';

    // -----------------

    // Get user to type in mouth.
    cout << "Type in mouth..." << endl;
    char mouth;
    cin >> mouth;
```

continues on next page...

continued...

```cpp
    // Check what symbol they typed.
    bool validMouth =  mouth == ')'  or  mouth == ']';

    // -----------------

    // Display what they typed in.
    cout << eyes;
    cout << nose;
    cout << mouth;

    // Display whether or not it is a valid smiley.
    if ( validEyes and validNose and validMouth )
        cout << " is a smiley.";
    else
        cout << " does not make a smiley.";

    cout << endl;


    return 0;
}
```

Here is an example that I tried on my Pi:

```
Type in eyes...
:
Type in nose...
o
Type in mouth...
]
:o] is a smiley.
```

The program considers that `:o]` is a valid smiley as the eye character, the nose character and the mouth character are all acceptable according to the simple `if` decisions.

The example below though is considered to be invalid as according to the `if` decision in the program, the mouth must either be a `)` or a `]` character:

```
Type in eyes...
:
Type in nose...
-
Type in mouth...
P
:-P does not make a smiley.
```

Setting Boolean variables using the result of a relational expression

The same approach applies to **relational expressions**, which compare two operands to each other. These expressions also produce a **true** or **false** value that can be stored in a Boolean variable to produce very readable code.

Take a look at the code below, which tests whether a value is either less than or exactly equal to zero:

```
bool frozen;

if ( waterTemp <= 0 )
    frozen = true;
else
    frozen = false;
```

Hopefully, you can see how the **if** statement decides which value to choose for the variable **waterTemp**.

The expression in the **( )** brackets of the **if** decision always gets evaluated to produce either a **true** or a **false** value.

Depending on the outcome of the expression, the code above will set the value of the variable **frozen** to either **true** or **false**.

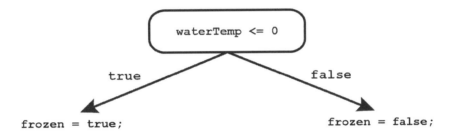

Instead of using an **if** decision to set **frozen** to **true** or **false**, we can simplify the code by directly assigning the result of the evaluated expression to the variable **frozen**:

```
bool frozen = ( waterTemp <= 0 ) ;
```

Thus, when this statement is executed, the computer tests whether the value of the variable **waterTemp** is less-than or equal-to **0**, giving either a **true** or **false** result. It then sets the value of the variable **frozen** to this result.

This approach works really well when working with more complex logical decisions, as you will see later in this chapter.

Combining several `if` decisions together to deal with more than two outcomes

Let's revisit one of our examples that used several `if` statements to make decisions about the value of a variable.

Consider these statements:

```
if ( num < 0 )
    cout << "It was negative" << endl;

if ( num > 0 )
    cout << "It was positive" << endl;

if ( num == 0 )
    cout << "It was exactly zero" << endl;
```

In the above code, all three `if` decisions will **always** be carried out, whatever the value of **num**. This means that the program will in some cases be inefficient.

Imagine if the value of **num** is **0**...

The **first** test will be carried out: **(num < 0)** giving the result **false**.

The **second** test will be carried out: **(num > 0)** also giving **false**.

The **third** test will be carried out: **(num == 0)** giving the answer **true**.

Now imagine what happens when the value of num is **−20**.

The first test will be carried out: **(num < 0)** giving the result **true**.

There is no need to carry out the other tests because **−20** is neither greater than zero nor equal to zero, but the code will go ahead and carry them out anyway, giving **false** results in both cases.

It would be better if our program didn't carry out any unnecessary tests. We can combine `if` statements together to simplify the decision-making process and to make our program more efficient:

```
if ( num < 0 )
    cout << "It was negative" << endl;
else
    if ( num > 0 )
        cout << "It was positive" << endl;
    else
        cout << "It was exactly zero" << endl;
```

Try tracing through the execution of this code with the value **0** for **num**, followed by the value **−20**. You should find that whatever value you choose for the variable **num**, only a maximum of two tests are ever carried out. In the case of a negative value, only the first test will be carried out.

This is called a **nested** `if` statement (one `if` statement that is embedded within another, to model a **"decision tree"** of possible outcomes). Unfortunately, depending on the number of possible outcomes, the code can become more difficult to read through. The nested `if` statement will however be more efficient to execute than many simple `if` statements.

Here is the program again, with the three `if` statements combined together as a single nested `if`:

Example 6.12 – nested_if.cpp

```cpp
#include <iostream>      // Program will be using keyboard and screen

using namespace std;     // Will be using standard identifiers cin, cout, endl

int main()
{
    cout << "Type in a whole number..." << endl;

    int num;

    cin >> num;


    // Decide whether the number was negative, positive or exactly zero

    if ( num < 0 )
        cout << "It was negative" << endl;
    else
        if ( num > 0 )
            cout << "It was positive" << endl;
        else
            cout << "It was exactly zero" << endl;


    return 0;
}
```

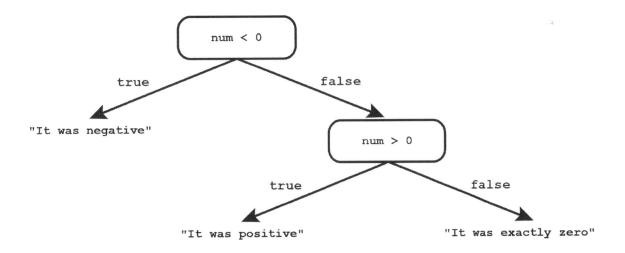

From the decision tree above, you can see how the program processes the value of **num**.

Finding the opposite of a value or expression using the ! NOT operator

You can find the **opposite** of a relational or a Boolean expression using the ! **NOT** operator. Another name for this is the *negation operator*. It is used when you want to find the opposite of an expression which evaluates to either `true` or `false`.

The simplest way to use the ! *negation operator* is to find the opposite of the value of a Boolean **variable**:

```
isNight  =  ! isDay

awake  =  ! asleep

inCredit  =  ! inDebt
```

It can also be used to find the opposite of an **expression**.

For instance, look at the following expressions below:

```
temperature < 100

( today == "Saturday" )  or  ( today == "Sunday" )

raining == true

( phoneCharged == true ) and ( credit > 0 )

myName.length() > 0
```

Each one of the above expressions can be evaluated by the computer to give either a `true` or `false` answer, depending on the value stored in each variable.

You can find the **opposite** of each of the expressions by prefixing it with the ! negation operator, as shown in the statements below:

```
waterBoiling =  ! ( temperature < 100 );

workingDay =  ! ( ( today == "Saturday" )  or  ( today == "Sunday" ) );

dryWeather =  ! ( raining == true );

problem =  ! ( phoneCharged == true ) and ( credit > 0 );

validSurname = ! ( myName.length() > 0 );
```

Adding extra ( ) brackets around parts of expressions to ensure the correct result

We have already seen that you can enclose parts of an arithmetic expression within ( ) brackets to change the order in which particular operations are carried out. Similarly, you may also enclose parts of a logical expression within ( ) brackets to force a particular logical operation to be carried out before others parts of the same expression.

Because the previous examples all contain one or more other operators, it is important to put ( ) brackets around each expression before applying the ! operator. If you don't do this, the ! operator may only affect **part** of the expression and will probably give an incorrect result.

In the example below, we need to use such a pair of extra ( ) brackets around the **whole** expression before applying the ! operator:

```
bool goToWork = ! ( ( today == "Saturday" ) or ( today == "Sunday" ) );
```

This means that it is a working day if it is **not** the case that today is either a Saturday or a Sunday, because whether I need to go to work is the opposite of whether it is the weekend (when it is Saturday or Sunday).

Without the extra pair or brackets, the statement will give the wrong answer, as it will mean something else:

```
bool goToWork = ! ( today == "Saturday" ) or ( today == "Sunday" );
```

In the above expression, the ! negation operator only acts upon the part of the expression that is shown in bold. This would mean that it is a working day either if it is not a Saturday, or alternatively if it is Sunday.

Using the **and** operator with **not** to check that a password is valid

This next program uses logical operators to check that a **string** value meets the rules for acceptable passwords:

Example 6.13 – validate_password.cpp

```cpp
#include <iostream>      // Program will be using keyboard and screen

using namespace std;     // Will be using standard identifiers string, cin, cout, endl

int main()
{
    // Instruct the user to type in a password
    cout << "Please type new password between 8 and 12 characters long." << endl;
    cout << "It must contain at least one letter and at least one digit." << endl;
    cout << "It must NOT contain any spaces." << endl;

    // Get user to type it in
    string password;
    cin >> password;

    // Find out how many characters they typed
    unsigned int numChars = password.length();
```

continues on next page...

```cpp
    // Check the length is acceptable, should be between 8 and 12 characters long
    bool lengthOK = ( numChars >= 8 ) and ( numChars <= 12 );

    // Check for at least one digit and one letter
    char symbol;
    bool foundDigit = false;
    bool foundLetter = false;

    // Examine each character that was typed, one by one
    for ( unsigned int position = 0;  position < numChars;  position++ )
    {
        // Get a character from the string
        symbol = password.at( position );

        // Find out whether it is a numeric digit or not
        if ( ( symbol >= '0' ) and ( symbol <= '9' ) )
            foundDigit = true;

        // Find out whether it is a lower-case letter or not
        if ( ( symbol >= 'a' ) and ( symbol <= 'z' ) )
            foundLetter = true;

        // Find out whether it is an upper-case letter or not
        if ( ( symbol >= 'A' ) and ( symbol <= 'Z' ) )
            foundLetter = true;

    }  // end of for loop

    // Decide whether the password meets all of the criteria
    // Length must be OK AND must have a digit AND must have a letter
    bool passwordOK = lengthOK and foundDigit and foundLetter;

    // Let user know if password is OK, or tell them what is wrong
    if ( passwordOK )
        cout << "Password is acceptable - thank-you." << endl;
    else
    {
      cout << "Sorry - this password is unacceptable." << endl;

      if ( not lengthOK )
          cout << "Password must be 8-12 characters long!" << endl;

      if ( not foundDigit )
          cout << "Password must contain at least one numeric digit!" << endl;

      if ( not foundLetter )
          cout << "Password must contain at least one letter from alphabet!" << endl;

    }  // end of if-else decision

    return 0;
}
```

Here are some examples of the different inputs and how they are handled when the program executes.

The first password is too short and does not contain any digits, thus it is rejected:

```
Please type new password between 8 and 12 characters long.
It must contain at least one letter and at least one digit.
It must NOT contain any spaces.
blob
Sorry - this password is unacceptable.
Password must be 8-12 characters long!
Password must contain at least one numeric digit!
```

The next password is too long and still does not contain any digits:

```
Please type new password between 8 and 12 characters long.
It must contain at least one letter and at least one digit.
It must NOT contain any spaces.
reallyreallylongpassword
Sorry - this password is unacceptable.
Password must be 8-12 characters long!
Password must contain at least one numeric digit!
```

Finally, the last password is a suitable length and contains a digit, making it acceptable:

```
Please type new password between 8 and 12 characters long.
It must contain at least one letter and at least one digit.
It must NOT contain any spaces.
justR1ght
Password is acceptable - thank-you.
```

Note that the decisions could be written in a slightly shorter form using the **isdigit()** and **isalpha()** character functions:

```
// Find out whether it is a numeric digit or not
if ( isdigit( symbol ) )
    foundDigit = true;

// Find out whether it is a letter or not
if ( isalpha( symbol ) )
    foundLetter = true;
```

Both of these functions can been found in the **<cctype>** library. It is not necessary however to add an **#include <cctype>** directive to our program as the **<iostream>** library already makes use of the same code. We will find out more about these character functions in *"Chapter 8: Characters and text strings"*.

Using a `switch` statement when there are many possible outcomes for a decision

So far, our programs have only made a very small number of decisions, using `if` statements that choose between very simple alternatives. We have also seen how the computer can choose a random number and display it on the screen.

Programs often need to choose between a larger number of possibilities. This next program uses a `switch` statement to respond to a randomly chosen value, deciding what to do from several possible alternatives:

Example 6.14 – switch_simon_says.cpp

```cpp
#include <iostream>    // Program will be displaying some text on the screen
#include <cstdlib>    // Uses the random() and srandom() functions
#include <ctime>    // Uses the time() function as the random seed
#include <unistd.h>    // Uses the sleep() function to pause during execution

using namespace std;    // Will be using standard identifiers string, cout and endl

int main()
{
    // Seed the random number generator so won't always select the same numbers
    srandom( time( 0 ) );

    int choice;
    string msg;

    cout << "Simon says..." << endl;

    // Infinite loop that will keep making random choices of what to do
    while ( true )
    {
        // Pick a random number between 0 and 3
        choice = random() % 4;

        // Set a message to display, depending on the random number that was chosen
        switch ( choice )
        {
            case 0:
                msg = "Put your hands on your head";
            break;

            case 1:
                msg = "Turn around three times";
            break;

            case 2:
                msg = "Sit down";
            break;

            case 3:
                msg = "Stand up";
            break;

        }  // end of switch statement
```

continues on next page...

continued...

```
        // Wait 3 seconds before displaying what to do
        sleep( 3 );
        cout << msg << endl;

    }   // end of infinite while loop

    return 0;
}
```

When the program runs, it displays random instructions that tell you what to do:

```
Simon says...
Sit down
Put your hands on your head
Turn around three times
Stand up
Sit down
Turn around three times
```

The **switch** statement takes up many lines of text in the source-code file. The code can be made a little easier to read by removing some of the line-breaks so that the statement takes up less space:

Example of a rewritten **switch** *statement using fewer lines on the screen*

```
        // Set a message to display, depending on the random number that was chosen
        switch ( choice )
        {

            case 0:  msg = "Put your hands on your head";  break;
            case 1:  msg = "Turn around three times";      break;
            case 2:  msg = "Sit down";                     break;
            case 3:  msg = "Stand up";                     break;

        }   // end of switch statement
```

Our program so far is a little bit simpler than the real game. Traditionally you are only supposed to carry out an instruction if it is preceded by the words "Simon says...".

The code could be changed to randomly bluff the player. It could choose a random number and then decide whether or not to display "**Simon says...** " before telling them what to do.

The program will need a new integer variable:

```
    int bluff;
```

Next, there will be a **1** in **4** chance that the program will try and bluff the player.

To make this happen, the program will choose an additional random number between **0** and **3**. This value will be used by a simple `if` decision to decide whether to display **"Simon says... "** or not.

The extra code will look like this:

```
// Choose a random number, between 0 and 3
bluff = random() % 4;

// If 1, 2 or 3 chosen display the message "Simon says "
// If 0 was chosen then do nothing - it's a bluff!
if ( bluff > 0 )
    cout << "Simon says... ";
```

Here's what happens after adding the random bluffing code to the original program:

```
Simon says... Turn around three times
Simon says... Stand up
Simon says... Put your hands on your head
Simon says... Sit down
Put your hands on your head
Simon says... Sit down
Turn around three times
Simon says... Turn around three times
Simon says... Turn around three times
Put your hands on your head
Simon says... Turn around three times
```

The final version of the program that uses the modified code is shown below:

*Example 6.14 modified – **switch_simon_says.cpp***

```
#include <iostream>     // Program will be displaying some text on the screen
#include <cstdlib>      // Uses the random() and srandom() functions
#include <ctime>        // Uses the time() function as the random seed
#include <unistd.h>     // Uses the sleep() function to pause during execution

using namespace std;    // Will be using standard identifiers string, cout and endl

int main()
{
    // Seed the random number generator so won't always select the same numbers
    srandom( time( 0 ) );

    int choice;
    string msg;
    int bluff;
```

continues on next page...

```
// Infinite loop that will keep making random choices of what to do
while ( true )
{
    // Choose a random number, between 0 and 3
    bluff = random() % 4;

    // If 1, 2 or 3 chosen display the message "Simon says "
    // If 0 was chosen then do nothing - it's a bluff!
    if ( bluff > 0 )
        cout << "Simon says... ";

    // Pick a random number between 0 and 3
    choice = random() % 4;

    // Set a message to display, depending on the random number that was chosen
    switch ( choice )
    {

        case 0:  msg = "Put your hands on your head";  break;
        case 1:  msg = "Turn around three times";      break;
        case 2:  msg = "Sit down";                     break;
        case 3:  msg = "Stand up";                     break;

    }  // end of switch statement

    // Wait 3 seconds before displaying what to do
    sleep( 3 );

    cout << msg << endl;

}  // end of infinite while loop

return 0;
}
```

A **switch** statement can also include a special **default** case that will get triggered if no other case has been matched. This is like a **"catch-all"** option and is very useful for dealing with values that your program did not expect:

```
switch ( singleCharacter )
{

    case '0':  cout << "Zero" << endl;  break;
    case '1':  cout << "One" << endl;   break;

    default:  cout << "Not a valid binary digit" << endl;  break;

}  // end of switch statement
```

When using a **switch** statement, note that the variable that it uses to determine which **case** has been matched must be a simple whole number, character or Boolean value. Unfortunately, **switch** statements cannot make decisions based on **string** or **float** values.

This example displays a message one letter at a time. It combines a **switch** statement with the result of a **%** modulus operation to decide on the colour to use for each letter, repeatedly choosing red, then green, then white:

Example 6.15 – switch_character_colours.cpp

```cpp
#include <iostream>      // Program will be displaying some text on the screen
#include <unistd.h>      // Uses usleep to delay display by fractions of a second

using namespace std;     // Will be using standard identifiers string, cout and endl

int main()
{
    const string MESSAGE = "GNU is not UNIX! ";

    const unsigned int LEN = MESSAGE.length();

    const string RED = "\e[31m";
    const string GREEN = "\e[32m";
    const string WHITE = "\e[37m";

    while ( true )
    {
        for ( unsigned int i = 0;  i < LEN;  i++ )
        {
            switch ( i % 3 )
            {

                case 0:    cout << RED;    break;  // Text colour red
                case 1:    cout << GREEN;  break;  // Text colour green
                case 2:    cout << WHITE;  break;  // Text colour white

            }  // end of switch statement

            cout << MESSAGE.at( i ) << flush;  // Display one character

            usleep( 10000 );  // Pause for one tenth of a second

        }  // end of for loop that obtains each character from the message

    }  // end of the infinite while loop

  return 0;
}
```

The individual letters in the message **"GNU is not UNIX! "** will be displayed forever across your screen using a repeating sequence of the three different colours:

Here is a similar example that uses the % modulus operator and a **switch** statement, although this time each whole message that is displayed on the screen uses only one single colour for the entire line of text:

Example 6.16 – switch_line_colours.cpp

```cpp
#include <iostream>     // Program will be displaying some text on the screen
#include <unistd.h>     // Uses the sleep() function to pause during execution

using namespace std;    // Will be using standard identifiers string, cout and endl

int main()
{
    const string MESSAGE = "1980s retro time-warp";

    const string RED = "\e[31m";
    const string BLUE = "\e[34m";
    const string GREEN = "\e[32m";
    const string MAGENTA = "\e[35m";

    int lineNumber = 0;

    while ( true )
    {
        switch ( lineNumber++ % 4 )
        {

            case 0:    cout << RED;     break;  // Text will be red
            case 1:    cout << BLUE;    break;  // Text will be blue
            case 2:    cout << GREEN;   break;  // Text will be green
            case 3:    cout << MAGENTA; break;  // Text will be magenta

        }  // end of switch decision about colours

        // Display the message, followed by a blank line
        cout << MESSAGE << endl << endl;

        usleep( 50000 );    // Pause for half a second

    }  // end of infinite while loop

    return 0;
}
```

When the program executes, it displays multi-coloured lines of text on the screen:

Using the ? conditional operator to decide between two possible values

As we saw earlier in this chapter, the **?** *conditional operator* is like a shorthand for making simple decisions that choose between one of two possible alternative values. It can be used instead of a simple `if-else` statement.

Consider this `if-else` statement:

```
if ( waterTemp <= 0 )
    message = "Frozen";
else
    message = "Not frozen";
```

This means...

> *"If the value of the variable called* **waterTemp** *is less than or the same as zero,*
> *then*
> > *set the value of the variable called* **message** *to* **"Frozen"**,
> *otherwise*
> > *set the value of the variable called* **message** *to* **"Not frozen".**"

The same statement can be rewritten in C++ using the **?** conditional operator in a slightly shorter form:

```
message =  ( waterTemp <= 0 ) ?  "Frozen" : "Not frozen";
```

> `( waterTemp <= 0 )` is the test to carry out.
> `"Frozen"` is the value that will be returned when the result of the test is **true**.
> `"Not frozen"` is the value that will be returned when the result of the test is **false**.

Similarly, the **?** conditional operator can return an **int** value as its result:

Example 6.17 – conditional_op.cpp

```cpp
#include <iostream>     // Program will be using keyboard and screen

using namespace std;    // Will be using standard identifiers cin, cout, endl

int main()
{
    cout << "Is the weather bad? y or n:" << endl;
    char letter;
    cin >> letter;

    // Decide which speed limit to use, depending on whether user typed the letter y
    int speedLimit = ( letter == 'y' ) ? 40 : 60;

    cout << "The speed limit is currently " << speedLimit << " mph" << endl;

    return 0;
}
```

The next program examines a whole number and tells you whether it is odd or even. It does this by obtaining the **remainder** that is left-over when the number is divided by 2:

Example 6.18 – conditional_odd_even.cpp

```cpp
#include <iostream>     // Program will be using keyboard and screen

using namespace std;    // Will be using standard identifiers string, cin, cout, endl

int main()
{
    // Get user to type in a number
    cout << "Enter a whole number:" << endl;
    int numValue;
    cin >> numValue;


    // Find the remainder when the number is divided by 2
    int remainder = numValue % 2;


    // Use the remainder to determine if the number is odd or even
    string message = ( remainder == 0 ) ? "even" : "odd";


    // Display the result on the screen
    cout << "That number is ";
    cout << message;

    cout << endl << endl;  // Display 2 blank lines


    return 0;
}
```

Here is a typical example of what might happen when the program runs:

```
Enter a whole number:
35
That number is odd
```

The example above was written using more statements than necessary in order to make the code as easy to understand as possible. Often when using the ? conditional operator, we can combine more than one statement together to make our C++ code shorter, although if you are not careful then it may become more difficult for people to understand at first glance.

Here is the same program after combining the statements together without using the unnecessary **remainder** and **message** variables:

Example 6.19 – simpler_odd_even.cpp

```cpp
#include <iostream>      // Program will be using keyboard and screen

using namespace std;     // Will be using standard identifiers cin, cout, endl

int main()
{
    cout << "Enter a whole number:" << endl;
    int numValue;
    cin >> numValue;

    cout << "That number is ";

    cout << ( ( numValue % 2 == 0 ) ? "even" : "odd" );

    cout << endl << endl;   // Display 2 blank lines

    return 0;
}
```

Finally, here is another example that makes use of the **?** conditional operator to decide which literal **string** values to display, based on several simple Boolean variables which hold either **true** or **false** values:

Example 6.20 – conditional_rainbow.cpp

```cpp
#include <iostream>      // Program will be displaying some text on the screen

using namespace std;     // Will be using standard identifiers cout and endl

int main()
{
    // Set up what the weather is like at the moment
    bool itIsRaining = true;
    bool itIsSunny = true;

    // Decide whether we have a rainbow, depending on whether we
    // have both rain AND sunshine at the same time
    bool canMakeARainbow = itIsRaining and itIsSunny;

    // Decide what the weather is like and which message to display
    cout << ( canMakeARainbow ? "Rainbow!" : "No rainbows." );

    cout << endl;

    return 0;
}
```

Summary of Chapter 6: Making decisions

Here's what we have covered in this chapter:

Simple `if` and `if-else` decisions evaluate an expression as **true** or **false** to determine what action they should take.

An expression can include the == < <= > >= != **relational operators**.

Several `if-else` decisions can be combined together to make **nested `if`** decisions that involve more than two possible outcomes.

A decision can test whether **all parts** of an expression are **true** using the `&&` **logical AND operator**.

A decision can test whether **one or more parts** of an expression are **true** using the `||` **logical OR operator**.

The `!` **negation operator** can be used to find the opposite of an expression or value.

The reserved words **and, or, not** can be used instead of the `&&` `||` `!` symbols to make code easier to read.

The reserved word `not_eq` can be used instead of the `!=` operator symbol.

A `switch-case` statement can make a decision from many different possible actions. It is an alternative to using many different `if` statements in your code.

A `switch-case` statement can include a `default` case that will be executed if no other matches are made for a value.

The `?` **conditional operator** evaluates an expression to choose which one of two possible values to return. It can be used as shorter alternative to an `if-else` statement.

1.	Write a program that asks you to type in how many sides a shape has.
	Make the program decide what kind of shape has this many sides, then display the name of the shape.
	For example, "*You typed 3 - the shape is a triangle*"
2.	What is the effect of mistakenly adding a ; semi-colon after the expression to be evaluated in an `if` statement?
	For instance:
	```\nint daysHoliday = 0;\n\n\nif (daysHoliday > 0);\n cout << "You still have some holiday left";\n```
3.	What value would be assigned to the **score** variable after executing this conditional statement?
	```\nscore = (time > 10) ? score + time * 100 : score + 500;\n```
	Assume that the current value of **score** is **5300** and the value of **time** is **20** before executing the statement.
4.	Write a program that allows you to enter text strings that contain only the character symbols '1', '0' or *space*.
	Any other symbols should trigger an error message: "*Contains characters that are not valid*"

Chapter 7:
Repetition using loops

A repetitive sequence of instructions

You can make the computer run through (or "**execute**") the same piece of C++ code again and again. You can tell it to repeatedly execute a single program statement, or a whole block of many statements. This is called "**iteration**", or "**looping**".

Imagine you wanted to count to ten. You could explicitly give the computer a sequence of simple, individual instructions, telling it exactly what to display on the screen for every single number, one instruction at a time:

Example 7.1 – sequence.cpp

```
#include <iostream>    // Program will be displaying some text on the screen

using namespace std;    // Will be using standard identifiers cout and endl

int main()
{
    // Manually display a sequence of numbers on the screen
    cout << "1" << endl;
    cout << "2" << endl;
    cout << "3" << endl;
    cout << "4" << endl;
    cout << "5" << endl;
    cout << "6" << endl;
    cout << "7" << endl;
    cout << "8" << endl;
    cout << "9" << endl;
    cout << "10" << endl;

    return 0;
}
```

The program above is very simple, but the code is rather repetitive. It contains quite a lot of statements that are extremely similar to each other. The only thing that changes about each statement is the literal value that gets displayed, such as `"7"`.

Now imagine how long the program would need to be if you wanted to display all of the numbers up to one million. The program would be massive, needing one simple statement to display each one of the million values.

Just to make things worse, the average human-being is extremely likely to make some sort of mistake in their typing somewhere in the million-or-so lines of program code. Try to spot the error in the code below:

```
    cout << "738952" << endl;
    cout << "738953" << endl;
    cout << "738954" << endl;
    cout << "738955" << endl;
    cout << "738556" << endl;
```

Did you find it? The last statement should actually be:

```
    cout << "738956" << endl;
```

It can be difficult enough to spot an error in only a few lines of code, let alone in a program that contains a million lines.

Repeatedly executing the same code one or more times using a `do-while` loop

Although it is very easy to understand what the previous program does, it is not very efficient code. Most of the time, we want to keep our programs as brief as we can without unnecessary statements. We also want to reduce the possibility of things going wrong, such as through mistakes in our typing.

A different approach would be to tell the computer to start at the number **1**, then repeatedly display this number and increase it by **1** until the number **10** has been displayed.

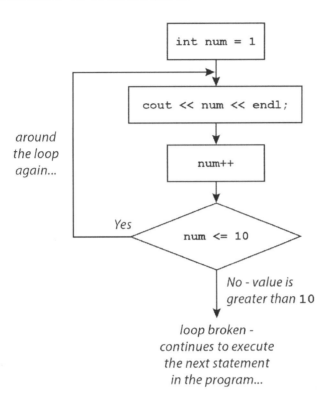

A **do-while** loop will always execute the **body** of the loop - the statements inside the **{ }** braces - at least once.
It will then **evaluate** the **while** condition contained within the **( )** brackets to check whether it should execute the body all over again.

```
do
{
    // Body of statements to execute one or more times

} while ( expression evaluates as true )
```

If the **while** expression evaluates as **true**, then the **{ }** body of statements needs to be executed again, so the flow of control jumps back up to the start of the **do-while** loop, ready to perform the body once again.

Alternatively, if the **while** condition evaluates to **false**, then the body of the loop will not be executed any more times. Execution continues instead with the next statement in the program.

Remember that the computer does not evaluate the controlling expression to decide whether to continue until **at least one** iteration has been carried out.

Below is a program that uses a **do-while** loop to count up from one to ten:

```cpp
#include <iostream>      // Program will be displaying some text on the screen

using namespace std;     // Will be using standard identifiers cout and endl

int main()
{
    // Set starting value to 1 before the do-while loop begins execution
    int num = 1;

    do
    {
        // This body of statements will be executed
        // again and again, 10 times

        cout << "The value of num is " << num << endl;     // Displays value of num

        num++;     // Increments num by 1

    } while ( num <= 10 );     // Stops once value of num is larger than 10


    // This part of the program will only be executed once the num
    // variable has reached a value greater than 10 i.e. 11
    // and the do-while loop has finished

    cout << "The do-while loop has now finished." << endl;


    return 0;
}
```

You can see the results below:

```
The value of num is 1
The value of num is 2
The value of num is 3
The value of num is 4
The value of num is 5
The value of num is 6
The value of num is 7
The value of num is 8
The value of num is 9
The value of num is 10
The do-while loop has now finished.
```

Using a `do-while` loop to make choices from a menu of options

Here's a program that displays a menu of choices and then allows you to choose an option by typing in a letter from the keyboard. It repeatedly does this until you choose to exit by typing '**x**'.

The program uses a `do-while` loop to repeatedly display the menu and then prompt for a choice. While the character that you type is **not** an '**x**', the body of the loop will be repeatedly executed again and again. Once '**x**' has been typed, the `do-while` loop terminates and execution continues with the rest of the program. In this case, once the `do-while` loop has completed, the program says "**Goodbye.**" and finishes.

Example 7.3 – *menu_loop.cpp*

```cpp
#include <iostream>      // Program will be using keyboard and screen

using namespace std;     // Will be using standard identifiers cin, cout, endl

int main()
{
    char choice;

    // Repeatedly get the user to type in a character from the keyboard
    do
    {
        // Body of the loop

        cout << "Type g for greeting," << endl;
        cout << "or type x to exit..." << endl;
        cout << "--------------------" << endl;

        cin >> choice;      // Lets the user type in a single character

        cout << "You chose the option: " << choice;

        cout << endl << endl;


        // Test whether the character was g - if it is then display a greeting
        if ( choice == 'g' )
            cout << "Hello! Hola! Bonjour!" << endl << endl;


    } while ( choice not_eq 'x' );      // Repeatedly execute loop unless 'x' typed

    // This part of the program will only get executed once the user has typed an 'x'
    cout << "Goodbye." << endl;


    return 0;
}
```

Repeatedly executing some code `while` an expression/condition is true

A **while** loop is similar to a **do-while** loop, except that the expression to check whether or not to execute the body of the loop gets evaluated at the **start** of the loop, **before** each iteration, rather than at the **end**.

Unlike the **do-while** loop, the body of a **while** loop may be executed once, many times, or even **not at all**. The **while** loop evaluates the controlling expression **before** each iteration. If the result of the evaluation is **true** then the body of the loop will be executed. But if the expression is evaluated to give **false**, the body of the loop will not get executed. This means that when the computer reaches the **while** loop in the program, if the very first time it evaluates the expression the answer is **false**, then the body of the loop will not be executed at all - it will simply be skipped over by the computer.

The program below uses a **while** loop to count downwards from a fixed starting value of **10** seconds. The statements inside the **while** loop are repeatedly executed until **secondsLeft** reaches **0**:

Example 7.4 – while_count_down.cpp

```
#include <iostream>      // Program will be displaying some text on the screen
#include <unistd.h>      // Uses the sleep() function to pause during execution

using namespace std;     // Will be using standard identifiers cout and endl

int main()
{
    int secondsLeft = 10;       // Start the countdown at 10

    while ( secondsLeft > 0 )
    {
        cout << secondsLeft << endl;    // Display the time remaining
        sleep( 1 );     // Wait for 1 second
        secondsLeft--;
    }  // end of while loop

    // Display message once countdown has finished
    cout << "\e[41m";    // Escape-sequence for white text on red
    cout << "BLAST OFF!" << endl;
    cout << "\e[0m";     // Escape-sequence for normal text

    return 0;
}
```

This can be changed to let you type in the starting value for **secondsLeft**. If you type **0** or less (such as **−60**) then the loop will not execute the body at all, because the expression **−60 > 0** will be evaluated to give the answer **false**:

```
    int secondsLeft;
    cout << "Please type in the starting point for the countdown:" << endl;
    cin >> secondsLeft;     // User types in starting value for the countdown

    while ( secondsLeft > 0 )
    {
        cout << secondsLeft << endl;    // Display the time remaining
        sleep( 1 );     // Wait for 1 second
        secondsLeft--;
    }  // end of while loop
```

This next `while` loop uses the expression `num * num < 100` to decide whether or not to execute the body of the loop:

```
while ( num * num < 100 )
```

The above expression contains both the `*` ("**multiply**") operator and also the `<` ("**less-than**") operator. How should the expression be evaluated by the computer? Which operator should it use first?

The C++ compiler uses operator precedence to decide how to make sense of the `while` loop. It treats the `*` multiply symbol with more importance than the `<` less-than symbol. This means that your Pi performs the multiplication of the value of `num` times itself **before** examining the final result to check whether it is less than the value `100`.

Example 7.5 – while_square_nums.cpp

```cpp
#include <iostream>     // Program will be displaying some text on the screen

using namespace std;    // Will be using standard identifiers cout and endl

int main()
{
    int num = 1;   // Start at the number 1

    while ( num * num < 100 )
    {
        // This block of statements will be executed repeatedly, but only
        // while the square is less than 100, then the loop will terminate.

        // Display the square of the number
        cout << num * num << endl;

        // Move on to the next number
        num++;
    }   // end of the while loop

    return 0;
}
```

This flowchart shows how the body of the `while` loop gets repeated until the value of `num * num` is `100` or more:

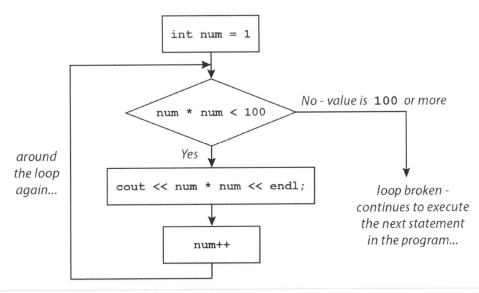

Here is another **while** loop that repeatedly calculates how far and how fast an object falls due to gravity:

Example 7.6 – while_gravity.cpp

```cpp
#include <iostream>    // Program will be displaying some text on the screen
#include <unistd.h>    // Uses the sleep() function to pause during execution

using namespace std;    // Will be using standard identifiers string, cout and endl

int main()
{
    const string GREEN = "\e[32m";
    const string NORMAL = "\e[0m";

    const float ACCEL = 9.8;

    float speed = 0;
    float distance = 0;

    int elapsedTime = 0;
    while ( elapsedTime <= 10 )
    {
        distance = distance + speed;

        // Display results so far - numbers will be shown using colour green
        cout << "Been falling for ";
        cout << GREEN << elapsedTime << NORMAL << " sec(s) ";

        cout << "Speed is " << GREEN << speed << NORMAL << " m/s ";

        cout << " Dist. fallen " << GREEN << distance << NORMAL << " m";

        cout << endl;

        speed = speed + ACCEL;

        elapsedTime++;

    }  // end of while loop elapsed

    return 0;
}
```

Below you can see the output produced at run-time:

```
Been falling for 0 sec(s) Speed is 0 m/s Dist. fallen 0 m
Been falling for 1 sec(s) Speed is 9.8 m/s Dist. fallen 9.8 m
Been falling for 2 sec(s) Speed is 19.6 m/s Dist. fallen 29.4 m
Been falling for 3 sec(s) Speed is 29.4 m/s Dist. fallen 58.8 m
Been falling for 4 sec(s) Speed is 39.2 m/s Dist. fallen 98 m
Been falling for 5 sec(s) Speed is 49 m/s Dist. fallen 147 m
Been falling for 6 sec(s) Speed is 58.8 m/s Dist. fallen 205.8 m
Been falling for 7 sec(s) Speed is 68.6 m/s Dist. fallen 274.4 m
Been falling for 8 sec(s) Speed is 78.4 m/s Dist. fallen 352.8 m
Been falling for 9 sec(s) Speed is 88.2 m/s Dist. fallen 441 m
Been falling for 10 sec(s) Speed is 98 m/s Dist. fallen 539 m
```

A `for` loop that executes a statement several times

Rather than a **while** or a **do-while** loop, you can use a **for** loop in your code when you know exactly how many times you would like to repeatedly execute a statement or block of statements. A **for** loop is a very compact way to repeatedly execute code in your program, although at first glance it may not appear quite as easy to understand as a **while** loop.

Here is an example that displays a greeting exactly three times using a **for** loop:

Example 7.7 – for_loop.cpp

```cpp
#include <iostream>      // Program will be displaying some text on the screen

using namespace std;     // Will be using standard identifiers cout and endl

int main()
{
    // Display the word "hello" (followed by a space) 3 times
    for ( int num = 0;  num < 3;  num++ )
        cout << "hello " << endl;

    // Display final message once only
    cout << "what's all this then?";

    return 0;
}
```

How does it work? Let's take a look at the **for** statement in more detail:

```cpp
for ( int num = 0;  num < 3;  num++ )
```

After the word **for**, within the **( )** brackets, there are three important parts:

A **controlling variable** which gets set to an initial starting value. You can either create a brand new variable here, or use an existing variable from elsewhere in your program code. The controlling variable in this example is a new **int** integer variable called **num**. The value of **num** is initially set to **0**.

An **expression** which will be evaluated or checked **each time** that the **for** statement executes: **num < 3**

A statement that **modifies** or **does something** to the controlling variable. In this case it increases the value of **num** by **1**.

In the program above, the **for** loop sets the value of the new controlling variable called **num** to **0**.

The loop then repeatedly executes the **cout** statement to display the message **"hello"** on the screen.

After each iteration of the **cout** statement, the loop increases the value of **num** by **1**.

The **for** statement then re-evaluates the controlling condition, checking whether the expression **num < 3** is still **true**. If it is **true**, then the loop begins another iteration. If it is **false** however, then the loop will terminate and execution moves on to the next statement in the program.

Execution of the loop stops when **num** reaches **3** because the controlling condition **num < 3** then evaluates to **false**, which causes the loop to terminate.

When you are using a **for** loop in your code, you can make use of the value of the controlling variable in exactly the same way that you would use any other variable in your program. The controlling variable is not just there to control the execution of the loop. The value of the controlling variable can be used by any statement in the body of the loop, such as to perform a calculation or make to make a logical decision.

This program uses the value of the controlling variable **num** to calculate a sequence of square numbers:

Example 7.8 – for_square_nums.cpp

```cpp
#include <iostream>     // Program will be displaying some text on the screen

using namespace std;    // Will be using standard identifiers cout and endl

int main()
{
    // Display the value of the variable called num
    // Starts with value 0, displays up to 9 i.e. values less than 10
    for ( int num = 1;  num <= 10;  num++ )
        cout << ( num * num ) << endl;  // Displays the square of the value num

    // At this point, the variable num does not exist anymore,
    // once the for statement has finished executing.
    // (It was part of the for statement.)

    return 0;
}
```

When the program runs, it should produce these results on the screen:

```
1
4
9
16
25
36
49
64
81
100
```

Each value displayed is the result of multiplying the value of the controlling variable **num** by itself.

Increasing or decreasing the value of a controlling variable

The controlling variable in a `for` loop does not always need to count upwards, or even in steps of one. You can increase or decrease its value it in any way that you like, as the next two examples show.

The first example makes the controlling variable **decrease** by **1** as long as its value remains above zero:

Example 7.9 – for_count_down.cpp

```
#include <iostream>     // Program will be displaying some text on the screen

using namespace std;     // Will be using standard identifiers cout and endl

int main()
{
    // Counting down in steps of 1
    // Value of the controlling variable decreases by 1 each time around the loop
    for ( int value = 100;  value > 0;  value-- )
        cout << value << endl;   // Display the value of controlling variable

    return 0;
}
```

This second example **doubles** the value of the controlling variable within each iteration of the `for` loop until reaching the value **128**:

Example 7.10 – for_doubling.cpp

```
#include <iostream>     // Program will be displaying some text on the screen

using namespace std;     // Will be using standard identifiers cout and endl

int main()
{
    // Value of the controlling variable gets doubled
    // each time around the loop 1, 2, 4, 8... until it reaches 128
    for ( int value = 1;  value <= 128;  value *= 2 )
        cout << value << endl;   // Display value of the controlling variable

    return 0;
}
```

The results for the second program are shown below:

```
1
2
4
8
16
32
64
128
```

Using the value of a `for` loop variable as part of a calculation

Here is a classic puzzle. Take a chessboard, which has 64 squares. Start at one corner of the board and place one single grain of rice on the first square. Now move along to the next square on the board and double the number of grains of rice that you put on it. Keep doing this until you have visited all squares on the board, covering each square with the appropriate number of grains.

Feel free to try this out for yourself with a real chessboard, but you'll need **a lot** of rice. You'll also need a **massive** board.

The program below calculates the solution to the chessboard puzzle. It uses a simple `for` loop to keep track of where we are on the board, using the integer variable **square**. The loop begins with square number **1**, increasing upwards until **square** reaches the value **64**. The program also uses another integer variable, called **grains**, to store the number of grains of rice that need to be placed on the current square. Thus, on the very first square, the value of **grains** starts at **1**. The value of **grains** then doubles as the program moves on to each new square.

Example 7.11 – for_chessboard.cpp

```cpp
#include <iostream>      // Program will be displaying some text on the screen

using namespace std;     // Will be using standard identifiers cout and endl

int main()
{
    // Begin with 1 grain of rice on the 1st square of the chessboard
    unsigned long long grains = 1;

    for ( int square = 1;  square <= 64;  square++ )
    {

        // Display the number of grains on this square
        cout << "On square no. " << square;
        cout << " there are " << grains;
        cout << " grains of rice." << endl;

        // Double the number of grains every time you move on to the next square
        grains *= 2;

    }  // end of for loop

    return 0;
}
```

In the above program, instead of declaring the variable **grains** as an integer:

```cpp
        int grains = 1;
```

...the code uses a different data-type, an **unsigned long long** variable:

```cpp
        unsigned long long grains = 1;
```

If you tried to use `int`, the first few results would appear to have been calculated correctly:

```
On square no. 1 there are 1 grains of rice.
On square no. 2 there are 2 grains of rice.
On square no. 3 there are 4 grains of rice.
On square no. 4 there are 8 grains of rice.
On square no. 5 there are 16 grains of rice.
On square no. 6 there are 32 grains of rice.
On square no. 7 there are 64 grains of rice.
On square no. 8 there are 128 grains of rice.
```

However, some of the results would start to appear a little odd after the 31st square:

```
On square no. 30 there are 536870912 grains of rice.
On square no. 31 there are 1073741824 grains of rice.
On square no. 32 there are -2147483648 grains of rice.
On square no. 33 there are 0 grains of rice.
On square no. 34 there are 0 grains of rice.
On square no. 35 there are 0 grains of rice.
```

This is because many of the values calculated by the program are far too large to hold using a variable of type `int`. The value of `grains` suddenly **overflows**, "wrapping around" to a negative value. Remember that the idea of "overflow" was introduced in *"Chapter 3: Data-types and values"*.

You could try using the `long` data-type instead of `int` for the `grains` variable, but this would still not be big enough:

```
On square no. 30 there are 536870912 grains of rice.
On square no. 31 there are 1073741824 grains of rice.
On square no. 32 there are -2147483648 grains of rice.
On square no. 33 there are 0 grains of rice.
On square no. 34 there are 0 grains of rice.
On square no. 35 there are 0 grains of rice.
On square no. 36 there are 0 grains of rice.
```

You could go even further and use the much larger `long long` data-type, but even this fails at the 64th square and cannot hold the final result:

```
On square no. 60 there are 576460752303423488 grains of rice.
On square no. 61 there are 1152921504606846976 grains of rice.
On square no. 62 there are 2305843009213693952 grains of rice.
On square no. 63 there are 4611686018427387904 grains of rice.
On square no. 64 there are -9223372036854775808 grains of rice.
```

By making the `long long` data-type **unsigned**, we tell the computer that we are not interested in negative values. It can use some of the arrangements of binary digits to represent even larger positive numbers. This is enough to hold the result for the 64th square of the chessboard.

```
On square no. 60 there are 576460752303423488 grains of rice.
On square no. 61 there are 1152921504606846976 grains of rice.
On square no. 62 there are 2305843009213693952 grains of rice.
On square no. 63 there are 4611686018427387904 grains of rice.
On square no. 64 there are 9223372036854775808 grains of rice.
```

Thus, if you need to use REALLY large positive numbers in your programs you can create a variable that has the `unsigned long long` data-type.

This program displays a range of characters on the screen. It uses a **for** loop to generate a sequence of integer values, starting at **32**, which is the ASCII code for *space* (the first printable character that is visible on the screen). The value of **asciiCode** increases by **1** until reaching the value **127**. Each integer value gets converted to a character using a **static_cast <char>** conversion and this is then displayed on the screen along with its ASCII character code.

Example 7.12 – for_ascii.cpp

```cpp
#include <iostream>    // Program will be displaying some text on the screen

using namespace std;    // Will be using standard identifiers cout and endl

int main()
{
    // Makes a list of all printable characters and their ASCII codes
    cout << "Characters and their ASCII codes:" << endl;

    for ( int asciiCode = 32;  asciiCode < 127;  asciiCode++ )
    {
        cout << "Symbol ";

        // Cast the integer value of asciiCode to a character, then display it
        cout << static_cast <char> ( asciiCode );

        cout << " has ASCII code ";

        cout << asciiCode;

        cout << endl;

    }  // end of for loop

    return 0;
}
```

Note that the program above does not actually attempt to display ASCII character **127**. This is because character **127** is a non-printable character.

Try changing the **for** loop so that it terminates when the value of **asciiCode** reaches **128**, rather than **127**:

```cpp
    for ( int asciiCode = 32;  asciiCode < 128;  asciiCode++ )
```

This will attempt to display the character **127**. Here is what happens when the modified program runs on my Pi:

```
Symbol { has ASCII code 123
Symbol | has ASCII code 124
Symbol } has ASCII code 125
Symbol ~ has ASCII code 126
Symbol ⌷ has ASCII code 127
```

Notice the appearance of the very last symbol in the screenshot above. This kind of symbol is used whenever your Pi tries to display a non-printable character. Your Pi displays the digits **007F** within the square symbol, which is the hexadecimal (base-16) equivalent for the number **127**.

Working directly with a range of characters in a loop

The previous example used a loop to display a range of characters. The loop was controlled by an integer variable. Each character was displayed by **casting** the integer value of the controlling variable to a character.

In C++ it is actually possible to iterate **directly** through a range of characters without the need for any such cast conversions, working through the character set in sequence, according to the order of the ASCII character codes. Your program can tell the Pi to start at a particular character, advancing through the ASCII character set, one symbol at a time.

The example below displays several different sequences of characters, using a **for** loop to generate each sequence. This time, the controlling variable **symbol** does not use the **int** data-type, but instead uses the **char** data-type. Thus, the program works directly with characters, rather than integer character codes. Conveniently, C++ also allows character variables to be incremented and decremented in exactly the same way as integers, using the **++** and **--** operators.

Example 7.13 – for_chars.cpp

```cpp
#include <iostream>     // Program will be displaying some text on the screen

using namespace std;    // Will be using standard identifiers cout and endl

int main()
{
    char symbol;  // This variable will be used to control all 3 loops

    // Display all the upper-case characters
    cout << "Upper-case letters" << endl;
    for ( symbol = 'A';  symbol <= 'Z';  symbol++ )
        cout << symbol;

    cout << endl;

    // Display lower-case letters
    cout << "Lower-case letters" << endl;
    for ( symbol = 'a';  symbol <= 'z';  symbol++ )
        cout << symbol;

    cout << endl;

    // Display all numeric digits IN REVERSE ORDER!
    cout << "Numeric digits" << endl;
    for ( symbol = '9';  symbol >= '0';  symbol-- )
        cout << symbol;

    cout << endl;

    return 0;
}
```

This approach is very handy if you don't know off-hand what the numeric ASCII code is for a particular letter or symbol. You can use the character symbol itself as the value of the controlling variable, enclosed within a pair of ' single quotation marks. You don't need to look up the equivalent numeric ASCII character codes that you might otherwise have needed to use.

Nesting: putting a loop within another loop

This program calculates the factorial for each of the whole numbers between **1** and **10**. To do this, the code contains two different **while** loops, one inside the body of the other.

The "**factorialToCalculate**" **while** loop is said to be inside the "**num**" **while** loop. We call "**num**" the "**inner**" loop and "**factorialToCalculate**" the "**outer**" loop. The inner **while** loop is said to be **nested** inside the outer **while** loop.

Example 7.14 – while_nested.cpp

```cpp
#include <iostream>     // Program will be displaying some text on the screen

using namespace std;    // Will be using standard identifiers cout and endl

int main()
{
    const string BOLD = "\e[1m";
    const string NORMAL = "\e[0m";

    cout << "FACTORIAL PROGRAM" << endl;
    cout << "=================" << endl;

    int factorialToCalculate = 1;

    // Outer while loop - controls WHICH factorial is being calculated
    while ( factorialToCalculate <= 10 )
    {
        cout << "Factorial of " << BOLD << factorialToCalculate << NORMAL << " is ";
        cout << factorialToCalculate;  // Working starts with the number itself

        int num = factorialToCalculate;
        unsigned long long resultSoFar = num;   // Builds up the product of all values

        // Inner while loop - calculates an individual factorial
        while ( num > 1 )
        {
            num--;

            cout << " x " << num;

            resultSoFar *= num;

        }   // end of inner while loop

        // Display the final result for this factorial
        cout << " = ";
        cout << BOLD << resultSoFar << NORMAL << endl;

        factorialToCalculate++;

    }   // End of outer while loop

    return 0;
}
```

If you are unfamiliar with factorials in mathematics, here is an example:

The factorial of **5** is: **5** x **4** x 3 x 2 x 1 = **120**
The factorial of **4** is: **4** x 3 x 2 x 1 = **24**
The factorial of **3** is: **3** x 2 x 1 = **6**

This flowchart shows the main steps that the program uses to calculate each factorial:

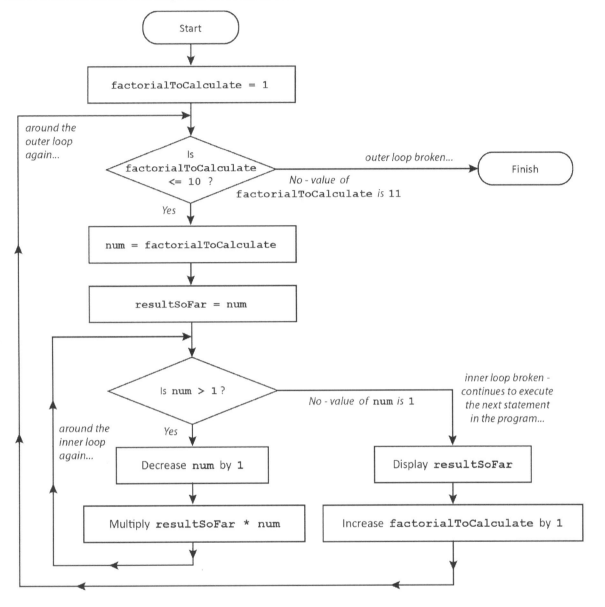

Running the program produces the following results:

```
FACTORIAL PROGRAM
=================
Factorial of 1 is 1 = 1
Factorial of 2 is 2 x 1 = 2
Factorial of 3 is 3 x 2 x 1 = 6
Factorial of 4 is 4 x 3 x 2 x 1 = 24
Factorial of 5 is 5 x 4 x 3 x 2 x 1 = 120
Factorial of 6 is 6 x 5 x 4 x 3 x 2 x 1 = 720
Factorial of 7 is 7 x 6 x 5 x 4 x 3 x 2 x 1 = 5040
Factorial of 8 is 8 x 7 x 6 x 5 x 4 x 3 x 2 x 1 = 40320
Factorial of 9 is 9 x 8 x 7 x 6 x 5 x 4 x 3 x 2 x 1 = 362880
Factorial of 10 is 10 x 9 x 8 x 7 x 6 x 5 x 4 x 3 x 2 x 1 = 3628800
```

As with the previous factorial example, the program below uses nested **for** loops to calculate a separate multiplication table for each of the whole numbers between **1** and **10**.

This time, "**row**" is the "**inner**" loop and "**table**" is the "**outer**" loop.

Example 7.15 – for_nested.cpp

```cpp
#include <iostream>     // Program will be displaying some text on the screen

using namespace std;    // Will be using standard identifiers cout and endl

int main()
{
    // Start with the 1 times table, go up to the 10 times table
    for ( int table = 1;  table <= 10;  table++ )
    {
        // Display an individual times-table
        for ( int row = 1;  row <= 12;  row++ )
        {
            cout << row;
            cout << " times ";
            cout << table;
            cout << " is ";

            cout << row * table << endl;

        }  // end of inner row loop that makes a single table

        // Leave blank lines after each complete table
        cout << endl << endl << endl;

    }  // end of outer loop that controls which table is being made

    return 0;
}
```

Notice that in this program the **table** and **row** loops don't merely execute one single statement repeatedly, each loop executes a block of statements that are enclosed in **{ }** braces.

```
1 times 1 is 1
2 times 1 is 2
3 times 1 is 3
4 times 1 is 4
5 times 1 is 5
6 times 1 is 6
7 times 1 is 7
8 times 1 is 8
9 times 1 is 9
10 times 1 is 10
11 times 1 is 11
12 times 1 is 12


1 times 2 is 2
2 times 2 is 4
3 times 2 is 6
```

Adding extra { } curly braces to make your code more readable

The code below also makes use of nested **for** loops to display a countdown using a large block of digits.

The outer **for** loop, which uses the variable **num**, controls which digit in the countdown is to be displayed. Within this loop, two other **for** loops are used to control the row and column numbers of the block of characters to be displayed on the screen.

The outer-most **for** loop uses the **num** variable to control the repeated execution a single statement, which is itself another **for** loop (and uses the **row** variable). This means that the body of the outer-most **for** loop does not need { } braces around the part of the code that it is going to repeat – it is going to repeatedly execute the entire **for** statement, which spans more than one line in the code.

Example without extra { } braces – shorter version

```
for ( char num = '9';  num > '0';  num-- )
    for ( int row = 0;  row < 6;  row++ )
    {
        for ( int col = 0;  col < 8;  col++ )
            cout << num;

        cout << endl;

    }  // end of the inner row loop
```

You can add extra additional { } curly braces to make the code slightly easier to read.

It is also helpful for the extra closing } brace to be labelled with a comment to clearly mark the end of the repeated section. This helps you to check that each opening { brace is paired with the correct closing } brace.

The example below does not actually need to use { } braces for the outer **num** loop, but they help to show which parts of the code will be repeatedly executed:

Example of extra { } braces to improve readability

```
for ( char num = '9';  num > '0';  num-- )
{
    for ( int row = 0;  row < 6;  row++ )
    {
        for ( int col = 0;  col < 8;  col++ )
            cout << num;

        cout << endl;

    }  // end of inner row loop

}  // end of outer num loop
```

What would happen if you tried to add a new statement that you wanted the `for` loop to repeat, but forgot to add a new pair of `{ }` braces around the body of statements? This is quite a common error that someone might make in a program.

To see what happens, consider this example of a loop that repeats only a single statement:

Example of a single statement that is executed repeatedly by a `for` loop

```
// Display a times table
for ( int table = 1;   table <= 10;   table++ )
    for ( int row = 1;   row <= 12;   row++ )
        cout << table << " times " << row << " is " << table * row << endl;
```

Supposing we want to add some code, such as to make an extra blank line appear after each result.

In the code below, an extra statement has been added to display a blank line:

Example of a `for` loop that repeats a single statement instead of a body of several statements

```
// Display a times table
for ( int table = 1;   table <= 10;   table++ )
    for ( int row = 1;   row <= 12;   table++ )
        cout << table << " times " << row << " is " << table * row << endl;
        cout << endl;   // THIS ONLY GETS EXECUTED ONCE!
```

Unfortunately, the newly-added statement would only be executed once. Without grouping the statements into a block using `{ }` braces, the inner `for` loop will only repeat the single statement that comes immediately after it in the C++ code.

To repeatedly execute both statements, they will need to be enclosed in `{ }` braces:

Example of extra `{}` braces being added to repeat a block of code

```
// Display a times table
for ( int table = 1;   table <= 10;   table++ )
    for ( int row = 1;   row <= 12;   row++ )
    {

        cout << table << " times " << row " is " << table * row << endl;

        cout << endl;   // NOW GETS EXECUTED WITHIN THE LOOP!

    }   // end of row for loop
```

Creating and using variables that are not local to a `for` statement

In the examples so far, the controlling variable **num** has been declared inside the **( )** brackets as part of the **for** statement. We say that the variable is a **"local variable"** that "belongs to" that particular **for** statement. The variable **num** can only be used by the code in the body of the **for** loop, not by any code that is outside the loop (either before the loop or after the loop).

In fact, once the **for** statement has been executed and the computer moves on to the next statement in the program, the variable **num** will not usually exist anymore as the computer cleans up old variables that are no longer needed in order to save memory space.

This tidying process is called **"garbage collection"**. It was invented in a time when computers had much less memory than they do today, but it is still especially important for programs that need to operate for long periods of time without slowing down or failing due to the gradual wastage of space.

If your code tries to access a local variable that no longer exists, such as a variable that was declared in the body of an earlier loop, the compiler will usually generate an error and your program will not run. Whilst you can force the compiler to be less careful by choosing the **-fpermissive** **"permissive compiling"** option, your program may well crash when it tries to access the non-existent variable.

If you want to keep the value of the controlling variable from a **for** statement to use after the loop has finished execution, you will need to declare it separately in your code **prior** to the loop, rather than as part of the **for** loop itself. This guarantees that the value of the variable will still exist once the loop has finished executing. The computer will not regard it as garbage or attempt to clear it away.

The following program makes use of a **for** loop that is controlled by such an existing variable called **num**, rather than declaring a brand new variable as part of the loop itself:

Example 7.16 – *for_scope.cpp*

```cpp
#include <iostream>      // Program will be displaying some text on the screen

using namespace std;     // Will be using standard identifiers cout and endl

int main()
{
    int num;   // num declared BEFORE using it in the for statement
               // It will still be usable once the loop has finished

    for ( num = 0;  num < 10;  num++ )
        cout << num << endl;

    // The for loop has finished executing, num variable still
    // exists and can be accessed here
    cout << "The value of num still exists." << endl;

    cout << "It is: " << num << endl;

    return 0;
}
```

In the above example, the scope of the variable **num** is the whole **main()** function. We say that the variable **num** is **local** to **main()**. Any part of the code in the **main()** function can successfully access the value of **num**.

Unlike the variables that were declared as part of **for** loops in the previous programs, the computer will not clear away the **num** variable as soon as the loop finishes. It will only do so once the entire **main()** function has completed execution. This means that we can still use **num** in our code once the **for** loop has terminated.

Global variables

A **global variable** is a variable that can be accessed and used **anywhere** in your program. It is not local to any one particular part of your code, such as within a `for` loop or within a **"function"** (functions are covered later in *"Chapter 10: Functions"*).

Global variables are declared **outside** of functions, thus they do not belong to any single part of your code in particular - they belong to and can be used by the **whole** program.

In general, the use of global variables is usually frowned upon by programmers because they can lead to changes to values that may be difficult to anticipate. These changes can make program code much more difficult to understand and debug. A seemingly innocent change to the value of a global variable can cause unexpected problems elsewhere in your program.

Here is an example of a typical problem that can occur. The following program compiles successfully but contains a run-time error – it will not display the times tables as originally planned by the programmer:

Example 7.17 – global.cpp

```cpp
#include <iostream>     // Program will be displaying some text on the screen

using namespace std;    // Will be using standard identifiers cout and endl

int num;    // Global variable that can be used anywhere in the program

void displayTimesTable( int table )
{
    // This function displays a particular times-table, determined by table argument
    // WATCH-OUT! It uses a global variable called num which gets changed elsewhere
    for ( num = 1;  num <= 10;  num++ )
    {
        cout << table << " times ";
        cout << num << " is ";
        cout << table * num << endl;
    }   // end of for loop

}   // end of the function

// --------------------

int main()
{
    for ( num = 1;  num <= 10;  num++ )
        displayTimesTable( num );   // Activates or "call" the function into action

    return 0;

}   // end of main function
```

Both the `main()` and `displayTimesTable()` functions attempt to use and modify the value of the global variable called **num**. This leads to erroneous results when the program is executed. In such a small program, the problem is quite easy to spot, but in a larger program it might not be so easy to find.

Infinite loops – programs that go on forever without ever stopping

You can make a program repeat a statement or a block of code **forever** by creating a simple loop that will never stop.

There are various different ways to this in C++, but two of the most popular are shown here.

An infinite loop that uses `while`

The first method is a `while` loop, just as we have used before, but with the literal value **true** instead of an expression that involves any variables.

It is perhaps the easiest method to read and understand when you look at the C++ code:

Example 7.18 – infinite_while.cpp

```cpp
#include <iostream>     // Program will be displaying some text on the screen

using namespace std;    // Will be using standard identifiers cout and endl

int main()
{
    while ( true )
        cout << "Still running." << endl;

    return 0;   // This statement will never be reached
}
```

How does it work?

Remember that a **while** statement evaluates whatever expression is written in the ( ) brackets. Whether or not the code inside the { } block will be executed depends upon the result of evaluating the expression enclosed in the ( ) brackets.

In general, if the expression evaluates as **true**, then the next statement or block of statements in { } braces will be executed. If the expression evaluates as **false**, then the next statement does not get executed. Once the loop has terminated, execution of the program moves on to the next statement in your code.

Because the **while** statement already contains the literal value **true** inside the pair of ( ) brackets, there is no need to break down their contents any further or to perform any evaluation - it is as though a result has already been reached. The **while** loop will automatically go ahead and execute the next statement or block of statements that make up the body of the loop.

After executing the body of the loop, the **while** statement attempts to evaluate the expression once again, finding that the contents of the ( ) are still **true**. There is no chance that the expression will ever change or that it will ever be anything else other than **true**, so the loop never terminates – it just goes on and on forever.

In this case, the **while** loop continues to execute the **cout** statement, displaying the message **"Still running."** The final **return 0** statement is never reached during the execution of the program.

> **Warning!** If you compile and run the above program, the infinite loop means that it will never stop. To terminate the program, you can press **Ctrl** and **C** at the same time on your keyboard.

A slightly less obvious method is to use a **for** loop that will never stop:

Example 7.19 – infinite_for.cpp

```cpp
#include <iostream>      // Program will be displaying some text on the screen

using namespace std;     // Will be using standard identifiers cout and endl

int main()
{
    for ( ; ; )
        cout << "Still running." << endl;

    return 0;   // This statement will never be reached
}
```

The controlling expression in the **( )** brackets of the **for** loop looks suspiciously empty, containing only a pair of semi-colons, but it actually means something quite clever.

The first **;** semi-colon marks the end of the loop initialisation. It effectively marks the end of an **empty statement**, so no variables are set or initialised!

The second **;** semi-colon marks the end of another empty statement, which would normally be the controlling condition that determines whether or not the loop should keep on running. Because there is no expression to decide whether or not to terminate the loop, the loop continues execution.

There is nothing else inside the **( )** brackets after the second semi-colon. The computer does not bother to increment or decrement any controlling variable, and this would have no effect on whether the loop should continue execution.

Both programs produce the same results, filling up the screen very quickly with the same message:

```
Still running.
Still running.
Still running.
Still running.
Still running.
Still running.
Still running.
Still running.
```

(Press **Ctrl** and **C** together to stop the program when you have seen enough.)

Forcing a loop to terminate using `break`

There is a way of telling a loop to stop repeating and to move on to the next statement in your C++ program. You can terminate a loop using a **break** statement. When the Pi encounters a **break** statement it will not attempt any further iterations of the current loop that is being executed. The program will merely finish the current iteration of that loop.

If you use **break** inside a { } block of statements, the rest of the statements in the { } block will still be executed, but the loop will no longer consider whether to run through them any further times once that iteration has finished.

This program uses an **if** decision to decide whether to terminate the loop using **break** or whether to let it continue:

Example 7.20 – break_loop.cpp

```
#include <iostream>      // Program will be displaying some text on the screen

using namespace std;     // Will be using standard identifiers cin, cout and endl

int main()
{
    char choice;

    // Infinite for loop
    for ( ; ; )
    {
        cout << "EXECUTING INSIDE for LOOP!" << endl;

        cout << "Type s to stop the loop, anything else to keep running..." << endl;

        cin >> choice;

        // Examine what the user typed - is it an s?
        if ( choice == 's' )
            break;  // This will immediately terminate the for loop if s is chosen
    }   // end of the infinite for loop

    // No longer in the loop - this code will only be reached
    // if the user chooses q and the break statement gets executed
    cout << "You have broken out of the loop." << endl;

    return 0;
}
```

```
EXECUTING INSIDE for LOOP!
Type s to stop the loop, anything else to keep running...
p
EXECUTING INSIDE for LOOP!
Type s to stop the loop, anything else to keep running...
g
EXECUTING INSIDE for LOOP!
Type s to stop the loop, anything else to keep running...
s
You have broken out of the loop.


------------------
(program exited with code: 0)
Press return to continue
```

Counting things that happen

The example below features three different variables: **pizzaVotes**, **curryVotes** and **noodleVotes**. These are used to count up votes that determine the most popular choice of food to eat tonight. At the start of the program, all three variables are given the starting value **0** as no choices have been recorded yet. Every time you type in a choice, the value of the corresponding variable for that kind of food is increased by **1**.

Example 7.21 – count_votes.cpp

```cpp
#include <iostream>     // Program will be using keyboard and screen

using namespace std;    // Will be using standard identifiers cin, cout, endl

int main()
{
    int pizzaVotes = 0;
    int curryVotes = 0;
    int noodleVotes = 0;

    // Type in a letter for each vote and count total votes for each person
    char choice;
    do
    {
        cout << "Type in a choice: p c n ( or * to quit )" << endl;

        cin >> choice;

        if ( ( choice == 'p' ) or ( choice == 'P' ) )
            pizzaVotes++;

        if ( ( choice == 'c' ) or ( choice == 'C' ) )
            curryVotes++;

        if ( ( choice == 'n' ) or ( choice == 'N' ) )
            noodleVotes++;

    } while ( choice not_eq '*' );  // Typing * terminates the loop

    // Display the results after all choices have been typed in
    cout << endl << "RESULTS TIME..." << endl;

    cout << "Pizza... " << pizzaVotes << endl;

    cout << "Balti-Curry... " << curryVotes << endl;

    cout << "Thai-Noodles... " << noodleVotes << endl;

    return 0;
}
```

Once the program executes, every time that the user enters **p** or **P**, the value of `pizzaVotes` increases by one. Similarly, every time that the user enters **c** or **C**, the value of `curryVotes` increases, and every time that they enter **n** or **N**, the value of **noodleVotes** increases.

After entering a character, the **while** loop checks whether it was the ***** asterisk symbol. If it was then the **while** loop terminates and the program goes on to display the values of `pizzaVotes`, `curryVotes` and `noodleVotes`.

```
Type in a choice: p c n ( or * to quit )
c
Type in a choice: p c n ( or * to quit )
c
Type in a choice: p c n ( or * to quit )
p
Type in a choice: p c n ( or * to quit )
n
Type in a choice: p c n ( or * to quit )
c
Type in a choice: p c n ( or * to quit )
n
Type in a choice: p c n ( or * to quit )
p
Type in a choice: p c n ( or * to quit )
p
Type in a choice: p c n ( or * to quit )
*

RESULTS TIME...
Pizza... 3
Balti-Curry... 3
Thai-Noodles... 2
```

As we will see in "**Chapter 8: Characters and text strings**", it is possible to simplify the **if** statements used in this code by using the **toupper()** function to ensure that all letters are upper-case before making each decision. This removes the need to consider lower-case letters during each **if** decision:

```cpp
cin >> choice;

choice = toupper( choice );

if ( choice == 'P' )
    pizzaVotes++;

if ( choice == 'C' )
    curryVotes++;

if ( choice == 'N' )
    noodleVotes++;
```

Here's what we have covered in this chapter:

Using **iteration**, your program can **repeatedly** execute one or more statements again and again.

Loops can lead to shorter programs as you don't need to write out similar or even identical statements in your code more than once.

A `do-while` loop will always execute a statement or group of statements **at least once**. It then evaluates a condition to determine whether the statements should be executed again.

A `while` loop will evaluate an expression before deciding whether to execute a statement or group of statements. **There is no guarantee that the statements will be executed at all** since the expression could be `false` to begin with. This means that a `while` loop executes the body of statements **zero or more times**.

A `for` loop can be used to execute a statement or group of statements a **fixed number of times**.

The variable that controls the execution of a `for` loop can be declared locally as part of the `for` statement. The value of this variable will no longer exist or be accessible to the rest of your code once the loop has finished execution.

Care should be taken when using **global** variables to control the execution of a loop. Other parts of your program code might unwittingly interfere with the execution of the loop if they change the value of such a global variable.

An **infinite** loop repeatedly executes a statement or group of statements **unconditionally**. It does not evaluate any statement to determine whether or not to repeat the body of the loop.

You can use either a `while` statement or a `for` statement to make an infinite loop.

A particular iteration around any of these kinds of loops can be terminated using a `break` statement.

1.	Write a program that uses a **for** loop to display the alphabet backwards.
2.	Write a program that uses a **do-while** loop to repeatedly ask the user to type in a word.
	The loop should only terminate when the word is exactly eight characters long, otherwise it should ask for another.
3.	Write a program that displays a sequence of numbers on the screen.
	The sequence should start at **50**, then increase by **25** until displaying the final value **150**.
4.	Write a program that repeatedly asks you to type in a character.
	It should count up how many of these characters are upper-case letters of the alphabet.
	After entering each character, the total number of upper-case letters typed so far should be displayed on the screen.
5.	Modify the code in *Example 7.6 – while_gravity.cpp* so that during each iteration of the **while** loop, the program checks that **speed** has not exceeded the maximum possible due to "terminal velocity".
	If the terminal velocity of **54 meters per second** has been reached, the code should no longer increase the speed of the falling object.

Chapter 8:
Characters and text strings

Working with single characters

Single character symbols can be typed in from the keyboard, assigned to `char` variables and displayed on the screen.

When working with characters, a literal character value must be enclosed between a pair of ' ' single quotes.

This next program displays different characters in several different ways. It displays them as **literal characters**, **character constants** and **character variables**.

Example 8.1 – characters.cpp

```cpp
#include <iostream>     // Program will be displaying some text on the screen

using namespace std;    // Will be using standard identifiers cout and endl

int main()
{
    // The letter R in the alphabet, stored as a literal character
    cout << "The 1st letter is... ";
    cout << 'R';
    cout << endl;

    // This constant is set to the character that has ASCII code 65,
    // which is the capital letter A in the alphabet
    const char NEVER_CHANGING_LETTER = 65;

    cout << "The 2nd letter is... ";

    cout << NEVER_CHANGING_LETTER;
    cout << endl;

    // The letter M in the alphabet, stored as a variable
    char letterThatGetsChanged = 'M';

    letterThatGetsChanged += 3;    // M gets changed to P (3 letters on from M)

    cout << "The 3rd letter is... ";
    cout << letterThatGetsChanged;
    cout << endl;


    return 0;
}
```

When setting the value for the character constant **NEVER_CHANGING_LETTER**, the program uses ASCII value **65**, which is the code for the capital letter **'A'**. Remember that ASCII codes and characters can be used interchangeably when working with the **char** data-type.

Because **letterThatGetsChanged** is a variable, it is possible to assign a new value to it or to change its value using arithmetic. In this case, the original value **'M'** has the integer value **3** added to it, which is like moving along three places in the alphabet from the letter **'M'** to the letter **'P'**.

Converting between ASCII character codes and character symbols

Sometimes a program may need to convert integer values to characters. This can be done by **casting**. (Casts were explained in *"Chapter 5: Using operators to process data"*.) The following code converts an `int` value to a `char` value, before displaying it on the screen:

```cpp
int asciiCode = 65;

cout << asciiCode;   // Displays the number 65 on the screen as an integer

cout << static_cast <char> ( asciiCode );  // Displays it as the letter 'A'
```

Here is a program that allows you to type in a whole number ASCII character code. The program casts the `int` value that you enter into a `char` and displays it on the screen:

Example 8.2 – cast_char.cpp

```cpp
#include <iostream>     // Program will be displaying some text on the screen

using namespace std;    // Will be using standard identifiers cin, cout, endl

int main()
{
    // User types in a whole number to be used as an ASCII code
    int asciiCode;
    cout << "Please type in a whole number between 33 and 126... ";
    cin >> asciiCode;

    // Display the number that they typed in
    cout << "The code " << asciiCode;

    // Display equivalent ASCII character symbol,
    // casting the integer ASCII code to a char
    cout << " is used for the symbol ";
    cout << static_cast <char> ( asciiCode );

    cout << endl;


    return 0;
}
```

Your Pi will take the whole number that you type in and use it as an ASCII code to display the corresponding character, providing that it is within the range of printable-characters that can be displayed:

```
Please type in a whole number between 33 and 126... 80
The code 80 is used for the symbol P
```

```
Please type in a whole number between 33 and 126... 43
The code 43 is used for the symbol +
```

Arithmetic operations on `char` values

As mentioned earlier, C++ allows arithmetic operations to be carried out on the data-type `char` in exactly the same way as with numeric data-types, which can be very convenient. This means that we can perform arithmetic not just with integers and floating point numbers, but also with characters.

Because every character symbol has a corresponding character code, you can add or subtract an integer to or from the value of a character variable.

Many other programming languages require you to explicitly carry out conversions or casts between characters and character-codes before a character can be manipulated in this way.

The program below creates three variables, each having the `char` data-type. An integer value is then added to or subtracted from the value of each variable. The modified character values then get displayed on the screen.

Example 8.3 – char_arithmetic.cpp

```cpp
#include <iostream>     // Program will be displaying some text on the screen

using namespace std;    // Will be using standard identifiers cout and endl

int main()
{
    char letter1 = 'G';
    char letter2 = 'N';
    char letter3 = 'U';

    cout << "Starting values:" << endl;

    cout << letter1 << letter2 << letter3 << endl;

    letter1 += 5;
    letter2 += 1;
    letter3 -= 9;

    cout << endl << "Final values:" << endl;

    cout << letter1 << letter2 << letter3 << endl;


    return 0;
}
```

If you execute the program above, the characters **G N U** are each transformed by adding or subtracting values from their character codes, changing them to **L O L** as shown in the screenshot below:

```
Starting values:
GNU

Final values:
LOL
```

Choosing character symbols at random

This next program fills the screen with random characters. It generates random integers within the range of ASCII codes for the 95 printable characters. Each integer value is converted to a character using a cast, then displayed on the screen.

Example 8.4 – char_random.cpp

```cpp
#include <iostream>     // Program will be displaying some text on the screen
#include <cstdlib>      // Program uses the random() and srandom() functions
#include <ctime>       // Program uses the time() function as the random seed

using namespace std;     // Will be using standard identifiers cout and endl

int main()
{
    // Seed random number generator so that the program gives
    // different results each time it runs
    srandom( time( 0 ) );

    int code;

    // Infinite loop that will never stop executing
    for ( ; ; )
    {
        // Choose a random number
        code = random();

        // Divide it by the number of printable ASCII characters 95
        // and obtain the remainder (in the range 0 to 94)
        code %= 95;

        // The printable ASCII chars are from code 32 onwards
        // so add an extra 32 on to the remainder
        code += 32;

        // The statements above could be combined efficiently as
        // code = random() % 95 + 32;

        // Display the final random character
        cout << static_cast <char> ( code );

    }   // end of the infinite loop block of statements

    return 0;
}
```

Once running, you will need to press **Ctrl** and **C** to stop this program as the infinite loop means that it will keep generating random characters forever.

To create each random character, the program chooses a random number, which is possibly a very large value. It then uses %= to obtain the remainder of the random number when dividing it by **95** in order to achieve a result that is between **0** and **94**. This remainder is added to **32**, which is the first printable character that would be possible to display on the screen (**32** is the ASCII code for a *space*).

The smallest ASCII code that the program can use is **32** (which is **0** + **32**). The largest will be **126** (which is **94** + **32**). This ensures that the range of ASCII codes generated is for the printable characters only.

Example 8.5 – char_at.cpp

```cpp
#include <iostream>      // Program will be displaying some text on the screen

using namespace std;     // Will be using standard identifiers string, cout and endl

int main()
{
    // Store a text value in a string variable
    string password = "Custard";

    // Find out which letters are in the 1st, 4th and 7th positions
    // in the text value (remember they are zero-indexed)
    char firstLetter = password.at( 0 );
    char middleLetter = password.at( 4 );
    char lastLetter = password.at( 3 );

    // Display the letters on the screen
    cout << firstLetter << endl;
    cout << middleLetter << endl;
    cout << lastLetter << endl;

    return 0;
}
```

This program picks out individual characters from a text value using the `at()` function, which is a part of the `string` data-type. Such a function is called a **member function**. We say that `at()` is a member function of the `string` class. You will learn more about functions and member functions in *"Chapter 10: Functions"* and *"Chapter 13: Objects and classes"*.

A call to `at( 0 )` always gives back the first character from a `string` value. Remember that the characters in a `string` are **"zero-indexed"**, which means that the first character is at position `0`, the second character is at position `1`, and so on.

In this case, positions `0`, `4` and `3` hold the characters `C`, `a` and `t` from the word `Custard`.

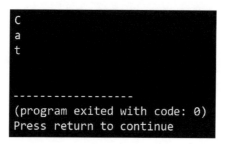

You can also use the `at()` function to change an individual character within a `string` value:

```cpp
    string animal = "Cat";  // Set the original value for the string
    animal.at( 0 ) = 'B';  // Change the first letter from C to B
```

The code above would change the first letter of `Cat` to produce the word `Bat`.

Finding whether a character is a numeric digit, letter of the alphabet, or other symbol

C++ allows many different ways to examine a single character to determine what kind of a symbol that character is.

One of the most common problems is to determine whether or not a character is a letter of the alphabet. Alternatively, your code might need to determine whether or not a particular character is a numeric digit.

Here are some functions that are part of the **<cctype>** library:

`isprint()`	Determines whether a character is a **printable** character or not.
`iscntrl()`	Determines whether a character is a **control** (non-printable) character or not.
`isdigit()`	Determines whether a character is a **numeric-digit** (between **0-9**) or not.
`isalpha()`	Determines whether a character is an **alpha-character** (letter of the alphabet) or not.
`islower()`	Determines whether a character is a **lower-case alpha-character** (between **a-z**) or not.
`isupper()`	Determines whether a character is an **upper-case alpha-character** (between **A-Z**) or not.
`ispunct()`	Determines whether a character is a **punctuation character** or not.
`isspace()`	Determines whether a character is the **space character** or not.

Each one of these functions takes a single argument, which can be either an **int** ASCII code or a single **char** value. The function then determines whether or not the character is of a particular kind and returns a **true** or **false** value as a result.

Note that your program will not need to include the **<cctype>** library explicitly if you have already included the **<iostream>** library in your code.

The following program shows several of these functions in action, using them to classify a character that corresponds to an ASCII code that the user types in:

Example 8.6 – classify_char.cpp

```cpp
#include <iostream>     // Program will be using keyboard and screen

using namespace std;    // Will be using standard identifiers cin, cout, endl

int main()
{
    // Allow user to type in an ASCII code for a character
    int typedIn;
    cout << "Type in an ASCII code: " << endl;
    cin >> typedIn;
```

Continued on next page...

```cpp
    // Determine whether the character is a printable character
    if ( isprint( typedIn ) )
    {
        cout << "It is a printable character" << endl;
        cout << "It is the code for the symbol ";
        cout << static_cast <char> ( typedIn );
        cout << endl;
    }
    else
        cout << "It is not a printable character" << endl;


    // Determine whether the character is a numeric digit
    if ( isdigit( typedIn ) )
        cout << "It is a numeric digit between 0 and 9" << endl;


    // Determine whether the character is a letter of the alphabet (either case)
    if ( isalpha( typedIn ) )
        cout << "It is a letter of the alphabet" << endl;


    // Determine whether the character is a lower-case letter of the alphabet
    if ( islower( typedIn ) )
        cout << "It is a lower-case letter of the alphabet between a and z" << endl;


    // Determine whether the character is an upper-case letter of the alphabet
    if ( isupper( typedIn ) )
        cout << "It is an upper-case letter of the alphabet between A and Z" << endl;


    // Determine whether the character is a punctuation mark
    if ( ispunct( typedIn ) )
        cout << "It is a punctuation mark" << endl;

    return 0;
}
```

Try typing in several ASCII codes. The program should tell you a little bit about the characters that they represent:

```
Type in an ASCII code:
71
It is a printable character
It is the code for the symbol G
It is a letter of the alphabet
It is an upper-case letter of the alphabet between A and Z
```

```
Type in an ASCII code:
33
It is a printable character
It is the code for the symbol !
It is a punctuation mark
```

Finding the number of characters in a `string` value using the `length()` function

If your program needs to examine or process all of the characters in a `string` value, then it will often need to visit each of the characters in order, from the first to the last. This means that your code needs to know **how many** characters that the `string` value contains in order to know where to stop.

The computer can find how many character symbols are in a `string` value by calling the `length()` member function.

As with the `at()` function, the `length()` function **belongs** to the `string` class, hence it is called using the `.` **membership operator**, which means *"is a part of..."* or *"belongs to..."*.

```
int numberOfChars = myStringValue.length();
```

Example 8.7 – string_length.cpp

```cpp
#include <iostream>    // Program will be displaying some text on the screen

using namespace std;    // Will be using standard identifiers string, cout and endl

int main()
{
    const string FIRST = "Apple";

    const string SECOND = "Strawberry";

    const string THIRD =  "Kiwi Fruit";


    // Find out and display how many letters in each string...

    cout << "Length of Apple is ";
    cout << FIRST.length() << endl;

    cout << "Length of Strawberry is ";
    cout << SECOND.length() << endl;

    cout << "Length of Kiwi Fruit is ";
    cout << THIRD.length() << endl;

    return 0;
}
```

When running this program, your Pi will report that the length of `"Apple"` is **5** characters, each one being a letter of the alphabet. Similarly, the length of `"Strawberry"` is displayed as **10** characters. Notice however that the program displays that the length of the string `"Kiwi Fruit"` is also **10**, even though the string only contains nine letters of the alphabet.

The computer regards the space in-between the words `"Kiwi"` and `"Fruit"` as a character, in exactly the same way as the letters of the alphabet that are used in each of the `string` values. This is an important point: although you cannot actually see a space on the screen, a space still counts as a character. In fact, a space is usually stored in a computer's memory using the ASCII character code **32** – whilst you don't see anything on the screen, the space is represented in the computer using this numeric character code.

As we have seen, C++ can be very flexible about how your code works with characters and their ASCII codes. This program uses the techniques described so far to examine each character in a **string** using a **for** loop. It then displays the ASCII code for each of the characters.

```cpp
#include <iostream>      // Program will be using keyboard and screen

using namespace std;     // Will be using standard identifiers string, cin, cout, endl

int main()
{
    // Get whole line of plain text from the keyboard
    cout << "Please type in a line of text:" << endl;
    string lineOfText;
    getline( cin, lineOfText );

    // Find out how long the string is
    unsigned int lengthOfMyText = lineOfText.length();

    // Look at each char in the string
    for ( unsigned int pos = 0;  pos < lengthOfMyText;  pos++ )
    {
        // Display the position in the string (how far along we are)
        cout << "The symbol at position ";
        cout << pos;

        // Display the current ASCII character symbol at this position in the string
        cout << " is ";
        cout << lineOfText.at( pos );

        // Cast (convert) the character to an integer ASCII code and display it
        cout << " which has the character code ";
        cout << static_cast <int> ( lineOfText.at( pos ) ) << endl;

    }  // end of for loop

    cout << endl;  // Display blank line



    return 0;
}
```

First of all, the program finds out how many characters are in the **string** value **lineOfText** using **length()**.

Starting with the first character, the program uses a **for** loop to obtain and display each character in **lineOfText**.

It displays each character on the screen, along with the corresponding ASCII code for that character. When displaying the ASCII code, the program uses a **cast** to force the **char** value to behave as an **int** value, thus a number is displayed on the screen rather than a character symbol:

```cpp
cout << static_cast <int> ( lineOfText.at( pos ) ) << endl;
```

Because the **char** data-type only uses eight bits to store a value, this can be a very compact and efficient way to store numbers that you know will only fall within a very limited range. However, as with other numeric data-types, you may run into problems when using them in your code if you attempt to use a value that is unexpectedly too large or too small.

All values that are stored in a computer's memory are held using patterns of **binary digits** (or "**bits**").

The data-type **char** stores values using **8** bits.

Using **8** bits gives **256** possible different values, each using a different 8-bit pattern of 0s and 1s.

You can make a list of these possible combinations, writing them out in order.

The first few would be:

```
00000000
00000001
00000010
00000011
00000100
00000101
```

...and so on, until reaching the final combinations:

```
11111100
11111101
11111110
11111111
```

You might expect that values of type **char** should range between 0 and positive 255, but values of type **char** are not always positive and can actually be negative. In fact, values of type **char** can range between −128 and 127.

The use of some of the combinations of 0s and 1s for negative numbers therefore leaves fewer combinations for representing positive values. Thus, this affects the largest number that can be used for a **char** variable.

You may find this a little confusing, especially as the ASCII character set begins at character code 0 and does not contain any characters that have negative character codes.

If you don't want to use negative values and want to use values larger than 127, you can **modify** the **char** data-type to represent only positive values by preceding it with the word **unsigned**.

Using **unsigned char** allows values that range between 0 and 255.

For example:

```
unsigned char myValue = 255;
```

Here is another program that examines the individual characters within a **string** value, although this time it examines and displays the characters in a different order.

The code uses a **while** loop that starts at the end of the original text that the user types in, working its way backwards towards the beginning, displaying each character along the way in reverse order.

Example 8.9 – *reverse_string.cpp*

```
#include <iostream>     // Program will be using keyboard and screen

using namespace std;    // Will be using standard identifiers string, cin, cout, endl

int main()
{
    // Infinite loop allows you to type in strings again and again
    while ( true )
    {
        // Person types in their text (which can include spaces)
        string lineOfText;
        cout << "Please type in some text:" << endl;
        getline( cin, lineOfText );

        // Count how many letters are in the name
        int lengthOfText = lineOfText.length();

        // Work backwards through the string from the end towards the beginning
        int position = lengthOfText - 1;

        while ( position >= 0 )
        {

            cout << lineOfText.at( position );  // Display current letter
            position--;

        }  // end of while loop that processes the string

        cout << endl << endl;  // Display blank line

    }  // end of infinite while loop

    return 0;
}
```

As with our other earlier examples, before it can begin, the **while** loop needs to know how many characters are in the **string** value.

It uses the **length()** member function to find this number, storing the result in the variable **lengthOfText**:

```
// Count how many letters are in the text
int lengthOfText = lineOfText.length();
```

The **while** loop now needs to begin at the final character in the **string** value.

Because the characters in a **string** are **zero-indexed** (with the first character in any **string** being at position **0**), the final character is at position **lengthOfText – 1**:

```
int position = lengthOfText - 1;
while ( position >= 0)
{
    cout << lineOfText.at( position );
    position--;
}
```

As with *Example 8.8 - ascii_codes.cpp*, during each iteration of the loop, a single character is obtained using the **at()** member function, which operates on **string** values to obtain a single character from a certain position in the text. The character is then displayed on the screen.

Once the character at position **0** (the first character in the **string** value) has been displayed and the value of **position** falls below **0**, the **while** loop ceases execution.

Here is an example of what happens at run-time:

```
Please type in some text:
GNU
UNG

Please type in some text:
Raspberry Pi
iP yrrebpsaR

Please type in some text:
wowee zowie!
!eiwoz eewow

Please type in some text:
tluciffid si sdrawkcab gnipyt
typing backwards is difficult

Please type in some text:
5-4-3-2-1
1-2-3-4-5
```

As you can see, whatever you type in to your Pi gets reversed and becomes a mirror image of the original text.

Detecting different kinds of characters in a `string` value

This program uses `if` decisions to identify capital letters, lower-case letters, numeric digits and spaces from a `string` value.

The program keeps a running total of the number of letters, digits and spaces found, using the variables `alphaTotal`, `numericTotal` and `spaceTotal`. The final values for these totals are then displayed at the end of the program.

Example 8.10 – char_totals.cpp

```cpp
#include <iostream>     // Program will be using keyboard and screen

using namespace std;    // Will be using standard identifiers string, cin, cout, endl

int main()
{
    cout << "Please type in some text:" << endl;
    string sentence;
    getline( cin, sentence );
    cout << endl << "Thanks" << endl << endl;

    // Find out how many character symbols are in the sentence
    unsigned int stringLength = sentence.length();

    // Examine each character and determine what kind it is, then update a total
    char currentChar;

    unsigned int alphaTotal = 0;
    unsigned int numericTotal = 0;
    unsigned int spaceTotal = 0;

    for ( unsigned int position = 0;  position < stringLength;  position++ )
    {
        currentChar = sentence.at( position );

        cout << currentChar << " ";

        if ( isupper( currentChar ) )
        {
            cout << "capital letter" << endl;
            alphaTotal++;
        }

        if ( islower( currentChar ) )
        {
            cout << "lower-case letter" << endl;
            alphaTotal++;
        }
```

continues on next page...

continued...

```cpp
        if ( isdigit( currentChar ) )
        {
            cout << "numeric digit" << endl;
            numericTotal++;
        }

        if ( isspace( currentChar ) )
        {
            cout << "space" << endl;
            spaceTotal++;
        }

    }  // end of the for loop


    // Display the summary of characters that were in the sentence
    cout << endl << "Your sentence contains:" << endl;

    cout << alphaTotal << " letters" << endl;

    cout << numericTotal << " digits" << endl;

    cout << spaceTotal << " spaces" << endl;


    return 0;
}
```

When the program runs, you will see the outcomes of the decisions that are made about each character. Once the end of the text is reached, your Pi will display the totals for the various kinds of characters.

```
Please type in some text:
If 6 was 9

Thanks

I capital letter
f lower-case letter
  space
6 numeric digit
  space
w lower-case letter
a lower-case letter
s lower-case letter
  space
9 numeric digit

Your sentence contains:
5 letters
2 digits
3 spaces
```

This next example asks the user to type in some text, which is then displayed on the screen as Morse code.

The text that the user types in is stored in the **string** variable called **myText**. The program enters a **for** loop to examine each individual character in **myText**, one-by-one, from the beginning.

Each individual character is temporarily stored in the variable **letterAtThisPos** and is used by a **switch** statement to decide which pattern of Morse code dots and dashes to display on the screen. Any unrecognised characters result in a **?** question-mark being displayed. (Note that I have omitted the Morse equivalents for numeric digits in order to shorten the program a little.)

Example 8.11 – morse_code.cpp

```cpp
#include <iostream>      // Program will be using keyboard and screen

using namespace std;     // Will be using standard identifiers string, cin, cout, endl

int main()
{
    // User types in some text from the keyboard
    cout << "Please type in some text:" << endl;
    string myText;
    getline( cin, myText );

    // Find out how long the text is
    unsigned int lengthOfMyText = myText.length();

    // Examine each character in the text
    char letterAtThisPos;

    for ( unsigned int position = 0;  position < lengthOfMyText;  position++ )
    {
        // Extract single character from the string
        letterAtThisPos = myText.at( position );

        cout << letterAtThisPos << " is ";

        // Convert character to lower-case - it may have been a capital
        letterAtThisPos = tolower ( letterAtThisPos );

        // If it is a letter of the alphabet, change to Morse code
        switch ( letterAtThisPos )
        {
            case 'a':    cout << ".-";       break;
            case 'b':    cout << "-...";     break;
            case 'c':    cout << "-.-.";     break;
            case 'd':    cout << "-..";      break;
            case 'e':    cout << ".";        break;
            case 'f':    cout << "..-.";     break;
            case 'g':    cout << "--.";      break;
            case 'h':    cout << "....";     break;
            case 'i':    cout << "..";       break;
            case 'j':    cout << ".---";     break;
```

continues on next page...

```
            case 'k':    cout << "-.-";        break;
            case 'l':    cout << ".-..";       break;
            case 'm':    cout << "--";         break;
            case 'n':    cout << "-.";         break;
            case 'o':    cout << "---";        break;
            case 'p':    cout << "-.-.";       break;
            case 'q':    cout << "--.-";       break;
            case 'r':    cout << ".-.";        break;
            case 's':    cout << "...";        break;
            case 't':    cout << "-";          break;
            case 'u':    cout << "..-";        break;
            case 'v':    cout << "...-";       break;
            case 'w':    cout << ".--";        break;
            case 'x':    cout << "-..-";       break;
            case 'y':    cout << "-.--";       break;
            case 'z':    cout << "--..";       break;
            case ' ':    cout << "(gap)";      break;

            // This will be chosen if none of the cases above have been selected...
            default:     cout << "?";          break;

        } // end of switch statement

        cout << endl;  // Move on to next line after displaying morse for the letter

    } // end of the for loop

    cout << endl;  // Display final blank line

    return 0;
}
```

Here's the program in action:

```
Please type in some text:
GNU is not Unix
G is --.
N is -.
U is ..-
  is (gap)
i is ..
s is ...
  is (gap)
n is -.
o is ---
t is -
  is (gap)
U is ..-
n is -.
i is ..
x is -..-
```

The program copes with both upper and lower-case letters thanks to the call to the **tolower()** function, which always converts any letter of the alphabet from **myText** to lower-case.

Replacing individual characters in a `string` value

The program below takes some text and **replaces** certain letters with numeric digits to produce a car number-plate style equivalent. All other symbols in the original text are unaffected.

Example 8.12 – replace_chars.cpp

```cpp
#include <iostream>    // Program will be displaying some text on the screen

using namespace std;    // Will be using standard identifiers string, cin, cout, endl

int main()
{
    // Allow the user to type in a line of text
    cout << "Type a line of text..." << endl;
    string lineOfText;
    getline( cin, lineOfText );

    // Change string to upper-case.
    unsigned int stringLen = lineOfText.length();

    // Examine each character, convert to upper-case and replace with digits if can
    char thisChar;

    for ( unsigned int position = 0;  position < stringLen;  position++ )
    {
        thisChar = lineOfText.at( position );

        thisChar = toupper( thisChar );

        // Swap special letters for other symbols
        switch ( thisChar )
        {
            case 'B':    thisChar = '8';    break;
            case 'I':    thisChar = '1';    break;
            case 'O':    thisChar = '0';    break;
            case 'E':    thisChar = '3';    break;
            case 'S':    thisChar = '5';    break;
        }   // end of switch statement

        lineOfText.at( position ) = thisChar;

    }   // end of for

    // Display final results
    cout << "It is now..." << endl;
    cout << lineOfText << endl << endl;


    return 0;
}
```

As with the previous Morse code program, the code above examines each character in the text that you type using a **switch** statement, deciding whether to substitute a particular character for a digit.

For instance:

```
Type a line of text...
egghead
It is now...
3GGH3AD
```

```
Type a line of text...
Bonkers
It is now...
80NK3R5
```

Determining whether two `string` values are the same

Very often, a program needs to test whether two **string** values are the same. Do both values have exactly the same number of characters in them? Do they both have exactly the same character at each position?

As with other data-types, your code can test whether two **string** values are the same using the **==** equivalence operator.

Example 8.13 – string_equiv.cpp

```cpp
#include <iostream>      // Program will be using keyboard and screen

using namespace std;     // Will be using standard identifiers string, cin, cout, endl

int main()
{
    const string OWNER = "Matilda Spaghetti";

    // Person types in their name (which can include spaces)
    cout << "Please type in your name..." << endl;
    string name;
    getline( cin, name );

    // Test whether the string values are exactly the same
    if ( name == OWNER )
        cout << "Hello Matilda!" << endl;
    else
        cout << "Greetings, oh mysterious one!" << endl;

    return 0;
}
```

Here's what you should see if you type in the name of the owner correctly:

```
Please type in your name...
Matilda Spaghetti
Hello Matilda!
```

Alternatively, here is what you would see if you type in someone else's name:

```
Please type in your name...
Bronwyn Flabbergast
Greetings, oh mysterious one!
```

Be aware that two **string** values are regarded as different if the **case** of each character is not exactly the same. An upper-case letter is **not** the same as a lower-case letter.

So:

```
Matilda Spaghetti
```

...is not considered to be the same as:

```
matilda spaghetti
```

```
Please type in your name...
matilda spaghetti
Greetings, oh mysterious one!
```

In the screenshot above, **matilda spaghetti** is considered by your Pi to be different to the value of the **string** constant **OWNER**, thus it does not display the **"Hello Matilda!"** message on the screen.

Another way to test whether the two **string** values are the same is to use the **compare()** member function:

```
if ( name.compare( OWNER ) == 0 )
    cout << "Hello Matilda!" << endl;
else
    cout << "Greetings, oh mysterious one!" << endl;
```

The **compare()** function returns an integer result. If this result is zero, then the two **string** values were found to be **exactly** the same, including their length and the exact sequence of characters that they contain.

Negative and positive results from this function can be used to diagnose **why** two particular **string** values are different. They can indicate differences in the length of the two values or which of them comes before the other when ordered alphabetically. Beware though: interpreting these different results can be a little complicated for beginners.

Appending – joining `string` values together

Text strings can be joined together using the **+ addition operator**. This is like adding the characters from one **string** value on to the end of another **string**. This is called "**appending**" text. You can also append single characters on to the end of **string** values, either using the **char** data-type or as ASCII codes (the latter using the **int** data-type).

```
string species = "eagle";     // set the value for the string variable

species = "golden " + species;    // add value on to beginning

species = "ant";    // replace value of string variable

species += "elope";    // add string on to end of value (append)

species += 's';    // add single character to end of string value

species += 33;    // add ! on to the end of the string (33 is ASCII code for !)
```

This next program joins several literal **string** and **char** values together:

Example 8.14 – append_strings.cpp

```cpp
#include <iostream>    // Program will be displaying some text on the screen

using namespace std;    // Will be using standard identifiers string, cout and endl

int main()
{
    // This program appends string variables together
    // It joins the values together to make a new string

    string day = "Tuesday";

    string when = "morning";

    string appointment = day + ' ' + when;

    // Add a single punctuation character to the end of the string
    appointment += '.';

    cout << "You are seeing the dentist on... ";
    cout << appointment;

    cout << endl;

    return 0;
}
```

Here is what your Pi should display when the program runs:

```
You are seeing the dentist on... Tuesday morning.
```

The following program appends a mixture of **string** and **char** values to another **string** value. It asks the user to type in a first name and a surname, which get stored in the **string** variables **firstName** and **lastName**. A new **string** value called **fullName** is created as a result of adding together the contents of the **firstName**, a single space character and then the contents of **lastName**. The resulting value of **fullName** is then displayed on the screen.

Example 8.15 – append_mixed.cpp

```cpp
#include <iostream>     // Program will be using keyboard and screen

using namespace std;    // Will be using standard identifiers string, cin, cout, endl

int main()
{
    // This program joins two string variables together to make a new string.

    // Get user to type in their first name
    cout << "Please type in your first name:" << endl;
    string firstName;
    cin >> firstName;

    // Get user to type in their surname
    cout << "Please type in your last name:" << endl;
    string lastName;
    cin >> lastName;

    // Join them together with a space in-between
    string fullName = firstName + ' ' + lastName;

    // Display joined name on the screen with a message
    cout << "Hello ";

    cout << fullName;

    cout << "! How are you?" << endl;

    return 0;
}
```

Notice that **without** the space, this statement:

```cpp
        string fullName = firstName + lastName;   // Two names joined WITHOUT a space
```

...would display the two names side-by-side without any gap whatsoever once the program is executed.

Jimi and **Hendrix** would be added together to make:

```
        JimiHendrix
```

...rather than:

```
        Jimi Hendrix
```

This is quite a common problem when writing programs that join pieces of text together. You sometimes want the parts of a **string** to appear separated by a space or by a punctuation mark, otherwise they might be difficult to read on the screen.

This program chooses a fixed number of random numeric digits to construct a PIN sequence. Once chosen, each random digit is appended to a **string** value called **pinString**. This continues until the PIN reaches the required length, which is specified by the constant **PIN_LENGTH**.

Example 8.16 – generate_pin.cpp

```cpp
#include <iostream>    // Program will be displaying some text on the screen
#include <cstdlib>     // Program uses the random() and srandom() functions
#include <ctime>       // Program uses the time() function as the random seed

using namespace std;    // Will be using standard identifiers string, cout and endl

int main()
{
    // Tell the computer how long each PIN will be
    const int PIN_LENGTH = 4;     // Change here for longer PINs

    // Make a new blank string to hold the PIN
    string pinString = "";

    // Set up (seed) the random number generator
    srandom( time( 0 ) );

    // We will be choosing random whole numbers
    int pos;
    int randomDigit;
    int asciiCode;

    for ( pos = 0;  pos < PIN_LENGTH;  pos++ )
    {
        // Choose a random digit between 0 and 9
        randomDigit = random() % 9;

        // Convert it to an ASCII char between 0 and 9
        asciiCode = 48 + randomDigit;     // Code for char '0' is 48

        // Convert ASCII code to a character
        // and then add it on to the end of the PIN string
        pinString += static_cast <char> ( asciiCode );
    }  // end of for loop

    // Display the finished PIN on the screen
    cout << "The new PIN is ";
    cout << pinString << endl;

    return 0;
}
```

When executed, the program will generate and display a random 4-digit PIN:

```
The new PIN is 0708
```

Following on from the previous example that generates a simple PIN, this program generates random passwords that are composed of letters of the alphabet.

The program allows you to choose how many passwords you want to generate and how long each password should be.

Each random password is constructed by appending a single random character, one at a time, to the **string** value called **password**.

Example 8.17 – random_password.cpp

```cpp
#include <iostream>     // Program will be using keyboard and screen
#include <cstdlib>      // Program uses the random() and srandom() functions
#include <ctime>        // Program uses the time() function as the random seed

using namespace std;    // Will be using standard identifiers string, cin, cout, endl

int main()
{
    // Seed random number generator
    // This only needs to be done ONCE during the program to ensure
    // that numbers do not follow a predictable pattern
    srandom( time( 0 ) );

    // ----------

    cout << "How many passwords do you want to be generated?" << endl;
    unsigned int numRequired;
    cin >> numRequired;

    // ----------

    cout << "How many characters should each password contain?" << endl;
    unsigned int howLong;
    cin >> howLong;

    // ----------

    string password;
    char randomChar;
    unsigned int numCharsAdded, chosenNumber, asciiCode;
```

continues on next page...

```cpp
    // Repeatedly make the passwords
    for ( unsigned int numMade = 0; numMade < numRequired; numMade++ )
    {
        password = "";  // Start with a blank string for a new password

        // Choose random characters and append them to the password
        for ( numCharsAdded = 0; numCharsAdded < howLong; numCharsAdded++ )
        {
            chosenNumber = random() % 26;

            asciiCode = 65 + chosenNumber;

            randomChar = static_cast <char> ( asciiCode );

            password += randomChar;

        }  // end of for loop that adds characters to a single password

        cout << password << endl;  // Display a completed password

    }  // end of for loop that controls how many passwords are made

    return 0;
}
```

You can see below what happened when I told my Pi to generate ten random passwords, each containing eight characters:

```
How many passwords do you want to be generated?
10
How many characters should each password contain?
8
OTKLKPUX
LDLXQYKZ
QHBZGRDH
ABTFUJLK
EYVONSOA
VZZNAJMS
SQSYJXGJ
YBQSKEDO
CAERSSTP
USDUDRMV
```

The previous program appended one single character at a time to a **string** value. Here is a program that uses a **for** loop to make a **string** value that gets longer and longer. It repeatedly appends a whole chunk of literal text to the **string** value, until reaching the desired length:

Example 8.18 – make_longer.cpp

```cpp
#include <iostream>      // Program will be displaying some text on the screen

using namespace std;     // Will be using standard identifiers string, cout and endl

int main()
{
    string myText = "Yo";   // Start with a simple word in the string value

    // Display the text and then add a word on to the end 10 times
    for ( int loop = 1;  loop <= 10;  loop++ )
    {
        // Display the contents of the string on the screen, followed by a ! char
        cout << myText << '!' << endl;

        // Add an extra word on to the end of the string value
        myText += "-Ho";

    }  // end of for loop

    return 0;
}
```

In the code above, the statement:

```cpp
myText += "-Ho";
```

...is used to add an extra word on to the end of the existing value of the **string** variable called **myText**, storing the new longer value back in the same variable. The phrase gets longer and longer until the loop has repeated the process ten times.

The += operator can be used either to append **string** values or single **char** values on to the end of another **string** value. Either are acceptable, just be sure to use **single** quotation marks when appending a single **char** value:

```cpp
myText += '!';   // Appends a single character to the end of string
```

When the program runs you should see this output on the screen:

```
Yo!
Yo-Ho!
Yo-Ho-Ho!
Yo-Ho-Ho-Ho!
Yo-Ho-Ho-Ho-Ho!
Yo-Ho-Ho-Ho-Ho-Ho!
Yo-Ho-Ho-Ho-Ho-Ho-Ho!
Yo-Ho-Ho-Ho-Ho-Ho-Ho-Ho!
Yo-Ho-Ho-Ho-Ho-Ho-Ho-Ho-Ho!
Yo-Ho-Ho-Ho-Ho-Ho-Ho-Ho-Ho-Ho!
```

Joining `string` values using the `append()` function

An alternative way to append one **string** value to the end of another is to use the **append()** member function. This takes a **string** literal, constant or variable and adds it on to the end of the original **string** value:

```
string finalStringValue = originalStringValue.append( extraStringValue )
```

Below is an example that makes use of **append()** to join several text values together to make a new **string** value:

Example 8.19 – append_function.cpp

```cpp
#include <iostream>      // Program will be using keyboard and screen

using namespace std;     // Will be using standard identifiers string, cin, cout, endl

int main()
{
    // This program joins two string variables together to make a new string.

    string operatingSystem = "Debian Linux";

    string version = "8.2";   // Note that number must be enclosed in quotation marks

    string nickName = "\"Jessie\"";

    // Join them together with a space in-between

    operatingSystem.append( " " );

    operatingSystem.append( version );

    operatingSystem.append( " " );

    operatingSystem.append( nickName );

    // Note that version number must be a string, not a float
    // You would not be able to append a float value to a string value

    // Display joined name on the screen
    cout << operatingSystem << endl;


    return 0;
}
```

Below, you can see the results:

```
Debian Linux
Debian Linux (8.2)
Debian Linux (8.2) "Jessie"
```

Below is another program that uses arithmetic on character values. It adds the character values of a secret code word to the character values in a text message to produce an encrypted result. Each scrambled character is appended to a new **string** value, building up the final scrambled message one letter at a time. The final scrambled message is then displayed.

Example 8.20 – scramble_string.cpp

```cpp
#include <iostream>     // Program will be using keyboard and screen

using namespace std;    // Will be using standard identifiers string, cin, cout, endl

int main()
{
    string originalMessage, codeWord;

    // Get user to type in their original message to be scrambled
    cout << "Please type in the message to be scrambled:" << endl;
    getline( cin, originalMessage );

    cout << endl;  // Display blank line

    // Get user to type in a code word(s)
    cout << "Please type in the code word(s):" << endl;
    getline( cin, codeWord );

    cout << endl;  // Display blank line

    // Find out how long message and code words are
    unsigned int messageLength = originalMessage.length();
    unsigned int codeWordLength = codeWord.length();

    // Scramble the message using the characters from the code words
    string scrambledResult = "";
    char charFromMessage, charFromCodeWord;
    int scrambledCode;
    for ( unsigned int charPos = 0;  charPos < messageLength;  charPos++ )
    {
        // Get letter from original message
        charFromMessage = originalMessage.at( charPos );

        // Get letter from code word using % modulus to make sure program does
        // not run out of letters if the code word is shorter than the message
        charFromCodeWord = codeWord.at( charPos % codeWordLength );

        // Add on extra places to the character in order to scramble it
        scrambledCode = charFromMessage + charFromCodeWord - 31;

        // If changed code has gone past last printable char, bring it back in range
        if ( scrambledCode > 126 )
            scrambledCode -= 95;

        // Append scrambled character to changed message
        scrambledResult += static_cast <char> ( scrambledCode );

    }  // end of for loop
```

continues on next page...

continued...

```
    // Display the final scrambled message once loop has finished

    cout << "The scrambled message is:" << endl;

    cout << scrambledResult << endl;

    return 0;
}
```

Here is an example of the encryption program running:

```
Please type in the message to be scrambled:
This text is secret.

Please type in the code word(s):
Egghead

The scrambled message is:
zQR]fWK?]hSZbY,L[O[p
```

You can see above that the message has been transformed into what looks like gibberish.

Notice that although the keyword was shorter than the original text message, every symbol in the message has been encrypted. This is because the program uses % **modulus** to determine which letter to use from the keyword.

The encryption loop takes the current position in the message and divides it by the length of the keyword to obtain a remainder. This remainder tells the computer which letter from the keyword to use. Thus, the encryption process never runs out of letters when it reaches the end of a short keyword.

Of course, now that the previous program has scrambled your text message, you will probably want to change the text back again to make it legible, so here's a program to unscramble the text:

Example 8.21 – unscramble_string.cpp

```
#include <iostream>      // Program will using keyboard and screen

using namespace std;     // Will be using standard identifiers string, cin, cout, endl

int main()
{
    string scrambledMessage, codeWord;

    // Get user to type in their original message to be unscrambled
    cout << "Please type in the message to be unscrambled:" << endl;
    getline( cin, scrambledMessage );

    cout << endl;  // Display blank line

    // Get user to type in a code word(s)
    cout << "Please type in the code word(s):" << endl;
    getline( cin, codeWord );
```

continues on next page...

```cpp
    cout << endl;  // Display blank line

    // Find out how long message and code words are
    unsigned int messageLength = scrambledMessage.length();
    unsigned int codeWordLength = codeWord.length();

    // Scramble the message using the characters from the code words
    string readableResult = "";
    char charFromMessage, charFromCodeWord;
    int unscrambledCode;
    for ( unsigned int charPos = 0;  charPos < messageLength;  charPos++ )
    {
        // Get letter from original message
        charFromMessage = scrambledMessage.at( charPos );

        // Get letter from code word using % modulus to make sure program does
        // not run out of letters if the code word is shorter than the message
        charFromCodeWord = codeWord.at( charPos % codeWordLength );

        // Subtract places from the code word character in order to unscramble it
        unscrambledCode = charFromMessage - ( charFromCodeWord - 31 );

        // If changed code has gone past last printable char, bring it back in range
        if ( unscrambledCode < 32 )
            unscrambledCode += 95;

        // Append unscrambled character to changed message
        readableResult += static_cast <char> ( unscrambledCode );

    }  // end of for loop

    // Display the final unscrambled message once loop has finished

    cout << "The unscrambled message is:" << endl;

    cout << readableResult << endl;

    return 0;
}
```

Here is what happens when the message from the previous example is unscrambled again:

```
Please type in the message to be scrambled:
zQR]fWK?]hSZbY,L[O[p

Please type in the code word(s):
Egghead

The scrambled message is:
This text is secret.
```

Using the same code word results in the original text being displayed.

Detecting a pattern of characters - finding whether a `string` contains a sub-string

The `find()` function is useful for searching through a `string` value to determine whether that value contains a certain **sub-string** of one or more characters. It always begins by searching for the first occurrence of the sub-string, starting from the beginning of the `string` value.

Similarly, you can use the `rfind()` **"reverse-find"** function to begin searching from the **end** of the `string`, rather than from the beginning.

This program uses the `find()` and `rfind()` functions to perform some simple validation on an email address. It tests whether an address that has been typed in contains one single @ *asquith* character and that the asquith character is not the very first character in the address. It also tests whether the email address contains at least one . *dot* character after the @.

```cpp
#include <iostream>     // Program will be using keyboard and screen

using namespace std;     // Will be using standard identifiers string, cin, cout, endl

int main()
{
    string address;

    int firstAsquithAt, lastAsquithAt;
    int dotAt;

    cout << "Type in your email address:" << endl;
    cin >> address;

    // Check for @ asquith symbol
    firstAsquithAt = address.find( "@" );

    if ( firstAsquithAt < 0 )
        cout << "No asquith at all!" << endl;
    else
        if ( firstAsquithAt == 0 )
            cout << "Can't put @ as start of address!" << endl;
        else
        {
            cout << "Has an asquith at position ";
            cout << firstAsquithAt << endl;

            // Check for other @ asquith symbols
            lastAsquithAt = address.rfind( "@" );

            if ( lastAsquithAt > firstAsquithAt )
                cout << "More than one asquith!" << endl;
        };
```

continues on next page...

```cpp
        // Check for . dots
        dotAt = address.find( "." );

        if ( dotAt < 0 )
            cout << "No dots found in the address!" << endl;
        else
            if ( dotAt == 0 )
                cout << "Email addresses can't start with ." << endl;
            else
                cout << "Has at least one . in it" << endl;

        // Check for spaces
        int spaceAt = address.find( " " );

        if ( spaceAt >= 0 )
            cout << "Can't have spaces!" << endl;

        return 0;
}
```

In the screenshots below, you can see that the program checks whether the address contains exactly one @ *asquith* symbol and that this symbol is not at the very beginning of the address. It also correctly identifies that the address contains at least one . *dot* symbol:

```
Type in your email address:
phil@egghead.fakemail.co.uk
Has an asquith at position 4
Has as least one . in it
```

Here is what happens if the email address has an @ *asquith* at the beginning as the first character:

```
Type in your email address:
@egghead.fakemail.co.uk
Can't put @ as start of address!
Has as least one . in it
```

Similarly, an error will be produced if the address does not contain any dots at all, or if it contains more than one @ *asquith*:

```
Type in your email address:
phil@egghead
Has an asquith at position 4
No dots found in the address!
```

```
Type in your email address:
phil@egghe@d.fakemail.co.uk
Has an asquith at position 4
More than one asquith!
Has as least one . in it
```

Finding more than one occurrence of a sub-string in a `string` value

Sometimes, a sub-string that you want to find may exist more than once within a `string` value. The `find()` function can search for the **first** occurrence of a sub-string, but how can you locate any further sub-strings within the `string` value?

Luckily, you can give the `find()` function an extra parameter, telling it not only what the sub-string is that you want to find, but also the position in the `string` value at which you want to start looking.

Example 8.23 – find_many.cpp

```
#include <iostream>     // Program will be using keyboard and screen

using namespace std;    // Will be using standard identifiers string, cout and endl

int main()
{
    string message;
    message = "The cow was in a bad mood so it mooed loudly.";

    int foundAt;

    int messLen = message.length();
    int startPos = 0;

    do
    {
        foundAt = message.find( "moo", startPos );

        if ( foundAt < 0 )
            cout << "End of search." << endl;
        else
        {
            cout << "Found sub-string at ";
            cout << foundAt << endl;

            startPos = foundAt + 1;
        }   // end of if-else decision

    } while ( foundAt >= 0  and  startPos < messLen );

    return 0;
}
```

The program will find the **first** occurrence of "**moo**" at position **21** in the `string` value, as part of the word "**mood**". It will also find a **second** occurrence at position **32**, as part of the word "**mooed**":

```
Found sub-string at 21
Found sub-string at 32
End of search.
```

| T | h | e | | c | o | w | | w | a | s | | i | n | | a | | b | a | d | | m | o | o | d | | s | o | | i | t | | m | o | o | e | d | | l | o | u | d | l | y | . |

Remember that the `string` value is **zero-indexed** - the first character is located at position **0**. Hence the 22nd character **m** is at position **21**, the 33rd character **m** is at position **32**.

Adding text characters inside a `string` value using the `insert()` function

The `insert()` function adds an extra sequence of characters into a `string` value at the position that you choose.

Example 8.24 – insert_function.cpp

```cpp
#include <iostream>      // Program will be displaying some text on the screen

using namespace std;     // Will be using standard identifiers string, cout and endl

int main()
{
    string sentence = "I'm hungry.";

    for ( int extraWords = 0;  extraWords < 5;  extraWords++ )
    {

        cout << sentence << endl;

        sentence.insert( 4, "very " );

    }  // end of for loop

    return 0;
}
```

Here is what happens when the program runs:

```
I'm hungry.
I'm very hungry.
I'm very very hungry.
I'm very very very hungry.
I'm very very very very hungry.
```

During each iteration through the `for` loop, the program displays the sentence on the screen. It the inserts the word "**very**" (followed by a space) into the sentence at position **4**. This is always directly after "**I'm** " in the text.

The `string` value grows in length by an extra **5** characters each time `insert()` is called. The `for` loop continues execution until the word has been inserted a total of five times.

Manually copying characters from one `string` to another

This next example copies characters from one **string** value into another. It uses a **for** loop to obtain and copy the characters, one at a time, until the desired number of characters has been added to the new **string** value. Manually copying single characters can be useful when your program needs to make some sort of useful decision about what to do with each one.

Example 8.25 – copy_chars.cpp

```cpp
#include <iostream>    // Program will be using keyboard and screen

using namespace std;    // Will be using standard identifiers string, cin, cout, endl

int main()
{
    // Person types in a word
    cout << "Type in a word... ";
    string word;
    cin >> word;

    // Person types in how long they want the final message to be
    cout << "How long should the final text be? ";
    unsigned int howManyWanted;
    cin >> howManyWanted;

    // Repeatedly add characters to the result string and check whether finished
    string resultString = "";
    unsigned int numberOfLetters = 0;
    unsigned int position = 0;

    while ( numberOfLetters < howManyWanted )
    {
        // Add the word on to the end of the result string
        resultString += word.at( position );

        // Check out how long the updated result string is
        numberOfLetters = resultString.length();

        // Move on to the next character in the word
        position++;

        // Go back to the start of the word if have gone past the end of it
        if ( position == word.length() )
            position = 0;

    }  // end of while loop


    // Display the final string
    cout << "Final string: " << resultString << endl;


    return 0;
}
```

If you ask for more characters than are in the original **string** value, the process returns back to the start again to obtain the next character to be copied. This means that the program will never run out of characters if the original text is too short.

For instance, if the original string that you type is **beep**, and you ask for **3** characters, the result displayed is **bee**.

However, if the original string that you type is **beep**, and you ask for **10** characters, the result is **beepbeepbe**.

```
Type in a word... Beep
How long should the final text be? 3
Final string: Bee
```

```
Type in a word... Beep
How long should the final text be? 10
Final string: BeepBeepBe
```

Notice that the variable **numberOfLetters** is an **unsigned int**. If instead we had chosen **int** as the data-type for **numberOfLetters** (which allows negative values as well as positive) then the compiler would generate a warning. This is because the program attempts to compare **numberOfLetters** with the length of **resultString**. Because the **length()** function always returns an **unsigned integer**, the compiler would consider that we are attempting to compare two different data-types - hence it displays the warning.

The character-by-character approach used here is useful for you to see how programs can obtain and make use of parts of text values (**sub-strings**). It is not the only approach though for obtaining a portion of a larger **string** value.

C++ includes a ready-made function to obtain a sub-string that most people find easier and more convenient to use than copying individual characters manually from one **string** value to another. Your program can instead copy a whole portion of a **string** value in one go.

Copying part of a `string` value using the `substr()` function

To make a copy of part of a **portion** of a **string** value in one single operation, you can use the **substr()** function.

The first way in which it can be used is to supply the **index** of the **first character** that will begin the substring, along with the **number of characters that you want to obtain**:

```
// Starts at position 1, makes a sub-string that is 3 characters long
string portion = original.substr( 1, 3 );
```

Alternatively, you can supply only the **index** of the **first character** that will begin the substring. This will obtain **all** subsequent characters until the end of the original **string** is reached:

```
// Starts at position 10, obtains all subsequent characters until the end
string portion = original.substr( 10 );
```

This program uses the **substr()** function to extract several different portions of a larger **string** value called **message**:

Example 8.26 – substring_function.cpp

```cpp
#include <iostream>     // Program will be using keyboard and screen

using namespace std;    // Will be using standard identifiers string, cin, cout, endl

int main()
{
    // Create a string value. Sub-strings will be obtained from this.
    string message = "Raspberry Pi";

    // Create a sub-string, copying from position 1, make it 3 characters long
    string snake = message.substr( 1, 3 );
    cout << snake << endl;

    // Create a sub-string, copying from position 4, make it 5 characters long
    string food = message.substr( 4, 5 );
    cout << food << endl;

    // Create a sub-string, copying from position 10 until the end of the original
    string computer = message.substr( 10 );
    cout << computer << endl;

    return 0;
}
```

Consider this text:

0	1	2	3	4	5	6	7	8	9	10	11
R	a	s	p	b	e	r	r	y		P	i

The statement:

```cpp
        string snake = message.substr( 1, 3 );
```

...creates a sub-string, starting at position **1** (which holds the letter **a**) and is **3** characters long, hence the sub-string is **"asp"**.

```cpp
        string computer = message.substr( 10 );
```

The statement above creates a sub-string that starts from position **10** (which holds the letter **P**) extending to the end of **message**, resulting in **"Pi"**.

You should see the following results:

```
asp
berry
Pi
```

Erasing and replacing parts of a `string` value

The `erase()` function can be used to **remove** one or more characters from a `string` value.

It can be used to erase part of a `string` value by specifying the index number at which to begin erasing characters.

The function will normally erase all characters until the end of the `string` from this point, unless you give it a second argument that tells it **how many** characters you want to erase.

The example below shows this function in use, first to erase all characters right up to the end of a `string` value, then to erase a sequence of exactly three characters.

Example 8.27 – erase_function.cpp

```
#include <iostream>      // Program will be using keyboard and screen

using namespace std;      // Will be using standard identifiers string, cin, cout, endl

int main()
{
    string message;
    message = "Ziggy played sitar";

    cout << message << endl;

    // Erase all characters from position 13 onwards in the string value (" sitar")
    message.erase( 13 );
    cout << message << endl;

    // Append a new word to the end of the string value
    message = message + "netball";
    cout << message << endl;

    // Erase 3 characters from position 13 onwards in the string value ("net")
    message.erase( 13, 3 );
    cout << message << endl;

    return 0;
}
```

Here is what happens on the screen when the above program runs:

```
Ziggy played sitar
Ziggy played
Ziggy played netball
Ziggy played ball
```

Example 8.28 – *erase_from_start.cpp*

```cpp
#include <iostream>      // Program will be using keyboard and screen

using namespace std;     // Will be using standard identifiers string, cout and endl

int main()
{
    string message = "Help! I'm being erased!";

    while ( not message.empty() )
    {
        // Display the string
        cout << message << endl;

        // Erase one single character from start of the string
        message.erase( 0, 1 );

    }  // end of while loop

    cout << "*** The sentence is now empty! ***" << endl;

    return 0;
}
```

The program above uses the **erase()** function to repeatedly remove characters from the beginning of a **string** value. It erases one character at a time from the beginning of the **string** value called **message**. This is achieved by starting at position 0, erasing 1 character from the value of **message** each time around the **for** loop:

```cpp
message.erase( 0, 1 );
```

```
Help! I'm being erased!
elp! I'm being erased!
lp! I'm being erased!
p! I'm being erased!
! I'm being erased!
 I'm being erased!
I'm being erased!
'm being erased!
m being erased!
 being erased!
being erased!
eing erased!
ing erased!
ng erased!
g erased!
 erased!
erased!
rased!
ased!
sed!
ed!
d!
!
*** The sentence is now empty! ***
```

Replacing part of a `string` using the `replace()` function

The `replace()` function can be used to **change** part of a `string` value. It replaces a sequence of characters in the original `string` value with a new sequence.

Example 8.29 – replace_function.cpp

```cpp
#include <iostream>      // Program will be using keyboard and screen

using namespace std;     // Will be using standard identifiers string, cout and endl

int main()
{
    string message = "I'm hungry.";

    // Display the original sentence
    cout << message << endl;

    cout << "(munch... munch... munch...)" << endl;

    // Replace the word "hungry" with the word "full"
    // "hungry" starts at position 4 in the sentence and is 6 letters long
    message.replace( 4, 6, "full" );

    // Display the new sentence
    cout << message << endl;


    return 0;
}
```

This is the original value for **message**:

0	1	2	3	4	5	6	7	8	9	10
I	'	m		h	u	n	g	r	y	.

Starting at position **4** in the value, the sequence of **6** characters will be replaced with **"full"**:

0	1	2	3	4	5	6	7	8	9	10
I	'	m		**h**	**u**	**n**	**g**	**r**	**y**	.

0	1	2	3	4	5	6	7	8
I	'	m		**f**	**u**	**l**	**l**	.

Here is what you should see when the program runs:

```
I'm hungry.
(munch... munch... munch...)
I'm full.
```

Here is another program that uses the **replace()** function to modify parts of a **string** value at run-time.

The program calls **replace()** to gradually change the text, one word at a time, replacing each complete word with a block of question marks.

```cpp
#include <iostream>        // Program will be using keyboard and screen

using namespace std;      // Will be using standard identifiers string, cout and endl

int main()
{
    // Display original sentence
    string message = "This message will self destruct";
    cout << message << endl;

    // Eliminate first word in message - starts at position 0, 4 letters long
    message.replace( 0, 4, "????" );
    cout << message << endl;

    // Eliminate second word in message - starts at position 5, 7 letters long
    message.replace( 5, 7, "???????" );
    cout << message << endl;

    // Eliminate third word in message - starts at position 13, 4 letters long
    message.replace( 13, 4, "????" );
    cout << message << endl;

    // Eliminate fourth word in message - starts at position 18, 4 letters long
    message.replace( 18, 4, "????" );
    cout << message << endl;

    // Eliminate fifth word in message - starts at position 23, 8 letters long
    message.replace( 23, 8, "????????" );
    cout << message << endl;

    return 0;
}
```

When the program executes, the individual words in the message are eliminated one-by-one:

```
This message will self destruct
???? message will self destruct
???? ??????? will self destruct
???? ??????? ???? self destruct
???? ??????? ???? ???? destruct
???? ??????? ???? ???? ????????
```

Finding characters in a `string` that are part of a certain set

The `find_first_of()` function can scan through a `string` value from the beginning, looking for any characters in a **set** of symbols that you are particularly interested in. As soon as it finds the **first** character in the `string` that is in the special set, the program returns the index of the character to show you where it has been found. If none of the characters in the `string` value are in the set of interest, the function returns a negative value to indicate this.

Note also that the `find_last_of()` function operates in a similar way to the `find_first_of()` function. It will find the position of the **last** character in a `string` value that is part of the set of characters that you are interested in.

Example 8.31 – find_first.cpp

```cpp
#include <iostream>     // Program will be using keyboard and screen

using namespace std;    // Will be using standard identifiers string, cout and endl

int main()
{
    string message = "It's as easy as 1-2-3!";

    // Repeatedly look for individual words in the message
    // Display each complete word, then remove it from the message

    int firstDigitPos, nextDigitPos, firstPuncPos;

    // Find first occurrence of a numeric digit in the message
    firstDigitPos = message.find_first_of( "0123456789" );

    // Find next occurrence of a numeric digit in the message
    // begin searching from next character after the previous digit that was found
    nextDigitPos = message.find_first_of( "0123456789", firstDigitPos + 1 );

    // Find first punctuation mark
    firstPuncPos = message.find_first_of( ".,;:-'!?" );

    // Display results
    cout << "First digit found at position: " << firstDigitPos << endl;

    cout << "Second digit found at position: " << nextDigitPos << endl;

    cout << "First punctuation mark found at position: " << firstPuncPos << endl;

    return 0;
}
```

Here's what happens when the program is executed:

```
It's as easy as 1-2-3!
First digit found at position: 16
Second digit found at position: 18
First punctuation mark found at position: 2
```

The first numeric digit, **1**, is found at position **16** in `message` (the 17th character).
The second numeric digit, **2**, is found at position **18** in `message` (the 19th character).
The first punctuation mark, **'**, is found at position **2** in `message` (the 3rd character).

Finding characters in a `string` that are not in a particular set

The `find_first_not_of()` function can scan through a `string` value from the beginning, looking for any characters that **do not** belong to a certain set that you are interested in. The function determines the index of the first character in the `string` that is not within the set of interest to show you where it has been found. If every single character in the `string` value is actually in the set though, the function returns a negative value instead.

This first example uses `find_first_not_of()` to determine whether a `string` value contains a valid Morse code message, or whether it contains characters that are not allowed:

Example 8.32 – find_first_not_of.cpp

```cpp
#include <iostream>      // Program will be using keyboard and screen

using namespace std;     // Will be using standard identifiers string, cout and endl

int main()
{
    // Prompt user to type in a message in Morse code
    cout << "Please type in a message in Morse code: " << endl;
    string morseMessage;
    getline( cin, morseMessage );

    // Starting at beginning of the message, look for any characters
    // that are unacceptable (can only contain dots, dashes or separators
    int badCharPos = morseMessage.find_first_not_of( ".- /" );

    // If a character was found that was not in the set of valid characters
    // then display it on the screen
    if ( badCharPos > -1 )
    {
        cout << "Contains unacceptable character: ";
        cout << morseMessage.at( badCharPos ) << endl;
    }
    else
        cout << "All characters in the message were acceptable." << endl;

    return 0;
}
```

```
Please type in a message in Morse code:
...--...  ...--...
All characters in the message were acceptable.
```

```
Please type in a message in Morse code:
...--...!  ...--...!
Contains unacceptable character: !
```

The `find_last_not_of()` function operates in a similar way to the `find_first_not_of()` function.

It determines the position of the **last** character in a `string` value that is **not** part of a set of characters that you are interested in.

Splitting a `string` value into individual words

Very often it is useful to **split** a line or a paragraph of text up into individual words so that some processing can be carried out. Each word or group of symbols is called a "**token**".

This program examines the sequence of characters in a `string` value, finding the beginning and end of individual words. Each completed word is displayed on the screen as it is found.

The code uses `find_first_not_of()` to analyse a `string` value, looking for complete words:

Example 8.33 – string_tokens.cpp

```cpp
#include <iostream>      // Program will be using keyboard and screen

using namespace std;     // Will be using standard identifiers string, cout and endl

int main()
{
    string sentence = "Whoa! This has... like, er... words?";

    // Repeatedly look for individual words in the sentence
    // Display each complete word, then remove it from the sentence

    int startPos, endPos;
    string wholeWord;

    do
    {
        // Display remaining sentence
        cout << "Sentence: " << sentence << endl;

        // Find start of word
        // (look for char that is not punctuation nor a space)
        startPos = sentence.find_first_not_of( ".,?! " );

        // If found start of word then look for end of word
        // (look for next char that is punctuation or is a space)
        if ( startPos >= 0 )
        {
            endPos = sentence.find_first_of( ".,?! ", startPos );

            // Create a substring out of the complete word
            wholeWord = sentence.substr( startPos, endPos-startPos );

            cout << "Word: " << wholeWord << endl << endl;

            // Erase the complete word from the sentence
            sentence.erase( 0, endPos );

        }   // end of if decision

    } while ( startPos >= 0 );

    return 0;
}
```

Below you can see the results that the program displays:

```
Sentence: Whoa! This has... like, er... words?
Word: Whoa

Sentence: This has... like, er... words?
Word: This

Sentence: has... like, er... words?
Word: has

Sentence: ... like, er... words?
Word: like

Sentence: , er... words?
Word: er

Sentence: ... words?
Word: words

Sentence:?
```

You should see that the program starts at the beginning of the sentence and isolates each individual word. After each word is displayed it is erased from the sentence and the remaining characters are displayed. This continues until no more words or alphabetical characters can be found in the **string** value.

Swapping the values of two **string** variables around

We have already seen earlier in the book how the values of two variables can be swapped around with the help of a third temporary variable.

If you have two different **string** variables in your code, you can swap their values using the **swap()** member function:

```
string firstCity = "Tacoma";
string secondCity = "Chicago";
firstCity.swap( secondCity );
```

This will take the value of **secondCity** and swap it with the value of **firstCity**.

Before swapping

firstCity `Tacoma`
secondCity `Chicago`

After swapping

firstCity `Chicago`
secondCity `Tacoma`

The program below shows the **swap()** function in action:

Example 8.34 – swap_whole_strings.cpp

```cpp
#include <iostream>      // Program will be using keyboard and screen

using namespace std;     // Will be using standard identifiers string, cout and endl

int main()
{
    string firstValue = "Tomato";

    string secondValue = "Ketchup";

    // Display both strings prior to swapping their values around

    cout << "The first value is originally " << firstValue << endl;

    cout << "The second value is originally " << secondValue << endl;


    cout << endl << endl;     // Display two blank lines


    firstValue.swap( secondValue );     // Swap the values of the string variables


    // Display both strings after swapping their values around

    cout << "The first value is now " << firstValue << endl;

    cout << "The second value is now " << secondValue << endl;


    return 0;
}
```

Note that the code above does not need to make use of a temporary variable when swapping the values.

You should see the following results at run-time:

```
The first value is originally Tomato
The second value is originally Ketchup


The first value is now Ketchup
The second value is now Tomato
```

Here's what we have covered in this chapter:

Character symbols and ASCII codes can be stored and used interchangeably using the **char** data-type.

A single literal character value should always be enclosed between a pair of ' single quotes.

A sequence of zero or more characters can be stored as a **string** value. To use this data-type, you usually need to include the **<string>** library in your program code.

A literal **string** value should be enclosed between a pair of " double quotation marks.

The **length()** function returns the number of characters that a **string** value contains, including any spaces.

The **at()** function obtains a single character from a **string** value. It checks that the index that you give it is within the bounds of the **string** and reports an error if the index is out-of-bounds (too large or too small).

Several functions allow you to determine whether or not a character is a **control character**, a **printable character**, a **numeric digit**, a **letter of the alphabet**, a **punctuation mark** or some other kind of symbol. These include **isprint()**, **iscntrl()**, **isdigit()**, **isalpha()**, **islower()**, **isupper()**, **ispunct()** and **isspace()**.

In the case of an **alpha-character**, the **toupper()** function converts a letter to upper-case. The **tolower()** function converts a letter to lower-case. Non-alpha characters are unaffected by these functions. Both **toupper()** and **tolower()** are part of the **<cctype>** library.

Characters and text strings can be **appended** (joined on to the end of) a **string** value using the **+** or **+=** operators. You may also use the **append()** function to join **string** values together.

The **substr()** function obtains a **portion** of a **string** value (a **sub-string**). You can control how large this portion is and where it is to be found in the original value.

Starting from the beginning of a **string** value, the **find()** function **searches for a particular sub-string** to check whether it can be found. If found, it returns the index of where the sub-string first occurs.

The **rfind()** function is similar, but begins searching from the **end** of the **string**, working towards the beginning.

The **replace()** function will replace part of a **string** value with characters from a second **string** that you specify. You can control which part of the original **string** is to be replaced.

The **insert()** function adds the characters from one **string** value into another **string** at a particular place.

The **erase()** function can be used to **remove** part of a **string** value. You can control which part of the original value is to be removed.

The function **find_first_of()** scans through a **string** value from beginning to end, looking for the first character that can be found from a particular set of characters that you have specified. If successful, the function returns the index of the first such character that has been found.

The function **find_first_not_of()** will give you the index of the first character that is found in a **string** value that is **not** part of a particular set of characters that you are interested in.

Problems and exercises for you to try

1.	Create a program that repeatedly asks you to enter individual characters, one at a time.
	Append each character to a **string** value and display it on the screen, before allowing you to type in the next character.
2.	Write a program that chooses two different letters at random from a **string** value and swaps them around.
	Repeat this process several times to create several anagrams of the original **string** value.
3.	Write a program that replaces numeric digits with their names.
	For instance, **"Easy as 1, 2, 3!"** would become **"Easy as one, two, three!"**
4.	Create a program that allows you to type in a simple word.
	The program should then capitalise each letter and insert a hyphen, as long as it is not the last letter in the word.
	For instance, **"cheese"** would become **"C-H-E-E-S-E"**.

Chapter 9:
Arrays of data

Working with several data values that have the same data-type

If you want to store many different things in the computer's memory, you could use lots of different variables.

For example, here are four variables from a game that allows different people to play against each other:

```
int player1Score = 0;
int player2Score = 0;
int player3Score = 0;
int player4Score = 0;
```

Notice that each of the four variables stores a whole number: an `int` value. They also have very similar names.

Here is another example of how you could store five separate items of `string` data:

```
string firstDay = "Monday";
string secondDay = "Tuesday";
string thirdDay = "Wednesday";
string fourthDay = "Thursday";
string fifthDay = "Friday";
```

Again, all of the items above are similar. They all have the same kind of data: they are all `string` values. Even their variable names follow a predictable pattern (you can probably guess that the next variable might be called `"sixthDay"`).

What is an array?

An **"array"** is a method of organising your data. It is a kind of **"data-structure"** which organises lots of data values together in a consistent way so that you can use them easily.

If you have lots of similar things, instead of making many different variables, you can **group** different values together. The group of values can be given one single **name** e.g. `playerScores`.

Each value in the array is given a **number**, called an **"index"**. This helps you to find the data value again when you want to use it. The index value tells you **where** in the array the data value is located. The index number is always written in between a pair of [ ] square brackets.

Here is a way to store the days of the week described in the example above, but using a single array that holds all of the various values together:

"**dayName**" an array of `string` values

Item number (index)	Data-value
0	Monday
1	Tuesday
2	Wednesday
3	Thursday
4	Friday

A word of warning! When you want to create and use an array, you should always make sure that all of the items of data in the array have the same data-type e.g. `string` or `int`. You cannot mix different data-types in the same array.

Creating a simple array of values

Here is how you could make an array to hold the scores for the four players of the game:

```
int playerScore[4];
```

This means that an array of exactly **4** different **int** values will be created. The array is called **"playerScore"**.

The **first** item in the array can be accessed using **playerScore[0]**.

The **last** item in the array (the fourth item) can be accessed using **playerScore[3]**.

Example 9.1 – array_scores.cpp

```
int main()
{
    // Create array of scores for each of the 4 players
    int playerScore[4];

    // Set starting scores at beginning of the game
    playerScore[0] = 0;
    playerScore[1] = 0;
    playerScore[2] = 0;
    playerScore[3] = 0;


    return 0;
}
```

Using index numbers to refer to the values in an array

In C++, the index numbers for arrays do **not** begin with 1, they begin with 0.

We say that C++ arrays are **"zero-indexed"**.

This is why the first item always has the index **0**.

In an array that holds *n* items, the last item always has an index that is *n - 1*.

Using the above rule, the score of the **third** player will be stored at position **2** in the array at **playerScore[2]**.

The example below would display the **fourth** item from the array that is called **playerScore**.

```
cout << playerScore[3];
```

Remember that the **first** item, the score for the first player, has the index **0** in the array. Because the index begins at zero, the **fourth** item in the array will have the index **3**.

You can also **set** (or "**assign**") data values to items in the array. Armed with the array name and an index value, you can use an array item in the same way that you would normally use a simple variable:

```
playerScore[3] = 0;        // Set the value of 4th array item to 0

playerScore[2] += 100;     // Add 100 to the value of the 3rd array item
```

Accessing an individual value from an array

Here is another example of how you could create an array to hold the names of the days of the working week:

```
string dayName[5];
```

This means that an array of **5** different **string** values will be created. Whilst the array will be called "**dayName**".

The **first** item in the array can be accessed using **dayName[0]**.

The **last** item in the array (the fifth item) can be accessed as **dayName[4]**.

Example 9.2 – array_days.cpp

```cpp
#include <string>      // Program will be using an array of string values

using namespace std;     // Will be using standard string identifier

int main()
{
    // Create array for the days of the working week
    string dayName[5];

    // Set the name of each day
    dayName[0] = "Monday";
    dayName[1] = "Tuesday";
    dayName[2] = "Wednesday";
    dayName[3] = "Thursday";
    dayName[4] = "Friday";

    return 0;
}
```

In the above example, the name of the **fourth** day is stored at **dayName[3]**.

To display the name of the first day of the week ("**Monday**") and the last day of the week ("**Friday**") you could use:

```
cout << dayName[0];     // Display the first item in the array
cout << dayName[4];     // Display the last item in the array
```

Using a loop to efficiently access more than one value in an array

It is possible to write a separate statement to access each individual item in an array:

```
cout << dayName[0] << endl;
cout << dayName[1] << endl;
cout << dayName[2] << endl;
cout << dayName[3] << endl;
cout << dayName[4] << endl;
```

This code is very simple, but is also very repetitive. It would not be very efficient if you had a very large array that holds a lot of data. An array that contains a thousand items would require a thousand lines of code to access all of the data that it holds.

Alternatively, a loop can be used to access or change more than one value in an array using only a few lines of code. Using arrays in conjunction with loops can make your program code much shorter. You don't need to write similar lines of code again and again in your program. By making use of a loop, the same statement or block of statements can be used repeatedly to access the items in an array and to carry out some processing on them.

The code below shows this more efficient way of displaying the days of the week. It uses a **for** loop to control the index to the array. The loop repeatedly executes a single statement to find out what is stored in each place in the array, displaying the data value as a line of text on the screen:

```
for ( int index = 0;  index < 5;  index++ )
    cout << dayName[index] << endl;
```

The code begins with a value of **0** for the integer **index** variable. It uses this to access the first item in the **dayName** array, which is **dayName[0]**.

Each iteration of the **for** loop increases the value of **index** by 1, thus it accesses **dayName[0]**, then **dayName[1]**, then **dayName[2]**, and so on.

The loop continues to execute as long as the value of **index** is less than **5**. It then terminates once **5** has been reached. This means that the last array item to be accessed and displayed is **dayName[4]**.

This next example could be used to set up initial starting values for each item in the array so that they are all the same:

```
for ( int index = 0;  index < 4;  index++ )
    playerScore[index] = 0;
```

Below is a program that uses the loop-based approach described on the previous page to assign and display an array of four player scores:

```cpp
#include <iostream>      // Program will be displaying some text on the screen

using namespace std;     // Will be using standard identifiers cout and endl

int main()
{
    // Create array of scores for each of the 4 players
    int playerScore[4];

    int index;  // This index will be used by both loops to access the array


    // Set scores at beginning of the game
    for ( index = 0;  index < 4;  index++ )
        playerScore[index] = 0;


    // Display scores
    for ( index = 0;  index < 4;  index++ )
    {
        cout << "Player " << index;
        cout << " has score " << playerScore[index] << endl;
    }


    return 0;
}
```

Here is what is displayed on the screen when the program runs:

```
Player 0 has score 0
Player 1 has score 0
Player 2 has score 0
Player 3 has score 0
```

This next program uses an array of **string** values to repeatedly display a simple ASCII graphic. Each line of the picture is held as an item in the array and gets displayed three times, using different colours.

Example 9.4 – array_face.cpp

```cpp
#include <iostream>      // Program will be displaying some text on the screen

using namespace std;     // Will be using standard identifiers string, cout and endl

int main()
{
    // Create an array of strings to hold the graphic
    string faceLine[5];

    faceLine[0] = "+-----+";
    faceLine[1] = "| O O |";
    faceLine[2] = "|  @  |";
    faceLine[3] = "| === |";
    faceLine[4] = "+-----+";

    // Display 3 copies of the face alongside each other
    // each face will be a different colour
    int num = 0;
    while ( num < 5 )
    {
        cout << "\e[31m";     // Escape-sequence - colour red
        cout << faceLine[num];    // Display part of face

        cout << "\e[32m";     // Escape-sequence - colour green
        cout << faceLine[num];    // Display part of face

        cout << "\e[34m";     // Escape-sequence - colour blue
        cout << faceLine[num];    // Display part of face

        cout << endl;     // Move on to next line of screen

        num++;     // Move on to next line in the array of text strings

    }  // end of while loop

    // Finished drawing, reset colours back to normal for your screen
    cout << "\e[0m";   // 0m means reset

    return 0;
}
```

When executed, the loop displays each individual part of the face 3 times, side-by-side:

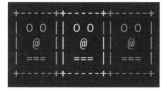

Similarly, this program will display all of the days of the week using only a single **cout** statement that is repeatedly executed by a **for** loop. The program then allows you to type in an index number, displaying the corresponding day from the array:

Example 9.5 – *array_access.cpp*

```cpp
#include <iostream>      // Program will be displaying some text on the screen

using namespace std;     // Will be using standard identifiers string, cin, cout, endl

int main()
{
    // Create array of days of the week
    string dayName[7];

    // Set the name of each day
    dayName[0] = "Monday";
    dayName[1] = "Tuesday";
    dayName[2] = "Wednesday";
    dayName[3] = "Thursday";
    dayName[4] = "Friday";
    dayName[5] = "Saturday";
    dayName[6] = "Sunday";

    // Display the names of the days of the week
    cout << "These are the days of the week:" << endl;

    for ( int index = 0;  index < 7;  index++ )
        cout << index << '\t' << dayName[index] << endl;

    // Type in the day number
    int dayNumber;
    cout << "Now please type in a number between 0 and 6" << endl;
    cin >> dayNumber;

    // Display the corresponding day of the week using the number
    cout << "This is " << dayName[dayNumber] << endl;

    return 0;
}
```

First of all, the **for** loop displays each of the days in the array, from **dayName[0]** to **dayName[6]**.

On typing the value **3** the program then displays the text that is stored in **dayName[3]**:

```
These are the days of the week:
0       Monday
1       Tuesday
2       Wednesday
3       Thursday
4       Friday
5       Saturday
6       Sunday
Now please type in a number between 0 and 6
3
This is Thursday
```

Going too far: attempting to use an index that is out-of-bounds

Remember that in the previous *Example 9.5 - array_access.cpp* program, the maximum index value that could be used for the **dayName** array was **6** (which corresponded to the seventh item of data - the last item in the array).

Try running the program again and then typing in an index value that is out of bounds, such as **7**, or **999**. You can even try a negative number.

What happens? Your Pi should display the following message:

> ```
> Segmentation fault
> ```

This is a technical term which means your program has tried to access some memory that it was not supposed to.

In short, you should never try to access an item in an array that does not exist. The index value must not be too small or too large. It must correspond to an item of data that really exists in the array.

A better approach would be to **validate** the index number that the user has typed in. The program code could check that any index number that you type in is not less than the index of the first data item in the array, and also that it is not larger than the index value of the last data item in the array:

Example of validation to prevent a segmentation fault

```cpp
// Type in the day number
int dayNumber;
cout << "Now please type in a number between 0 and 6" << endl;
cin >> dayNumber;

// Check whether the day number is too small or too large
// If so, the number cannot be used as an index for the array
// as it would cause a segmentation fault
if ( ( dayNumber < 0 ) or ( dayNumber > 6 ) )
    cout << "This is not an acceptable number!" << endl;
else
{
    // This is an acceptable index number so
    // display the corresponding day of the week
    cout << "This is " << dayName[dayNumber] << endl;
}
```

If we were to modify *Example 9.5 - array_access.cpp* to include this check, the program would be able to cope with both valid and invalid data:

```
Now please type in a number between 0 and 6
-1
This is not an acceptable number!
```

```
Now please type in a number between 0 and 6
7
This is not an acceptable number!
```

This next example uses an array to store the names of the planets in the solar system. It creates an array of eight **string** values, called **planetName**. The names of the planets are stored one-by-one in this array. The program then uses a simple **for** loop to display the name of each planet.

Note that both the array declaration and the **for** loop make use of a constant called **NUM_PLANETS**, which has the value 8. This makes it a little easier to understand what is going on when you read the code. It also ensures that all parts of the program consistently access or search through the correct number of items in the array.

Example 9.6 – *array_planets.cpp*

```cpp
#include <iostream>      // Program will be displaying some text on the screen

using namespace std;     // Will be using standard identifiers string, cout and endl

int main()
{
    // Create array of planets

    const int NUM_PLANETS = 8;

    string planetName[NUM_PLANETS];

    // Store the name of each planet in the array
    planetName[0] = "Mercury";
    planetName[1] = "Venus";
    planetName[2] = "Earth";
    planetName[3] = "Mars";
    planetName[4] = "Jupiter";
    planetName[5] = "Saturn";
    planetName[6] = "Uranus";
    planetName[7] = "Neptune";


    // Display position and name of planet
    for ( int index = 0;  index < NUM_PLANETS;  index++ )
    {
        cout << "Planet number " << index << " is ";
        cout << planetName[index] << endl;

    }  // end of for loop

    return 0;
}
```

You should see these results on the screen:

```
Planet number 0 is Mercury
Planet number 1 is Venus
Planet number 2 is Earth
Planet number 3 is Mars
Planet number 4 is Jupiter
Planet number 5 is Saturn
Planet number 6 is Uranus
Planet number 7 is Neptune
```

I haven't forgotten Pluto – it's a "dwarf-planet", rather than a "real" planet. Sorry Pluto.

Recording raw data from user inputs using arrays

This program allows the user to record the scores for a 200m running race. As each person reaches the finishing line, their time in seconds is entered into the computer. The times are recorded in an array of **float** values, called **raceTime**.

Example 9.7 – array_times.cpp

```cpp
#include <iostream>    // Program will be displaying some text on the screen

using namespace std;    // Will be using standard identifiers cin, cout, endl

int main()
{
    const int MAX_RUNNERS = 9;  // Maximum 9 lanes on standard running track

    float raceTime[MAX_RUNNERS];  // Records finish time in seconds for each runner

    // Make every time in the array start with the value 0
    int index = 0;
    while ( index < MAX_RUNNERS )
    {
        raceTime[index] = 0;
        index++;
    }  // end of while loop

    // Store times for runners as they finish
    // Stop when reaching maximum number of runners or when enter 0
    int runnersFinished = 0;

    float seconds;

    do
    {
        cout << "Type in a finish time: (or 0 if all runners finished) ";
        cin >> seconds;

        if ( seconds > 0 )
        {
            raceTime[runnersFinished] = seconds;
            runnersFinished++;
        }  // if seconds decision

    } while ( ( seconds > 0 ) and ( runnersFinished < MAX_RUNNERS) );


    // Display the fastest and the slowest times
    cout << endl << endl;
    cout << "SUMMARY OF RESULTS" << endl;

    cout << "Fastest time: ";
    cout << raceTime[0];
    cout << " seconds" << endl;
```

continues on next page...

```
    cout << "Slowest time: ";
    cout << raceTime[runnersFinished-1];
    cout << " seconds" << endl;

    // Display list of all finish times, starting with the fastest
    cout << "HERE ARE THE TIMES" << endl;

    index = 0;
    while ( index < runnersFinished )
    {
        cout << "Runner in position " << index + 1;
        cout << " - time " << raceTime[index] << " seconds" << endl;
        index++;
    }


    return 0;
}
```

The program allows you to enter times for up to nine different runners (this is how many lanes there are on a running track). Each of these times is typed in as a floating-point number until a time for every runner has been entered. Typing 0 as a time indicates to the computer that there are no more times to enter for any other runners.

Here's what my Pi displayed when I typed in some data for four runners:

```
Type in a finish time: (or 0 if all runners finished) 8.25
Type in a finish time: (or 0 if all runners finished) 10.3
Type in a finish time: (or 0 if all runners finished) 12.7
Type in a finish time: (or 0 if all runners finished) 17.5
Type in a finish time: (or 0 if all runners finished) 0


SUMMARY OF RESULTS
Fastest time: 8.25 seconds
Slowest time: 17.5 seconds
HERE ARE THE THE TIMES
Runner in position 1 - time 8.25 seconds
Runner in position 2 - time 10.3 seconds
Runner in position 3 - time 12.7 seconds
Runner in position 4 - time 17.5 seconds
```

Each finishing time is stored in an array of floating point values called **raceTime**. The program uses the variable **runnersFinished** to keep count of how many non-zero times were entered, checking that the value of this does not exceed the maximum number of runners allowed.

After all of the finish times have been entered, the program displays the fastest time, which it assumes was the first to be entered. This first finish time will have been stored at position 0 in the **raceTime** array, hence it displays the value of **raceTime[0]**.

It now uses the value of **runnersFinished** to determine the last time that was entered, which is stored at position **runnersFinished-1** in the **raceTime** array, hence the value of **raceTime[runnersFinished-1]** is displayed.

Finally, the program displays a list of all of the finishing times, using a **while** loop to iterate through and display each value that has been stored in the **raceTime** array.

Categorising or counting up user inputs using arrays

Here is a re-written version of the **Example 7.21 - count_votes.cpp** example from *"Chapter 7: Repetition using loops"* that determines the most popular choice of take-away food. Instead of using three different variables to store the number of choices for each kind of food, the program uses an array of integer values.

Example 9.8 – array_votes.cpp

```cpp
#include <iostream>     // Program will be displaying some text on the screen

using namespace std;    // Will be using standard identifiers string, cin, cout, endl

int main()
{
    const int NUM_OPTIONS = 3;

    string name[NUM_OPTIONS];

    name[0] = "Pizza";
    name[1] = "Balti-Curry";
    name[2] = "Thai-Noodles";

    int totalChosen[NUM_OPTIONS];
    int index;

    // Make each food start with zero choices
    for ( index = 0;  index < NUM_OPTIONS;  index++ )
        totalChosen[index] = 0;

    // Loop to type in a letter for each food and count up totals
    char choice;
    do
    {
        cout << "Type in a choice: p c n (or * to quit)" << endl;
        cin >> choice;

        switch ( choice )
        {
            case 'p': case 'P':    totalChosen[0]++;    break;
            case 'c': case 'C':    totalChosen[1]++;    break;
            case 'n': case 'N':    totalChosen[2]++;    break;
        }   // End of switch statement

    } while ( choice not_eq '*' );    // Typing * terminates the loop

    // Display the results after all votes have been typed in
    cout << endl << "RESULTS TIME" << endl;

    for ( index = 0;  index < NUM_OPTIONS;  index++ )
        cout << name[index] << " = " << totalChosen[index] << endl;

    return 0;
}
```

Below is an example of some test data being typed into the program:

```
Type in a choice: p c n (or * to quit)
c
Type in a choice: p c n (or * to quit)
c
Type in a choice: p c n (or * to quit)
p
Type in a choice: p c n (or * to quit)
n
Type in a choice: p c n (or * to quit)
p
Type in a choice: p c n (or * to quit)
c
Type in a choice: p c n (or * to quit)
*

RESULTS TIME
Pizza = 2
Balti-Curry = 3
Thai-Noodles = 1
```

The array that holds the number of choices for each kind of takeaway is called **totalChosen**. At the start of the program, each item in the array is set to the value **0** using a simple **for** loop, before we begin counting each of the choices that the user types in.

The main work is carried out by the **do-while** loop, which repeatedly asks the user to type in a single character to indicate their choice of takeaway - either **'p'**, **'c'** or **'n'**. A **switch** statement determines which (if any) of these characters was entered, updating the relevant item in the **totalChosen** array.

Once the user types **'*'** the **do-while** loop terminates. The program will then display the value from each item in the **totalChosen** array using a second **for** loop.

Searching through an array of data values to find what you want: a linear search

We can search through an array to find a particular item of data. The program below allows you to search through our **planetName** array for a particular planet to check that it exists. It begins with the first item in the array (at position **0**), comparing the item to the search target that the user wants to find. If the two match then the name of the planet is displayed on the screen. Otherwise, the search moves on to the next item in the array until reaching the end. Because the search uses a **while** loop, it will only continue searching until the item is found, at which point the loop terminates. This means that it does not continue searching right up to the end of the array unless it is absolutely necessary. This kind of search is called a **"linear search"** as it proceeds in a straight-line from the first data item in the array towards the last.

Example 9.9 – array_search_item.cpp

```cpp
#include <iostream>     // Program will be displaying some text on the screen

using namespace std;    // Will be using standard identifiers string, cin, cout, endl

int main()
{
    // Create array of planets
    const int NUM_PLANETS = 8;

    string planetName[NUM_PLANETS];
```

continues on next page...

```
      // Store the name of each planet in the array
      planetName[0] = "Mercury";
      planetName[1] = "Venus";
      planetName[2] = "Earth";
      planetName[3] = "Mars";
      planetName[4] = "Jupiter";
      planetName[5] = "Saturn";
      planetName[6] = "Uranus";
      planetName[7] = "Neptune";

      // Decide which planet to search for
      cout << "Which planet are you searching for?" << endl;
      string searchTarget;
      cin >> searchTarget;

      // Search to determine whether the planet exists in the array
      bool found = false;
      int index = 0;
      while ( ( not found ) and ( index < NUM_PLANETS ) )
      {
          if ( searchTarget == planetName[index] )
          {
              cout << "Planet number " << index;
              cout << " in the array is " << planetName[index] << endl;
              found = true;   // This terminates the search once found
          }  // end of if decision

          index++;
      }  // end of while loop

      // Report whether the planet could be found successfully in the array
      if ( not found )
          cout << "No matching planet found" << endl;

      return 0;
}
```

If you try to search for a non-existent planet, the program will tell you that it can't find it:

```
Which planet are you searching for?
Rasperrian-VI
No matching planet found
```

This is what happened however when I searched for **Saturn**:

```
Which planet are you searching for?
Saturn
Planet number 5 in the array is Saturn
```

Be aware that the program will only find an **exact** match, including the case of each letter. To successfully find **Saturn**, the search value must be spelled with a capital **S** and not a lower-case **s**. The program could be improved by making it less fussy when comparing the search value with each array value. *"Chapter 10: Functions"* includes an example of how you could convert entire **string** values to upper or lower-case to help you do this.

Searching through an array of data values to find a partial match

The previous example searched through the array of planets to find an **exact** match. It compared the name of each planet with the search target to determine whether the two values were exactly the same.

This next program searches for a **partial** match rather than a **complete** match. It will find any planet that **begins with** a particular letter. To do this, the program examines the first letter of each `string` value in the array of planet names, one by one. If the first letter matches the letter that you are searching for, then the name of the planet gets displayed on the screen.

The search code uses the following `if` decision:

```
if ( planetName[index].at( 0 ) == searchLetter )
```

The `if` decision above checks whether the first letter of the current planet name is the same as the letter that the user has typed in as a search value.

> `planetName[index]` is the current planet name being examined in the loop.
>
> `.at( 0 )` obtains the first letter, which is at position `0` in the current planet name.

Example 9.10 – array_search_first_letter.cpp

```cpp
#include <iostream>      // Program will be displaying some text on the screen

using namespace std;     // Will be using standard identifiers string, cin, cout, endl

int main()
{
    // Create array of planets
    const int NUM_PLANETS = 8;

    string planetName[NUM_PLANETS];

    // Set values for name of each planet
    planetName[0] = "Mercury";
    planetName[1] = "Venus";
    planetName[2] = "Earth";
    planetName[3] = "Mars";
    planetName[4] = "Jupiter";
    planetName[5] = "Saturn";
    planetName[6] = "Uranus";
    planetName[7] = "Neptune";

    // Find out which letter to search for
    cout << "What letter does the planet begin with?" << endl;
    char searchLetter;
    cin >> searchLetter;
```

continues on next page...

```
    // Search for planets that begin with the search letter
    cout << "SEARCHING..." << endl;

    int resultsFound = 0;
    for ( int index = 0;  index < NUM_PLANETS;  index++ )
    {

        if ( planetName[index].at( 0 ) == searchLetter )
        {
            cout << planetName[index] << endl;
            resultsFound++;
        }  // end of if decision


    }  // end of for loop


    // Display the number of matching planets that were found
    cout << resultsFound << " planets found" << endl;



    return 0;
}
```

Below you can see an example of a search carried out on my Pi. When asked to find planets that begin with "M", the program first finds **Mercury** at position 0 in the **planetName** array. Even once a match has been found, the **for** loop continues searching, subsequently finding **Mars** at position 3 in the array:

```
What letter does the planet begin with?
M
SEARCHING...
Mercury
Mars
2 planets found
```

When asked to find a planet beginning with the letter "T", the **for** loop fails to find any such planet. Once it has finished searching through all items in the **planetName** array, the program reports that no planets have been found that begin with this letter:

```
What letter does the planet begin with?
T
SEARCHING...
0 planets found
```

How to pick something at random from an array of values

As with previous examples, the program below uses the `%` **modulus operator** when picking a random number. The random number is used as an index to the array of possible greetings. The appropriate **string** value from the **greeting** array is then displayed on the screen, along with the name that the user typed in.

Example 9.11 – array_random.cpp

```cpp
#include <iostream>    // Program will be using keyboard and screen
#include <cstdlib>     // Program uses the random() and srandom() functions
#include <ctime>       // Program uses the time() function as the random seed

using namespace std;    // Will be using standard identifiers string, cin, cout, endl

int main()
{
    cout << "Please type in your name..." << endl;
    string name;
    cin >> name;

    // Makes an array that holds 5 strings
    const int NUM_GREETINGS = 5;
    string greeting[NUM_GREETINGS];

    greeting[0] = "Hello";
    greeting[1] = "Bonjour";
    greeting[2] = "Hola";
    greeting[3] = "Top o' the morning to you";
    greeting[4] = "Howdy";

    srandom( time( 0 ) );    // Seed the random number generator using current time

    int choice = random() % NUM_GREETINGS;    // Pick random number between 0 and 4

    cout << greeting[choice];    // Use it to display greeting

    cout << " " << name << endl;    // Display the person's name

    return 0;
}
```

As you can see, each time that I ran the program on my Pi, it gave a different result:

```
Please type in your name...
Alonso
Bonjour Alonso
```

```
Please type in your name...
Alonso
Howdy Alonso
```

```
Please type in your name...
Hurdy-Gurdy-Man
Top o' the morning to you Hurdy-Gurdy-Man
```

Example 9.12 – array_smileys.cpp

```cpp
#include <iostream>    // Program will be displaying some text on the screen
#include <cstdlib>    // Program uses the random() and srandom() functions
#include <ctime>     // Program uses the time() function as the random seed

using namespace std;     // Will be using standard identifiers string, cout and endl

int main()
{
    // Define how many different kinds of eyes, noses and mouths there are
    const int POSSIBLE_EYES = 3;
    const int POSSIBLE_NOSES = 2;
    const int POSSIBLE_MOUTHS = 3;

    // Define all the possibilities for eyes
    string eyes[POSSIBLE_EYES];
    eyes[0] = ":";
    eyes[1] = ";";
    eyes[2] = ">:";

    // Define all the possibilities for a nose
    string nose[POSSIBLE_NOSES];
    nose[0] = "-";
    nose[1] = "O";

    // Define all the possibilities for mouth
    string mouth[POSSIBLE_MOUTHS];
    mouth[0] = ")";
    mouth[1] = "]";
    mouth[2] = "|";

    srandom( time( 0 ) );    // Seed the random number generator

    // Create and display 10 smileys at random
    int choice;
    for ( int face = 0;  face < 10;  face++ )
    {
        choice = random() % POSSIBLE_EYES;    // Pick a number between 0 and 3
        cout << eyes[choice];    // Display the eyes using this number

        choice = random() % POSSIBLE_NOSES;    // Pick a number between 0 and 2
        cout << nose[choice];    // Display the nose using this number

        choice = random() % POSSIBLE_MOUTHS;    // Pick a number between 0 and 3
        cout << mouth[choice];    // Display the mouth using this number

        cout << endl << endl;    // Display blank line after each completed face
    }  // end of for loop

    return 0;
}
```

Matching related items from more than one array

Here is a program that uses two different arrays to store the names and populations of several cities.

The names of the cities are stored in an array of **string** values, called **cityName**.

The population for each city is stored in an array of **int** values, called **population**.

When using more than one array to store different kinds of data about things, if you organise your array values in a consistent way, you can use the same index number to access several related items of data from the different arrays.

For instance, everything to do with the city of Paris has the index value **1**. The name **"Paris"** is found at **cityName[1]**, the corresponding population of Paris is stored in **population[1]**.

Example 9.13 – related_arrays.cpp

```cpp
#include <iostream>      // Program will be displaying some text on the screen

using namespace std;     // Will be using standard identifiers string, cout and endl

int main()
{
    // Create array of city names
    const int NUM_CITIES = 3;
    string cityName[NUM_CITIES];

    // Set values for city names
    cityName[0] = "London";
    cityName[1] = "Paris";
    cityName[2] = "New York";

    // Create array of populations
    float population[NUM_CITIES];

    // Set values for populations
    population[0] = 8.6;
    population[1] = 2.2;
    population[2] = 8.4;

    // Display name of a city and population
    cout << cityName[1];

    cout << " has ";

    cout << population[1];

    cout << " million residents." << endl;


    return 0;
}
```

An array of arguments – passing input values to a program when you run it.

When working at the command-line, many Linux commands take one or more values as input. Build the program below, calling it "***newcommand***".

Example 9.14 – program_arguments.cpp

```
#include <iostream>      // Program will be displaying some text on the screen

using namespace std;     // Will be using standard identifiers cout and endl

int main( int argc, char *argv[] )
{
    cout << "Here are the arguments that I gave the program:" << endl;

    for ( int index = 1;  index < argc;  index++ )
    {
        cout << "Argument number " << index << " is... ";
        cout << argv[index] << endl;
    }

    return 0;
}
```

Note: In the program above `*argv[]` means an array of C-style character strings - the convention for programs that take arguments at the command-line.

Once built, you can run the executable from the command-line, giving it several arguments. For instance, try the following:

```
./newcommand yellow red blue
```

This should produce the output:

```
Here are the arguments that I gave the program:
Argument number 0 is... yellow red blue
Argument number 1 is... yellow
Argument number 2 is... red
Argument number 3 is... blue
```

Notice that argument `0` in the **argv** array of C-style character strings always automatically holds the complete list of all arguments that you supply to the program. Each single argument that you type in is held using the remaining items in the **argv** array from item **1** onwards.

This technique could be used by a program to control the way that it behaves at run-time. For instance, a program could search through a list of music tracks to find all songs by a particular artist before or after a certain date:

```
findsongs Motorhead before 1981
findsongs Trio
findsongs "The Ramones" after 1977
```

In the examples on the previous page, the same program (called "***findsongs***") can search for different music depending upon the argument values that you supply when you run it, such as the name of the artist or band.

Here is a program that will allow you type in a list of values as arguments when it is executed from the command-line. The program will choose one of the argument values at random.

For instance, assuming that you build the program with the filename "***pick***", you could type:

```
./pick strawberry chocolate vanilla
```

The program would randomly pick one of the arguments that you supplied: **strawberry**, **chocolate** or **vanilla**.

The code determines the number of values that you have supplied by examining the standard variable **argc** (which means "**argument count**"). Once it knows how many arguments have been supplied to the program, the computer picks a random number between **1** and this number. This is used as an index into the **argv** array of C-style character strings that holds the argument text values.

Example 9.15 – pick.cpp

```cpp
#include <iostream>     // Program will be displaying some text on the screen
#include <cstdlib>      // Program uses the random() and srandom() functions
#include <ctime>       // Program uses the time() function as the random seed

using namespace std;    // Will be using standard identifiers cout and endl

int main( int argc, char *argv[] )
{
    const int NUM_ARGUMENTS = argc - 1;  // Find how many arguments were supplied

    cout << "No. of arguments supplied to program by user: ";
    cout << NUM_ARGUMENTS << endl;

    // If any arguments were supplied when running the program then display them
    // and pick one at random (ignore arg[0] as this stores list of all arguments)
    if ( argc > 1 )
    {
        // Have some arguments (other than the program name) so display them
        for ( int index = 1;  index < argc;  index++ )
            cout << "argv[" << index << "] = " << argv[index] << endl;

        // Now generate a random number to use an an index for the argv array
        srandom( time( 0 ) );  // seed random number generator
        int choice = 1 + random() % ( NUM_ARGUMENTS );  // Choose random index

        // Use the randomly chosen index to display the corresponding argument
        cout << "I have chosen ";
        cout << argv[choice];
        cout << " from the " << NUM_ARGUMENTS << " arguments supplied" << endl;
    }
    else
        cout << "No arguments supplied - nothing to choose from!" << endl;

    return 0;
}
```

Below you can see the program in action:

```
pi@eno  ~ $ ls -l pick
-rwxr-xr-x 1 pi pi 7924 Aug 22 09:32 pick
pi@eno  ~ $ ./pick strawberry chocolate vanilla
No. of arguments supplied to program by user: 3
argv[1] = strawberry
argv[2] = chocolate
argv[3] = vanilla
I have chosen strawberry from the 3 arguments supplied
pi@eno  ~ $ ./pick Paris Berlin Rome Madrid
No. of arguments supplied to program by user: 4
argv[1] = Paris
argv[2] = Berlin
argv[3] = Rome
argv[4] = Madrid
I have chosen Rome from the 4 arguments supplied
pi@eno  ~ $
```

Inserting items of data into an array at a particular point

Unfortunately, when you want to add an item of data anywhere other than at the end of the array, it is necessary to make room for the new item. The process involves finding the place in the array where the new item is to be inserted and then copying all subsequent items one place lower down in the array. This "opens up" a space in the array to store the new item.

Example 9.16 – array_insert.cpp

```cpp
#include <iostream>     // Program will be displaying some text on the screen
#include <cstdlib>      // Program uses the random() srandom() exit() functions

using namespace std;    // Will be using standard identifiers string, cout and endl

int main()
{
    //Define the maximum number of items that the array will be able to hold
    const int MAX_ITEMS = 10;

    // Create array of city names
    string cityName[MAX_ITEMS];

    // Set values for city names
    cityName[0] = "London";
    cityName[1] = "Paris";
    cityName[2] = "New York";
    cityName[3] = "Berlin";
    cityName[4] = "Cardiff";
    cityName[5] = "Glasgow";
    cityName[6] = "Delhi";

    // These variables will be used to access items in the array
    unsigned int index;
    unsigned int itemsStoredInArray = 7;
```

continues on next page...

continued...

```cpp
    // Display the contents of the array
    for ( index = 0;  index < itemsStoredInArray;  index++ )
    {
        cout << "The item at position " << index;
        cout << " is " << cityName[index] << endl;
    }  // end of for
    cout << endl;

    // Allow user to choose where to insert the new city name
    cout << "Which index number would you like to use for the new city?" << endl;
    unsigned int placeToInsert;
    cin >> placeToInsert;
    cout << endl;

    // Check the array index is sensible
    if ( placeToInsert < 0  or  placeToInsert > itemsStoredInArray )
    {
        cout << "This index is not valid." << endl;
        exit( 1 );
    }  // end of if

    // Copy the bottom items to one place below in the array
    cout << "Making room for new item to be inserted." << endl;
    for ( index = itemsStoredInArray;  index > placeToInsert;  index-- )
        cityName[index] = cityName[index-1];

    itemsStoredInArray++;

    // Redisplay the contents of the array
    for ( index = 0;  index < itemsStoredInArray;  index++ )
    {
        cout << "The item at position " << index;
        cout << " is now " << cityName[index] << endl;
    }  // end of for
    cout << endl;

    // Store new city name where old item used to be
    cout << "Storing the new item in the array." << endl << endl;
    cityName[placeToInsert] = "Rome";

    // Redisplay the final contents of the array
    for ( index = 0;  index < itemsStoredInArray;  index++ )
    {
        cout << "The item at position " << index;
        cout << " is now " << cityName[index] << endl;
    }  // end of for
    cout << endl;

    return 0;
}
```

The insertion technique can be used to **sort** a collection of data values, adding them one-by-one to the appropriate place in the array. See *Example 10.15 - function_insertion_sort.cpp* in *"Chapter 10: Functions"* for an example of an **"insertion-sort"**.

Here is what happens when you choose to add the new data item somewhere in the middle of the array of values:

```
The item at position 0 is London
The item at position 1 is Paris
The item at position 2 is New York
The item at position 3 is Berlin
The item at position 4 is Cardiff
The item at position 5 is Glasgow
The item at position 6 is Delhi

Which index number would you like to use for the new city?
3

Making room for new item to be inserted.
The item at position 0 is now London
The item at position 1 is now Paris
The item at position 2 is now New York
The item at position 3 is now Berlin
The item at position 4 is now Berlin
The item at position 5 is now Cardiff
The item at position 6 is now Glasgow
The item at position 7 is now Delhi

Storing the new item in the array.

The item at position 0 is now London
The item at position 1 is now Paris
The item at position 2 is now New York
The item at position 3 is now Rome
The item at position 4 is now Berlin
The item at position 5 is now Cardiff
The item at position 6 is now Glasgow
The item at position 7 is now Delhi
```

The program also allows you to insert the new item either at the very beginning or the very end of the array, rather than in the middle:

```
Which index number would you like to use for the new city?
0

Making room for new item to be inserted.
The item at position 0 is now London
The item at position 1 is now London
The item at position 2 is now Paris
The item at position 3 is now New York
The item at position 4 is now Berlin
The item at position 5 is now Cardiff
The item at position 6 is now Glasgow
The item at position 7 is now Delhi

Storing the new item in the array.

The item at position 0 is now Rome
The item at position 1 is now London
The item at position 2 is now Paris
The item at position 3 is now New York
The item at position 4 is now Berlin
The item at position 5 is now Cardiff
The item at position 6 is now Glasgow
The item at position 7 is now Delhi
```

Multi-dimensional arrays

The array examples used so far have been straightforward numbered collections of similar items. Each item has used a simple data-type such as `int` or `string`. All of the items in each array have been of the **same** type.

Here is a reminder of the array used in our earlier program *Example 9.10 – array_search_first_letter.cpp*:

"`planetName`" an array of `string` values

Item number (index)	Data-value
0	Mercury
1	Venus
2	Earth
3	Mars
4	Jupiter
5	Saturn
6	Uranus
7	Neptune

You can see that the first item in the array is **Mercury** and it has the index **0**.

The next item in the array is **Venus**, which has the index **1**.

The line of items continues downwards until **Neptune**, which has the index **7**.

You can think of them as being items that are organised in a straight line that extends in one direction from their starting point (in this case, downwards). These kind of arrays are called "**one-dimensional arrays**".

Two-dimensional arrays

It is possible for arrays to spread out in two or more directions.

Arrays that spread out in more than one direction are called "**multi-dimensional arrays**".

Here is an example of an array to represent a game of noughts-and-crosses, played on a 3 x 3 grid:

"`grid`" an array of `char` values

Item number (index)	0	1	2
0	X		O
1		X	
2	O	O	X

As you can see, the array above spreads out in two different directions, across and down, thus it is called a "**two-dimensional**" or "**2D array**".

Creating and accessing a two-dimensional array

The example below stores and displays some noughts-and-crosses data using a two-dimensional array.

Each item in the array uses two different index numbers, with each index number being enclosed inside [ ] braces.

The first index number indicates the **row** number of the grid. The second number indicates the **column** number.

Example 9.17 – array_2d.cpp

```cpp
#include <iostream>    // Program will be displaying some text on the screen

using namespace std;    // Will be using standard identifiers cout and endl

int main()
{
    // 2D array to store positions of O and X symbols
    char grid[3][3];

    // Store the data of symbols, as in the example

    // Top row - row 0
    grid[0][0] = 'X';    // Row 0, Col 0
    grid[0][1] = ' ';    // Row 0, Col 1
    grid[0][2] = 'O';    // Row 0, Col 2

    // Middle row - row 1
    grid[1][0] = ' ';    // Row 1, Col 0
    grid[1][1] = 'X';    // Row 1, Col 1
    grid[1][2] = ' ';    // Row 1, Col 2

    // Bottom row - row 2
    grid[2][0] = 'O';    // Row 2, Col 0
    grid[2][1] = 'O';    // Row 2, Col 1
    grid[2][2] = 'X';    // Row 2, Col 2

    // Display the grid on the screen using loops to access the items
    int row, col;
    for ( row = 0;  row < 3;  row++ )
    {

        for ( col = 0;  col < 3;  col++ )
            cout << grid[row][col];

        cout << endl;  // Move on to new line at end of finished row

    }  // end of for loop for rows

    return 0;
}
```

This final program is a simple "treasure hunt" hit-or-miss game. Five locations are chosen at random on a 4 x 6 grid to hide the treasure. The user has to type in the row and column number for each location where they think that some treasure might have been hidden.

You can change the values of the constants **NUM_ROWS**, **NUM_COLS**, **NUM_LIVES** and **ITEMS_TO_BURY** to make the game easier or more difficult to win.

Example 9.18 – array_treasure_hunt.cpp

```cpp
#include <iostream>     // Program will be displaying some text on the screen
#include <cstdlib>      // Program uses the random() and srandom() functions
#include <ctime>        // Program uses the time() function as the random seed

using namespace std;    // Will be using standard identifiers cin, cout and endl

const int NUM_ROWS = 4;
const int NUM_COLS = 6;
const int NUM_LIVES = 5;
const int ITEMS_TO_BURY = 5;

int main()
{
    // 2D array to store possible locations of treasure
    char island[NUM_ROWS][NUM_COLS];

    int row, col;

    // Clear each location on the island so the whole array is "blank"
    for ( row = 0;  row < NUM_ROWS;  row++ )
        for ( col = 0;  col < NUM_COLS;  col++ )
            island[row][col] = '.';

    // Seed random number generator so that does not always select the same numbers
    srandom( time( 0 ) );

    // Hide some treasure in three random places
    int randomRow, randomCol;
    for ( int timesHidden = 0;  timesHidden < ITEMS_TO_BURY;  timesHidden++)
    {
        // Pick a random place on the island to hide some treasure
        randomRow = random() % NUM_ROWS;
        randomCol = random() % NUM_COLS;

        island[randomRow][randomCol] = 'X';

    }  // end of for loop

    cout << "TREASURE HUNT" << endl << endl;
```

continues on next page...

```cpp
    // Allow user to repeatedly guess a place where the treasure is hidden
    int rowGuessed, colGuessed;

    int guessesLeft = NUM_LIVES;

    while ( guessesLeft > 0 )
    {
      cout << "Which column across? 0-" << NUM_COLS-1 << ": ";
      cin >> colGuessed;

      cout << "Which row down? 0-" << NUM_ROWS-1 << ": ";
      cin >> rowGuessed;

      // Check whether any treasure is buried where the user guessed
      if ( island[rowGuessed][colGuessed] == 'X' )
      {
          // Mark the treasure as found
          cout << "Found some treasure at (";
          cout << colGuessed << ", " << rowGuessed << ")" << endl;
          island[rowGuessed][colGuessed] = 'F';
      }
      else
      {
          // No treasure at that spot - lose a life
          cout << "Nothing there." << endl;
          guessesLeft--;
      }  // end of if-else

      cout << endl;  // Display blank line after each guess

    }  // end of while loop

    // Game over
    cout << endl << "Out of guesses!" << endl << endl;

    // Display the grid on the screen using loops to access the items
    for ( row = 0;  row < NUM_ROWS;  row++ )
    {

        for ( col = 0;  col < NUM_COLS;  col++ )
            cout << island[row][col];

        cout << endl;  // Move on to new line at end of finished row

    }  // end of for loop for rows


    return 0;
}
```

The screenshot below shows one of the games that I played:

```
TREASURE HUNT

Which column across? 0-5: 4
Which row down? 0-3: 2
Nothing there.

Which column across? 0-5: 5
Which row down? 0-3: 3
Nothing there.

Which column across? 0-5: 1
Which row down? 0-3: 3
Nothing there.

Which column across? 0-5: 2
Which row down? 0-3: 3
Found some treasure at (2, 3)

Which column across? 0-5: 0
Which row down? 0-3: 0
Nothing there.

Which column across? 0-5: 5
Which row down? 0-3: 2
Nothing there.


Out of guesses!

......
...X.X
.X....
..F.X.
```

Note that at the end of the game, the program shows you where the undiscovered treasure was actually hidden (using '**X**') and all of the treasure that you successfully found (using '**F**').

Here's what we have covered in this chapter:

An "**array**" is a way to organise your data. It is a type of "**data-structure**". It groups numerous data values together in a consistent way so that you can use them easily.

The group of values has one single name, the **name** of the array.

All of the items of data stored in the array **must have the same data-type**, such as `int` or `string`.

A **one-dimensional array** is an array where the data items are organised in a straight line that extends in one direction from their starting point.

Arrays that spread out in more than one direction are called **multi-dimensional arrays**. A **two-dimensional array** spreads out in two-directions.

An individual item of data in an array can be **accessed** (examined or altered) using one or more **index numbers**. Each dimension in the array has an index.

Each index number is always written in between a pair of `[ ]` **square brackets**.

A one-dimensional array requires only one index number to identify and access a particular item of data.
e.g. `score[5]`

A two-dimensional array requires two index numbers, one for each dimension. The first index is the row number, the second index is the column number. The combination of these two indices allow any item of data in the two-dimensional array to be found and accessed.
e.g. `island[3][2]`

Arrays in C++ are "**zero-indexed**". The **first item** in an array has an index value of **zero**.
e.g. `planetName[0]`.

A loop can be used to efficiently access more than one item of data from an array, using the value of a variable as an index to the array.

You should take care not to use an index value that is **out-of-bounds**. Trying to access an array using an index value for which there is no corresponding item of data will cause a run-time error, such as when an index value is too large for the number of items in the array.

When running a C++ program from the command-line, the program can be passed one or more **arguments** as input from the command-line - items of data for it to use. To allow arguments to be passed in to your program, the convention is to specify that the `main()` function takes `argc` and `argv[]` as arguments.

Arguments to a program are always automatically stored in an array of C-style character strings called `argv[]`. Once running your program code can access the text values in this array.

The number of arguments supplied to your program is automatically stored using the `argc` integer variable. The value of `argc` indicates how many items in the `argv` array are available to use.

Problems and exercises for you to try

1.	Modify *Example 9.13 - related_arrays.cpp* so that it allows you to type in a whole number.
	The program will use this number as an index into the array of city names.
	It will tell you the name of the city that corresponds to the number that you typed in.
	If you type in a number that is either below zero or larger than the index of the last city, the program should tell you that the number was not a valid index.
2.	Write a program that creates a 10 x 10 grid of random digits between **0** and **9**.
	Display the contents of the grid on the screen.
3.	Create a program that contains an array of **20** integer values called `fibonacci`.
	Set the first and second items to the value **1**.
	Use a loop to set the value for each of the remaining values in the array.
	The value of each array item should be the sum of the previous two array items.
	For instance, the value of `fibonacci[6]` should be the result of adding `fibonacci[5]` to `fibonacci[4]`.
4.	Create a program that contains an array of **100** different `bool` values.
	Use a loop to set the value of each item to **true** if it has an index number that is exactly divisible by **5**.
	Run through the array and create a sum total for the **true** and **false** values.

Chapter 10:
Functions

What are functions?

In the early days of computing, many computer programs were a lot shorter and simpler than they are now. Programs were often comprised of only one single file of code, as with many of the examples in this book. Modern programs have become more and more sophisticated, containing more features and lines of code than ever before. Most programmers find it essential to split their programs up into different sections to make their code easier to understand.

One of the most common ways to organise your program code in this way is to use **functions**. Functions are very similar to **function machines** in mathematics – they are like machines that do useful jobs for you. A function is a named block of code to perform a certain task that can be activated by another part of your program.

We can create a function to perform each particular task that the program needs to carry out, such as to sort some data or save data to a file. Functions are incredibly important in creating programs that are easy to understand. They can also help you to find and correct errors in your code as they often help you to know where to start looking for a problem if your program does not work correctly.

Once created, other parts of your program can activate (or "**call**") the function code using the name that you have given it. A single function can be activated many times during the execution of a program, reducing the number of lines of program code needed. Using repeated calls to a function can significantly reduce the number of statements in your program.

Here is an example of a function that a program might use:

A function always needs to be given a **name**, to distinguish it from other parts of your program and to allow the function code to be activated from elsewhere. In the example above, the name of the function is `makeStringUpperCase`.

A function can be given some data to work with as **input**. It will then usually perform some sort of **processing** on the data, before giving you back a **result** as output. In the example above, the function `makeStringUpperCase()` is given a `string` value as input, the value `"Hello"`.

Many functions produce some sort of result as **output**, once they have finished execution. The function `makeStringUpperCase()` processes the original input value `"Hello"` and gives back a different `string` value as a result: `"HELLO"`.

We can activate the same `makeStringUpperCase()` function one or more times from elsewhere in our program code, giving it different `string` values as input each time to produce different results as output:

Repeatedly activating the same function code in this way means that we don't have to write several copies of the same code in our program. We write the function code **once**, then call it as many times as we need to. This usually leads to shorter C++ programs that contain fewer errors.

Creating a function in C++

How can we actually create such functions in C++?

First of all, when creating a function, we need to consider each of these things:

> The **name** of the function, which will be used to call it into action from other parts of our code.
>
> Any **inputs** that the function will need, including **what type of data each input has** and **the name of each input**.
>
> The **output – what type of data (if any) that will be returned** back to the calling code. At most, a function can only return one single value at a time.

We also need to create a **body** for the function. This is a block of C++ statements that will be executed each time that the function is called.

Below are some examples of functions, along with the arguments they take and the type of data that will be returned by each one. Each function includes a set of **{ }** curly braces to contain the body of the function that actually does the work. In these examples I have left the body of each function empty for now.

```cpp
// This function called main takes no arguments at all.
// It returns an integer value as a result.
int main()
{
}



// This function called scrambleMessage requires one string, called originalText,
// and one integer, called lettersToShiftBy
string scrambleMessage( string originalText, int lettersToShiftBy )
{
}



// This function called findSmallestValue requires two integers,
// one called firstNumber and the other called secondNumber
int findSmallestValue( int firstNumber, int secondNumber )
{
}
```

In each case, the code begins with the **data-type** that the function returns, followed by the **name of the function**, then the **arguments** that it takes as input within a pair of **()** brackets, followed by the **body of the function** which is enclosed within a pair of **{}** curly braces.

If the function does not take any arguments at all as input, an empty set of **()** brackets needs to be used. This makes it clear to the compiler that we haven't forgotten to define them. In the three examples above, we can see that the **main()** function does not take any data as arguments, but the functions named **scrambleMessage()** and **findSmallestValue()** do.

The following sections now consider each of the parts of a function in more detail.

Function names

Every function created in a C++ program must be given a unique **name**. The name **identifies** the block of code that the function will carry out. It will be used to **activate** or **"call"** the function into action.

We have already seen in the previous examples that `main()`, `scrambleMessage()` and `findSmallestValue()` are acceptable names for functions. When choosing a name for a function, use the same guidelines as you would for choosing a variable name. Choose a descriptive name that helps people to understand what the function is meant to do. You should make sure that the name does not contain any spaces or forbidden characters. You should also try not to make the name of the function too long, as statements that call the function may become difficult to read or type without making mistakes.

You must always be careful not to make two functions that have the **same** name in your program. This can become a particular problem when working with **libraries** of code written by other programmers. Remember that a library is a collection of code written by others that you can use in your own program code. It is typically a collection of functions that are defined in a separate file. You must avoid creating your own functions that the computer could confuse with existing functions from any other libraries that you plan to use.

Arguments – input values for a function

When creating a new function, we must tell the computer whether or not the function expects some input data or not.

As already described, many functions take in one or more data values as input when they get activated. These input values are often called **"arguments"**. The function will usually make use of the input values and do something with them.

Because there is often more than one single input value that is fed into a function, each input value also has to be given an **argument name** so the function can make use of it whilst not confusing it with the other input values. The code inside the function can use the argument name to refer to each separate input value when processing the data.

We must also tell the computer what **type** of data the function is expecting to work with for each of the arguments (such as whether it is a **string**, an **int** or a **float** value).

It is important for the compiler that each call to a function supplies that function with the correct kind of input values, otherwise the function may not be able to correctly process the data. Imagine if the function `makeStringUpperCase()` was given a **float** value when it has been told to expect a **string** value. Trying to change a **float** value to upper-case makes no sense, hence the compiler gives an error.

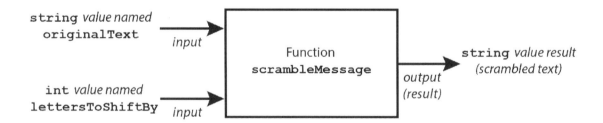

The diagram above shows a function that would use the Caesar Cipher to scramble a message. It would take two arguments as input: a message called `originalText` and a number that tells it how many places to shift each letter by in the message, `lettersToShiftBy`. It would produce one single result as output – a **string** value containing the scrambled message.

The C++ code inside the function can use the named values `originalText` and `lettersToShiftBy` in statements just as if they were local variable names. See ***Example 10.11 - function_scramble.cpp*** later in this chapter.

Functions that do not take any arguments as input

Some functions do not need to be given any data at all to do their job. They don't take any arguments as input and we can simply call them using their name without needing to supply them with any values.

For example, a function might display lots of text on the screen, but not actually process any data values. Note that an empty pair of **()** brackets is always needed when calling such a function, even though it does not require any arguments:

```
displayMenu();
```

Another example of a function that takes no input values at all is the C++ function **random()** which we have already used in some of our previous programs:

No input values to be passed in to the function

Function
random

output (result)

*Produces an **int** value e.g. 2374*

We might make use of a call to the **random()** function like this:

```
int chosenNumber = random();
```

You can see that it has been used as part of an assignment statement. The integer variable called **chosenNumber** is set to the **result** of the call to the **random()** function.

The body and return value of a function

Once a function has finished execution it may give something back in return to the code that called it. This "returned" result can be used by the program for further processing. The data value that the function gives back on completion is called a "**return**" value. But how does this happen?

Firstly, when creating a function, we must define what **kind** of data the function gives back (if any) once it has finished execution. This is called its "**return type**". We must also give the function a **name** and define any data that it needs as input - the **arguments** of the function.

We can now tell the computer what the function should actually do. This is called the "**body**" of the function. It is a group of one or more statements that the function will execute when it is called by another part of your program. The statements are placed inside a pair of **{ }** braces, along with one or more **return** statements to pass a result back to the calling code.

Below is the standard **main()** function for a program, which in this case does not take any arguments as input, but which returns a single **int** value once the execution of the function has completed:

```
int main()
{
    // This function is called main. It does not take any arguments as input.
    // The body of the function contains statements to do something useful.
    // It returns the integer value zero once it has finished execution.
    return 0;
}
```

The function below takes two different values as arguments: a **string** and an **int** value. It scrambles the original contents of the **string**. When finished, it returns the scrambled result:

```cpp
string scrambleMessage( string originalText, int lettersToShiftBy )
{
    // This function is called scrambleMessage.
    // It takes two input values: a string called originalText
    // and an integer called lettersToShiftBy.
    // It returns a string once it has finished execution.

    string scrambledResult = "";

    for ( unsigned int pos = 0;  pos < originalText.length();  pos++ )
        scrambledResult += originalText( pos ) + lettersToShiftBy;

    // Gives back finished string value
    return scrambledResult;
}
```

This final function takes two separate **int** values as input. It decides which is the smallest of the two inputs, returning this smallest value as the **int** result:

```cpp
int findSmallestValue( int firstNumber, int secondNumber )
{
    // This function is called findSmallestValue.
    // It takes two input values called firstNumber and secondNumber, both
    // of these are integers.
    // It returns an integer value once it has finished execution.

    // Gives back an int value, whichever was the smallest input value
    return ( firstNumber < secondNumber ) ? firstNumber : secondNumber;
}
```

Note that it is the **return** statement inside each function body that actually gives the result back to the code that called it.

We have already encountered the C++ word **return** in many of our programs. In fact, nearly all of our C++ programs so far have been comprised of a single function called **main()** that takes no data values as input and which returns an **int** value as an "**error code**" to the Linux operating system. In this way, you can actually consider a C++ program itself as a kind of function.

The **return** statement is often, but not always, the last statement in the body of the function. Some functions may even contain more than one **return** statement, perhaps as the result of a decision making process.

Remember that as soon as a **return** statement is executed, the flow of execution in your program passes back from the function to the code that called it, along with the returned result.

Calling a function

Once a function has been created it can be activated from another part of your program. We can **call** the function into action using its **name**.

For instance:

```
displayRandomWords( 10 );
```

This might call the function that has the name **displayRandomWords()**, telling it to pick out **10** words at random from the dictionary. In this case it is a **void** function that does not produce any result - no value is returned, the values are simply displayed on the screen.

The same function can do different things depending on the input value that you give it. The function could be called again, but this time telling it to only display **3** random words, thus the input values supplied to a function affect how it behaves:

```
displayRandomWords( 3 );
```

The program below calls a function called **factorial()**. This function takes a positive integer as an argument, then returns the factorial of this number as a result.

If you are unfamiliar with factorials in mathematics, here is an example:

The factorial of **5** is: **5 x 4 x 3 x 2 x 1 = 120**

Example 10.1 – function_factorial.cpp

```cpp
#include <iostream>      // Program will be using screen

using namespace std;     // Will be using standard identifiers cout and endl

// --------------------

int factorial( int num )
{
    cout << "Now in factorial function" << endl;

    int result = 1;

    for ( int index = 1;  index <= num;  index++ )
        result = result * index;

    cout << "About to return result";
    cout << " and jump back to main" << endl;


    return result;
}

// --------------------
```

continues on next page...

continued...

```cpp
int main()
{
    cout << "About to call function from main" << endl;

    // Calls function to calculate factorial of 5
    int result = factorial( 5 );

    cout << "Back in main again" << endl;

    cout << result << endl;


    return 0;
}
```

How a call to a function affects the flow-of-execution within your program

How does the computer execute the previous example? Take a look at the diagram below to see what happens at run-time.

The arrows show the **flow of execution** through the program. You can see what happens when the `main()` function calls the `factorial()` function:

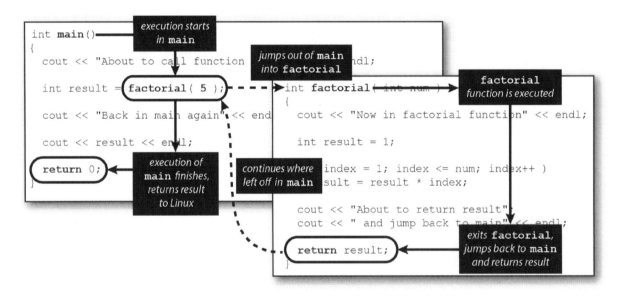

Upon calling a function from some other place in your program code, execution at that point in the program effectively pauses. The newly-called function then begins execution. Upon finishing execution of the function and returning its value, the flow-of-control is transferred back from the function to the code that called it.

How does the computer keep track of where it was in the execution of your program? When a function is called, the computer makes a note of exactly where it had got to in your program before jumping elsewhere to begin executing the code in the body of the function. This information is stored in a special part of the computer's memory, called the **"program stack"**.

Once the function has finished execution, the computer uses the information held on the stack to decide where to resume execution of the program. It jumps back to the point in the program where the function had previously been called, obtaining this information from the stack. Any returned result from the function is then passed back for the calling code to make use of.

Here is another example that illustrates the flow of execution through a program:

Example 10.2 – *function_roll.cpp*

```cpp
#include <iostream>     // Program will be using screen
#include <cstdlib>      // Program uses the random() and srandom() functions
#include <ctime>        // Program uses the time() function as the random seed

using namespace std;    // Will be using standard identifiers cout and endl

const char TAB = '\t';

// --------------------

int rollSingle( int numSides )
{
    cout << endl << TAB << "In rollSingle function" << endl;

    int result = 1 + ( random() % numSides );  // Choose number between 1 and numSides

    cout << TAB << "Finishing rollSingle function" << endl << endl;

    return result;
}

// --------------------

int main()
{
    cout << "Started in main function" << endl;

    srandom( time ( 0 ) );  // Seed the random number

    int first = rollSingle( 12 ); // Call function to choose num between 1 and 12

    cout << "I rolled " << first << endl;

    int second = rollSingle( 100 ); // Call function to choose num between 1 and 100

    cout << "Then I rolled " << second << endl;

    int third = rollSingle( 4 ); // Call function to choose num between 1 and 4

    cout << "Finally I rolled " << third << endl;

    cout << endl << "Finishing main function" << endl;

    return 0;
}
```

When the program runs, you can see how the flow of execution is affected by the call to the **rollSingle()** function:

```
Started in main function

        In rollSingle function
        Finishing rollSingle function

I rolled 9

        In rollSingle function
        Finishing rollSingle function

Then I rolled 50

        In rollSingle function
        Finishing rollSingle function

Finally I rolled 2

Finishing main function
```

Making use of a result that gets returned from a call to a function

As we have seen, when calling a function, your program often expects some sort of result to be returned that is useful to the rest of the code.

There are various ways in which the value returned from a function can be used.

To activate the function called **makeUpperCase()** from our earlier examples and obtain the result, we could write:

```
makeUpperCase( "Hello" );   // Calls function, with "Hello" as input
```

This in itself does not do anything with the returned **string** value (which for the input **"Hello"** is **"HELLO"**). It does not actually **use** the result that the function gives back to the calling code. The compiler would issue a warning if you tried to compile a program that contains such a call. It would warn you that the returned value from the function never gets used and that it has effectively been thrown away.

One possible use of a returned value is to display it on the screen. We could direct the value returned from the function to *channel-out* (the screen):

```
cout << makeUpperCase( "Hello" );   // Calls function, displays result
```

This would take the value **"Hello"** as input, change it to capitals and then display the result **"HELLO"** on the screen.

We could call the same function again, giving it some different input data and obtaining a different result:

```
cout << makeUpperCase( "gnu" );
```

Given the original **string** value **gnu**, this would display the result **GNU** on the screen.

Very often, after going to the trouble of creating a function, we might want to use it more than once in a program.

The example below uses a streamlined version of the factorial function from **Example 10.1 - function_factorial.cpp**. Notice that I have removed the **cout** statements that were previously used to help us trace the flow of execution through the running program.

The program contains a simple **for** loop, which uses the controlling integer variable **number** to count from **1** up to **10**.

Each iteration of the **for** loop calls the **factorial()** function, passing the value of **number** into it. The result that is returned from the function is then displayed as part of the **cout** statement.

Example 10.3 – function_factorial_loop.cpp

```cpp
#include <iostream>     // Program will be using screen

using namespace std;    // Will be using standard identifiers cout and endl

// --------------------

unsigned int factorial( unsigned int num )
{
    unsigned int result = 1;

    for ( unsigned int index = 1;  index <= num;  index++ )
        result = result * index;

    return result;
}

// --------------------

int main()
{
    // Repeatedly call the factorial() function to display the factorials for the
    // numbers between 1 and 10
    for ( unsigned int number = 1; number <= 10; number++ )
        cout << number << "! is " << factorial( number ) << endl;

    return 0;
}
```

When executed, you should see the following results:

```
1! is 1
2! is 2
3! is 6
4! is 24
5! is 120
6! is 720
7! is 5040
8! is 40320
9! is 362880
10! is 3628800
```

Below is another function would take a whole number and multiply it by itself:

```cpp
int squareMyNumber( int startingNumber )
{
    return startingNumber * startingNumber;
}
```

We could call **squareMyNumber()** and then display the result that it returns:

```cpp
cout << "The square of 5 is " << squareMyNumber( 5 ) << endl;
```

This would display:

```
The square of 5 is 25
```

Alternatively, we could take the returned result and **store** it in a **variable**, which other statements can then make use of:

```cpp
int answer = squareMyNumber( 5 );
```

Finally, we could take the returned value and feed it as input to another function call:

```cpp
cout << "5 to the power of 4 is ";
cout << squareMyNumber( squareMyNumber( 5 ) );
```

This would display:

```
5 to the power of 4 is 625
```

Creating a function that changes a **string** value to upper-case

The program on the following page uses one of the previous examples to change a **string** value so that any letters of the alphabet that it contains are converted to upper-case.

This is achieved by calling the **makeUpperCase()** function. The function is passed the original **string** value **iTyped** as an argument, which takes the argument name **originalText** within the function. The function then iterates through the characters in **originalText** using a **for** loop.

Each character is converted to upper-case by a call to **toupper()**. The converted upper-case character is then appended to a new **string**, called **finalText**.

Once completed, the value of **finalText** is returned by **makeUpperCase()** back to the **main()** function of the program, where it gets displayed on the screen:

```
Type line of text...
Mumble, JuMbLE, iT wiLL crUMBLe
It is now...
MUMBLE, JUMBLE, IT WILL CRUMBLE
```

Example 10.4 – *function_upper_case.cpp*

```cpp
#include <iostream>     // Program will be using keyboard and screen

using namespace std;    // Will be using standard identifiers string, cin, cout, endl

// --------------------

string makeUpperCase( string originalText )
{
    // This function examines each character in a string and changes it to upper-case
    // It takes a string called originalText as input
    // It returns a string as when finished

    unsigned int stringLen = originalText.length();  // Find num of chars to process

    string finalText = "";    // This will be used to hold the final upper-case text

    // Examine each character in the original string

    char currentChar;

    for ( unsigned int position = 0;  position < stringLen;  position++ )
    {
        // Obtain a single character
        currentChar = originalText.at( position );

        // Convert it to upper-case and append to the result string
        finalText += toupper( currentChar );

    }  // end of for loop

    return finalText;    // Returns the result to the code that called this function
}

// --------------------

int main()
{
    string iTyped, changed;

    // Allow user to type in a line of text
    cout << "Type line of text..." << endl;
    getline( cin, iTyped );

    // Call function to convert what they typed into upper-case letters
    changed = makeUpperCase( iTyped );

    // Display the changed text on the screen
    cout << "It is now..." << endl;
    cout << changed << endl << endl;

    return 0;
}
```

This next program features a function called **numberIsEven()** which uses the **% modulus operator** to determine whether an integer is an even number or not, returning either a **true** or **false** Boolean value:

Example 10.5 – *function_even.cpp*

```cpp
#include <iostream>     // Program will display some text on the screen as output

using namespace std;    // Will be using standard identifiers cin, cout, endl

// --------------------

bool numberIsEven( int numToCheck )
{
    // This function determines whether or not a number is an even number.

    // It takes a single integer as input, called numToCheck.

    // It checks what the remainder is when the number is divided by 2,
    // a remainder of zero indicates that it is an even number.

    // It returns a bool value, which is true if numToCheck is found to be even,
    // but false if numToCheck is found to be odd.

    return ( numToCheck % 2 ) == 0;
}

// --------------------

int main()
{
    // Get user to type in a number
    cout << "Type in a whole num: ";
    int myNum;
    cin >> myNum;

    // Call function to determine whether the number was even or not
    // and display the result on the screen.
    if ( numberIsEven( myNum ) )
        cout << "That was an even number.";
    else
        cout << "That was an odd number.";

    cout << endl;

    return 0;
}
```

Here is an example of what happens at run-time when the number **53** is entered:

```
Type in a whole num: 53
That was an odd number.
```

This further example uses a function called **makeRandomPassword()** to generate a password. The function takes an integer as input to determine how long the password should be. It then constructs the password by repeatedly picking out random characters and adding them to the end of a **string** value. The final **string** value is then returned as output.

Example 10.6 – function_random_password.cpp

```cpp
#include <iostream>     // Program will be using keyboard and screen
#include <cstdlib>      // Program uses the random() and srandom() functions
#include <ctime>        // Program uses the time() function as the random seed

using namespace std;    // Will be using standard identifiers string, cout and endl

// --------------------

string makeRandomPassword( int passLen )
{
    string password = "";    // Start with a new blank password
    char ranChar;
    int count = 0;    // count will keep track of how many digits have been chosen

    // Repeatedly choose random numeric characters and add to password
    while ( count < passLen )
    {
        ranChar = ( random() % 10 ) + 48;  // Choose ASCII code between 48 and 57
        password += ranChar;  // Add chosen character on to end of password
        count++;
    }  // end of while loop

    return password;
}

// --------------------

int main()
{
    srandom( time( 0 ) );  // Seed the random number process using the current time

    cout << "Here is your first password: ";
    cout << makeRandomPassword( 4 );  // Call function to create 4-digit password
    cout << endl;

    cout << "Here is your second: ";
    cout << makeRandomPassword( 20 );  // Call function to create 20-digit password
    cout << endl;

    return 0;
}
```

Here you can see that the same function gets called twice to produce two different passwords, each with a different length:

```
Here is your first password: 5331
Here is your second: 10365580709877850645
```

Good luck remembering the second password...

The program below calls the function **checkPasswordIsOK()** to obtain a **bool** value (which will always be either **true** or **false**). This will indicate whether a particular password has an acceptable length or not:

Example 10.7 – function_check_length.cpp

```cpp
#include <iostream>      // Program will be using keyboard and screen

using namespace std;      // Will be using standard identifiers string, cin, cout, endl

// --------------------

bool checkPasswordIsOK( string password )
{
    // Check that the password is between 8 and 12 characters long
    // Returns true if it is, false if it is not
    return password.length() >= 8  and  password.length( )<= 12;
}

// --------------------

int main()
{
    // Allow user to type in some text
    cout << "Please type a password (8-12 characters): ";
    string newPassword;
    cin >> newPassword;

    // Call function to check length of password is acceptable
    if ( checkPasswordIsOK( newPassword ) )
        cout << "Thanks." << endl;
    else
        cout << "Not accepted!" << endl;

    return 0;
}
```

The body of the function shown above contains only one single **return** statement, which evaluates an expression as either **true** or **false**, depending on the length of the password value that was passed to the function as input.

The code in **main()** then uses the result returned from **checkPasswordIsOK()** to decide which message to display.

A password that is **8** characters long or more, but also **12** characters or less is **acceptable**:

```
Please type a password (8-12 characters): m0t0rhead
Thanks.
```

A password that is less than **8** characters long or more than **12** characters long is **unacceptable**:

```
Please type a password (8-12 characters): abba
Not accepted!
```

This program allows the user to type in a single whole number. It then tests whether or not that number is a **prime number** - a number that is only divisible by itself or by the number **1**.

Most of the hard work is carried out by the **testForPrime()** function, which uses a **while** loop to check whether a range of different whole numbers can be divided into the chosen number to give a remainder of zero.

Finding a number that yields a zero remainder means that number is a **factor** of the number being tested. If any such factors exist (other than **1** and the original number itself) then the number being tested cannot be a prime. If no such factors are found though, this means that the number **must** be a prime.

Example 10.8 – function_prime.cpp

```cpp
#include <iostream>     // Program will be using keyboard and screen
#include <cstdlib>      // Program uses the exit() function

using namespace std;    // Will be using standard identifiers cin, cout, endl

bool testForPrime( int numToTest )
{
    int divisor = 2;

    bool foundExactDivision = false;

    while ( divisor < numToTest )
    {

        if ( numToTest % divisor == 0 )
        {
            foundExactDivision = true;

            cout << divisor << " goes into " << numToTest  << endl;

            // Uncomment break statement to make more efficient
            // Will find first factor only
            // break;

        }  // end of if

        divisor++;

    }  // end of while

    return not foundExactDivision;

}  // end of the function testForPrime

// ----------
```

continues on next page...

```cpp
int main()
{
    int userInput;

    cout << "PRIME TESTER" << endl;
    cout << "------------" << endl << endl;

    cout << "Type in an integer to test:" << endl;
    cin >> userInput;

    if ( userInput < 2 )
    {
        cout << "Must type a whole number, 2 or above." << endl;
        cout << "Program aborted." << endl;

        exit( 1 );

    }  // end of if


    // Call function to test whether the number entered
    // is a prime number or not, then display result on screen

    if ( testForPrime( userInput ) == true)
        cout << userInput << " is a prime number.";
    else
        cout << userInput << " is NOT a prime number";

    cout << endl;

    return 0;
}
```

Here's what happens when the program is given a prime number:

```
PRIME TESTER
------------

Type in an integer to test:
11
11 is a prime number.
```

Meanwhile, the program will show the **factors** for any number that it finds **not** to be a prime number:

```
PRIME TESTER
------------

Type in an integer to test:
65
5 goes into 65
13 goes into 65
65 is NOT a prime number
```

This next example builds on the previous program. It tests a **range** of positive integer values in order to determine which of them are prime numbers. As with the previous example, most of the work is carried out by the **testForPrime ()** function.

Rather than the user typing in which number they would like to test, they are asked for the **highest** number that they would like to test, which gets stored as **userInput**. The computer then uses a **for** loop to supply all of the values between **2** and **userInput** to the **testForPrime ()** function.

Unlike the previous example, the program is capable of working with a much larger range of values. This is because it makes use of the **unsigned long long** data-type, rather than **int**. This larger data-type can handle values up to approximately 54 billion.

The **testForPrime ()** function also saves some work by only trying potential divisors up until the **square-root** of each number being tested. There is no point in testing divisors that are larger than the square-root as they can only exist if a smaller corresponding factor has already been found by the function.

Example 10.9 – primes_in_range.cpp

```
#include <iostream>    // Program will be using keyboard and screen
#include <cstdlib>     // Program uses the exit() function
#include <cmath>       // Program uses the sqrt() function

using namespace std;    // Will be using standard identifiers cin, cout, endl

bool testForPrime( unsigned long numToTest )
{
    unsigned long long divisor = 2;

    unsigned long long stopValue = (unsigned long) sqrt( numToTest );

    bool foundExactDivision = false;

    while ( divisor <= stopValue )
    {
        if ( numToTest % divisor == 0 )
        {

            foundExactDivision = true;

            break;  // Stops once has found a factor

        }  // end of if decision that decides whether divisor is a factor

        divisor++;  // Move on to the next number to try

    }  // end of while loop that looks for factors in the current number

    return not foundExactDivision;

}  // end of function

// ----------
```

continues on next page...

```cpp
int main()
{
    long primesFound = 0;   // Records number of primes found so far.
    unsigned long long userInput;

    cout << "ULTRA-MEGA PRIME TESTER" << endl << endl;

    cout << "Type in maximum integer to test:" << endl;
    cout << "(program will test all whole numbers up to and including this)" << endl;
    cin >> userInput;

    // ----------

    if ( userInput < 2 )
    {
        cout << "Max integer must be whole number, 2 or above.";
        cout << endl << "Program aborted." << endl;

        exit( 1 );

    }   // end of if

    // ----------

    for ( unsigned long long loop = 2;  loop <= userInput;  loop++ )
    {
        // Display whether this number is prime or not.
        cout << endl << "Testing: " << loop << endl;
        cout << loop << " is ";

        if ( testForPrime( loop ) )
            primesFound++;
        else
            cout << "not ";

        cout << "a prime number." << endl;

    }   // end of for loop that drives the function

    // ----------

    // Finished testing the range of numbers,
    // display the total number of primes found in this range.
    cout << endl << endl;

    cout << "FOUND " << primesFound << " PRIMES IN THIS RANGE.";

    cout << endl << endl;

    return 0;
}
```

Here is what happens when asking the program to search for all prime numbers, up to and including 5:

```
ULTRA-MEGA PRIME TESTER

Type in maximum integer to test:
(program will test all whole numbers up to and including this)
5

Testing: 2
2 is a prime number.

Testing: 3
3 is a prime number.

Testing 4:
4 is not a prime number.

Testing 5:
5 is a prime number.

FOUND 3 PRIMES IN THIS RANGE.
```

You can ask it to search for prime numbers up to a much larger maximum if you like, but it will take longer to find the results. Here are some of the results and the final summary that is shown when asking to find all primes up to one million:

```
Testing 999997:
999997 is not a prime number.

Testing 999998:
999998 is not a prime number.

Testing 999999:
999999 is not a prime number.

Testing 1000000:
1000000 is not a prime number.


FOUND 78498 PRIMES IN THIS RANGE.
```

Validating a sequence of binary digits

Here is another function in use. It checks whether a **string** value is a valid 8-bit number – a pattern composed entirely of the characters **0** or **1** that is exactly eight characters long. If the **string** value is found to be a valid 8-bit binary pattern then the function **convertBinStringToDenary()** is called to convert it to a denary (base-10) number.

Example 10.10 – function_binary.cpp

```cpp
#include <iostream>    // Program will be using keyboard and screen
#include <cmath>    // Program uses the pow() function

using namespace std;    // Will be using standard identifiers string, cin, cout, endl

// --------------------
```

continues on next page...

```
int convertBinStringToDenary( string bitPattern )
{
    int result = 0;

    for ( int place = 0;  place < 8;  place++ )
        if ( bitPattern.at( place ) == '1' )
            result += pow( 2, 7 - place );  // Digit at pos 0 represents 2 to power 8

    return result;
}

// --------------------

int main()
{
    // Type in string of digits
    cout << "Type in 8-bit binary number..." << endl;
    string binString;
    cin >> binString;

    // Assume to begin with that the string is going to be OK
    bool valid = true;

    // Check the string is 8 chars long
    int stringLen = binString.length();

    if ( stringLen not_eq 8 )
    {
        cout << "Not 8 characters long." << endl;
        valid = false;
    }
    else
    {
        // Use a loop to check for any characters that are not 0 or 1
        char thisChar;
        for ( int pos = 0;  pos < 8;  pos++ )
        {
            thisChar = binString.at( pos );
            if ( thisChar != '0'  and  thisChar != '1' )
            {
                cout << "Invalid: " << thisChar << endl;
                valid = false;
            }  // end of if decision

        }  // end of for loop

    }  // end of if-else decision

    // Tell the user if the string was valid
    if ( valid )
    {
```

continues on next page...

continued...

```
            cout << "This is a valid 8-bit binary number." << endl;
            cout << "In base-10 it is: ";
            cout << convertBinStringToDenary( binString );
    }
    else
            cout << "Not a valid 8-bit binary number.";

    cout << endl;


    // Pass back success/error status to Linux
    return ( valid ? 0 : 1 );  // If valid returns 0, if not valid returns 1
}
```

The program begins by asking the user to type in an 8-bit binary pattern, which is stored as the **string** value **binString**.

It then determines the length of this, checking whether or not it is exactly **8** characters long. If not, an error message is displayed and the **string** is marked as invalid by setting the **valid** Boolean variable to **false**:

```
Type in 8-bit binary number...
0110100
Not 8 characters long.
Not a valid 8-bit binary number.
```

Alternatively, if **binString** holds exactly **8** characters, then a **for** loop iterates through them from beginning to end, checking that each individual character is either **1** or **0**.

If any of the characters are found to be anything other than **1** or **0** then the pattern is marked as invalid and the offending character is displayed on the screen with an error message:

```
Type in 8-bit binary number...
01230400
Invalid: 2
Invalid: 3
Invalid: 4
Not a valid 8-bit binary number.
```

Because a **for** loop is used in this way, the program will examine every single character in the **string** and will detect more than just a single invalid character - it always checks all eight characters.

If all characters are found to be valid, then the program attempts to convert the bit-pattern to a base-10 number:

```
Type in 8-bit binary number...
01101010
This is a valid 8-bit binary number.
In base-10 it is: 106
```

The actual conversion is performed by the function **convertStringToDenary()** which is passed the value of **binString** as an value when it is called. The function iterates through the characters from left to right. If an individual character is found to be a **1** then the function uses the **pow()** function to calculate the base-2 place-value of that particular position in the bit-pattern. This calculated value is added to the integer variable **result**, which is used to hold the overall total for all of the columns that have been processed so far.

Once all eight characters in the bit-pattern have been examined and processed, the value of **result** is passed back to the calling code in the **main()** function and is displayed on the screen.

A function that accepts more than one argument as input

Now let's put everything that we have learned about functions so far into practice. This program is based on one of the examples at the start of the chapter.

As with our other examples, the program contains a **main()** function, where execution will begin when the program runs. It also contains another function called **scrambleMessage()**.

Function **scrambleMessage()** takes two different inputs: a **string** value called **originalText** and an **int** value called **lettersToShiftBy**.

The function creates a new **string** value called **scrambledResult** by adding the value of **lettersToShiftBy** to the ASCII code of each character in **originalText**.

It then returns the newly built **string** value to the statement in **main()** that called it.

Example 10.11 – function_scramble.cpp

```
#include <iostream>       // Program will be using keyboard and screen

using namespace std;      // Will be using standard identifiers string, cin, cout, endl


// --------------------

string scrambleMessage( string originalText, int lettersToShiftBy )
{
    string changedResult = "";

    // Find out how long original string is
    int len = originalText.length();

    // Look at each char in the original string
    unsigned char singleChar;
    for ( unsigned int charPos = 0;  charPos < len;  charPos++ )
    {
        // Add on extra places to the character in order to scramble it
        singleChar = originalText.at( charPos ) + lettersToShiftBy;

        // If changed char has gone past last printable char, bring it back in range
        if ( singleChar > 126 )
            singleChar -= 95;
        else
            if ( singleChar < 32 )
                singleChar += 95;

        // Append the changed char to the result string
        changedResult += singleChar;

    }   // end of for loop

    // Finished whole string, pass back the result
    return changedResult;
}
```

continues on next page...

```
// -------------------

int main()
{
    // Type in line of text to be scrambled or unscrambled
    cout << "Please type in a line of text:" << endl;
    string lineOfText;
    getline( cin, lineOfText );

    cout << endl;   // Display blank line

    // Type in the number of places to scramble/unscramble by
    cout << "Number of places to scramble/unscramble by:" << endl;
    int numberOfPlaces;
    cin >> numberOfPlaces;

    cout << endl;   // Display blank line

    // Call the Scramble function to scramble it
    // and display the scrambled result on the screen
    cout << "This becomes..." << endl;

    // Call function to scramble the plain text and then display result
    cout << scrambleMessage( lineOfText, numberOfPlaces );

    cout << endl;


    return 0;
}
```

On running the program, you are asked to enter a message to scramble or unscramble, which gets stored as `lineOfText`. You are then asked to type in a number which will be used to adjust the characters in the message, which is stored as `numberOfPlaces`. This number can be with a positive or negative integer.

The call to `scrambleMessage()` passes both of these values into the function as the arguments `originalText` and `lettersToShiftBy`.

The function uses a `for` loop to examine each character in `originalText`, adding on the value of `lettersToShiftBy` to produce an ASCII code for a different character.

A check is then made to ensure that the new ASCII code is within the range of printable characters, adjusting it if necessary. This is required because adding or subtracting a value to a character code could result in a value that is either less than 32 (the first printable character, a *space*) or greater than 126 (the last printable character, ~ *tilde*).

Each adjusted character is appended to the `changedResult` variable. Once the entire text has been examined and adjusted, the value of `changedResult` is returned to the calling function `main()` to be displayed on the screen.

Below, you can see the effect of scrambling a message by moving each character along one single place:

```
Please type in a line of text:
My Raspberry Pi fell down from the sky.

Number of places to scramble/unscramble by:
1

This becomes...
Nz!Sbtqcfssz!Qj!gfmm!epxo!gspn!uif!tlz/
```

Here's what happens when the program is given a negative number of places, causing it to unscramble the message again:

```
Please type in a line of text:
Nz!Sbtqcfssz!Qj!gfmm!epxo!gspn!uif!tlz/

Number of places to scramble/unscramble by:
-1

This becomes...
My Raspberry Pi fell down from the sky.
```

You can see that characters which are scrambled using a high number are adjusted so that they remain within the range of printable characters - namely between **32** (*space*) and **126** (*~ tilde*):

```
Please type in a line of text:
The Pi in the sky (is a bit dented)

Number of places to scramble/unscramble by:
30

This becomes...
r'$>n(>(->3'$>2*8>F(2> >!(3>#$-3$#G
```

The same applies to messages that need to be unscrambled:

```
Please type in a line of text:
r'$>n(>(->3'$>2*8>F(2> >!(3>#$-3$#G

Number of places to scramble/unscramble by:
-30

This becomes...
The Pi in the sky (is a bit dented)
```

Functions that do not return any result

Although many functions return some data after completing their execution, some functions don't give anything back at all. A function that does not return a value is called a "**void**" function. Such a function does not need to include a `return` statement in its body because it does not give back any result to the code that called it.

C++ void functions operate in the same way as "**procedures**" that you can create in many other programming languages. You can think of them as **named sequences of instructions** that can be called from elsewhere in your program.

Here is an example of a **void** function:

```
void startNewGame()
{
    score = 0;
    lives = 3;
    // No return statement necessary - this is a "void" function
}
```

The example below shows a call being made to activate a **void** function with the name **sayHi()** from within **main()**:

Example 10.12 – function_void.cpp

```
#include <iostream>    // Program will be using keyboard and screen

using namespace std;    // Will be using standard identifiers cout and endl

// --------------------

void sayHi( int times )
{
    int completed = 0;
    while ( completed < times )
    {
        cout << "***    ***    ********" << endl;
        cout << "***    ***    ********" << endl;
        cout << "********       ***    " << endl;
        cout << "********       ***    " << endl;
        cout << "***    ***    ********" << endl;
        cout << "***    ***    ********" << endl << endl << endl;

        completed++;

    } // end of while loop
}

// --------------------

int main()
{
    sayHi( 3 );  // Single call to the function to display the message 3 times

    return 0;
}
```

When the program runs, the call to function **sayHi()** passes it the value **3** as an argument. This tells the function to repeatedly display the message three times. It does not however attempt to return any result, since all of the useful work that the **sayHi()** function does is displayed on the screen.

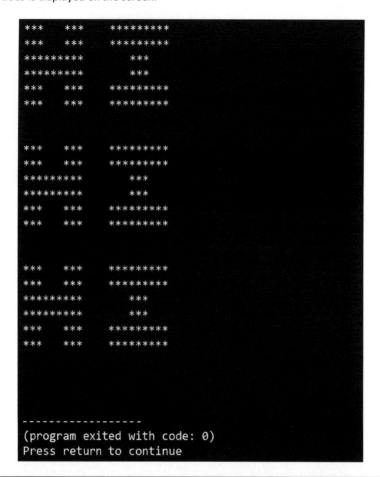

```
***    ***    *********
***    ***    *********
********       ***
********       ***
***    ***    *********
***    ***    *********


***    ***    *********
***    ***    *********
********       ***
********       ***
***    ***    *********
***    ***    *********


***    ***    *********
***    ***    *********
********       ***
********       ***
***    ***    *********
***    ***    *********


-----------------
(program exited with code: 0)
Press return to continue
```

Navigating your source-code to find a particular function

Note that if you are using Geany, you can use the **Symbols** pane on the left-side of the window to jump to the source-code of a particular function that you have written without scrolling up or down in the text-editor pane.

If you look under the **Functions** heading, you should see the **name** of each function that you have created in your program, including the **main()** function. Displayed alongside the name is the **line number** (shown in square-brackets) at which this function begins in your source-code. All you need to do is click on the name of the function that you want to jump to. As your programs get larger this can make it much easier to find a particular function that you want to work on.

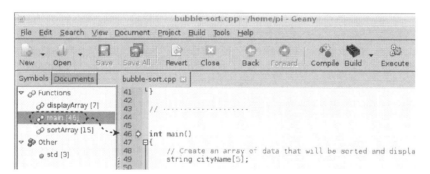

If for some reason you cannot see the sidebar or the **Symbols** pane, go to the **View** menu in the Geany window and select the **Show Sidebar** option.

Later on during *"Chapter 13: Objects and classes"*, you will learn about "classes". The **Symbols** pane can also display the names of any classes that you have made in your code along with the line-numbers at which they are declared.

The next example is slightly more useful. It uses a **void** function to display a menu of choices:

Example 10.13 – function_menu.cpp

```cpp
#include <iostream>     // Program will be using keyboard and screen

using namespace std;    // Will be using standard identifiers cin, cout, endl

// -------------------

void displayMenuOptions()
{
    // This function displays a menu of choices on the screen.
    // It does not take any arguments as input.
    // It does not return any value once executed.

    cout << "*** C D - F I N D E R ***" << endl << endl;

    cout << "MAIN-MENU" << endl;
    cout << "---------" << endl;

    cout << "t Search for a CD using title" << endl;
    cout << "a Search for all CDs by a particular artist" << endl;
    cout << "l Search for all CDs released by a particular record label" << endl;
    cout << "y Search for all CDs released in a particular year" << endl;

    cout << endl;

    cout << "* Exit the program" << endl;

    cout << endl << endl;
}

// ----------

int main()
{
    char choice;

    // Infinite loop to allow menu choices - gets broken by * to exit
    for ( ; ; )
    {
        // Activate the function to display the menu...
        displayMenuOptions();

        cin >> choice;

        if ( choice == '*' )
            break;

    }  // end of for loop

    return 0;
}
```

As you can see, the function **displayMenuOptions()** has the return-type **void**, thus the body of the function does not contain a **return** statement as it does not need to give anything back to the code that calls it.

The call to the function simply uses the name of the function, without passing it any arguments or attempting to do anything with any such returned value:

```
displayMenuOptions();
```

Here is an example of what gets displayed on the screen when the **void** function is called as part of the menu loop:

```
*** C D - F I N D E R ***

MAIN-MENU
---------
t Search for a CD using title
a Search for all CDs by a particular artist
l Search for all CDs released by a particular record label
y Search for all CDs released in a particular year

* Exit the program


t
*** C D - F I N D E R ***

MAIN-MENU
---------
t Search for a CD using title
a Search for all CDs by a particular artist
l Search for all CDs released by a particular record label
y Search for all CDs released in a particular year

* Exit the program


y
*** C D - F I N D E R ***

MAIN-MENU
---------
t Search for a CD using title
a Search for all CDs by a particular artist
l Search for all CDs released by a particular record label
y Search for`all CDs released in a particular year

* Exit the program



*

-----------------
(program exited with code: 0)
Press return to continue
```

More about function arguments – copies of values

When you activate a function, passing data-values as arguments to it, unless you tell the computer otherwise, these input values are said to be "**local**" to the function. Code outside the function will not be able to access the local values. The local values will only last temporarily while the function is active. Once the function has finished execution, the data-values will no longer exist. They do not affect any of the original values of the variables in any other part of your program.

So what happens if you pass the value of a variable as an input (an **argument**) to a function? Let's consider in more detail what happens to the arguments that are passed in.

Imagine we have this program code:

```cpp
#include <iostream>     // Program will be displaying some text on the screen

using namespace std;     // Will be using standard identifiers cout and endl

int main()
{
    int myNumber = 25;

    cout << "Value of original variable is " << myNumber << endl;

    displayTenTimesBigger( myNumber );

    // Will display 25 as function has no effect on the original variable
    cout << "Value of original variable is n" << myNumber << endl;

    return 0;
}
```

Now, here is the code for the `displayTenTimesBigger()` function that is called from the `main()` function:

```cpp
void displayTenTimesBigger( int numberToMakeBigger )
{
    numberToMakeBigger *= 10;

    cout << "Multiplied by 10 gives " << numberToMakeBigger << endl;
}
```

Notice that inside the `displayTenTimesBigger()` function, the value of the variable `numberToMakeBigger` gets changed and displayed on the screen.

But what happens to the value of the original variable `myNumber` from the `main()` function that was passed in as an argument to the function `displayTenTimesBigger()`? The answer is nothing.

The value of `myNumber` in `main()` is unaffected by what happens inside the `displayTenTimesBigger()` function. This is because the function works on a **copy** of the value of `myNumber`. Inside the function, this copy has the name `numberToMakeBigger`.

The function does not work on the **actual** value of the `myNumber` variable itself. The value of the original variable `myNumber` in `main()` is unaffected by changes that are made to the variable `numberToMakeBigger` inside the `displayTenTimesBigger()` function.

Functions that operate directly on their input data using & references to values

With a slight change to the previous function `displayTenTimesBigger()`, we can tell the computer to operate directly on the **actual** variable that is being used as an input value, rather than working on a mere copy of the variable.

The **&** (**"reference"**) symbol may be placed at the start of any variable name when defining the arguments of a function.

This means that instead of working on a **copy** of an argument, the function will operate on the real thing, referencing the **actual value** of the variable that we supply as input. To do this, your Pi will use the **address** of the variable in memory:

```
void displayTenTimesBigger( int &numberToMakeBigger )
{
    numberToMakeBigger *= 10;

    cout << numberToMakeBigger << endl;
}
```

This time, the **memory address** of the actual variable **myNumber** is passed as input to the `displayTenTimesBigger()` function to process, rather than a copy of its value.

If the value of **myNumber** is originally **25**, the function multiples that value of the variable by **10**, giving it the result **250**. The variable will retain this value even once the function has completed execution. Thus, when using references to variables as function arguments, what goes on inside a function can have lasting effects once the function has finished execution.

```
int myNumber = 25;

// Will display 25 prior to calling the function displayTenTimesBigger
cout << myNumber << endl;

// Call to function that makes the number 10 times bigger and then displays it
displayTenTimesBigger( myNumber );

// Will display 250 as function has changed the actual variable, not a copy of it
cout << myNumber << endl;
```

This can sometimes be very useful, particularly when writing functions that work on organised collections of data values, such as arrays. For instance, as we have seen earlier in this chapter, it is possible to sort an array of values into order by passing a reference to the array into a sorting function, permanently sorting the values.

Passing an array as an input to a function

This program stores some data in an array called **cityName**. In addition to **main()** it also contains two other functions:

displayArray() displays the contents of an array of **string** values.

sortArray() performs a simple "**bubble-sort**" on an array of **string** values.

Example 10.14 – function_bubble_sort.cpp

```cpp
#include <iostream>    // Program will display some text on the screen as output

using namespace std;    // Will be using standard identifiers string, cout and endl

// --------------------

void displayArray( string value[], int numItems )
{
    for ( int index = 0;  index < numItems;  index++ )
        cout << "Item no. " << index << " is " << value[index] << endl;
}

// --------------------

void sortArray( string value[], int numItems )
{
    string tempValue;    // Used when swapping a pair of data values with each other
    bool performedASwap;

    do
    {
        performedASwap = false;

        for ( int index = 0;  index < numItems-1;  index++ )
        {

            if ( value[index] > value[index+1] )
            {
                // Swap the pair of items around (via the temporary variable)
                tempValue = value[index];
                value[index] = value[index+1];
                value[index+1] = tempValue;

                performedASwap = true;
            }  // end of if decision that performs a swap

        }  // end of for loop that performs one whole pass through the array

    } while ( performedASwap );  // Keeps repeating passes until no swaps made

}

// --------------------
```

continues on next page...

continued...

```cpp
int main()
{
    // Create an array of data that will be sorted and displayed
    const int NUM_CITIES = 5;
    string cityName[NUM_CITIES];

    cityName[0] = "Chicago";
    cityName[1] = "New York";
    cityName[2] = "San Francisco";
    cityName[3] = "Detroit";
    cityName[4] = "Miami";

    // Call the displayArray function to display the array called cityName
    cout << "BEFORE sorting, the array looks like this..." << endl;
    displayArray( cityName, NUM_CITIES );

    // Call the sortArray function to sort the itmes in the array called cityName
    sortArray( cityName, NUM_CITIES );

    // Call the displayArray function again to display the updated cityName array
    cout << endl << "AFTER sorting, the array looks like this..." << endl;
    displayArray( cityName, NUM_CITIES );

    return 0;
}
```

When passing an array as an argument to a function, C++ treats it as a **reference** to the array, just as though you had used the **& reference operator** when creating the function. Thus **sortArray()** permanently changes the **actual** values of the **cityName** array that belongs to the **main()** function, rather than working on a **copy** of the array.

This is very convenient because if a reference to the array were not used, it would result in the original **cityName** array remaining unsorted when the **displayArray()** function gets called a second time at the end of the program.

Why does a reference to an array get passed, rather than a complete copy of the values that the array contains? As we have seen, passing arguments to functions uses the fixed area of memory called the **program stack**, which is also used by your Pi to manage the variables used by each function in your program and to keep track of the flow of execution as your program jumps into and returns from other functions. The array of items could easily be so large that it takes up too much space from the stack memory, hence it is more efficient to pass only a single memory address instead of the data itself.

Here's what happens on my Pi when the program runs, showing the original contents of the **cityName** array before sorting, followed by the final values from the same array after the call to the **sortArray()** function:

```
BEFORE sorting, the array looks like this...
Item no. 0 is Chicago
Item no. 1 is New York
Item no. 2 is San Francisco
Item no. 3 is Detroit
Item no. 4 is Miami

AFTER sorting, the array looks like this...
Item no. 0 is Chicago
Item no. 1 is Detroit
Item no. 2 is Miami
Item no. 3 is New York
Item no. 4 is San Francisco
```

If you want to see how the sorting works, one step at a time, you can add an extra call to the **displayArray()** function to show you the contents of the array after every single swap that is made:

```cpp
void sortArray( string value[], int numItems )
{
    string tempValue;
    bool performedASwap;

    do
    {
        // Single pass through the array of items
        performedASwap = false;

        for ( int index = 0;  index < numItems-1;  index++ )
        {

            if ( value[index] > value[index+1] )
            {
                // Swap the pair of items around (via the temporary variable)
                tempValue = value[index];
                value[index] = value[index+1];
                value[index+1] = tempValue;

                performedASwap = true;

                // Display the updated array now that two items
                // have been swapped around
                cout << endl << endl;  // Display a gap

                // After making a swap, display the progress of the sort so far
                displayArray( value, numItems );  // Display the array items

                cout << endl << endl << endl;  // Display a gap

            }  // end of if-decision that performs a swaps

        }  // end of for-loop that performs one whole pass through the array

    } while ( performedASwap );    // Keeps repeating passes until no swaps made

}
```

Whilst this bubble-sort program will work, as we saw in "*Chapter 8: Characters and text strings*" there is a simpler way to swap two different **string** values around using the **swap()** function. This removes the need for the temporary variable **tempValue**:

```cpp
                // Swap the pair of items around
                value[index].swap( value[index+1] );
```

Here is another program that sorts data from an array. Unlike the bubble-sort method, this program **inserts** data items one-by-one into a new sorted array at the correct place, hence this approach is called an **"insertion sort"**.

The program contains an array of `string` values called `unsortedData` that holds the names of the first ten chemical elements from the periodic table. In the `main()` function, a `while` loop is used to repeatedly call the `insertItem()` function.

Each time that it does this, the name of one of the chemical elements is passed into `insertItem()` which finds the correct place in the array of sorted data at which to add the element. Once the item has been inserted into the array of sorted values, the `while` loop displays the contents of the sorted array so far, allowing you to inspect how the sort is progressing.

Example 10.15 – function_insertion_sort.cpp

```
#include <iostream>     // Program will display some text on the screen as output

using namespace std;    // Will be using standard identifiers string, cout and endl

// --------------------

void displayArray( string value[], unsigned int numItems )
{
    for ( unsigned int index = 0;  index < numItems;  index++ )
        cout << "\tItem no. " << index << " is " << value[index] << endl;

    cout << endl << "--------------------" << endl;
}

// --------------------

void insertItem( string newItem, string sortedArray[], unsigned int numItems )
{
    cout << endl << "Now adding " << newItem;
    cout << " into the array of sorted items..." << endl;

    // Determine where the new item needs to go in the sorted array
    unsigned int insertAt, itemIndex;

    // Decide whether the array of sorted items was previously empty or not
    if ( numItems == 0 )
    {
      insertAt = 0;
      cout << "Array of sorted items previously empty - is the only item" << endl;
    }
    else
    {
        unsigned int indexOfLastItem = numItems - 1;
        if ( newItem >= sortedArray[indexOfLastItem] )
        {
            cout << "Adding to end of sorted items" << endl;
            insertAt = numItems;
        }
        else
```

continues on next page...

```
        {
            cout << "Adding in middle - need to search for insertion point" << endl;

            itemIndex = 0;
            bool foundPlaceToInsert = false;

            while ( itemIndex < numItems and not foundPlaceToInsert )
            {
                cout << "Comparing " << newItem;
                cout << " with " << sortedArray[itemIndex];
                cout << " at position " << itemIndex << endl;

                if ( newItem < sortedArray[itemIndex] )
                {
                        cout << "Found place to add item" << endl;
                        insertAt = itemIndex;
                        foundPlaceToInsert = true;
                }
                else
                    itemIndex++;

            }  // end of while

            // Copy the bottom items to one place below in the array
            cout << "Making room in sorted array so that ";
            cout << newItem << " can be inserted" << endl;

            for ( unsigned int copyIndex = numItems;
                            copyIndex > insertAt;
                            copyIndex -- )
                sortedArray[copyIndex] = sortedArray[copyIndex-1];

        }  // end of if else decision about where to add

    }  // end of decision aboutwhether sorted array was previously empty or not

    // Store the new item into the array
    sortedArray[insertAt] = newItem;

}  // end of function

// --------------------
```

```cpp
int main()
{
    // Create two different arrays to hold the unsorted and sorted data

    const unsigned int NUMBER_OF_ELEMENTS = 10;

    string unsortedData[NUMBER_OF_ELEMENTS];
    string sortedData[NUMBER_OF_ELEMENTS];

    unsortedData[0] = "Hydrogen";
    unsortedData[1] = "Helium";
    unsortedData[2] = "Lithium";
    unsortedData[3] = "Beryllium";
    unsortedData[4] = "Boron";
    unsortedData[5] = "Carbon";
    unsortedData[6] = "Nitrogen";
    unsortedData[7] = "Oxygen";
    unsortedData[8] = "Flourine";
    unsortedData[9] = "Neon";

    // Call the displayArray function to display the array called cityName
    cout << "The unsorted array looks like this..." << endl;
    displayArray( unsortedData, NUMBER_OF_ELEMENTS );

    unsigned int unsortedIndex = 0;
    while  ( unsortedIndex < NUMBER_OF_ELEMENTS )
    {
        // Insert single item from unsorted array into correct place in sorted array
        insertItem( unsortedData[unsortedIndex], sortedData, unsortedIndex );

        unsortedIndex++;

        // Call the displayArray function to display sorted items so far
        cout << endl << "The sorted array now looks like this..." << endl;
        displayArray( sortedData, unsortedIndex );

    }  // end of for loop

    cout << endl << "*** All items now added to the sorted array ***" << endl;

    return 0;
}
```

Here you can see the program in action, showing the first few data items **Hydrogen**, **Helium**, **Lithium** and **Beryllium** being inserted into the **sortedData** array:

```
The unsorted array looks like this...
        Item no. 0 is Hydrogen
        Item no. 1 is Helium
        Item no. 2 is Lithium
        Item no. 3 is Beryllium
        Item no. 4 is Boron
        Item no. 5 is Carbon
        Item no. 6 is Nitrogen
        Item no. 7 is Oxygen
        Item no. 8 is Flourine
        Item no. 9 is Neon


--------------------

Now adding Hydrogen into the array of sorted items...
Array of sorted items previously empty - is the only item

The sorted array now looks like this...
        Item no. 0 is Hydrogen


--------------------

Now adding Helium into the array of sorted items...
Adding in middle - need to search for insertion point
Comparing Helium with Hydrogen at position 0
Found place to add item
Making room in sorted array so that Helium can be inserted

The sorted array now looks like this...
        Item no. 0 is Helium
        Item no. 1 is Hydrogen


--------------------

Now adding Lithium into the array of sorted items...
Adding to end of sorted items

The sorted array now looks like this...
        Item no. 0 is Helium
        Item no. 1 is Hydrogen
        Item no. 2 is Lithium


--------------------

Now adding Beryllium into the array of sorted items...
Adding in middle - need to search for insertion point
Comparing Beryllium with Helium at position 0
Found place to add item
Making room in sorted array so that Beryllium can be inserted

The sorted array now looks like this...
        Item no. 0 is Beryllium
        Item no. 1 is Helium
        Item no. 2 is Hydrogen
        Item no. 3 is Lithium


--------------------
```

Eventually, the final item of data **Neon** is inserted and the finished sorted array looks like this:

```
Now adding Neon into the array of sorted items...
Adding in middle - need to search for insertion point
Comparing Neon with Beryllium at position 0
Comparing Neon with Boron at position 1
Comparing Neon with Carbon at position 2
Comparing Neon with Flourine at position 3
Comparing Neon with Helium at position 4
Comparing Neon with Hydrogen at position 5
Comparing Neon with Lithium at position 6
Comparing Neon with Nitrogen at position 7
Found place to add item
Making room in sorted array so that Neon can be inserted

The sorted array now looks like this...
        Item no. 0 is Beryllium
        Item no. 1 is Boron
        Item no. 2 is Carbon
        Item no. 3 is Flourine
        Item no. 4 is Helium
        Item no. 5 is Hydrogen
        Item no. 6 is Lithium
        Item no. 7 is Neon
        Item no. 8 is Nitrogen
        Item no. 9 is Oxygen


--------------------

*** All items now added to the sorted array ***
```

This sorting technique will be revisited later *Example 10.24 – function_recursive_binary_search.cpp* to illustrate a more efficient method of searching through the array of items using a **"binary search"**.

Deciding where to put functions in your code

Here is a program which uses two functions, called **sayHi()** and **sayGoodBye()**. Both functions are called from the **main()** function of the program. However, at the point in **main()** where they are called, the compiler does not yet know that they even exist because they don't get created until the last part of the program, after the **main()** function.

Example 10.16 – function_unknown.cpp

```
#include <iostream>    // Program will be displaying some text on the screen

using namespace std;    // Will be using standard identifiers cout and endl

int main()
{
    // Tries to call two functions to display some messages...
    sayHi();  // Compiler does not yet know about this function!
    sayGoodbye();  // Compiler does not yet know about this function!


    return 0;
}

// -------------------

void sayHi()
{
    cout << "Hi!" << endl;
}

// -------------------

void sayGoodbye()
{
    cout << "Goodbye!" << endl;
}
```

If you try to compile the above program, you will see the error message:

```
error: 'sayHi' was not declared in this scope
```

The problem is that you can't call a function that the compiler does not yet know about. This could make it difficult for you to write a program that needs to make use of several functions that will call each other.

In this case, the problem is easily solved. All you need to do is add the code for the two functions **before** creating the code for the **main()** function which calls them:

Example 10.17 – function_order.cpp

```
#include <iostream>      // Program will be displaying some text on the screen

using namespace std;     // Will be using standard identifiers cout and endl

void sayHi()
{
    cout << "Hi!" << endl;
}

// -------------------

void sayGoodbye()
{
    cout << "Goodbye!" << endl;
}

// -------------------

int main()
{
    // Calls two functions here to display messages...
    // The functions have already been made earlier in the program
    // and the compiler is aware that they exist, so it is okay
    // to call them - the compiler will recognise their names

    sayHi();
    sayGoodbye();


    return 0;
}
```

In more complex programs though, it is not always so easy (or even possible) to put all of your functions into such a straightforward order to avoid this kind of problem.

Declaring a function: telling the compiler that a function will exist later in your code

To make sure that a program never tries to call an as-yet unknown function, we can "**declare**" to the compiler in advance that it **will** exist later in our code:

```
int makeNewPassword();
```

This is like saying "this program will *definitely* have a function that is called **makeNewPassword()**, and I promise that the code will be somewhere later on in the program". This declaration of a function is called a "**function prototype**" or "**forward declaration**".

Here is the previous program, but this time it **declares** in advance that there are two functions called `sayHi()` and `sayGoodbye()`. The `main()` function is then able to call them before reaching the point at which they are defined in the program:

Example 10.18 – *function_declarations.cpp*

```cpp
#include <iostream>      // Program will be displaying some text on the screen

using namespace std;     // Will be using standard identifiers cout and endl

// Declare to compiler that these functions that will be defined later in the code
void sayHi();
void sayGoodbye();

// --------------------

int main()
{
    sayHi();      // Calls function here to say "Hi!"
    sayGoodbye();      // Calls function here to say "Goodbye!"

    return 0;
}

// --------------------

void sayHi()
{
    cout << "Hi!" << endl;
}

// --------------------

void sayGoodbye()
{
    cout << "Goodbye!" << endl;
}
```

Once your program has declared that a function will exist later on, you can call it from **anywhere** in your C++ code. Just make sure you don't break your promise to actually create the function – otherwise, the **linker** will give you an error message during the build process if it cannot find a body for the declared function anywhere in the source-code.

Declarations for C++ functions are often put in separate files called "**header files**". Header files can be included in source-code files using `#include` directives. They contain all of the details about the functions that are available to use, arguments that these functions take and the kind of results that they give back. Header files make it very easy to define and re-use your own functions in all of the different programs that you write, saving you from re-writing them again and again for each new program.

The convention is for the header files to use filenames that end in "*.h*" rather than the "*.cpp*" ending used by source-code files.

Creating your own re-usable library of useful functions

Programs often need to do similar things, such as converting text to upper-case or lower-case. Rather than writing code to do this every time we create a new program, we can place reusable code in a file that all of our programs can use.

We can create our own reusable library files, such as the one shown below, which contains two functions that operate on **string** values. All you need to do is create a **.cpp** file to contain the functions, then use a **#** directive to **include** the file in any program that you create in the future. Indeed, nearly all of the programs so far in this book have made use of standard C++ library files in this way.

Let's try making a simple library file of our own:

Example 10.19a – *string_functions.cpp*

```cpp
#include <string>     // These functions use variables of type string

using namespace std;     // Will be using the string standard identifier

// ------------------

string convertToCapitals( string textString )
{
    unsigned int len = textString.length();

    for ( unsigned int pos = 0;  pos < len;  pos++ )
        textString.at( pos ) = toupper( textString.at( pos ) );

    return textString;
}

// ------------------

string convertToLowerCase( string textString )
{
    unsigned int len = textString.length();

    for ( unsigned int pos = 0;  pos < len;  pos++ )
        textString.at( pos ) = tolower( textString.at( pos ) );

    return textString;
}
```

Once you have created the above file, your programs can add the following **#include** directive to make use of it:

```cpp
#include "string_functions.cpp"
```

Your program is now able to call the **convertToCapitals()** and **convertToLowerCase()** functions, as you will see in the example shown on the next page.

Note that it is **not** necessary to compile your new library file. The code will simply be added to any program that chooses to include it. The combined source-code will then be compiled in one go.

Example 10.19b – uses_string_functions.cpp

```cpp
#include <iostream>      // Program will display some text on the screen as output

#include "string_functions.cpp"     // Will be using own library of functions

using namespace std;      // Will be using standard identifiers string, cout and endl


int main()
{

    string textToDisplay = "Hello GNU!";

    cout << "Original text is " << textToDisplay << endl;


    // Call functions from the library of reusable string functions

    cout << "Upper-case text is " << convertToCapitals( textToDisplay ) << endl;

    cout << "Lower-case text is " << convertToLowerCase( textToDisplay ) << endl;


    return 0;
}
```

Below, you can see the library code in action:

```
Original text is Hello GNU!
Upper-case text is HELLO GNU!
Lower-case text is hello gnu!
```

There are several advantages to creating your own libraries of functions. Firstly, they save you work, as in theory you do not need to create code for the same function more than once. By writing the function code once and storing it in an external file, it can be included and called by many different programs.

Another advantage is that once you have tested a library function and you are sure that it works without errors, you can rely on that function to work correctly when it is used by programs that you write in future. Repeatedly writing the same code several times without libraries though could mean that you make a mistake somewhere, leading to an error.

Inline functions

Breaking your code into functions can make your program easier to understand and can also reduce the overall number of statements that your program contains if those functions are called more than once. Unfortunately, the down-side is that functions can make the process of compiling and execution a little more complex. When calling a function, argument values get copied from one place in memory to another. Execution also jumps between different parts of the program and this requires some behind-the-scenes work by the computer.

Some functions are very small. Often they may consist of only one or two statements in their body. When jumping into or out of such a small function, the computer may be going to a lot of trouble just to carry out a very small number of instructions.

For instance, consider this small function that displays a line of text on the screen:

```
void displayLine( string textToDisplay )
{
    cout << textToDisplay << endl;
}
```

The function body contains only a single statement that sends the value of **textToDisplay** to *channel-out*, followed by **endl** to indicate the end of that line.

An alternative approach is to create an "**inline function**". When compiling your code, the compiler **replaces** every call to the inline function with the source-code for the body of that function.

So if we had the following function calls in our code:

```
displayLine( "This displays a line of text." );
displayLine( "So does this." );
displayLine( "This does too." );
```

...when compiling, the compiler would replace each of the three calls to **displayLine()** with the **cout** statement from the body of the function:

```
cout << "This displays a line of text." << endl;
cout << "So does this." << endl;
cout << "This does too."<< endl;
```

As you should be able to see in the example above, any arguments that were being passed as input values to the **displayLine()** function have automatically been substituted into the modified code by the compiler.

To make a function into an inline function, you need to precede the function definition with the reserved word **inline**:

```
inline void displayLine( string textToDisplay )
{
    cout << textToDisplay << endl;
}
```

Here is a program that uses this technique to define and call the inline function **displayLine()** to enable several messages to be displayed on the screen:

Example 10.20 – function_inline.cpp

```cpp
#include <iostream>      // Program will be using keyboard and screen

using namespace std;     // Will be using standard identifiers string, cout and endl

// --------------------

inline void displayLine( string textToDisplay )
{
    cout << textToDisplay << endl;
}

// --------------------

int main()
{
    displayLine( "This is some literal text." );

    string lineOfText = "This text was stored in a variable.";
    displayLine( lineOfText );

    string firstPart = "This text";
    string secondPart = " was joined together";
    displayLine( firstPart + secondPart + '!' );

    return 0;
}
```

When executed, the program produces the following output:

```
This is some literal text.
This text was stored in a variable.
This text was joined together!
```

Using inline functions can make your code more compact and easier to read, especially if the function is called many times throughout your program.

Even if they don't know any C++ and have never used **cout** before, most programmers would be able to understand what this call does:

```cpp
        displayLine( "This is some literal text." );
```

Recursive functions: functions that call themselves

This program creates a function that contains a call to **itself** – a process called "**recursion**". A function that calls itself is called a "**recursive function**".

Try running the program and you should see that it repeatedly goes into the function **simpleFunction()** again and again, displaying the message **"Gone into simpleFunction!"** each time that it does so. What you won't see though is the message **"Exiting simpleFunction!"**. Why not?

Here's why: every time part of your C++ program calls a function, the computer puts the current code "on hold". It pauses execution of the code at the point where the function was called. Execution now jumps to the code of the newly-activated function. Once the code for the function has been executed, the computer jumps back to the point where the function was called and resumes execution of the original code again.

In the recursive code below, every time the function **simpleFunction()** gets called, it activates another separate copy of the same function. This means that the program should never end – it just goes on recursively calling **simpleFunction()** into action again and again. None of the activated functions ever get a chance to finish as they always activate a new copy of the same function. The program effectively sets up an ever-increasing chain of functions that are waiting for a chance to end, but which never actually get a chance to do so.

In theory, this could go on forever, but in practice a computer can only manage a finite number of active function calls using the program stack. Once the stack fills up and can no longer hold any more details of active functions, a critical error is triggered called a "**stack overflow**". The program will display a "**Segmentation fault**" error message and then cease execution. This takes approximately fifteen minutes on an older Model B Pi!

Example 10.21 – function_trace_recursion.cpp

```cpp
#include <iostream>    // Program will be displaying some text on the screen

using namespace std;    // Will be using standard identifiers cout and endl

void simpleFunction()
{
    cout << "Gone into simpleFunction!" << endl;

    simpleFunction();  // Function recursively calls itself again here

    // This next statement will never get executed!
    cout << "Exiting simpleFunction!" << endl;
}

// -----------

int main()
{
    // First call to the function from the main part of the C++ program
    simpleFunction();

    // This next statement will never get executed!
    // Execution will never get back to the main function
    return 0;
}
```

You can even count how far the chain of function calls reaches by creating a variable to count them.

In the next recursive program, a variable called **callLimit** is used to track how many recursive instances of **simpleFunction()** have been activated. It places a limit on the number of recursive calls. When the number of active functions reaches **10** it no longer calls itself again, thanks to the constant **CALL_LIMIT**.

This means that the tenth time that **simpleFunction()** is called, it finally has a chance to finish execution. The computer now passes control back to the part of the code that called it – the ninth called instance of **simpleFunction()**. This ninth instance gets a chance to finish execution, then passes control back to the eighth instance... and so on until all of the recursive function instances have completed execution.

Example 10.22 – function_recursion_limit.cpp

```cpp
#include <iostream>     // Program will be displaying some text on the screen

using namespace std;    // Will be using standard identifiers cout and endl

// Change this to control how far the recursion goes
const int CALL_LIMIT = 10;

void simpleFunction( int functionsActive )
{
    cout << "Gone into simpleFunction! Functions now active: ";
    cout << functionsActive << endl;

    // Recursion alert! This function now calls itself again
    if ( functionsActive < CALL_LIMIT )
        simpleFunction( functionsActive + 1 );

    // Tell the user which version of the function is now finishing
    cout << "Exiting simpleFunction number: ";

    cout << functionsActive << endl;
}

// -----------

int main()
{
    // Call the function once from the main part of the C++ program
    simpleFunction( 1 );

    // This next statement will only get executed once the whole chain
    // of recursively called functions has completed!
    return 0;
}
```

The screenshot below shows the flow of execution when the program runs. The **main()** function calls **simpleFunction()** once, which displays the first message to say that it is now being executed and how many copies of the function are active:

```
        Functions now active: 1
```

This first activate instance of **simpleFunction()** calls itself, activating a second instance. There are now two active instances of **simpleFunction()** running. The second instance now activates a third instance, the third instance activates a fourth, and so on.

This process carries on repeatedly, creating a chain of active functions until **CALL_LIMIT** is reached, which then prevents any further instances from being activated.

Eventually, all active instances of **simpleFunction()** have completed their execution and control finally returns to the **main()** function in the program.

Here is what you should see on your Pi:

```
Gone into simpleFunction! Functions now active: 1
Gone into simpleFunction! Functions now active: 2
Gone into simpleFunction! Functions now active: 3
Gone into simpleFunction! Functions now active: 4
Gone into simpleFunction! Functions now active: 5
Gone into simpleFunction! Functions now active: 6
Gone into simpleFunction! Functions now active: 7
Gone into simpleFunction! Functions now active: 8
Gone into simpleFunction! Functions now active: 9
Gone into simpleFunction! Functions now active: 10
Exiting simpleFunction number: 10
Exiting simpleFunction number: 9
Exiting simpleFunction number: 8
Exiting simpleFunction number: 7
Exiting simpleFunction number: 6
Exiting simpleFunction number: 5
Exiting simpleFunction number: 4
Exiting simpleFunction number: 3
Exiting simpleFunction number: 2
Exiting simpleFunction number: 1
```

Recursion can be used to solve many kinds of problems using very little program code. The final program in this chapter uses recursion to determine whether a **string** value is a palindrome or not. If the sentence is a palindrome, then it should contain a symmetrical sequence of letters that appear to be the same, regardless of whether you read them from left-to-right or right-to-left.

For instance, "**OXO**" and "**Madam, I'm Adam**" are both palindromes. Note that spaces and punctuation marks don't count - the process is only concerned with the actual letters of the alphabet. It is also case-insensitive, meaning that it does not matter whether each letter is upper-case or lower-case.

The program asks the user to type in a sentence. It then examines the characters to make sure that the left-half and the right half of the sentence are mirror images of each other.

Example 10.23 – function_palindromes.cpp

```cpp
#include <iostream>     // Program will be displaying some text on the screen

using namespace std;     // Will be using standard identifiers string, cin, cout

// --------------------

string removeSpacesEtc( string original )
{
    // Makes new copy of original string, but containing only letters of alphabet
    // Any spaces or punctuation will not be included in the new string
    string cleaned = "";

    unsigned int textLength = original.length();

    char currentChar;

    for ( unsigned int pos = 0;  pos < textLength;  pos++ )
    {
        currentChar = original.at( pos );   // Obtain single character

        // If the character is a letter then convert to upper-case and add to copy
        if ( isalpha( currentChar ) )
            cleaned += toupper( currentChar );

    }  // end of for loop

    return cleaned;
}

// --------------------
```

continues on next page...

```cpp
bool isPalindrome( string textToCheck )
{
    // This function determines whether a string value is a palindrome or not.
    // It returns a true value if the string is found to be a palindrome,
    // otherwise returns a false value.

    bool bothSidesSame;

    int textLen = textToCheck.length();

    if ( textLen >= 2 )
    {
        // Examine the first and last characters of the string
        char first = textToCheck.at( 0 );
        char last = textToCheck.at( textLen-1 );

        // If they are the same then determine whether the rest of the string
        // is a palindrome using a recursive call
        if ( first == last )
        {
            bothSidesSame = true;
            if ( textLen > 2 )
                bothSidesSame &= isPalindrome( textToCheck.substr( 1, textLen-2 ) );
        }
        else
            bothSidesSame = false;

    }
    else
        if ( textLen == 1 )
            bothSidesSame = true;   // String contains a single character - palindrome

    return bothSidesSame;
}

// --------------------

int main()
{
    string sentence;

    // Infinite loop
    while ( true )
    {
        // Allow user to type in a line of text
        cout << "Type in a sentence: " << endl;
        getline( cin, sentence );

        // Remove any character that is not a letter of the alphabet
        sentence = removeSpacesEtc( sentence );
```

continues on next page...

continued...

```
        // Activate the function to check for palindrome and display results
        if ( isPalindrome( sentence ) )
            cout << "The sentence IS a palindrome." << endl;
        else
            cout << "The sentence is NOT a palindrome." << endl;

        cout << "--------------------";
        cout << endl << endl;

    }   // end of while

    return 0;
}
```

You can see below what happens when if you try running the program with a few well-known palindromes:

```
Type in a sentence:
Ada
The sentence IS a palindrome.
--------------------

Type in a sentence:
Madam, I'm Adam
The sentence IS a palindrome.
--------------------

Type in a sentence:
Go deliver a dare, vile dog!
The sentence IS a palindrome.
--------------------

Type in a sentence:
Madam, I'm bonkers
The sentence is NOT a palindrome.
--------------------
```

Execution of the program begins with the **main()** function, which repeatedly asks the user to type in some text. Each line of text that the user types in will then be processed. When checking whether what the user types in is a palindrome or not, the process will only need to consider the letters from the text, thus all spaces and punctuation need to be removed.

For each line of text that is typed in, the function **removeSpacesEtc()** is called to ensure that it does not contain any characters that are not letters of the alphabet. The function builds up a new version of the text called **cleaned**, which is eventually passed back to the **main()** function. To build the new value for **cleaned**, the program iterates through the line of text using a **for** loop. Each character is examined using **isalpha()** to determine whether is it is a letter of the alphabet. If it is, then **toupper()** is also called to ensure that the letter is upper-case. The upper-case letter is then appended to the cleaned **string** value

The **main()** function now calls the **isPalindrome()** function, passing it the clean text value. This function first decides how many characters are in the text. A single character is automatically counted as a palindrome. If there are two or more characters in the text, the first and last characters are compared to determine whether they are the same, which is essential if the text is to be regarded as a palindrome. If the characters are the same, the function then considers whether there are any more characters still to check - it determines whether the length of the text was more than **2**. If so, the function recursively calls itself again, passing the remaining text in as an argument, without the first and last letters. This continues, breaking the text down two letters at a time to produce shorter and shorter **string** values, until eventually reaching either the final pair of letters or only one single letter.

As the execution of each recursive **isPalindrome()** function completes, a **true** or **false** Boolean value is passed back to indicate whether the first and last letters of the particular **string** value were the same. These result values are combined together with a logical AND operation, using the **&=** operator. If all of the returned results are **true** then the text is considered to be a palindrome.

As you can see below, the program can also deal with the special cases of a single letter, or only two letters:

```
Type in a sentence:
a
The sentence IS a palindrome.
--------------------

Type in a sentence:
ab
The sentence is NOT a palindrome.
--------------------

Type in a sentence:
aa
The sentence IS a palindrome.
--------------------
```

Both of these cases result in the recursive function **isPalindrome()** being called only once to examine the sequence of letters - the function does not need to recursively call itself again to determine whether such a short **string** value of only one or two characters is a palindrome or not as there is no need to break it down further.

Searching efficiently through sorted data

We have already seen how to search through an array of values using a loop to find a data item that we are looking for. The previous programs have all started at the first data item in the array, examining each one until the desired item has been found. This kind of search is called a **"linear search"**. It proceeds in a straight-line from the start of the array to the end.

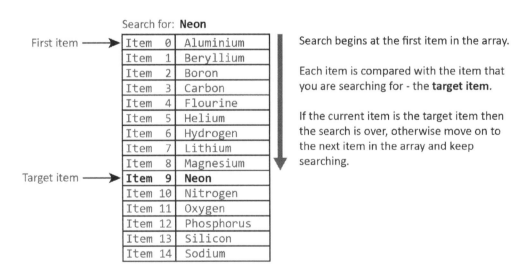

Search for: **Neon**

First item →

Item	0	Aluminium
Item	1	Beryllium
Item	2	Boron
Item	3	Carbon
Item	4	Flourine
Item	5	Helium
Item	6	Hydrogen
Item	7	Lithium
Item	8	Magnesium
Item	**9**	**Neon**
Item	10	Nitrogen
Item	11	Oxygen
Item	12	Phosphorus
Item	13	Silicon
Item	14	Sodium

Target item →

Search begins at the first item in the array.

Each item is compared with the item that you are searching for - the **target item**.

If the current item is the target item then the search is over, otherwise move on to the next item in the array and keep searching.

A linear search is not always the most efficient way to find data that is stored in an array. Once an array of data values has been sorted, instead of examining every single data item from start to finish, we can use a technique called a **"binary search"** to search through the data.

A binary search is especially useful when you have a very large number of data items to search through. In general, the larger the number of items to be searched, the more time a binary search saves when compared to a linear search as it repeatedly narrows down the number of items to search through, rather than laboriously checking through every single data item.

The binary search always needs to work with a **sorted** collection of items, such as an array of integer or text values.

When looking for a particular item of data, we determine which item lies in the middle of the collection of values. We use a simple calculation to find the halfway point between the first item and the last item.

The middle data item is examined. If this is the data that you are looking for then the search ends - the item has been found.

If the item is **not** the one that you are looking for, then the remaining collection of items that you are searching through gets divided or "split" into two halves: those that are before the middle item and those that come after it in the sorted collection.

The search then continues using only one half of the data. The other half will be completely ignored. The search process calls itself recursively to search through the smaller, newly divided collection of data.

Which half does it choose to use? It decides to use the first half if the target item that you are trying to find occurs **before** the middle item. It decides to use the second half if the target item occurs **after** the middle item.

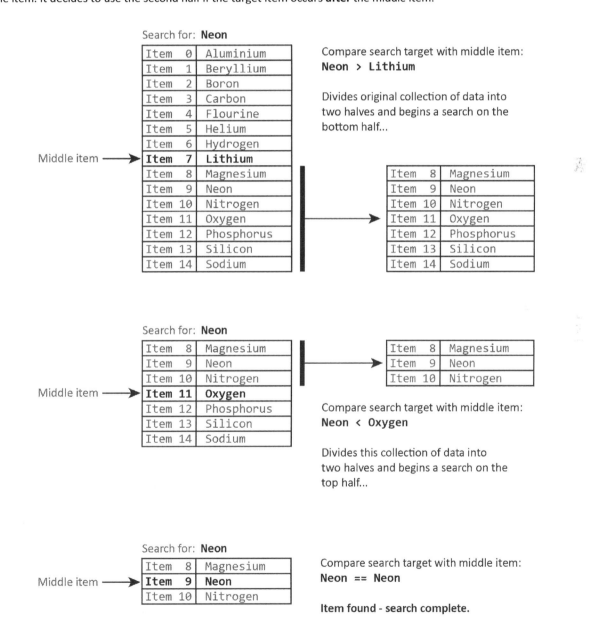

Search for: **Neon**

Item	0	Aluminium
Item	1	Beryllium
Item	2	Boron
Item	3	Carbon
Item	4	Flourine
Item	5	Helium
Item	6	Hydrogen
Item	**7**	**Lithium**
Item	8	Magnesium
Item	9	Neon
Item	10	Nitrogen
Item	11	Oxygen
Item	12	Phosphorus
Item	13	Silicon
Item	14	Sodium

Middle item →

Compare search target with middle item:
Neon > Lithium

Divides original collection of data into two halves and begins a search on the bottom half...

Item	8	Magnesium
Item	9	Neon
Item	10	Nitrogen
Item	11	Oxygen
Item	12	Phosphorus
Item	13	Silicon
Item	14	Sodium

Search for: **Neon**

Item	8	Magnesium
Item	9	Neon
Item	10	Nitrogen
Item	**11**	**Oxygen**
Item	12	Phosphorus
Item	13	Silicon
Item	14	Sodium

Middle item →

Item	8	Magnesium
Item	9	Neon
Item	10	Nitrogen

Compare search target with middle item:
Neon < Oxygen

Divides this collection of data into two halves and begins a search on the top half...

Search for: **Neon**

Item	8	Magnesium
Item	**9**	**Neon**
Item	10	Nitrogen

Middle item →

Compare search target with middle item:
Neon == Neon

Item found - search complete.

Here is a recursive example of a binary search that searches through a sorted array to locate a particular chemical element:

```cpp
#include <iostream>     // Program will be displaying some text on the screen

using namespace std;     // Will be using standard identifiers string, cout and endl

const char TAB = '\t';

// -------------------

void displayArray( string value[], unsigned int numItems )
{
    for ( unsigned int index = 0;  index < numItems;  index++ )
        cout << TAB << "Item no. " << index << " is " << value[index] << endl;

    cout << endl << "--------------------" << endl;

}  // end of displayArray function

// -------------------

void insertItem( string newItem, string sortedArray[], unsigned int insertedSoFar )
{
    // Determine where the new item needs to go in the sorted array
    unsigned int insertAt, itemIndex;

    // Decide whether the array of sorted items was previously empty or not
    if ( insertedSoFar == 0 )
        insertAt = 0;
    else
    {
        unsigned int indexOfLastItem = insertedSoFar - 1;
        if ( newItem >= sortedArray[indexOfLastItem] )
            insertAt = insertedSoFar;
        else
        {
            itemIndex = 0;
            bool foundPlaceToInsert = false;

            while ( itemIndex < insertedSoFar and not foundPlaceToInsert )
            {
                if ( newItem < sortedArray[itemIndex] )
                {
                        insertAt = itemIndex;
                        foundPlaceToInsert = true;
                }
                else
                    itemIndex++;

            }  // end of while
```

continues on next page...

```
            // Copy the bottom items to one place below in the array
            for ( unsigned int copyIndex = insertedSoFar;
                                copyIndex > insertAt;
                                copyIndex-- )
                sortedArray[copyIndex] = sortedArray[copyIndex-1];


        }   // end of if else decision about where to add

    }   // end of decision aboutwhether sorted array was previously empty or not

    // Store the new item into the array
    sortedArray[insertAt] = newItem;

}   // end of insertItem function

// --------------------

bool searchUsingBinarySplit( string itemToFind, string sortedArray[],
                             int startOfRange, int endOfRange )
{
    bool foundElement = false;

    unsigned int itemsInRange = ( endOfRange + 1 ) - startOfRange;

    cout << endl << "Searching through part of array" << endl;
    cout << TAB << "Number of items in this portion of the array: ";
    cout << itemsInRange << endl;

    if ( itemsInRange == 1 )
    {
        cout << TAB << "Only single element to compare with search item" << endl;
        foundElement = ( itemToFind == sortedArray[startOfRange] );
        return foundElement;
    }
    else
    {
        unsigned int middleIndex = startOfRange + itemsInRange / 2 ;
        string middleItem = sortedArray[middleIndex];

        cout << TAB << "First item is " << sortedArray[startOfRange];
        cout << " at index " << startOfRange << endl;
        cout << TAB << "Last item is " << sortedArray[endOfRange];
        cout << " at index " << endOfRange << endl;

        cout << endl;
        cout << TAB << "Middle item is " << middleItem;
        cout << " at index " << middleIndex << endl;
        cout << endl;
```

continues on next page...

```
        if ( itemToFind == middleItem )
        {
            cout << TAB << "The middle item is the same as the search item" << endl;
            return true;
        }
        else
        {
            unsigned int newStartOfRange;
            unsigned int newEndOfRange;

            if ( itemToFind < middleItem )
            {
                cout << TAB << "Search item " << itemToFind;
                cout << " is before middle item " << middleItem << endl;

                newStartOfRange = startOfRange;
                newEndOfRange = middleIndex - 1;

            }
            else
            {
                cout << TAB << "Search item " << itemToFind;
                cout << " is after middle item " << middleItem << endl;

                newStartOfRange = middleIndex + 1;
                newEndOfRange = endOfRange;

            }   // end of if-else

            cout << endl;
            cout << TAB << "Search continues in smaller part of the array..." << endl;
            cout << endl << "----------" << endl << endl;

            foundElement = searchUsingBinarySplit( itemToFind, sortedArray,
                                                   newStartOfRange, newEndOfRange );
        }   // end of if-else


    }   // end of if-else

    return foundElement;

}   // end of searchUsingBinarySplit function

// --------------------
```

```cpp
int main()
{
    // Create two different arrays to hold the unsorted and sorted data
    const unsigned int NUMBER_OF_ITEMS = 15;
    string unsortedData[NUMBER_OF_ITEMS];
    string sortedData[NUMBER_OF_ITEMS];

    unsortedData[0] = "Hydrogen";
    unsortedData[1] = "Helium";
    unsortedData[2] = "Lithium";
    unsortedData[3] = "Beryllium";
    unsortedData[4] = "Boron";
    unsortedData[5] = "Carbon";
    unsortedData[6] = "Nitrogen";
    unsortedData[7] = "Oxygen";
    unsortedData[8] = "Flourine";
    unsortedData[9] = "Neon";
    unsortedData[10] = "Sodium";
    unsortedData[11] = "Magnesium";
    unsortedData[12] = "Aluminium";
    unsortedData[13] = "Silicon";
    unsortedData[14] = "Phosphorus";

    unsigned int unsortedIndex = 0;
    while  ( unsortedIndex < NUMBER_OF_ITEMS )
    {
        // Insert single item from unsorted array into correct place in sorted array
        insertItem( unsortedData[unsortedIndex], sortedData, unsortedIndex );

        unsortedIndex++;

    }  // end of for loop


    // Call the displayArray function to display the sorted array items
    cout << endl << "The sorted array contains these items..." << endl;
    displayArray( sortedData, unsortedIndex );

    cout << endl;

    // Prompt user to type in name of a chemical element to search for
    string elementToFind;
    cout << "Search for which chemical element?" << endl;
    cin >> elementToFind;

    cout << endl;

    // Start the recursive search
    bool exists = searchUsingBinarySplit( elementToFind, sortedData,
                                    0, NUMBER_OF_ITEMS - 1 );

    cout << endl;
```

continues on next page...

continued...

```
    // Report whether search was successful
    if ( exists )
        cout << "*** Found this element ***" << endl;
    else
        cout << "*** Element not found in the array ***" << endl;

    return 0;
}
```

Here you can see how the binary search locates the data item **Neon** in the sorted array:

```
Search for which chemical element?
Neon


Searching through part of array
        Number of items in this portion of the array: 15
        First item is Aluminium at index 0
        Last item is Sodium at index 14

        Middle item is Lithium at index 7

        Search item Neon is after middle item Lithium

        Search continues in smaller part of the array...

----------


Searching through part of array
        Number of items in this portion of the array: 7
        First item is Magnesium at index 8
        Last item is Sodium at index 14

        Middle item is Oxygen at index 11

        Search item Neon is before middle item Oxygen

        Search continues in smaller part of the array...

----------


Searching through part of array
        Number of items in this portion of the array: 3
        First item is Magnesium at index 8
        Last item is Nitrogen at index 10

        Middle item is Neon at index 9

        The middle item is the same as the search item

*** Found this element ***
```

The first thing that the program does is sort the array of **string** values. The array is then ready to be searched.

The search begins by considering the whole **sortedData** array, beginning at item number **0** (which is **"Aluminium"**) and ending with item number **14** (which is **"Sodium"**).

The program determines how many items are in this range between **0** and **14**:

```
unsigned int itemsInRange = ( endOfRange + 1 ) - startOfRange;
```

The result is that there are **15** items in the range, from item number **0** to item number **14**.

If there is only one single item in the range, then the program can immediately check whether this item is the data value that it is searching for. This will result in a **true** or **false** answer.

If there is more than a single data item in the range though, the program now determines which item is the middle item in the range of array items. To do this it uses the following calculation:

```
unsigned int middleIndex = startOfRange + itemsInRange / 2 ;
```

In our example, when the value of **startOfRange** is **0** and the value of **itemsInRange** is **15**, the middle item in this range will be item number **7**.

The program then obtains the **middle** item from the range:

```
string middleItem = sortedArray[middleIndex];
```

It now checks whether the middle item is the data item that it is searching for:

```
if ( itemToFind == middleItem )
{
    cout << TAB << "The middle item is the same as the search item" << endl;
    return true;
}
```

If the middle item is not the item being searched for, the program decides whether the search item is located before or after the current middle item.

It divides the range of items being searched in half and then recursively calls the search process again on one of the halves. The other half of the range is effectively ignored from this point on.

This is how the range of data items is split when the search item is found to be **before** the middle item in the current range:

```
if ( itemToFind < middleItem )
{
    cout << TAB << "Search item " << itemToFind;
    cout << " is before middle item " << middleItem << endl;

    newStartOfRange = startOfRange;
    newEndOfRange = middleIndex - 1;
}
```

Alternatively, a similar split is made when the search item is found to be located somewhere **after** the middle item:

```
else
{
    cout << TAB << "Search item " << itemToFind;
    cout << " is after middle item " << middleItem << endl;

    newStartOfRange = middleIndex + 1;
    newEndOfRange = endOfRange;
}
```

How do you find a middle item in an even number of data values?

It is worth pointing out that if the array to be searched contains an even number of values then there will not be an item that is in the exact middle of the array - this is only possible if the array contains an **odd** number of values.

When there is an **even** number of values, the split will result in an unequal number of items in the two halves - there will be one more value in one half than in the other. This does not affect the overall efficiency of the search though.

Searching through a larger number of data items

Here you can see I have modified the program so that it contains more of the chemical elements from the periodic table. The screenshots below show the top and bottom ends of the sorted array:

```
The sorted array contains these items...
        Item no. 0 is Actinium
        Item no. 1 is Aluminium
        Item no. 2 is Americium
        Item no. 3 is Antimony
        Item no. 4 is Argon
```

```
        Item no. 110 is Xenon
        Item no. 111 is Ytterbium
        Item no. 112 is Yttrium
        Item no. 113 is Zinc
        Item no. 114 is Zirconium


--------------------
```

Whilst it is true that you still need to have sorted the data beforehand to carry out this more efficient method of searching, the data only needs to have been sorted once. As long as none of the data items change after the sort has been performed, searches can be carried out repeatedly, making the extra time and effort of sorting the data worthwhile.

Note that some searches take very few comparisons before they find their target value. When searching for "**Mercury**" the binary search immediately finds the target value with the first comparison that it tries. This is because **Mercury** is exactly halfway through the sorted array. In the case of **Mercury**, the search process never even makes a single split:

```
Search for which chemical element?
Mercury


Searching through part of array
        Number of items in this portion of the array: 115
        First item is Actinium at index 0
        Last item is Zirconium at index 114

        Middle item is Mercury at index 57

        The middle item is the same as the search item

*** Found this element ***
```

The above example shows what we call the "**best-case scenario**". The search item was the very first data item that we considered... it got lucky!

Where a linear search of these chemical elements would take over a hundred comparisons to determine whether the element "Zinc" exists in the array, the binary search reduces the number of comparisons necessary down to a maximum of seven:

```
Search for which chemical element?
Zinc


Searching through part of array
        Number of items in this portion of the array: 115
        First item is Actinium at index 0
        Last item is Zirconium at index 114

        Middle item is Mercury at index 57

        Search item Zinc is after middle item Mercury

        Search continues in smaller part of the array...


----------


Searching through part of array
        Number of items in this portion of the array: 57
        First item is Molybdenum at index 58
        Last item is Zirconium at index 114

        Middle item is Seaborgium at index 86

        Search item Zinc is after middle item Seaborgium

        Search continues in smaller part of the array...


----------


Searching through part of array
        Number of items in this portion of the array: 28
        First item is Selenium at index 87
        Last item is Zirconium at index 114

        Middle item is Titanium at index 101

        Search item Zinc is after middle item Titanium

        Search continues in smaller part of the array...


----------
```

Even with a large number of data items, the amount of data to be searched is very quickly reduced to smaller and smaller portions of the sorted array until the target item is found:

```
Searching through part of array
        Number of items in this portion of the array: 6
        First item is Vanadium at index 109
        Last item is Zirconium at index 114

        Middle item is Yttrium at index 112

        Search item Zinc is after middle item Yttrium

        Search continues in smaller part of the array...

----------


Searching through part of array
        Number of items in this portion of the array: 2
        First item is Zinc at index 113
        Last item is Zirconium at index 114

        Middle item is Zirconium at index 114

        Search item Zinc is before middle item Zirconium

        Search continues in smaller part of the array...

----------


Searching through part of array
        Number of items in this portion of the array: 1
        Only single element to compare with search item

*** Found this element ***
```

Here's what we have covered in this chapter:

A **function** is a named block of code to perform a certain task. It can be activated by another part of your program.

A function must be given a **unique** name. The name identifies the block of. It is used to **activate** (or "**call**" the function into action) from elsewhere in your code.

The **body** of a function is a group of one or more statements that will be executed when the function is called using its **name**.

The body of the function is always placed inside a pair of { } curly braces.

A function can be passed data values as input, called **arguments**, for it to work with.

The arguments to a function are always enclosed within a pair of ( ) brackets.

Because more than one single input value might be fed into a function, each input value has to be given an **argument name** so that the body of the function can make use of it and can distinguish it from other arguments.

Each argument that is passed to a function as input must have the correct **data-type**. The function will expect to work with a particular kind of data for each argument e.g. `float`.

Some functions do not take any data values at all as input. These functions require an **empty** pair of () brackets to show that no arguments are being used.

Many functions produce some sort of result when executed. This result is **returned** to the program code that called the function. The `return` statement passes a value back from a function to the code that called it.

A function with the return-type `void` does not pass back any value at all to the code that calls it. The function will not need to contain a `return` statement.

Upon calling a function from some other place in your program code, execution at that point in the program effectively pauses. The newly-called function then begins execution. Upon finishing execution of the function, the flow-of-control is transferred back from the function to the code that called it. Any returned result from the function is then passed back for the calling code to make use of.

If a function is passed a **reference** to some argument data, the function may process that **actual data**. Otherwise, a function usually processes a **local copy** of that data.

To show that a function accepts a reference as an argument, the **name** of the argument is preceded with the **&** symbol:

```
int displayTenTimesBigger( int &originalNumber )
```

A program can "**declare**" a function to the compiler. This allows your code to call the function before the body of the function has actually been defined at that point.

Declarations for C++ functions are often put in separate files called "**header files**". The convention is for these files to have filenames that end in "**.h**"

Header files can be included in source-code files using the `#include` directive. They make it easy to define and re-use functions in many different programs.

A function that **calls itself** is called a "**recursive function**". Recursion can be used to solve many kinds of problems using very little program code, although the same problems can usually be solved using iteration instead.

1.	Create another function called **displayColourLine** that displays a **string** value in a chosen colour.
	
	It should take two parameters: a **string** value to display and a **char** that determines the colour.
	
	For instance, it could be called using:
	
	      `displayColourLine( "Fire engine", 'r' );`
	
	      `displayColourLine( "Rain forest", 'g' );`

2.	Write a simple function called **trimString**. The function should that will take a single **string** value as input and return a new **string** value as output. The function should remove any spaces from the beginning and the end of the original **string** value.
3.	Create a function called **promptForInteger** that asks the user to type in a whole number. The function should display a prompt message which is passed into it as a **string** value. It should return the integer value that the user typed in. You can even include validation in the function using `.good()` to refuse any values that are not valid integers.
4.	Create a function takes two **string** values as input. The function should determine whether the two values are mirror images of each other. It should return either **true** or **false** as a result.

Chapter 11:
Files of data

Why do we need to use files?

While your program is being executed, all of the data that it is using, including anything that you type in at run-time for it to process, is being stored using electricity in the computer's **random access memory** (RAM). This memory is **"volatile"** – it does not store the data permanently. It can only store data while the computer is switched on. Once the computer is switched off, any values that were stored in memory will be lost. What is needed is a way to store data even when your Pi is switched off.

In computing, a **"file"** is a persistent **repository** – a place to store a collection of data, either on a device such as a hard-disk drive, removable storage media such as a USB flash-drive, or on the SD-card of a Raspberry Pi.

Once running, a program can read the data in from a file, storing it in the RAM of your Pi. The program can then process the data, either to take some kind of action or to produce useful results as output.

To allow data to flow in and out between programs and stored files, your code needs to use **"streams"**. You can think of a stream as a **"channel"** or "pipeline" that data flows through, in a similar way to how we have used **"*channel-in*"** for the keyboard and **"*channel-out*"** for the screen. This time though, the stream is connected to a storage medium for your files.

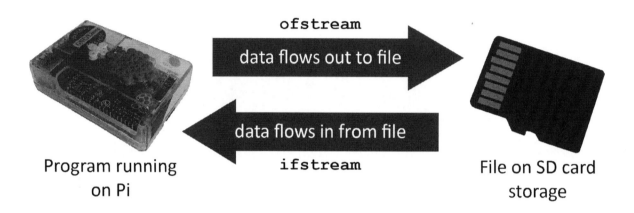

ofstream
data flows out to file

data flows in from file
ifstream

Program running on Pi

File on SD card storage

Using file streams to read and write data

When working with files and streams, your programs always need to include the C++ **file-handling code**. As with other libraries, such as **<iostream>**, someone else wrote the code but **you** get to use it. The file-handling code is stored in the **<fstream>** library and you can include it in your own source-code.

The **#include** directive should be placed at the start of your code along with all other directives that you use:

```
#include <fstream>     // code for using file streams
```

You will also need to tell your Pi whether you are going to be **writing data out** to a file, or **reading data in** from a file.

First of all, we will consider how to write data out to a file. Once we have successfully created a file of data, we can proceed to read it back in again into the memory of your Pi.

To write data **out** from your computer to a stored file, your program will need to make an **output stream**. Data will flow along this stream, out of your program, to be collected by the file of your choice...

```
// Create a stream of data that will flow out to a file
ofstream myNewFile;
```

The statement above creates a new output file stream (or "**buffer**") called **myNewFile**. Any data that you want to store in your file travels along this stream. Note that **ofstream** stands for "**output file stream**".

Next we need to make the file on your Pi to collect the flow of data. To do this we will use the **open()** member function:

```
// Create and open up a new file, called "passwords.txt"
myNewFile.open( "passwords.txt" );
```

Now that you have created your file and it is open, you can start putting things in it. You can "push" text and values into the file. It is very similar to "pushing" things on to the screen, but uses the name of the file buffer **mynewfile**, rather than **cout** (otherwise, your data would be displayed on the screen instead of being stored in the file):

```
// Write a literal string value to the file using the file stream
myNewFile << "Here is what I typed in..." << endl;
```

Finally, when you have finished using the file, you must **close** it. This tells the computer that you have finished working with the data. Other programs and users will then be able to use the file once it has been closed. If you don't close it, the file will be locked by your Pi and no-one will be able to make any changes to it. This "locking" stops two people working on the same file at the same time, preventing them from accidentally overwriting each other's work.

```
// Tell computer you have finished using the file
myNewFile.close();
```

Where will the program look when trying to find a file? Unless you include a **pathname** with your filename, the computer will attempt to use the current directory that you were working in when you began execution of your program.

You can tell the computer to look in a specific directory by providing an **absolute path**:

```
myNewFile.open( "/home/pi/Desktop/passwords.txt" );
```

Assuming that you are logged in as the user "**pi**", the statement above would create a new text file called "***passwords.txt***" on the desktop.

Using an output stream to create a file of text

Here is a program that will create a new file in your current working directory. It will fill the file with a sequence of even numbers. Each number written to the file is separated from the next with a , *comma*.

Example 11.1 – save_numbers.cpp

```cpp
#include <iostream>     // Program will be displaying some text on the screen
#include <fstream>      // Program will be using files

using namespace std;    // Will be using standard identifiers cout and endl

int main()
{
    cout << "Making file called \"even-numbers\" in your current directory." << endl;

    // Create a new file, called "even-numbers"
    ofstream myNewFile;
    myNewFile.open( "even-numbers" );

    // Write an explanatory comment as the first line in the file
    myNewFile << "Even numbers:" << endl;

    // Fill the file with the sequence of even numbers
    for ( int num = 1;  num <= 20;  num++ )
    {
        // Write the number to the file
        myNewFile << ( 2 * num );

        // If not the last number in the sequence, add a separating comma
        if ( num < 20 )
            myNewFile << ",";

    }  // end of for loop

    myNewFile << endl;  // Move on to new line after sequence of numbers

    // Let the computer know you have finished using the file
    myNewFile.close();

    cout << "The file has been created." << endl;

    return 0;
}
```

The following statement uses the special \" character to allow quotation marks to be included within the literal string that is displayed on the screen:

```cpp
cout << "Making file called \"even-numbers\" in your current directory." << endl;
```

Without this special character you would not be able to display quotation marks around the filename **even-numbers**, as these are used to denote the start and end of the literal text being displayed.

When you run this program, assuming that your SD card is not full and that you have permission to write to the current directory that your program is running in, the new file should be created:

```
Making file called "even-numbers" in your current directory.
The file has been created.
```

From the command-line, you should be able to check whether the new file has successfully been created. Using the `ls` command you can ascertain that the file now exists. Assuming it does, you can then examine the contents using the `cat` command:

```
pi@eno ~/Desktop $ ls
even-numbers
pi@eno ~/Desktop $ cat even-numbers
Even numbers:
2,4,6,8,10,12,14,16,18,20,22,24,26,28,30,32,34,36,38,40
pi@eno ~/Desktop $
```

Saving user inputs to a file

Programs often need to save data that has typed in by the user at run-time. In some cases, the amount of data that will be typed in is predictable, but in other cases the program does not know how much data to expect or how much it will need to save.

We will start with a simple program that asks for a small fixed amount of data.

This example on the next page asks the user to type in three separate words, storing each one in a separate variable. The program creates a new file on your computer, called "***verysafedata***". The value of each of the three variables is then written to the file as a separate line of text. Finally, the program closes the newly created data file.

Example 11.2 – save_text.cpp

```cpp
#include <iostream>     // Program will be displaying some text on the screen
#include <fstream>      // Program will be using files

using namespace std;    // Will be using standard identifiers string, cin, cout, endl

int main()
{
    // Make a new file on SD card
    ofstream myNewFile;
    myNewFile.open( "verysafedata" );

    // Type in three words and store them in memory using variables
    string firstWord, secondWord, thirdWord;
    cin >> firstWord;
    cin >> secondWord;
    cin >> thirdWord;

    // Store the words in the file on the card
    myNewFile << "First I typed this... ";
    myNewFile << firstWord << endl;

    myNewFile << "Then I typed this... ";
    myNewFile << secondWord << endl;

    myNewFile << "Finally I typed this... ";
    myNewFile << thirdWord << endl;

    // Let the computer know you have finished using the file
    myNewFile.close();

    return 0;
}
```

Again, once you run the program and type in your text, you can check from the Linux command-line that your Pi has successfully created the file to store the data.

The screenshot below shows the **cat** command being used to check that the text has been stored successfully in the "*verysafedata*" file:

```
pi@eno ~/Desktop $ ls verysafedata
verysafedata
pi@eno ~/Desktop $ cat verysafedata
First I typed this... Albatross
Then I typed this... Squirrel
Finally I typed this... Vampire
pi@eno ~/Desktop $
```

This program is very predictable. It always saves exactly three values, although you could change what these three values are. Unfortunately, we don't always know for certain how much data a computer may be wanting to write to a file. The amount of data to be saved can be much more unpredictable.

This next program is more flexible. No matter how many lines of text you choose to type in, it will save each line until you decide to stop typing any more, which is signalled by entering a blank line with the **enter** key.

```cpp
#include <iostream>    // Program will be displaying some text on the screen
#include <fstream>     // Program will be using files

using namespace std;   // Will be using standard identifiers string, cout and endl

int main()
{
    // Tell the user what to do
    cout << "Please type in some lines of text." << endl;
    cout << "Enter a blank line when you have finished." << endl;

    // Open file stream or writing to "my-data" in append mode
    ofstream myFile;
    myFile.open( "my-data" );

    // Let the user type in lines of text. Stop when they type a blank line
    string lineOfText;

    do
    {
        // Get a whole line of text from the keyboard
        getline( cin, lineOfText );

        // If the line contains some text, write it to the file
        if ( lineOfText.length() > 0 )
            myFile << lineOfText << endl;

    } while ( lineOfText.length() > 0 );    // Finish when it is blank

    myFile << "*** End of file! ***" << endl;

    // Tell computer you have finished using the file
    myFile.close();

    // Tell the user what has happened
    cout << "Thank you - text saved to \"my-data\"." << endl;

    return 0;
}
```

Of course, this assumes that everything went well: that there is enough file-space on your Pi and that you have permission to create a file in the current working directory. You will find out in later programs how to guard against anything going wrong when attempting to create files.

A word of warning: when you run the program, if you already have a file called "**my-data**" on your Pi in the current directory then it will be overwritten by the new file and any data that it held will be lost.

To test that the program works, type in several words, followed by a blank line:

```
Please type in some lines of text.
Enter a blank line when you have finished.
one
two
big
GNU

Thank you - text saved to "my-data".
```

Below you can see that the file of data has been created and that it contains the values that you typed in:

```
pi@eno ~/Desktop $ ls -l my-data
4 -rw-r--r-- 1 pi pi 37 Dec  4 01:11 my-data
pi@eno ~/Desktop $ cat my-data
one
two
big
GNU
*** End of file! ***
pi@eno ~/Desktop $
```

The **ls** command shows that the "*my-data*" file contains **37** bytes of data. The **cat** command displays the text data that the file contains. As you can see above, each of the lines of text that I typed in have been saved to the file.

Note also that the final blank line that signalled that I had finished typing data was not actually saved to the file. The program did not send this to the **myFile** stream to be saved.

Appending data on to the end of an existing file

So far, our programs have used a simple call to the **open()** function to create the output file-stream, passing in the name of the file that the data will be written to:

```
myFile.open( "my-data" );
```

Remember that when opening a file-stream in this way, any existing file that exists with that name will be over-written and any data that it contains will be lost.

If your program needs to **add** data to the end of an existing file, rather than overwriting it, you can specify an extra option when opening the output file-stream to **append** the data.

A program can create an output file-stream using the "**file append mode**", which is indicated by an additional argument:

```
myFile.open( "my-data", ios::app );
```

This means that data that is written to the file-stream will be added **after** any existing data in the file. New lines of data will be added to the end.

What happens if the file does not exist? How can your program append data to a non-existent file? If no such file existed previously and it is the first time that any data is being written to a file of this name, then the file will automatically be created by the call to **open()** so that data can be added to it.

The program below makes use of file append mode when opening an output file:

```cpp
#include <iostream>     // Program will be displaying some text on the screen
#include <fstream>      // Program will be using files

using namespace std;    // Will be using standard identifiers string, cout and endl

int main()
{
    // Tell the user what to do
    cout << "Please type in some lines of text." << endl;
    cout << "Enter a blank line when you have finished." << endl;

    // Open file stream or writing to "my-data" in append mode
    ofstream myFile;
    myFile.open( "my-data", ios::app );

    // Let the user type in lines of text. Stop when they type a blank line
    string lineOfText;

    do
    {
        // Get a whole line of text from the keyboard
        getline( cin, lineOfText );

        // If the line contains some text, write it to the file
        if ( lineOfText.length() > 0 )
            myFile << lineOfText << endl;

    } while ( lineOfText.length() > 0 );    // Finish when it is blank

    myFile << "*** End of data-entry session. ***" << endl;

    // Tell computer you have finished using the file
    myFile.close();

    // Tell the user what has happened
    cout << "Thank you - text added to \"my-data\"." << endl;

    return 0;
}
```

Here is what you the program displays when it is executed:

```
Please type in some lines of text.
Enter a blank line when you have finished.
C
C++
Pascal
BASIC

Thank you - text added to "my-data".
```

Running the program a second time allows further data to be entered:

```
Please type in some lines of text.
Enter a blank line when you have finished.
Prolog
Lisp
Python
Rust

Thank you - text added to "my-data".
```

This data is saved to the same file and gets added on after the existing data from the first time that the program was executed. Examining the contents of "*my-data*" should show that all of the inputs have been saved to the same file:

```
pi@eno ~ $ cat my-data
C
C++
Pascal
BASIC
*** End of data-entry session. ***
Prolog
Lisp
Python
Rust
*** End of data-entry session. ***
pi@eno ~
```

After running the program several times, you should see that any new text that you add gets appended to the bottom of the existing data in the file, followed by the message ***** End of data-entry session. ***** to help you distinguish one section from another.

Detecting whether a file exists

Before a program tries to read data from a file into memory, it should check whether the file really exists.

Imagine telling your Pi to open up a particular file that does not reside in the current directory or even anywhere else on your storage device. An attempt to open such a file would fail, often resulting in a message on the screen to report that an error has occurred. Alternatively the file might exist, but you might not have permission to open it up and to access its contents. It is worth knowing that in some cases, these kinds of problems with files could cause a program to crash.

Once your program has attempted to create an input file-stream to read data in from a file, it can use the **good()** member function to test whether or not the stream now exists and whether it contains any data:

```
ifstream myFileOnTheCard;

// Look for the file and try to open it ready to read data into the program
myFileOnTheCard.open( "my-data" );

if ( myFileOnTheCard.good() )
    cout << "FOUND THE FILE AND IT CONTAINS DATA TO READ IN" << endl;
else
    cout << "COULD NOT FIND THE FILE OR IT IS EMPTY" << endl;
```

Note that we have previously used the **good()** member function when validating keyboard input from the **cin** stream.

This simple program checks for the existence of the file called "**my-data**" that was created by the previous **Example 11.3 - save_inputs.cpp** program. The program reports whether the file exists and whether it can be opened:

```cpp
#include <iostream>     // Program will be displaying some text on the screen
#include <fstream>      // Program will be using files

using namespace std;    // Will be using standard identifiers cout and endl

int main()
{
    int errorCode = 0;

    ifstream myFileOnTheCard;

    // Look for the file and try to open it ready to read data into the program
    myFileOnTheCard.open( "my-data" );

    if ( myFileOnTheCard.good() )
    {
        cout << "FOUND THE FILE - OK TO TAKE A LOOK INSIDE!" << endl;
        myFileOnTheCard.close();
    }
    else
    {
        cout << "No data file found - program terminating." << endl;
        errorCode = 1;   // This will indicate to Linux that there was a problem
    }

    return errorCode;
}
```

The code above calls the file-stream member function **good()** to check the status of the **myFileOnTheCard** stream. This determines whether the file exists and can be accessed. If the file is found and opened successfully then the function will return a **true** value, otherwise it will return the value **false**.

This is achieved by the **if** statement below:

```cpp
    if ( myFileOnTheCard.good() )
    {
        cout << "FOUND THE FILE - OK TO TAKE A LOOK INSIDE!" << endl;
        myFileOnTheCard.close();
    }
    else
    {
        cout << "No data file found - program terminating." << endl;
        errorCode = 1;   // This will indicate to Linux that there was a problem
    }
```

The above code only attempts to **close** the file stream if it was able to successfully open it in the first place. If the file cannot be found then the program does not attempt to close the file stream.

Using an input stream to read text in from a file

Our programs can now detect whether a file exists or not and whether it can be accessed, but how can you read the data back into the computer from the file so that it can be displayed or processed?

This next program reads in the text from one of the standard Linux files on your system, the Bash **"history file"** (a file that records the most recent commands that you have typed into your Bash shell):

Example 11.6 – read_whole_lines.cpp

```cpp
#include <iostream>     // Program will be displaying some text on the screen
#include <fstream>      // Program will be using files

using namespace std;     // Will be using standard identifiers string, cout and endl

int main()
{
    // Tell the user what is going to happen
    cout << "This program will display your Bash history commands:" << endl << endl;

    // Try to open the history file for the user that is logged in at the moment
    ifstream historyFile;
    historyFile.open( "/home/pi/.bash_history" );

    // Check whether the file exists and has been opened
    if ( historyFile.good() )
    {
        // Read in the text if the file was successfully opened
        string lineOfText;

        // Read each line until there is no more data to be read in from file-stream
        while ( historyFile.good() )
        {
            // Read in the next whole line of text from the file
            getline( historyFile, lineOfText );

            cout << lineOfText << endl;  // Display it on the screen

        }  // end of while - finishes when last line has been read in

        cout << endl << "*** End of file reached ***" << endl;

        // Tell computer you have finished using the file
        historyFile.close();

        cout << endl << endl << "File closed."  << endl;

    }
    else
        cout << "ERROR! Could not read from the Bash history file!" << endl;


    return 0;
}
```

The program creates a new input file-stream called **historyFile** to allow data to flow from the Bash history file into memory. This file is usually called *.bash_history* and is stored in your home directory, hence the file-stream attempts to open "*/home/pi/.bash_history*". Note that you will need to use a different path if you are not logged in with the username "*pi*".

Note also that the filename of the history file begins with "**.**" which makes it a **hidden file**. This means that it is normally hidden from view at the command-line, unless you specify the **-a** option when using the **ls** command.

The code first uses the **good()** function to check whether or not the file has been successfully located and opened. If not, an error message is displayed and the program finishes.

If successful though, the program enters a **while** loop, which also uses the **good()** function to repeatedly check whether there is any data left in the file to read in. If there is, your Pi reads in a complete line of text and displays it on the screen. Once the **good()** function indicates that the end of the file has been reached, the **while** loop terminates. The file-stream is then closed and the program finishes.

```
This program will display your Bash history commands:

ls
ls c*
clear
cat mycommands | sort | more
pwd

*** End of file reached ***


File closed.
```

Example 11.6 - read_whole_lines.cpp above does very little with the data as it reads it in from the file. It merely displays each line of text on the screen before moving on to the next line in the file. It is easy for your program to process or do something more meaningful with the data as it is read in from a file.

Reading in one single character from a file at a time

Note that **getline()** brings in a whole line of text, reading in all characters until encountering a **\n** *new-line* character, which indicates the end of the current line in the file.

Alternatively, you can read in **individual characters** using the **get()** member function of **ifstream**, rather than reading in a whole line. This can be especially useful for simple files that are not organised as individual lines of text, containing instead a single unbroken block of character data.

The code below uses this approach:

```
char singleChar;

// Determine whether there is still data in the file that can be read in
while ( myFile.good() )
{
    myFile.get( singleChar );  // Read in a single character
    cout << singleChar << endl;  // Display it on the screen
}
```

The program below uses this single-character approach to read in the same file, pausing briefly after displaying each individual character:

```cpp
#include <iostream>    // Program will be displaying some text on the screen
#include <fstream>     // Program will be using files
#include <unistd.h>    // Uses the sleep() function to pause 1 second

using namespace std;    // Will be using standard identifiers string, cout and endl

int main()
{
    // Tell the user what is going to happen
    cout << "This program will display your Bash history commands:" << endl << endl;

    // Try to open the history file for the user that is logged in at the moment
    ifstream historyFile;
    historyFile.open( "/home/pi/.bash_history" );

    // Check whether the file exists and can be opened
    if ( historyFile.good() )
    {
        // Read in the text if the file was successfully opened
        char singleChar;

        // Determine whether there is still data in the file that can be read in
        while ( historyFile.good() )
        {

            historyFile.get( singleChar );  // Read in a single character
            cout << singleChar << flush;  // Display it on the screen
            usleep( 50000 );  // Pause for 1/20th of a second

        }  // end of while - finishes when last line has been read in

        cout << endl << "*** End of file reached ***" << endl;

        // Tell computer you have finished using the file
        historyFile.close();

        cout << endl << endl << "File closed."  << endl;

    }
    else
        cout << "ERROR! Could not read from the Bash history file!" << endl;


    return 0;
}
```

On running the program, you should see the contents of your Bash history file being displayed gradually, character-by-character, as though on an old tele-type computer terminal, rather than at the full speed of your Raspberry Pi.

Processing data as it is read in from an input stream

The next example reads in a list of words from a file called "**_wordlist_**", picking out those words that are a certain number of characters in length. For instance, it could automatically find all words in the file that are twelve letters long.

Before we look at how this would be done, we first need to create a new file of words, or find an existing file that we can use.

Creating a dictionary file of words for the program to use

Quite a few Linux programs make use of a "**dictionary file**". This is a list of words that is used to look up correct spellings. Popular word-processors such as Libre Office Writer make use of such files. There are also several stand-alone spell-checking tools available in Linux, including "**_aspell_**" and "**_ispell_**".

In the UK, many Linux systems use a file called "**_british-english_**", which can be found in the "**_/usr/share/dict_** " directory.

To check whether this file is already present on your Pi, try typing the following at the command-line:

```
ls -als /usr/share/dict/british-english
```

Hopefully, you should find that you already have this file on your system. If not, to install the list of words on your system, from the command-line you can try:

```
sudo apt-get install wbritish
```

Assuming that all goes well with the install, if you try the `ls` command again exactly as before, you should now find that the file "**_/usr/share/dict/british-english_**" exists on your Pi.

If you want to check the contents of this file, try:

```
cat /usr/share/dict/british-english
```

This will display the contents of the file as a scrolling list of words, with one word shown on each line.

Alternatively, you may choose to use a different dictionary file for any other language that you want to work with. There are many others available for downloading over the Internet, including Open Source files that are frequently updated with new words.

If you are still unable to find a dictionary file on your Pi, or you cannot download one from the Internet, you can make your own simple file that contains a few different words. Simply create a new text file in Nano and type each word on a different line before saving your finished file.

Below is a very short file of simple words that I created to test **Example 11.8 - word_lengths.cpp**. The file has been saved as "**wordlist**" in the same directory as the program. You may notice that the words have been arranged in alphabetical order - this will be useful later on.

As you can see, I have seen chosen some of the most important words known to the English language:

```
alien
awesome
camera
cat
dog
frisbee
pizza
octopus
otter
toast
```

In the next program, it is important that you supply the correct filename for the list of words that you want to use.

If you want to use the file "**/usr/share/dict/british-english**" dictionary, your code will need the following **open()** statement:

```
dictionaryFile.open( "/usr/share/dict/british-english" );
```

If your dictionary of words is a "**wordlist**" file that you have created yourself then your code should use:

```
dictionaryFile.open( "wordlist" );
```

I have included both of these **open()** statements in the program below, although the latter is commented out. Which filename you choose is up to you. Comment out the line that you don't want, or leave it out altogether.

Example 11.8 – word_lengths.cpp

```cpp
#include <iostream>    // Program will be displaying some text on the screen
#include <fstream>     // Program will be using files

using namespace std;   // Will be using standard identifiers string, cout and endl

int main()
{
    int numEntriesFound = 0;

    cout << "Enter number of chars to search for" << endl;
    unsigned int chars;
    cin >> chars;
    cout << endl;   // Display blank line

    // Try to open the dictionary file - USE THE CORRECT FILENAME FOR YOUR SYSTEM
    ifstream dictionaryFile;
    dictionaryFile.open( "/usr/share/dict/british-english" );
    // dictionaryFile.open( "wordlist" );
```

continues on next page...

```
    // Read in the text if the file was successfully opened
    if ( dictionaryFile.good() )
    {
        // Read in contents of file, line-by-line
        string lineOfText;
        while ( getline( dictionaryFile, lineOfText ) )
        {
            // Determine whether this word has the desired number of characters
            if ( lineOfText.length() == chars )
            {
                cout << lineOfText << endl;
                numEntriesFound++;
            }
        }  // end of while loop

        cout << endl << "*** End of file reached ***" << endl;

        // Tell computer you have finished using the file.
        dictionaryFile.close();

        cout << endl << endl;  // Display blank lines

        // Display summary of words found
        cout << "Found " << numEntriesFound;
        cout << " entries with this number of characters." << endl;
    }
    else
        cout << "ERROR! COULD NOT READ FROM FILE!!!" << endl;

    return 0;
}
```

The example below shows the results of a search for words that contain exactly twenty characters. Ten such words were found in the file (some of which include ' *apostrophe* symbols):

```
Enter number of chars to search for
20

Andrianampoinimerina
chlorofluorocarbon's
counterrevolutionary
disenfranchisement's
electrocardiograph's
electroencephalogram
oversimplification's
telecommunications's
transubstantiation's
uncharacteristically

*** End of file reached ***


Found 10 entries with this number of characters.
```

As each word is read in from the file, the `length()` function is used to determine how many characters it contains. If the word contains the specified number of characters then it is displayed on the screen and the **numEntriesFound** counter that records the number of words that have been found is increased. After the search is finished, the number of matching entries is also displayed as a summary.

Refining the search process

A slight twist would be to ask the computer to search for words that begin with a certain letter.

It would be very easy to add some extra code at the start of the program to prompt the user for this:

```cpp
// Prompt user for a letter - will search for words that begin with this letter
cout << "Starting with letter (or * for all)" << endl;
char firstLetter;
cin >> firstLetter;

firstLetter = toupper( firstLetter );  // The search will be case-insensitive
```

Note the use of `'*'` as a "**wild-card**" character. This indicates that **any** letter will be acceptable as the start of a word.

When checking each word that is read in from the file, as well as checking the length of the word, the program can also check the very first character to see whether that word begins with the particular letter that the user is looking for:

```cpp
// Check whether the word from the file is what the user is looking for
if ( lineOfText.length() == chars )
    if ( firstLetter == '*' or ( toupper( lineOfText.at( 0 ) ) == firstLetter ) )
    {
        cout << lineOfText << endl;
        numEntriesFound++;
    }  // end of nested-if that checks for a match
```

Here is the improved program:

Example 11.9 – *word_search.cpp*

```cpp
#include <iostream>    // Program will be displaying some text on the screen
#include <fstream>     // Program will be using files

using namespace std;    // Will be using standard identifiers string, cout and endl

int main()
{
    int numEntriesFound = 0;

    cout << "Enter number of chars to search for" << endl;
    unsigned int chars;
    cin >> chars;
```

continues on next page...

```cpp
    cout << endl;  // Display blank line

    // Prompt user for a letter - will search for words that begin with this letter
    cout << "Starting with letter (or * for all)" << endl;
    char firstLetter;
    cin >> firstLetter;

    firstLetter = toupper( firstLetter );  // The search will be case-insensitive

    cout << endl;  // Display blank line

    // Try to open the dictionary file - USE THE CORRECT FILENAME FOR YOUR SYSTEM
    ifstream dictionaryFile;
    dictionaryFile.open( "/usr/share/dict/british-english" );
    // dictionaryFile.open( wordlist" );

    // Read in the text if the file was successfully opened
    if ( dictionaryFile.good() )
    {
        // Read in contents of file, line-by-line
        string lineOfText;
        while ( getline( dictionaryFile, lineOfText ) )
        {
            // Check whether the word from the file is what the user is looking for
            if ( lineOfText.length() == chars )
                if ( firstLetter == '*'
                or ( toupper( lineOfText.at( 0 ) ) == firstLetter ) )
                {
                    cout << lineOfText << endl;
                    numEntriesFound++;
                }  // end of nested-if that checks for a match

        }  // end of while loop

        cout << endl << "*** End of search ***" << endl;

        // Tell computer you have finished using the file.
        dictionaryFile.close();

        cout << endl << endl;  // Display blank lines

        // Display summary of words found
        cout << "Found " << numEntriesFound;
        cout << " entries with this number of characters." << endl;
    }
    else
        cout << "ERROR! COULD NOT READ FROM FILE!!!" << endl;

    return 0;
}
```

You can see below what happened when I searched for three letter words beginning with the letter **'z'**:

```
Enter number of chars to search for
3

Starting with letter (or * for all)
z

Z's
Zen
Zoe
zap
zed
zip
zit
zoo

*** End of search ***


Found 8 entries with this number of characters.
```

You can also see that the **'*'** *wild-card* works for all first-letters:

```
Enter number of chars to search for
23

Starting with letter (or * for all)
*

electroencephalograph's

*** End of search ***


Found 1 entries with this number of characters.
```

Searching more efficiently through sorted data

The program could actually be made more efficient for files of words that are in alphabetical order. If the user wants to find all letters that begin with a particular letter, once all of the words have been found that begin with this letter, there is no point in reading in the rest of the file since no more matching words will be found.

The **while** loop that reads in the file one line at a time could be made to terminate once a word has been found that begins with a letter that is beyond the particular one that the user is interested in. For instance, if you wanted to find all words that begin with the letter **'s'**, there is no point in searching beyond this as the program is guaranteed not to find anything useful:

```cpp
// Terminate the search if have gone past the letter that user wants
if ( lineOfText.at( 0 ) > firstLetter )
    break;
```

Note that the contents of the "*/usr/share/dict/british-english*" file are **not** actually in alphabetical order though. If you examine the file in a text editor, you should see that the words that begin with capitals are listed first, followed by those that begin with lower-case letters, then followed by those that begin with special characters such as accents.

Why is the "**/usr/share/dict/british-english**" file in this order rather than the strict alphabetical order that you would find in a printed dictionary on your book shelf? It is because the file was originally sorted by someone using the ordering of characters in the **Extended-ASCII** character-set.

Notice that in ASCII, the character **A** always appears before **a** in the character-set. Similarly, in extended-ASCII, special "roman" characters appear after the lower-case letters. This means that É, ê, é and ê appear after a conventional lower-case **e**.

Because the order of the character codes in a character-set is very often used to sort data in memory or in a file, this creates data that is not strictly sorted in "**alphabetic order**". The data is said to be "**lexicographically sorted**" - sorted in order of the different symbols as they are ordered in the character-set. Hence the entry "**ESP's**" can be found before "**earthworm**", which is also before "**émigré**" in the dictionary file.

Using an array to store and process the data from a file

Sometimes, data from a file needs to be used repeatedly by a program. To save time, it can be helpful to read all of the data in once, storing it in the computer's memory to use again and again. (This assumes that there is enough space in memory to hold the contents of the entire file.)

For this next example, make a text file containing some simple data and save it with the filename "**places**".

Here is an example of a "**places**" file that I created using Nano:

```
Exeter
Portree
London
Dundee
Swansea
Bristol
Glasgow
Belfast
Leeds
Cardiff
Manchester
Sheffield
Plymouth
```

Example 11.10 - read_into_array.cpp on the next page reads the names from the **places** file into the computer's memory. It stores them in a single array of **string** values, called **placeName**.

The program then picks a random number, called **choice**. It uses this random number as an index into the **placeName** array to select a mystery place name, calling it **secretName**. The user is then asked to guess the place that the computer has picked. To make it a little easier, the computer displays how many letters are in the mystery place name and also what letter it begins with.

Example 11.10 – *read_into_array.cpp*

```cpp
#include <iostream>    // Program will be displaying some text on the screen
#include <fstream>     // Program will be using files
#include <cstdlib>     // Program uses the random() and srandom() functions
#include <ctime>       // Program uses the time() function as the random seed

using namespace std;     // Will be using standard identifiers string, cout and endl

int main()
{
    int errorCode = 0;
    const int MAX_PLACES = 30;

    // Array to store the different place names that are read in from the file
    string placeName[MAX_PLACES];
    int howManyPlaces = 0;

    // Try to open the file of place names
    ifstream myFile;
    myFile.open( "places" );

    // Exit the program if the file cannot be opened - no point in continuing
    if ( not myFile.good() )
    {
        cout << "CAN'T FIND FILE." << endl;
        exit( 1 );
    }   // end of if decision

    // Opened the file, so read in the place names and store them in the array
    string onePlace;

    while ( myFile.good()  and  howManyPlaces < MAX_PLACES )
    {
        getline( myFile, onePlace );

        placeName[howManyPlaces] = onePlace;

        howManyPlaces = howManyPlaces + 1;
    }   // end of while

    // Seed the random numbers to make choices more random
    srandom ( time( 0 ) );

    // Pick a place by choosing a random index number for the array
    int choice = random() % howManyPlaces;

    string secretName = placeName[choice];

    // Display length of the place name as a clue
    cout << "I have got " << secretName.length() << " letters..." << endl;
```

continues on next page...

continued...

```
    // Display first letter of the place name as another clue
    cout << "My first letter is " << secretName.at( 0 ) << endl;

    // Ask the user to guess the place name
    string guess = "";

    while ( guess != secretName )
    {
        cout << "Guess the place..." << endl;

        cin >> guess;

        if ( guess == secretName )
            cout << "YOU GOT IT!" << endl;
        else
            cout << "Nope! Keep trying." << endl;
    }  // end of while loop that controls guesses


    return errorCode;
}
```

Here is an example of the program in action:

```
I have got 8 letters...
My first letter is P
Guess the place...
Penzance
Nope! Keep trying.
Guess the place...
Plymouth
YOU GOT IT!
```

It's quite easy to guess the place since it is chosen from such a small file of data. To make the game more challenging you can edit your data file to add more place names. When you run the program again, any additional place names that you have added will be read into the computer and stored in the array.

The advantage of using a separate data file is that we can make changes to the stored data without needing to edit or recompile the C++ program code in order to recognise the changes to the place names.

Just imagine if we had not used a data file with our program. We would have needed to manually set the values in the placeName array using C++ statements in our program, such as in the code below:

```
placeName[0] = "Exeter";
placeName[1] = "Portree";
placeName[2] = "London";
placeName[3] = "Dundee";
```

If we had embedded the place name data directly in the program as in the example above, then every time we make a change to the data or add new place names, the entire program would need to be recompiled. We would also need to manually assign the value for the howManyPlaces variable to keep track of the number of items in the placeName array.

This next program makes use of the techniques that we have learned so far to open a file and read values into an array so that they can be searched.

The program mimics a simple spell-checker that you might use in a word-processor. It reads a list of acceptable spellings from the "*wordlist*" dictionary file (used earlier in *Example 11.8 - word_lengths.cpp*) and stores them in an array called **wordArray**. When the user types in a **string** value, the computer searches for the corresponding word in the array. If it can be found, then it is judged to have been spelled correctly, otherwise it is judged to be an unrecognised word or one that contains a spelling mistake.

Example 11.11 – spell_check.cpp

```cpp
#include <iostream>     // Program will display some text on the screen as output
#include <fstream>      // Program will be using files

using namespace std;    // Will be using standard identifiers string, cin, cout, endl


// --------------------

// This constant value will be used by all parts of the program (global constant)
const int MAX_WORDS = 100000;  // This is enough for a typical dictionary file


// --------------------

string convertToCapitals( string wordString )
{
    unsigned int len = wordString.length();

    for ( unsigned int pos = 0;  pos < len;  pos++ )
        wordString.at( pos ) = toupper( wordString.at( pos ) );

    return wordString;

}  // end of convertToCapitals function


// --------------------

int readInFileOfWords( string wordArray[] )
{
    int wordsAdded = 0;

    ifstream wordFile;  // Connect to the file of words

    wordFile.open( "wordlist" );  // Attempt to open the file from current directory
    // wordFile.open( "/usr/share/dict/british-english" ); // Alternative file to use

    // Check whether or not the file could be opened
    if ( not wordFile.good() )
        cout << "CAN'T READ THE FILE." << endl;
```

continues on next page...

```
        else
        {
            string newWord;

            // Read in each word and convert to upper-case, then store it in the array
            while ( wordFile.good()  and  wordsAdded < MAX_WORDS )
            {
                getline( wordFile, newWord );
                if ( newWord.length() > 0 )
                {
                    wordArray[wordsAdded] = convertToCapitals( newWord );
                    wordsAdded++;
                }   // end of if decision
            }   // end of while loop that reads words in

            wordFile.close();

        }   // end of if-else decision

        return wordsAdded;

}   // end of readInFileOfWords function

// --------------------

bool canFindWordInArray( string wordArray[], int totalWords, string wordToCheck )
{
    bool foundIt = false;

    // Start at the top of the array of words
    int index = 0;

    // Look at each word in the array of known words
    while ( ( not foundIt ) and  index < totalWords )
    {
        // Display the current word from the array that is being examined
        cout << "Comparing with item " << index << ": " << wordArray[index] << endl;

        // Compare wordToCheck with current word in the array of known words
        if ( wordToCheck == wordArray[index] )
        {
            cout << "Item matches the word you are searching for." << endl;
            foundIt = true;
        }   // end of if

        index++;   // Move on to the next word in the array

    }   // end of while loop that searches through the array

    return foundIt;

}   // end of canFindWordInList function
```

continues on next page...

```
// -------------------

int main()
{
    string wordArray[MAX_WORDS];  // Array of known words that get read in from file

    int differentWords = 0;  // Indicates how many words are stored in the array

    // Read the words in from the file and store them in the array in memory
    // (is told how many got read in)
    differentWords = readInFileOfWords( wordArray );

    // Display how many words are now stored in the array
    cout << "There are ";
    cout << differentWords;
    cout << " words in the dictionary." << endl << endl;

    // Type in a word to search for
    string typedIn;
    while ( true )
    {
        cout << "Type in a word:" << endl;
        cin >> typedIn;
        typedIn = convertToCapitals( typedIn );

        // Search for the word in the list and display whether it could be found
        if ( canFindWordInArray( wordArray, differentWords, typedIn ) )
            cout << "This spelling exists in the dictionary." << endl;
        else
            cout << typedIn << " is not a recognised spelling." << endl;

        cout << "---------------------------" << endl;

    }  // end of infinite while loop

    return 0;

}  // end of main function
```

When the program begins, it calls the function **readInFileOfWords()** to read in the contents of the "*wordlist*" file. Each line in this file contains a separate word, which gets stored in memory in **wordArray**. The program displays how many words were read in from the file before allowing the user to repeatedly type in words to search for.

After entering the target word to search for and storing this using the **typedIn** variable, the program calls **convertToCapitals()** to make sure that the target is composed entirely of capital letters, before searching for it in **wordArray** through a call to the function **canFindWordInArray()**. The program then displays the outcome of the search on the screen.

The **canFindWordInArray()** function is a simple linear search that starts at the first item in **wordArray**, comparing each item to the target word, returning a Boolean result to indicate whether the target word could be found.

Normally, comparing two **string** values using the **==** equivalence operator is case-sensitive. For this reason, when reading in the file at the start of the program, each word is converted to capital letters before storing it in **wordArray**. Similarly, the target word that the user types in is also converted to capitals by calling the function **convertToCapitals()**.

After comparing the target word with the current item in `wordArray`, the `canFindWordInArray()` function decides whether a match has been found or not. If the word matches the current item in `wordArray` then the search is over and the `while` loop terminates, otherwise the search moves on to the next item if the end of the array has not yet been reached.

```
There are 10 words in the dictionary.

Type in a word:
frisbee
Comparing with item 0: ALIEN
Comparing with item 1: AWESOME
Comparing with item 2: CAMERA
Comparing with item 3: CAT
Comparing with item 4: DOG
Comparing with item 5: FRISBEE
Item matches the word you are searching for.
This spelling exists in the dictionary.
----------------------------
```

```
There are 10 words in the dictionary.

Type in a word:
flimtox
Comparing with item 0: ALIEN
Comparing with item 1: AWESOME
Comparing with item 2: CAMERA
Comparing with item 3: CAT
Comparing with item 4: DOG
Comparing with item 5: FRISBEE
Comparing with item 6: PIZZA
Comparing with item 7: OCTOPUS
Comparing with item 8: OTTER
Comparing with item 9: TOAST
Not a recognised spelling.
----------------------------
```

As with *Example 11.8 - word-lengths.cpp*, I have created my own simple version of the "*wordlist*" file that contains a very small number of words. The program could easily be used with a much larger list of spellings, such as the "*/usr/share/dict/british-english*" dictionary file described earlier:

```
There are 99156 words in the dictionary.

Type in a word:
memory
Comparing with: A
Comparing with: A'S
Comparing with: AA'S
Comparing with: AB'S
Comparing with: ABM'S
Comparing with: AC'S
Comparing with: ACTH'S
```

After thousands of comparisons with words from the dictionary file, this search eventually reaches the target word:

```
Comparing with: MEMORISING
Comparing with: MEMORY
FOUND AT POSITION 61007 IN THE ARRAY
Found this word in the dictionary.
```

Another possible use for *Example 11.11 - spell_check.cpp* could be to look for banned words in an email or to help you skim through some text to find relevant keywords.

Reading from files that contain columns of tab-delimited data

Before trying the next program, you will need to make another new text file for it to read in.

Type in the following data using a text editor:

```
LAX     Los Angeles International, USA
KTM     Kathmandu, Nepal
LHR     London Heathrow, UK
DEL     New Delhi Indira Gandhi, India
HND     Tokyo International, Japan
LGW     London Gatwick, UK
CCS     Caracas, Venezuela
PEK     Beijing Capital, China
FRA     Frankfurt International, Germany
IST     Istanbul Ataturk International, Turkey
BKK     Bangkok, Thailand
PER     Perth International, Australia
MAD     Madrid, Spain
ICN     Incheon International, South Korea
KUL     Kuala Lumpur International, Malaysia
LIM     Lima, Peru
AMS     Amsterdam Schipol, Netherlands
YQB     Quebec International, Canada
CDG     Paris Charles De Gaulle, France
SOF     Sofia, Bulgaria
BLR     Bangalore, India
IQT     Iquitos, Peru
PIT     Pittsburgh International Airport, USA
SFO     San Francisco, USA
```

After the three-letter code that begins each line, press the *tab* key once before typing in the name of the airport.

Once you have finished, save the file as "*airportdata*".

Example 11.12 - tabbed_cols.cpp on the next page reads in the "*airportdata*" file that you have just created. Each line of data that is read in gets split into two parts: The first part of each line is the 3-letter code for a particular airport. The second part of the line is the name of the airport. Note that these parts are separated by the invisible *tab* character on each line.

Once the data is read into your Pi, the program stores all of the airport codes in an array of **string** values called **code**. It stores the names of the airports in another array called **name**. The first few items in each array are shown in the diagram below:

Array of airport codes: **code**

0	LAX
1	KTM
2	LHR
3	DEL
4	HND
5	LGW
6	CCS

Array of airport names: **name**

0	Los Angeles International, USA
1	Kathmandu
2	London Heathrow, UK
3	New Delhi Indira Gandhi, India
4	Tokyo International, Japan
5	London Gatwick, UK
6	Caracas, Venezuela

Example 11.12 – *tabbed_cols.cpp*

```cpp
#include <iostream>     // Program will be displaying some text on the screen
#include <fstream>      // Program will be using files

using namespace std;    // Will be using standard identifiers string, cin, cout, endl

int main()
{
    int errorCode = 0;  // No errors so far
    const int MAX_AIRPORTS = 100;   // Maximum number of airports that array can hold

    // Check that the file exists on your storage card and open it ready to read data
    ifstream airportFile;
    airportFile.open( "airportdata" );

    if ( airportFile.good() )
    {
        string code[MAX_AIRPORTS];  // Airport initials
        string name[MAX_AIRPORTS];  // Name of each airport

        int airportCount = 0;
        string chunkOfText;

        while ( airportFile.good()  and  airportCount < MAX_AIRPORTS )
        {
            // Read in the airport code (first part) until reaching tab char
            getline( airportFile, chunkOfText, '\t' );

            // Store the chunk of text in the airport code array
            code[airportCount] = chunkOfText;

            // Read in the name of the airport (second part) until end of line char
            getline( airportFile, chunkOfText, '\n' );

            // Store the chunk of text in the airport name array
            name[airportCount] = chunkOfText;

            airportCount++;

        }  // while loop that reads data in

        airportFile.close();
```

continues on next page...

```
        // Search for aiports using 3-letter code
        string searchingFor;
        bool foundYet;
        int index;

        // Infinite loop - repeatedly allows user to search for an airport
        while ( true )
        {
            cout << "Type in 3-letter airport code to search for: " << endl;
            cin >> searchingFor;

            // Start at first item in the array, compare 3-letter code
            // to the one that you are searching for
            foundYet = false;
            index = 0;
            while ( ( not foundYet ) and ( index < airportCount ) )
            {
                if ( searchingFor == code[index] )
                {
                    cout << "FOUND! The airport is ";
                    cout << name[index] << endl;

                    foundYet = true;
                }
                else
                    index++;
            }  // while loop that examines the items in the array

            if ( !foundYet )
                cout << "NOT FOUND." << endl;

            cout << endl;  // Display a blank line once search has been completed

        }  // end of infinite while loop that lets you search

    }
    else
    {
        // File could not be opened
        cout << "No data file found - program terminating." << endl;
        errorCode = 1;  // This will indicate to Linux that there was a problem

    }  // end of if decision that looks for file

    return errorCode;
}
```

Once running, the program above attempts to open the "***airportdata***" file from the current working directory. If the file cannot be found then there is no point in the program continuing since there will not be any airport data to populate the **code** and **name** arrays, hence it will display an error message:

```
No data file found - program terminating.
```

If however the file can be successfully opened, then the contents will be read into the computer.

The program enters the first **while** loop to begin reading data in from the open file. For each line in the file, the computer reads in the first part of the text, up until reaching the invisible **tab** character. This part of the line of text is then stored in the **code** array. The program now reads the remaining characters up until the end of the line, signified by the **new-line** character, storing these in the **name** array.

The **getline()** statement shown below explicitly reads characters from the file until reaching the **new-line** character:

```
getline( airportFile, chunkOfText, '\n' );
```

Note that this could have been written in a shorter form, which will **automatically** assume that **new-line** will be the character at which to stop reading:

```
getline( airportFile, chunkOfText );
```

Once the whole file has been read in and the two arrays have been filled with data, the program enters an infinite loop, asking the user to type in an airport code, the **string** value called **searchingFor**.

It will use this value to search through the **code** array for such an airport, reporting the result on the screen:

```
Type in 3-letter airport code to search for:
CDG
FOUND! The airport is Charles De Gaulle, France

Type in 3-letter airport code to search for:
IQT
FOUND! The airport is Iquitos, Peru

Type in 3-letter airport code to search for:
GNU
NOT FOUND.
```

Whilst it might seem that we have gone to quite a lot of trouble, checking that the file exists, reading it in and filling up the arrays, it is worth remembering that you can now make changes to your "*airportdata*" text file and then run the program again without compiling it. You will notice that your newly-added airports exist, along with the others. The same short program could allow you to search through hundreds of airports just by adding data about them to the "*airportdata*" file.

Reading from files that contain comma-separated data values

Many data files contain values that are separated by **,** *comma* symbols. This kind of file is often called a "**CSV file**" as it contains "**comma separated values**".

An example of such data might look something like this:

```
Hazel,Forder,paintball
Bill,Mackaye,bowling
Sam,Hodgson,paintball
Lucy,Gates,high-ropes
Maya,Taylor-Wright,water-park
```

Unless it is the last value on a line, each value is followed by a **,** comma. This is a very flexible method for storing data for files that need to contain many short text values. It allows the text values to contain spaces, hyphens or other special characters.

The program below will use this CSV data. Type it in and save the file as "*activities*".

As with tab-delimited files, `getline()` can be used to read characters in from a file stream until reaching a **,** comma:

```
getline( dataFile, singleValue, ',' );
```

Thus, each separate value could be read in one at a time from the data file and stored in the computer's memory, discarding the **,** comma symbols that mark the end of each value.

The program below reads in the CSV data, storing the values in three different arrays called **firstName**, **surname** and **activity**.

Example 11.13 – read_CSV.cpp

```cpp
#include <iostream>     // Program will be displaying some text on the screen
#include <fstream>      // Program will be using files

using namespace std;    // Will be using standard identifiers string, cin, cout, endl

int main()
{
    int errorCode = 0;   // No errors so far
    const int MAX_PEOPLE = 100;   // Maximum number of people that arrays can hold

    // Check that the file exists on your storage card and open it ready to read data
    ifstream csvFile;
    csvFile.open( "activities" );

    if ( csvFile.good() )
    {
        string firstName[MAX_PEOPLE];
        string surname[MAX_PEOPLE];
        string activity[MAX_PEOPLE];
```

continues on next page...

```
        int peopleCount = 0;
        string singleValue;

        while ( csvFile.good()  and  peopleCount < MAX_PEOPLE )
        {
            // Read in chars for the first name until reaching comma char then store
            getline( csvFile, firstName[peopleCount], ',' );

            // Read in chars for the surname until reaching comma char then store
            getline( csvFile, surname[peopleCount], ',' );

            // Read in chars for the activity until reaching end of line then store
            getline( csvFile, activity[peopleCount], '\n' );

            peopleCount++;

        }   // while loop that reads data in

        // --------------------

        // Find which people are interested in which activity

        string activityToSearchFor;
        bool foundAny;

        // Infinite loop - repeatedly allows user to search for an activity
        while ( true )
        {
            cout << "Type in the name of an activity: " << endl;
            cin >> activityToSearchFor;

            // Start at first item in the activity array,
            // compare each item to the one that you are searching for
            foundAny = false;
            for ( int index = 0;  index < peopleCount;  index++ )
            {
                // Check whether this activity is the one you are searching for
                if ( activityToSearchFor == activity[index] )
                {
                    // Display the name of person
                    cout << firstName[index] << " ";
                    cout << surname[index] << endl;

                    foundAny = true;
                }

            }   // for loop that examines the items in the array
```

```
            if ( !foundAny )
                cout << "NOT FOUND." << endl;

            cout << endl;   // Display a blank line once search has been completed

        }  // end of infinite while loop that lets you search for an activity
    }
    else
    {
        // File could not be opened
        cout << "No data file found - program terminating." << endl;
        errorCode = 1;   // This will indicate to Linux that there was a problem

    }  // end of if decision that looks for file


    return errorCode;
}
```

When executed, the program creates an input file-stream, with the name **csvFile**. Using this stream, the program then attempts to open up a file of CSV data called **activities**. It uses the **good()** member function to test that the file is now open and that the stream contains some data that is ready to be read in.

The program creates three arrays of **string** values, called **firstName, surname** and **activity**. These store details about people and the activities that they have chosen. It then begins executing a **while** loop that repeatedly reads in a sequence of three values in from each line in the file, storing these values in the three different arrays. Once the end of the file has been reached, or once the arrays are full if the file is too large, the **while** loop terminates.

Now that the arrays contain the data from the file they can be searched. The program begins an infinite **while** loop that allows the user to type in the name of a particular activity that they want to search for. It then searches through the **activity** array for the text that the user has typed in. If found, the first name and surname of each person that has chosen that particular activity is displayed. In the event that no-one is found to have chosen the target activity, the program displays **"NOT FOUND."** on the screen.

```
Type in the name of an activity:
water-park
Maya Taylor-Wright

Type in the name of an activity:
paintball
Hazel Forder
Sam Hodgson

Type in the name of an activity:
yodelling
NOT FOUND.
```

Choosing files: typing in the filename for the file that you want to use

In the previous examples, we have seen that you can create a file stream to bring data into the computer's memory from a file. Your program tells the computer to open a file that has a certain name. So far this filename has been built into the program code as literal text, which has then been used when calling the **open()** member function of the file-stream:

```
// Check that the file exists on your storage card and open it ready to read data
ifstream originalFile;
originalFile.open( "airportdata" );
```

Often though, the person running the program may want to **choose** which file to open. We could ask the user to type in the name of the file that they want, store it in a **string** variable, then use this to try to open the file:

Example showing how to choose a filename and then open that particular file

```
// Find out what the file is called
cout << "Please type in the filename:" << endl;
string fileName;
cin >> fileName;

// Create the file "buffer" to read data from
ifstream airportFile;

// Try to open the file - THIS NEXT LINE WILL NOT WORK!
airportFile.open( fileName );
```

Unfortunately, the **open()** function was created before the C++ language existed – it is code from the language "C", the predecessor to C++. In fact, quite a few common functions that people use in C++ actually come from C.

The C language handled text strings in a different way to C++. In C, there was no such thing as the "**string**" data-type. When you wanted to create and use a variable to store text data, you had to create an array of characters, including a special invisible **null** character to mark the end of the text. These were called "**null-terminated strings**" or "**C-style strings**".

Many older C functions expect C-style strings as arguments (input values) when you call them. If you try to give a C function a C++ **string** value to work with when it expects to be given a null-terminated character string, the function will not recognise this as a valid argument and the compiler will report an error. What is needed is a way to convert a C++ **string** value to a C-style null-terminated string so that the value can be used as an argument.

Fortunately, it is very easy to change a C++ **string** value to a C-style string. The **c_str()** function will do this for us:

Example showing how to choose a particular file using a C-style null-terminated string for a filename

```
// Find out what the file is called as a C++ string value
cout << "Please type in the filename:" << endl;
string fileName;
cin >> fileName;    // Note this is a C++ string

// Create the file "buffer" to read data from
ifstream originalFile;

// Convert the filename to a C-style null-terminated string, then open the file
originalFile.open( fileName.c_str() );
```

Working with more than one file at the same time

The next example works with more than one file. It reads in text from a file of your choice, creating a copy of the file that has double line-spacing by inserting an extra blank line after each line of text in the new file. To choose the file to be copied, the program uses the technique described on the previous page, allowing the user to type in the filename of their choice.

The program uses two different file-streams – an **input** file-stream and an **output** file-stream. Both of these file-streams remain open simultaneously. As with any program that works with files, you should make sure that every file stream that your program opens eventually gets closed again once the program has finished working with it.

Example 11.14 – *two_files.cpp*

```cpp
#include <iostream>    // Program will be displaying some text on the screen
#include <fstream>     // Program will be using files
#include <cstdlib>     // Program uses the exit() and c_str() functions

using namespace std;     // Will be using standard identifiers string, cout and endl

int main()
{
    // Type in what the input file is called
    cout << "Name of the original file that contains the text:" << endl;
    string inputFileName, outputFileName;
    cin >> inputFileName;     // Note this is a C++ string
    outputFileName = inputFileName + ".new";

    // Create file "buffer" and try to open the original file
    ifstream originalFile;
    originalFile.open( inputFileName.c_str() );

    // Read in the text if the file was successfully opened
    if ( originalFile.is_open() )
    {
        // Create a new file of same name, ending in ".new"
        ofstream newFile;
        newFile.open( outputFileName.c_str() );

        // Only proceed if the new file was successfully created
        if ( newFile.is_open() )
        {
            string lineOfText;
            while ( originalFile.good() )
            {
                getline( originalFile, lineOfText );  // Reads whole line from file

                // Write the line to the new file, followed by an extra blank line
                newFile << lineOfText << endl << endl;
            }  // Finish when last line has been read in

            newFile.close();  // Finished using the new file
        }
        else
            cout << "ERROR! COULD NOT CREATE NEW FILE!!!" << endl;
```

continues on next page...

continued...

```
        originalFile.close();   // Finished using the original file

        cout << endl << "Done - look in " << outputFileName << endl;
    }
    else
        cout << "ERROR! COULD NOT READ FROM ORIGINAL FILE!!!" << endl;

    return 0;
}
```

Once running, the user is asked for the name of the text file to read in, which is stored as **inputFileName**.

A new **string** value called **outputFileName** is then created to serve as a filename for the new file. This is simply a case of appending "**.new**" to the original value of **inputFileName**.

The program now attempts to create both an input file-stream (called **originalFile**) to read in the original text file and an output file-stream (called **newFile**) to write out the text with the additional blank lines inserted. It checks whether or not both of these file streams are open using the **is_open()** member function before starting to read in the contents of the original file, one line at a time. This is an alternative method to the **good()** member function for checking that the file has been opened successfully.

After reading in a line from the original file, the line of text is written to the new file by directing it to the **newFile** stream, followed by an extra blank line.

Finally, when all lines have been read in from the original file, the program closes both file streams using the **close()** member function.

Below you can see what happens to a text file when the program executes. Here is the original text file that I used:

```
C
C++
Pascal
BASIC
```

When the program runs, this text file is chosen as the file to be transformed:

```
Name of the original file that contains the text:
my-data

Done - look in my-data.new
```

The contents are transformed by the program to produce the following text file:

```
C

C++

Pascal

BASIC
```

The original file remains unchanged, but the newly created file (whose filename ends in "*.new*") contains an extra blank line between each line of text.

Converting between text and numeric values using `stringstream`

C++ can convert between text values that are stored using the **string** data-type and numeric values, such as those that are stored using the **int** or **float** data-types.

Before we begin, you will need to create a text file called "***numbers***" containing the following simple data:

```
32
27
12
199
```

Although the contents of the file **appear** to be numeric, they are actually text values. Unfortunately, **string** values cannot be processed as numbers - your programs cannot perform common numeric calculations on text.

To convert between text and numeric data, your program can make use of a special feature called a **stringstream**, which is part of the **<sstream>** library.

Data values can be fed into a **stringstream** object, ready to be converted to some other data-type. They can then be extracted or "pulled" out of the **stringstream** again in the form of the data-type that you wish to use.

For instance, a particular **string** value **"1.75"** can be fed into a **stringstream**. It can then be pulled out again as the numeric value **1.75**, represented using the **float** data-type. Once it is in the form of a **float** value, mathematical operations can be performed on it that would not be possible on a **string** value.

The **int** value **2001** could be fed into the same **stringstream**. The value could be pulled out again as the **string** value **"2001"**. Once it is in the form of a **string** value, operations can be performed on parts of the text, even on individual characters within it. You can imagine that the **string** might get split into individual characters - something that is easy to do for a text value, but not for a value that is stored as a numeric data-type.

To use a **stringstream** in your program, you must include the **<sstream>** library:

```
#include <sstream>
```

You may then create an object of the type **stringstream** in your code:

```
stringstream conversionStream;
```

You can now feed a value **into** the **stringstream** so that it is ready for conversion:

```
int numValue = 123;
conversionStream << numValue;
```

The value can then be pulled back **out** of the **stringstream** to be stored in a variable that has a different data-type:

```
string textValue;
conversionStream >> textValue;
```

In the above example, once the **int** value **123** has been converted to a **string** value, text and character operations such as **length()** or **at()** can be carried out on it. These would not be possible for a value that has a numeric data-type.

Here is a program that will read in your "*numbers*" file, using `stringstream` to convert `string` values to `int` values.

Once the values have been converted to integers, they are added together to create a running total which is displayed once the end of the text file has been reached.

Example 11.15 – convert_to_integers.cpp

```cpp
#include <iostream>     // Program will be displaying some text on the screen
#include <fstream>      // Program will be using files
#include <sstream>      // Program will be using stringstream to convert values

using namespace std;    // Will be using standard identifiers string cout and endl

int main()
{
    // Try to open text file that contains the data
    ifstream dataFile;
    dataFile.open( "numbers" );

    // Check whether the file exists and can be opened
    if ( dataFile.is_open() )
    {
        stringstream conversionStream;    // This converts text values to integers

        string lineOfText;    // The text value read in from the file
        int dataValue;     // The value once converted to an integer

        int sumTotal = 0;    // Adds up total of all integer values from the file

        // Read in lines of text data if the file was successfully opened

        while ( dataFile.good() )
        {
            // Read in the next whole line from the file
            getline( dataFile, lineOfText );

            // Check whether the line was blank or not
            if ( lineOfText.length() > 0 )
            {
                // Display the original text value on the screen
                cout << "Text value " << lineOfText;

                // Put the text value into the stringstream for conversion
                conversionStream << lineOfText;

                // Get the converted integer value out from the stringstream
                conversionStream >> dataValue;

                // Display the converted integer value on the screen
                cout << " converted to integer value " << dataValue << endl;

                // Now that the data is a numeric value, add it to the total
                sumTotal += dataValue;
```

continues on next page...

```
                    // Clear contents of conversion stream ready to convert next value
                    conversionStream.str( "" );

                    // Reset status of conversion stream in case encountered errors
                    conversionStream.clear();
              }
           else
              cout << "Blank line - ignored" << endl;   // end of if-else decision

       }   // end of while - finishes when last line has been read in

       cout << endl << "*** End of file reached ***" << endl;

       // Tell computer you have finished using the file
       dataFile.close();

       // Display results of processing the numeric data
       cout << endl << endl;
       cout << "The total of all of the values is " << sumTotal << endl;

   }
   else
       cout << "ERROR! Could not read from the data file!" << endl;


   return 0;
}
```

Note that the program also contains these additional statements:

```
    // Clear contents of conversion stream ready to convert next value
    conversionStream.str( "" );

    // Reset status of conversion stream in case encountered errors
    conversionStream.clear();
```

These are necessary to "reset" the **stringstream** converter so that any new value that is converted is unaffected by any of the characteristics of the previous value that was handled. The previously converted value is effectively wiped out by calling the **str()** member function of **stringstream** to empty the text value that it holds. Any error indicators that were set during previous conversions are also reset by calling the **clear()** member function. These steps ensure that any problems with a particular data value that gets read in from the file do not affect all of the subsequent values that are read in from the rest of the file.

```
Text value 32 converted to integer value 32
Text value 27 converted to integer value 27
Text value 12 converted to integer value 12
Text value 199 converted to integer value 199

*** End of file reached ***


The total of all of the values is 270
```

How does the program cope with values that cannot be converted to valid integers? Try changing your "**numbers**" file so that it contains a few blank lines and a word:

```
32
27

12
Aloha!

199
```

Here is what you should see when the program reads in the above data:

```
Text value 32 converted to integer value 32
Text value 27 converted to integer value 27
Blank line - ignored
Text value 12 converted to integer value 12
Text value Aloha! converted to integer value 0
Blank line - ignored
Text value 199 converted to integer value 199
Blank line - ignored

*** End of file reached ***

The total of all of the values is 270
```

Notice that the blank lines are simply ignored - they do not contain any data to convert into a number. The text **"Aloha!"** however is passed into the **stringstream** converter, which gives back the integer value **0** as a result.

If you wanted to customise the code to reject any values from the file that contain letters of the alphabet or punctuation, you could add statements to check for unacceptable characters in the text value before passing it into the **stringstream** converter. This could easily be in the form of a simple **for** loop that uses the **isdigit()** function to check that each character in the original value is a digit:

```
unsigned int pos;
bool foundProblem;

// Code below checks that a text value is composed only of numeric digits
foundProblem = false;
for ( pos = 0;  pos < lineOfText.length();  pos++ )
    if ( not isdigit( lineOfText.at( pos ) ) )
        foundProblem = true;
```

Note that in the code above, because we have already included **<iostream>** in the program, we can make use of the **isdigit()** function without explicitly including the **<cstdlib>** library.

In the event that a problem is found with the text value, an error message can then be displayed on screen instead of attempting to convert the value to an integer.

Here is the final program that validates each value that is read in from the file before attempting to convert it to an integer:

Example 11.16 – validate_integers.cpp

```cpp
#include <iostream>    // Program will be displaying some text on the screen
#include <fstream>     // Program will be using files
#include <sstream>     // Program will be using stringstream to convert values

using namespace std;    // Will be using standard identifiers string, cout and endl

int main()
{
    // Try to open text file that contains the data
    ifstream dataFile;
    dataFile.open( "numbers" );

    // Check whether the file exists and can be opened
    if ( dataFile.is_open() )
    {
        stringstream conversionStream;    // This converts text values to integers

        string lineOfText;    // The text value read in from the file
        int dataValue;    // The value once converted to an integer

        unsigned int pos;    // The position in the text when checking is valid
        bool foundProblem;    // Indicates non-digit character found in text value

        int sumTotal = 0;    // Adds up total of all integer values from the file

        // Read in lines of text data if the file was successfully opened

        while ( dataFile.good() )
        {
            // Read in the next whole line from the file
            getline( dataFile, lineOfText );

            if ( lineOfText.length() > 0 )
            {
                // Display text value on the screen
                cout << "Text value " << lineOfText;

                // Check that text value contains only numeric digit characters
                foundProblem = false;
                for ( pos = 0;  pos < lineOfText.length();  pos++ )
                    if ( not isdigit( lineOfText.at( pos ) ) )
                        foundProblem = true;
```

continues on next page...

```cpp
                    if ( not foundProblem )
                    {
                         // Put the text value into the stringstream for conversion
                         conversionStream << lineOfText;

                         // Get the converted integer value out from the stringstream
                         conversionStream >> dataValue;

                         // Display the converted integer value on the screen
                         cout << " converted to integer value " << dataValue << endl;

                         // Now that the data is an integer value, add it to the total
                         sumTotal += dataValue;

                         // Clear the contents of the conversion stream
                         conversionStream.str( "" );

                         // Reset status of stringstream to make it ready for a new value
                         conversionStream.clear();
                    }
                    else
                         cout << " - can't convert to integer" << endl;
               }
               else
                    cout << "Blank line - ignored" << endl;   // end of if-else decision

               cout << endl;   // Display blank line

          }   // end of while - finishes when last line has been read in

          cout << endl << "*** End of file reached ***" << endl;

          // Tell computer you have finished using the file
          dataFile.close();

          // Display results of processing the numeric data
          cout << endl << endl;
          cout << "The total of all of the values is " << sumTotal << endl;

     }
     else
          cout << "ERROR! Could not read from the data file!" << endl;


     return 0;
}
```

Here's what we have covered in this chapter:

A **file** is a persistent repository – a place to store a collection of data, either on a device or on removable storage media.

Data travels between your Pi and a file using **file-streams**.

Code for working with files and file-streams is located in the **`<fstream>`** library.

To **read** data from a file into the computer, your program needs to create an **input file-stream** of type **`ifstream`**.

To **write** data from your Pi to a file, your program needs to create an **output file-stream** of type **`ofstream`**.

Once a file-stream has been created, you must **open** the file up, ready to read or write data.

To open a file-stream, call the **`open()`** member function, supplying a **filename** as an argument. You may also supply either a **relative** or an **absolute path** to help your Pi to find the file.

The filename may be a **literal string value** enclosed in a pair of `"` quotes, or it may be a C-style null-terminated character string variable. To use the value of variable that has the C++ **`string`** data-type your code can use the **`c_str()`** function to convert the C++ **`string`** value to a C-style character string.

It is possible to check whether a file-stream has been successfully opened by calling the **`is_open()`** member function. This returns the value **`true`** if the file-stream has been opened successfully.

Your program can check whether a file-stream contains any data to read using the **`good()`** member function. This can prevent your program from attempting to read past the end of a file.

You can work with more than one open file-stream at a time, such as one for reading in and one for writing out.

Your code can read in a whole line at a time from a text file using the **`getline()`** function. This reads in characters until encountering a `'\n'` *new-line* character. An additional argument can be supplied when calling **`getline()`** so that it stops reading data upon reaching the character of your choice. This is useful for both **comma separated values** and **tab-delimited files**.

A program can read in a single character using the **`get()`** function.

To process the contents of a file, many programs read the data in from the file and then store it in an **array** in the computer's memory. Once processed, the contents of the array are written back out to a file of the same name.

When creating an output file-stream, any existing file that has the same filename and location as the one that you are creating will be **overwritten** unless your program tells the computer not to do so.

A program can **append** data to the contents of an existing file, rather than overwriting it. To do this it should use the **`ios::app`** option when calling **`open()`** to create the output file-stream.

Your program should always ensure that all file-streams have been **closed** when you have finished working with them. To close a file-stream, call the **`close()`** function.

You can force your program to terminate by calling the **`exit()`** function. When working with files it may be necessary for your program to do this if it is not possible to carry out a particular operation. The **`exit()`** function is located in the **`<cstdlib>`** library.

When calling **`exit()`** you can pass back an error code from your program to indicate to Linux why your program chose to exit.

1.	Write a program that reads in a file that consists of several lines of text.
	After reading the file, display a summary of the number of blank lines and non-blank lines that were read in.
2.	Create another program that reads in a similar text file.
	For each letter of the alphabet (upper or lower-case) count the number of times that the letter appears in the file.
3.	Write a program that uses a loop to generate five different file names.
	For example "**data1**", "**data2**", "**data3**", "**data4**" and "**data5**".
	Generate some simple text data and save copies of it to five different files using these filenames.
4.	Create a program that reads in a file and highlights the white-space that it contains.
	Make it display the contents of the file on the screen using a green background colour when displaying a space and a red background colour when displaying a tab.
	Use the usual default background colour for all other text characters.

Chapter 12:

Structures, pointers and memory

Creating structures to group data values together

Named values that are related to each other in some way can be grouped together to make a larger "**structure**" using the keyword **struct**. This new structure can itself be given an overall name to describe what it is for or what it means.

For instance, various different data values can be put into a group to describe a music festival. The combined structure can then be given the name **musicFestival**:

```
struct
{
    string nameOfFestival;
    string location;
    string startDate;
    int numberOfDays;
} musicFestival;
```

As you should be able to see from the example above, the **musicFestival** structure contains several values. It contains the name of the festival, the place where it will be held, when it will take place and how many days the festival lasts for. Each of these values is called a **member** of the structure. These members are all stored together as one neat parcel of data and it is relatively obvious which value is which by looking at the descriptive name that each member has.

Once created, there are two ways that your code can set values for each individual member that makes up the structure.

The first method is to use the **.** **membership operator** to access each single value of the structure using its member name:

```
musicFestival.nameOfFestival = "Roskilde";
musicFestival.location = "Roskilde, Denmark";
musicFestival.startDate = "25th June 2016";
musicFestival.numberOfDays = 9;
```

Alternatively, as long as you arrange the individual values in the correct order, you can supply them within **{ }** curly braces:

```
musicFestival = { "Roskilde", "Roskilde, Denmark", "25th June 2016", 9 };
```

Either approach is acceptable, although you may find that the second requires less typing.

Using a structure to create your own data-type

Sometimes, you may want to use the same kind of structure more than once. You might want to make several variables that all have identical structures or groupings of data values. With the previous example, what would happen if you wanted to store details for five different music festivals? Would you want to define the same structure five times?

Rather than redefining exactly the same structure again and again for each new variable, it is possible to create a single general structure that can be used as a new custom data-type. Your program may then declare variables that use this new structured data-type.

To create a new re-usable structure for music festivals, your program can define the following general structure:

```cpp
// Define a new data-type called musicFestival
// Your code will be able to declare variables that have this data-type
struct musicFestival
{
    string nameOfFestival;
    string location;
    string startDate;
    int numberOfDays;
};
```

Note the slight change in the order in which the structure is named and the parts are declared. The name of the new data-type **musicFestival** now follows straight after the word **struct**, rather than after the closing **}** curly-brace.

Your code can now make use of the newly defined structured data-type when declaring and using variables. Here's a complete program which defines the new data-type, then creates four variables that use it. The program also assigns the values from one of the structures to those of another, just as you might do with variables that have simple data-types.

Example 12.1 – struct_festival.cpp

```cpp
#include <iostream>     // Program will be displaying some text on the screen

using namespace std;    // Will be using standard identifiers string, cout and endl

// -------------------

// Define a new data-type called musicFestival
// Your code will be able to declare variables that have this data-type
struct musicFestival
{
    string nameOfFestival;
    string location;
    string startDate;
    int numberOfDays;
};

// -------------------
```

continues on next page...

```
void displayFestivalDetails( musicFestival festivalToDisplay )
{
  // This function displays the data members for a festival.

  cout << festivalToDisplay.nameOfFestival << " (";
  cout << festivalToDisplay.location << " - ";
  cout << festivalToDisplay.startDate << " - ";
  cout << festivalToDisplay.numberOfDays << " days)";

  cout << endl << endl;
}

// --------------------

int main()
{
    // Create three new variables using the new musicFestival data-type

    musicFestival lastSummer = { "Roskilde", "Roskilde, Denmark",
        "25th June 2016", 9 };

    musicFestival thisSummer = { "Tomorrowland", "Boom, Belgium",
        "21st July 2017", 10 };

    musicFestival nextSummer = { "Download Festival", "Derby, UK",
        "9th July 2018", 3 };


    // Create another festival, copying the member values from another

    musicFestival bestYet = lastSummer;


    // Display member values for several festivals

    cout << "Last summer was ";
    displayFestivalDetails( lastSummer );

    cout << "Looking forward to ";
    displayFestivalDetails( nextSummer );

    cout << "Best one so far? ";
    displayFestivalDetails( bestYet );

    return 0;
}
```

The new **musicFestival** data-type is very flexible in how it can be used and what you can do with it.

When declaring constants or variable that will use the new data-type, values can be assigned to data members straight away as part of the declaration. Your code can also create arrays using the new type. You can even pass variables of this type as arguments to functions. Note that in the above program, the function **displayFestivalDetails()** takes an argument of type **musicFestival**, the argument being called **festivalToDisplay**.

Here is another program which uses a new structured data-type called **point2D** to represent a place on a map. The program creates three variables of this type, explicitly setting co-ordinates for the two of the places. It then calls a function **findMidPoint()** to calculate the co-ordinates for the third location, half-way between the first two points. Finally, the program displays the details of all three points.

Example 12.2 – struct_point2D.cpp

```cpp
#include <iostream>      // Program will be displaying some text on the screen

using namespace std;     // Will be using standard identifiers string, cout and endl

// -------------------

// Create new structure. Several variables will use this later in the program.
struct point2D
{
    float xCoord;
    float yCoord;
    string textDescription;
};

// -------------------

void displayPointDetails( point2D pointToDisplay )
{
    // This function displays the data members for a point.
    cout << pointToDisplay.textDescription;

    cout << " - co-ordinates ( ";

    cout << pointToDisplay.xCoord << ", " << pointToDisplay.yCoord;

    cout << " )";
}

// -------------------

point2D findMidPoint( point2D firstPoint, point2D secondPoint )
{
    // This function takes two points, calculates the mid-point that is half-way
    // between them, then returns the mid-point to the calling code.
    point2D midPoint;

    float xSmallest = min( firstPoint.xCoord, secondPoint.xCoord );
    float xLargest = max( firstPoint.xCoord, secondPoint.xCoord );

    float ySmallest = min( firstPoint.yCoord, secondPoint.yCoord );
    float yLargest = max( firstPoint.yCoord, secondPoint.yCoord );

    midPoint.xCoord = xSmallest + ( xLargest - xSmallest ) / 2;
    midPoint.yCoord = ySmallest + ( yLargest - ySmallest ) / 2;

    return midPoint;
}
```

continues on next page...

```
// --------------------

int main()
{
    point2D routeStart = { 5, 2, "the row-boat" };
    point2D routeFinish = { 10, 4, "Dead-Man's Creek" };

    point2D halfWay = findMidPoint( routeStart, routeFinish );
    halfWay.textDescription = "Skull Rock";

    cout << "I started at ";
    displayPointDetails( routeStart );
    cout << endl << endl;

    cout << "I stopped half-way at ";
    displayPointDetails( halfWay );
    cout << endl << endl;

    cout << "I buried the treasure at ";
    displayPointDetails( routeFinish );
    cout << endl << endl;

    return 0;
}
```

When the program is executed, the new **point2D** structured data-type is defined.
This contains several data members: an x coordinate and a y coordinate, as well as a text label that describes the point.
These are called **xCoord**, **yCoord** and **textDescription** respectively.

The code in the **main()** function declares two new variables called **routeStart** and **routeFinish**, both of which have the data-type **point2D**.

The co-ordinates and descriptions are then set for both **routeStart** and **routeFinish** before calling the function **findMidPoint()** to calculate the co-ordinates of the point half-way between the two and giving it a descriptive label.

Finally, all three points are displayed on the screen by calling the function **displayPointDetails()** for each:

```
I started at the row-boat - co-ordinates ( 5, 2 )

I stopped half-way at Skull Rock - co-ordinates ( 7.5, 3 )

I buried the treasure at Dead-Man's Creek - co-ordinates ( 10, 4 )
```

Arrays of structures

It is possible to make an **array** of **structured values** in the same way as when making an array of simple data values:

```
point2D buriedTreasure[20];    // Array of 20 different point2D structures
```

Once created, the individual data items within a particular structure in the array can be accessed using the . membership operator:

```
buriedTreasure[0].xCoord = 100;    // Assign value to part of a structure
buriedTreasure[0].yCoord = 275;
buriedTreasure[0].textDescription = "Golden Cabbage";
```

Below is a program that makes use of a structure called **car** to hold the details about a single car that might be owned by a company employee. An array of these structures called **carArray** is used to hold the details for each car that is allowed to park in the company car-park.

Example 12.3 – array_of_struct.cpp

```cpp
#include <iostream>     // Program will be displaying some text on the screen

using namespace std;    // Will be using standard identifiers cout and endl

struct car
{
    // Holds all details about a single car
    string regPlate;
    string make;
    string model;
    string colour;
    string owner;
};

// -----------------------------

int main()
{
    // Data that the program will use
    const int MAX_CARS = 30;  // How many car structs the array will be able to hold

    car carArray[MAX_CARS];  // Array of car structures

    int numCars = 0;   // Indicates how many cars have been entered by the user

    const int MAX_REG_LEN = 7;   // Maximum length of car registration plate

    // -----------------------------

    cout << "CAR-PARK-O-TRONIC" << endl;
```

continues on next page...

```cpp
    // Menu of choices

    string choice;
    do
    {
        cout << endl << "Choose add, display, search-reg or exit: ";
        getline( cin, choice);

        // Menu choice - add new car if there is room in the array of structures
        if ( choice == "add"  and  numCars < MAX_CARS )
        {
            // Type in registration plate and check length is acceptable
            string textVal;
            int len;
            do
            {
                cout << "Registration? ";
                getline( cin, textVal );

                len = textVal.length();  // Determine length of reg plate typed in

            } while ( len > MAX_REG_LEN );  // Keeps asking if length is too long

            // Registration accepted - store in array of structures
            carArray[numCars].regPlate = textVal;

            cout << "Make? ";
            getline( cin, carArray[numCars].make );

            cout << "Model? ";
            getline( cin, carArray[numCars].model );

            cout << "Colour? ";
            getline( cin, carArray[numCars].colour );

            cout << "Owner? ";
            getline( cin, carArray[numCars].owner );

            // Update count of car details currently stored in array of structures
            numCars++;

        }  // end of if decision for menu choice

        // -----------------------------
```

continues on next page...

```
    // Menu-choice - display all cars
    if ( choice == "display" )
    {
        int index = 0;
        while ( index < numCars )
        {
            // Display all facts about this car
            cout << carArray[index].regPlate << " ";
            cout << carArray[index].make << " ";
            cout << carArray[index].model << ", ";
            cout << carArray[index].colour << " - ";
            cout << carArray[index].owner << endl;

            // Move on to next car in the array of structures
            index++;
        }   // end of while loop

    }   // end of if decision for menu choice


    // ----------------------------


    // Menu-choice - search for particular registration plate
    if ( choice == "search-reg" )
    {
        cout << "Search for which registration? ";
        string target;
        getline( cin, target);

        bool found = false;
        int index = 0;

        // Linear search through array until target found or end reached
        while ( index < numCars and not found )
        {
            if ( target == carArray[index].regPlate )
            {
                cout << carArray[index].make << " ";
                cout << carArray[index].model << ", ";
                cout << carArray[index].colour << " - ";
                cout << carArray[index].owner << endl;

                found = true;  // Prevents "Not found." message being displayed
            }   // if target found

            index++;
        }   // end of while loop

        if ( not found )
            cout << "Not found." << endl;

    }   // end of if decision for menu choice
```

continues on next page...

```
        // ------------------------------

        // Validate menu choices and report if not a valid choice typed in

        if ( choice != "add" and choice != "display"
            and  choice != "search-reg"  and choice != "exit" )
                cout << "Not a valid choice." << endl;

    } while ( choice != "exit" );  // end of menu do-while loop

    // ----------------------------

    return 0;
}
```

As you can see below, the **car** structure is used to store all of the details about a single car:

```
struct car
{
    // Holds all details about a single car
    string regPlate;
    string make;
    string model;
    string colour;
    string owner;
};
```

The code allows for thirty of these structures, ready to hold the details of each car that is typed in:

```
    const int MAX_CARS = 30;  // How many car structs the array will be able to hold

    car carArray[MAX_CARS];  // Array of car structures

    int numCars = 0;  // Indicates how many cars have been entered by the user
```

The program enters a **do - while** loop, allowing the user to choose between adding the details of a new car, displaying all cars entered so far, searching through the array of structures for a particular registration plate, or exiting the system. Any other options will result in a simple error message being displayed:

```
        Not a valid choice.
```

Note that when choosing to enter the details of a new car, the program only allows data to be entered if the array is not already full. It also checks that the new registration plate does not exceed the maximum length allowed, which is defined by the constant **MAX_REG_LEN**.

Static and dynamic data

Up until now we have made use of the simple C++ data-types, such as `int`, `float`, `bool`, `char` and `string`. We have created arrays of values and even our own structured data-types that group related data items together. Even when creating arrays of values though, we have tended to work with small amounts of data. For instance, several of our arrays have contained fewer than ten items.

So far, the way that the Pi manages memory has mostly been hidden from us. We have written programs that tell the Pi to store a certain kind of value using a particular name. We have not been concerned with **where** the Pi will store our values in memory or whether or not there will be enough storage space in memory for all of our data.

Let's consider what happens when a program begins execution. When we begin running a program, the Pi **"allocates"** or **reserves** a **fixed** amount of memory space for the program to use. The amount of memory available to the program will not change once the program has started execution. Unless the program tells the computer otherwise, any data values that it needs to store and process will make use of this fixed amount of memory. This kind of data is called **"static data"**.

Unfortunately, limiting a program to using a fixed amount of memory during execution can lead to problems. Whilst static data is good enough for many small programs, it can be very limiting for programs that need to use large amounts of data.

Problems with static data

We have seen that you can make an array of integer values, giving the array a name to describe its purpose:

```
int creditScore[10];
```

The above declaration would create an array of credit scores for up to ten different people, each credit score being a whole number. What happens if a program needs to process a very large amount of data? Imagine a program that needs to create an array that holds **millions** of integer values, such as to hold a credit score for each adult in the UK:

```
int main()
{
    // This array holds a credit score for each of the 50 million UK adults
    int massiveArray[50000000];

    for ( unsigned long long index = 0;  index < 50000000;  index++ )
        massiveArray[index] = 100;  // Person starts with perfect credit score

    return 0;
}
```

This program will compile without errors on the Pi, although upon **execution** it displays the following error message:

```
Segmentation fault
```

During the compilation of a program, the GNU g++ compiler determines the amount of memory that the program will need in order to store that program's static data and it attempts to reserve this fixed amount of space. The space reserved is usually more than enough for programs that don't use extreme amounts of data. Unfortunately though, once the program is running, any attempt to exceed this fixed amount of memory by storing too much data will cause the program to cease execution as it is not possible to obtain further memory.

There is also the further complication that arrays are only allowed to contain a certain number of items, due to the maximum allowable index number that can be used. Even if enough fixed memory is available for your static data, one single array may not be able to store and access the required number of data items as the index value may be too large to represent. This is the case for the program above, the number of items in **massiveArray** is too large for the compiler to handle.

Sometimes programs need to use very large amounts of data, more than static memory allows. As the program executes, the amount of data that it stores may grow and grow. Fortunately, there is another way for a program to obtain memory to store values: "**dynamic data**".

Once running, a program can **ask** for memory to be **allocated** (given to it) from a much larger reserve of memory, usually from an area called "**the heap**". If the computer is able to grant some heap memory, the program may then go ahead and store some data there. Data that is stored in memory in this way is called **dynamic data** (the opposite of static data).

The amount of memory used by such a program can change - it can grow or even shrink - hence the description "dynamic". The space available is not limited by the static memory space that has been reserved at compile time for that program. The heap provides a much larger pool of memory that all programs can use.

To make use of dynamic data, we now need some way of knowing **where** our data will be stored. We need to be able to store our data in the correct place and then access it again when we need it. This requires us to make use of **memory addresses** and **pointers** - variables (or in some cases constants) that store memory addresses.

Memory locations and addresses

You can imagine that memory is like a collection of storage boxes, or "**memory locations**". These are all arranged in a very long line. Each location can be used to contain one thing at a time - called the "**contents**" of a location. Every time that you type in a value or your program generates an item of data, the data is stored in memory using one or more locations. To distinguish one location from another, each needs some sort of label so that they don't get mixed up. Thus, each memory location is numbered with a "**memory address**".

Below is a <u>very</u> simple example of a computer's memory:

Memory address (helps you find a particular location)	Contents (what is stored in this location)	
0	0	*Unused by our program*
1	0	*Unused by our program*
2	76	ASCII code for **L**
3	73	ASCII code for **I**
4	78	ASCII code for **N**
5	85	ASCII code for **U**
6	88	ASCII code for **X**
7	0	ASCII code for *null*
8	0	*Unused by our program*
9	0	*Unused by our program*

You can see above that there are ten possible "boxes" (memory locations) in which data can be stored.

Each box is labelled with a number between 0 and 9. This is the **memory address** of the location. Every single location has its own address - they are all different and no location has the same address as any other location. The first location has address 0, whilst the last location has address 9. Using such addresses allows the computer to distinguish between one memory location and another without any confusion between them.

Each memory location contains a value: it has some **contents**. Whatever the kind of data, the value will be represented in memory as a number - this is what "**digital**" means in computing. You can imagine that unused boxes contain the number zero (representing "nothing") rather than being completely empty. (In actual fact, an unused location in a real computer system may contain some other value where it has previously been used by a different program).

I have stored a few values in memory, each one in a different location: 76, 73, 78, 85, 88 and 0. These are the ASCII codes for the symbols **L**, **I**, **N**, **U**, **X**, followed by 0, the code for the *null* character '**\0**', which marks the end of the text.

A computer actually stores these numbers as base-2 using patterns of binary digits. This is a very simple example, so I have shown both the memory addresses and their contents using base-10.

The previous example features a ridiculously small amount of memory. In a real computer such as the Pi, there would be more than just ten memory locations... there would be millions or billions of them!

As described in the previous example, any value that is stored in the memory of a computer is actually represented using a pattern of binary digits. These patterns have a fixed size - they always contain the same number of digits. In the case of the Raspberry Pi, each individual memory location that can be accessed always contains exactly 8 binary-digits, commonly referred to as one single "**byte**".

Meanwhile, the number that is used to address each location is represented using a pattern of 32 binary digits, which allows a massive range of different memory addresses. This means that the Pi can make use of large amounts of RAM. The Raspberry Pi Model A has 256 MB of RAM, whereas the Raspberry Pi 2 has 1 GB of RAM. Both of these have a massive number of memory locations available to them for storing data.

When storing a single item of data, the Pi will use one or more of the memory locations, depending upon the type of value. For instance, a value that has type `char` can be represented using only 8 binary digits, or 1 byte. Thus any `char` value only requires one single memory location to be stored on the Pi.

A value with the data-type `int` uses 32 binary digits, or 4 bytes. Thus a single `int` value requires four adjacent memory locations to hold the 32-bit pattern for the integer value.

A value with the data-type `long int` uses 64 binary digits, or 8 bytes. Thus a `long int` value requires eight adjacent memory locations.

As mentioned above, a Model A Pi has 256 MB of RAM. If each individual memory location holds a pattern of 8 binary digits (or a single byte), then the number of bytes in 256 MB is:

`1000 x 1000 x 256 = 256,000,000` memory locations, each able to store a single byte.

Later versions of the Raspberry Pi have **1** GB of RAM. This means that the number of memory locations is:

`1000 x 1000 x 1000 = 1,000,000,000` memory locations, each able to store a single byte.

Whatever model of Pi you have, because each memory address is 32-bits long, meaning that if you had enough RAM, the Pi would be able to access up to `4,294,967,296` different memory locations. Over 4 billion boxes!

When working with high-level program code, most people seldom need to work directly with memory addresses if they are writing short, simple programs that use a small amount of data. When a statement in your code needs to access a variable or a constant value, it uses an **identifier** - a name for the data value - making your program easier to understand than if addresses were to be used.

When writing programs in C++ that use variable or constant identifiers, your Pi keeps track of **where** each corresponding data value is held in memory. For each identifier in your program, the computer knows where in memory the particular data value is stored. When using a variable or constant identifier, the computer determines which memory location(s) are used to store this data and retrieves the contents from the appropriate location(s). Remember that larger data-types may require more than one memory location.

Imagine that your program uses a variable called `textString`. This identifier might refer to the data that is stored beginning at memory location `2`. When a program statement tries to use the value of `textString`, such as to display the text on screen, the computer looks at location `2` for the first character code to use. It then looks at the contents of each successive memory location until encountering the marker for the end of the string value, a '`\0`' *null* character. The addresses are the computer's problem. All you need to know is the name of the variable that you want to use.

Contrast this approach with the early days of computers, when programmers had to tell the computer **where** in memory each value would be stored, making programming much more challenging.

References: obtaining the memory address of a data value

Imagine that you have created several variables in a program and assigned values to each one. It is possible to find out where your Pi has stored each value in memory. You can obtain the memory address for the value of a variable using the **&** **reference operator**. You can also find out how many bytes your Pi uses to store a particular value using the `sizeof()` function.

Here is a simple program that creates several variables. It finds where their values are stored and then displays their corresponding memory addresses on the screen. It also displays how many bytes are used to store each value.

Example 12.4 – *addresses.cpp*

```cpp
#include <iostream>     // Program will be displaying some text on the screen

using namespace std;    // Will be using standard identifiers cout and endl

int main()
{
    // Create several variables and assign values to them
    short smallNumber = 13;
    int largeNumber = 123456;
    unsigned long long muchLargerNumber = 987654321000;

    // Find where each value is stored and display on the screen

    cout << "The value of smallNumber is " << smallNumber << endl;

    cout << "It is stored at address ";
    cout << &smallNumber << endl;

    cout << "It uses ";
    cout << sizeof( smallNumber ) << " bytes" << endl << endl;

    // --------------------

    cout << "The value of largeNumber is " << largeNumber << endl;

    cout << "It is stored at address ";
    cout << &largeNumber << endl;

    cout << "It uses ";
    cout << sizeof( largeNumber ) << " bytes" << endl << endl;

    // --------------------

    cout << "The value of muchLargerNumber is " << muchLargerNumber << endl;

    cout << "It is stored at address ";
    cout << &muchLargerNumber << endl;

    cout << "It uses ";
    cout << sizeof( muchLargerNumber ) << " bytes" << endl << endl;

    return 0;
}
```

Here is what you should see when you run the program:

```
The value of smallNumber is 13
It is stored at address 0xbebcc4be
It uses 2 bytes

The value of largeNumber is 123456
It is stored at address 0xbebcc4b8
It uses 4 bytes

The value of muchLargerNumber is 987654321000
It is stored at address 0xbebcc4b0
It uses 8 bytes
```

Notice that the addresses begin with **"0x"**, which indicates that these numbers have been written as **hexadecimal** (base-16).

Why do computers often display numbers using hexadecimal?

The hexadecimal (base-16) number system is a more compact way to such write numbers than denary (base-10) or binary (base-2). This is because hexadecimal can represent the same value using fewer digits.

Any 8-bit binary number can be represented using only two hexadecimal digits.

A 16-bit binary number requires only four hexadecimal digits.

A 32-bit binary number requires only eight hexadecimal digits.

Thus, because memory addresses can be very large numbers, they are often displayed using hexadecimal. The contents of a memory location can also be displayed in this way. When displaying the contents of a whole computer program or data file as hexadecimal values on the screen, we call this a **"hex-dump"**.

You should find that you already have a hex-dump feature installed on your Pi as part of Linux. See the **"Useful Linux commands"** section in the Appendices at the back of the book for details of how to use the **xxd** command.

In the screenshot above, the hexadecimal address **0xbebcc4be** is another way of writing the same base-10 address **3,200,042,174**:

Place value	16^7 (268,435,456)	16^6 (16,777,216)	16^5 (1,048,576)	16^4 (65,536)	16^3 (4,096)	16^2 (256)	16^1 (16)	16^0 (1)		
Hexadecimal digit	b	e	b	c	c	4	b	e		
Base 10 equivalent of this digit	11	14	11	12	12	4	11	14		Base 10 Total
Base 10 equivalent of this value	11 x 268,435,456 2,952,790,016	14 x 16,777,216 234,881,024	11 x 1,048,576 11,534,336	12 x 65,536 786,432	12 x 4,096 49,152	4 x 256 1,024	11 x 16 176	14 x 1 14	>>>	3,200,042,174

Notice also that our three values are not stored in the very first memory locations of the Pi. The value of the first variable **smallNumber** has not been stored at address **0**. This is because the Pi is using location **0** to store some other data. The starting address of the block of memory that our program is allowed to use to store static data has been determined by the Pi when the executable was loaded into memory, prior to beginning execution.

Pointers

So far our programs have made extensive use of variables. Recall that a variable is a named value, and that such a value can change during the execution of a program. You can store literal values in the memory of the computer using variable names (or identifiers) to access these values from your program code.

We have now seen how data values are stored in memory and how we can obtain memory addresses to them using the **&** reference operator. But, once you have obtained the address to an item of data, how can actually do something **useful** with it? To make use of and to manipulate memory addresses, C++ makes use of "**pointers**".

A pointer is a special kind of variable or constant. It is used to store a **memory address** for an item of data. As with other variables, a pointer is given a descriptive name (an identifier) that typically describes how the pointer will be used.

Imagine that your program creates a literal **string** value in static memory:

```
string holidayDestination = "Monster Island";
```

A pointer to this value could be created. To tell the computer to make a *pointer* to a **string**, rather than an *actual* **string** when declaring the pointer, the data-type is followed by an ***** asterisk:

```
// Create a pointer to a string value
string* pDestination;
```

The pointer variable above is called **pDestination**. You can think of the **"p"** as standing for "*pointer to*", thus you could pronounce the variable name as "*pointer to* **Destination**". Many programmers begin the names of pointer identifiers in this way.

As mentioned above, the literal string is stored in the static memory that has been allocated to our program. Using the **&** reference operator, it is possible to find out **where** in memory the value begins. Our pointer can be used to store this memory address so that it can be used later by our program:

```
// Set the pointer to the address of the holidayDestination value
pDestination = &holidayDestination;
```

It is also possible to create a pointer to something more complex than a simple data-value, such as to some data that has the type **musicFestival**, which we defined earlier. A pointer variable could be created, with the name **pMusicFestival**. This pointer could hold the memory address of a newly created structure so that all of the details about a particular festival could be held on the heap as dynamic data, rather than in static memory.

Thus, a pointer variable is like a sign-post that "shows the way" or "points to" some data that is held in memory. When using a pointer to access an item of data, we say that the computer "follows a pointer", just as a person might follow some directions to find a particular place or thing. The computer examines the value of the pointer to obtain a memory address. This memory address tells the computer where in memory the required data is stored. The computer can then retrieve or alter the data that is stored at that location.

Accessing data from a pointer using the * de-reference operator

Below are two statements that look very similar. What is the difference between them?

```
cout << pTemperatureToDisplay;
```

This first statement tells the computer to display the **value** of the pointer variable called **pTemperatureToDisplay**. This value is a **memory address** and it would normally be displayed on the screen using hexadecimal notation.

```
cout << *pTemperatureToDisplay;
```

The second statement tells the computer to **follow** the pointer. The computer **uses** the pointer value, which is a memory address, to locate the actual data value which is to be displayed on the screen. This would display the actual floating point temperature value.

The * symbol in this context is called the *de-reference operator*. Whenever you see that it precedes the name of a pointer variable it means that the pointer will be followed to locate and access a value that is held in memory.

Rather than examining or setting the value of a variable directly, when you follow or de-reference a pointer to obtain a data value and then examine or change that value, this is called "**indirect access**" or "**pointer indirection**".

Here is a simple example that creates a data value to record the current temperature of a city. A pointer is created to the temperature value, which is then used both to display and to update the value.

The value is not updated by **directly** adding 0.5 to the variable. The value is updated **indirectly** by following the pointer to the value and then adding 0.5 to the value that is found there.

Example 12.5 – indirect.cpp

```
#include <iostream>    // Program will be displaying some text on the screen

using namespace std;   // Will be using standard identifiers cout and endl

int main()
{
    // Create a variable that has the float data-type and assign a value to it
    float parisTemp = 23.5;

    // Create a pointer for a float value
    float* pTemperatureToDisplay;

    // Set the pointer value to hold the address of the Paris data
    pTemperatureToDisplay = &parisTemp;

    // Display the memory address stored in the pointer
    cout << "The temperature is stored starting at location ";
    cout << pTemperatureToDisplay;
    cout << endl;
```

continues on next page...

```
    // Follow the pointer to find the value, then determine the size of it in bytes
    cout << "The value takes up ";
    cout << sizeof(*pTemperatureToDisplay);
    cout << " bytes" << endl;

    // Follow the pointer to find the value, then display the value on the screen
    cout << "The actual temperature value is ";
    cout << *pTemperatureToDisplay;
    cout << endl << endl;

    // Follow the pointer to find the value, then increase the value by 1
    *pTemperatureToDisplay += 1;
    cout << "The pointer has been followed and the value increased" << endl;

    // Display the Paris variable directly, after it has been indirectly updated
    cout << "The new temperature value is ";
    cout << parisTemp;
    cout << endl;

    return 0;
}
```

Running the program should produce results similar to the screenshot below:

```
The temperature is stored starting at location 0xbeb2a4b0
The value takes up 4 bytes
The actual temperature value is 23.5

The pointer has been followed and the value increased
The new temperature value is 24.5
```

Of course, your computer is almost certain to choose a different memory location to the one shown on my Pi when storing the temperature data for the variable.

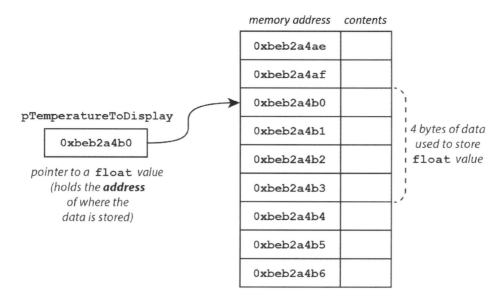

When de-referencing a pointer in order to locate a value, it is very important to make sure that the pointer holds a **legitimate** memory address and not some other value.

Imagine a program that creates a pointer but which does not actually set a value for it. The pointer might contain an unpredictable value, depending upon what the computer had previously stored at that location (possibly even after running a different program). If a statement attempts to de-reference the pointer then it will attempt to use the arbitrary value to locate an item data in memory as though it was a memory address. The value obtained will probably be meaningless and in all probability it would not even be one that exists within the block of memory that your Pi has granted to the program to use during execution. Thus your program would be attempting to access a memory location that it was not supposed to. Attempting to access such a memory location or use the data stored there will usually cause your program to crash.

Here is such an example that attempts to use an unassigned pointer value:

Example 12.6 – unassigned_pointer.cpp

```
#include <iostream>      // Program will be displaying some text on the screen

using namespace std;     // Will be using standard identifiers cout and endl

int main()
{
    // Create a pointer but do no set any value for it
    int* pWholeNumber;

    // Display the arbitrary memory address stored in the pointer
    cout << "The pointer contains this address: ";
    cout << pWholeNumber << endl;

    // Attempt to follow the pointer to find a value, then display the value
    cout << "After following the pointer value, this is what was found ";
    cout << *pWholeNumber << endl;

    return 0;
}
```

Note that the program attempts to follow a pointer which has not been assigned any value. This causes a warning to be generated when you compile it, although the program will still successfully compile without any actual *errors*.

Running the program should produce results that are similar to the screenshot below:

```
The pointer contains this address: 0
Segmentation fault


-------------------
(program exited with code: 139)
Press return to continue
```

The uninitialized pointer holds the value 0, which is interpreted as a memory address. When attempting to access this location the computer triggers a "**segmentation fault**", meaning that it has detected that the program is attempting to access a memory location that it has not been given permission to access. Your program is not supposed to try to access memory location 0. You can also see above that the program exits with the **error code 139** rather than 0 to indicate what has gone wrong.

Null pointers

Very often, a pointer may be marked as **unused** so that the computer will not attempt to follow it. This is particularly useful when setting up new pointer variables that have yet to be assigned meaningful values by statements in your program.

Your program code can set any pointer to a special value called **NULL**. This tells the computer that the pointer does not actually contain a sensible memory address and that the pointer should not be followed. Note that **NULL must** be written in capitals as the value is case-sensitive.

For example:

```
// Create a pointer to a float value
float* pTemperatureToDisplay = NULL;
```

Your program can perform checks before attempting to use such a pointer, testing to see whether it holds the special **NULL** value. This will tell your code whether pointer is useable or not. If a pointer holds the **NULL** value then the program should **not** attempt to follow it. If the pointer holds any value **other than NULL** then it can be assumed that the pointer holds a usable memory address that will lead to some useful data in memory.

For instance:

```
// Check whether the pointer leads to some data, if so follow the pointer
if ( pTemperatureToDisplay != NULL )
    cout << *pTemperatureToDisplay;
else
    cout << "No temperature data to display.";
```

Here is the modified program that will correctly detect that there is no temperature data to display:

Example 12.7 – null_pointer.cpp

```cpp
#include <iostream>     // Program will be displaying some text on the screen

using namespace std;    // Will be using standard identifiers cout and endl

int main()
{
    // Create a pointer to a float value
    float* pTemperatureToDisplay;
    pTemperatureToDisplay = NULL;

    // Check whether the pointer leads to some data, if so follow the pointer
    if ( pTemperatureToDisplay != NULL )
        cout << *pTemperatureToDisplay;
    else
        cout << "No temperature data to display." << endl;

    cout << endl;

    return 0;
}
```

Using pointers to create and access dynamic data stored on the heap

The examples so far have used addresses that refer to static data. Programs can also create data values in dynamic memory. The data from the previous example could easily be stored on the heap, rather than in static memory.

To create a new value on the heap, the program uses the **new** operator. As part of the **new** operation, the computer must be told what **kind** of data is to be created. It will also usually be told what value should be assigned to it:

```
new string( "Monster Island" )
```

The above operation tells the computer to create a **string** with the literal value **"Monster Island"**. The computer returns the memory address of where the data is stored on the heap.

To **use** the **string** value in the future, your code will need to know **where** in memory the data is stored. It can keep the memory address that was returned by the **new** operation for later use, storing the address using a pointer variable:

```
string* pHolidayDestination = new string( "Monster Island" );
```

The above statement means:

> 'Create a new pointer to a **string** and call this pointer **pHolidayDestination**.
>
> Set the value of this pointer to the address of a new **string** on the heap that has the value **"Monster Island"**.'

As well as simple data, it is possible to create **structured** data on the heap.

Here is a structure that has been defined in a program:

```
struct point2D
{
    float xCoord;
    float yCoord;
    string textDescription;
};
```

It is possible to create a pointer to a new instance of this structure on the heap. The statement below does this, creating a pointer called **pFirstPoint** to a newly created **point2D** structure:

```
point2D* pFirstPoint = new point2D;
```

With this approach, it is only once the structure has been created with the **new** operator that you can begin to set values for individual data members. To set each value it is necessary to follow the pointer using the **->** *pointer-to-member* operator:

```
pFirstPoint->xCoord = -10;
pFirstPoint->yCoord = 5;
pFirstPoint->textDescription = "Crashed alien spaceship";
```

One possible approach to dealing with large amounts of data is to store the actual data dynamically on the heap, whilst storing the *pointers* to the dynamic data using the ordinary static memory in your program. Only a relatively small amount of memory is needed to store the pointers, compared to the amount of memory that is used to store the dynamic data.

Here is an example that uses the two-dimensional point structure from our previous examples, but this time the program stores each 2D point dynamically:

Example 12.8 – heap.cpp

```cpp
#include <iostream>      // Program will be displaying some text on the screen

using namespace std;     // Will be using standard identifiers string, cout and endl

// --------------------

// Create new structure. Several variables will use this later in the program.
struct point2D
{
    float xCoord;
    float yCoord;
    string textDescription;
};

// --------------------

void displayPoint( point2D* pPoint )
{
    // Check whether the pointer is NULL or not
    // Can only follow pointer and display data about point if is not NULL pointer

    if ( pPoint != NULL )
    {
        // Follow the pointer to display the data values for the point

        cout << pPoint->textDescription;

        cout << " is located at co-ordinates (";

        cout << pPoint->xCoord;

        cout << ", ";

        cout << pPoint->yCoord;

        cout << ")" << endl;

    };  // end of if

}  // end of function

// --------------------
```

continues on next page...

```
int main()
{
    // Create a new 2-dimensional point, storing data about it on the heap
    point2D* pFirstPoint = new point2D;


    // Follow the pointer to set each data value that is a member of the structure

    pFirstPoint->xCoord = -10;

    pFirstPoint->yCoord = 5;

    pFirstPoint->textDescription = "Crashed alien spaceship";


    // Pass the pointer to the function that displays a point
    displayPoint( pFirstPoint );

    // --------------------

    // Create another 2-dimensional point, storing data about it on the heap
    point2D* pSecondPoint = new point2D;


    // Follow the pointer to set each data value that is a member of the structure

    pSecondPoint->xCoord = 35;

    pSecondPoint->yCoord = 10;

    pSecondPoint->textDescription = "Drive-Thru";


    // Pass the pointer to the function that displays a point
    displayPoint( pSecondPoint );


    return 0;
}
```

As already mentioned, the program stores the data dynamically on the heap. The address of each **point2D** structure is stored using the pointer variables **pFirstPoint** and **pSecondPoint**:

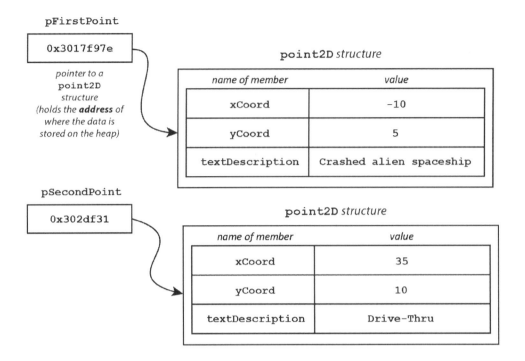

In addition to the **main()** function, which creates the points and sets values for their co-ordinates and text-descriptions, the program also features a function called **displayPoint()**.

The **displayPoint()** function takes a pointer to a **point2D** structure and checks whether or not it is safe to follow.

If the pointer is not **NULL**, the function displays each of the data members from the **point2D** structure on the screen.

Note the use of the **->** *pointer-to-member* operator to access each data-member:

```
cout << pPoint->textDescription;
```

The **displayPoint()** function is called twice by the **main()** function, once for each of the points that are stored on the heap.

The results are shown below:

```
Crashed alien spaceship is located at co-ordinates (-10, 5)
Drive-Thru is located at co-ordinates (35, 10)
```

This next example allows the user to dynamically add contact details about one or more people that are typed in at run-time.

It creates an array of pointers in memory. As the user types in new details for each person, a new **person** structure is created dynamically on the heap to store their data. The address of the newly created data is stored as a pointer in an array called **pContact**.

Example 12.9 – array_of_pointers.cpp

```cpp
#include <iostream>     // Program will be displaying some text on the screen

using namespace std;    // Will be using standard identifiers string, cout and endl

const char TAB = '\t';

// --------------------

// Create new structure. Several variables will use this later in the program.
struct person
{
    string firstName;
    string emailAddress;
    bool sendNewsletter;
};

// --------------------

int main()
{
    const int MAX_PEOPLE = 100;
    person* pContact[MAX_PEOPLE];

    int numberOfPeopleEntered = 0;

    person* pNewPerson;
    string newName, newEmail, wantNewsletter;

    // --------------------

    // Type in details of people until array of pointers has reached maximum size
    // or you choose to quit

    do
    {
        cout << "Type in name of new person, or quit when finished:" << endl;
        getline( cin, newName );
```

continues on next page...

```cpp
        if ( newName != "quit" )
        {
            cout << "Type in their email address: " << endl;
            getline( cin, newEmail );

            cout << "Do they want a monthly newsletter? y or n:" << endl;
            getline( cin, wantNewsletter );

            // Creates new person on heap
            pNewPerson = new person;

            // Set their details
            pNewPerson->firstName = newName;
            pNewPerson->emailAddress = newEmail;
            pNewPerson->sendNewsletter = ( wantNewsletter == "y" );

            // Store pointer in array to use later when displaying mailing list
            pContact[numberOfPeopleEntered] = pNewPerson;

            numberOfPeopleEntered++;

        }  // end of if decision

        cout << endl;  // Display blank line before prompting again

    } while ( newName != "quit"  and  numberOfPeopleEntered < MAX_PEOPLE );

    // --------------------

    // Display all people that have opted in to the mailing list for a newsletter
    if ( numberOfPeopleEntered > 0 )
    {
        cout << "Mailing list:" << endl;
        cout << "-------------" << endl;

        // Use each pointer in the array to access details of a person
        person* pCurrentPerson;
        for ( int index = 0;  index < numberOfPeopleEntered;  index++ )
        {
            pCurrentPerson = pContact[index];
            // If not NULL pointer, decide whether on mailing list or not
            if ( pCurrentPerson != NULL  and  pCurrentPerson->sendNewsletter )
            {
                cout << pCurrentPerson->firstName << TAB << TAB;
                cout << pCurrentPerson->emailAddress << endl;
            }  // end of if decision - whether person wants newsletter

        }  // end of for loop

    }  // end of if decision - whether to display list

    return 0;
}
```

Here is what happened when I typed in details for three different people:

```
Type in name of new person, or quit when finished:
Daisy Westberg
Type in their email address:
daisy@superduper.fakemail.com
Do they want a monthly newsletter? y or n:
y

Type in name of new person, or quit when finished:
Thor Stollingter
Type in their email address:
ts@neat-web.fakemail.com
Do they want a monthly newsletter? y or n:
n

Type in name of new person, or quit when finished:
Zhou Lum
Type in their email address:
zhou@mega-mega.fakemail.co.uk
Do they want a monthly newsletter? y or n:
y
```

(Note that only two of these people have chosen to be on the mailing list.)

Once the user chooses to quit, or the array of pointers reaches its maximum size, the **while** loop terminates. The program then displays a list of all of the people that were entered who opted in to the mailing list for the monthly newsletter.

Here are the results from my Pi after I added a few more people:

```
Type in name of new person, or quit when finished:
quit

Mailing list:
-------------
Daisy Westberg      daisy@superduper.fakemail.com
Zhou Lum            zhou@mega-mega.fakemail.co.uk
Kenzubero Tanaka    ken@tekno.fakemail.co.jp
Jay Schutter        jschutter@flow3d.fakemail.com
Helena Meyer        hm92@zmailer.fakemail.net
```

Note that **Thor Stollingter** is not included in the list above. This is because when entering their details I typed **'n'** to indicate that they did not want to receive a monthly newsletter. The only people shown are those for whom I typed **'y'**.

Another advantage of managing data using pointers is that certain processes can be made more efficient, such as sorting.

When sorting a large amount of data, instead of copying data from one place in memory to another as part of each individual swap operation, the computer can simply change two different pointer values around. The actual data that the pointers refer to stays in the same place in memory as the sorting process takes place. This is called a "**detached sort**".

It is much faster to swap two pointer values around than to swap a relatively large amount of data, such as a structured data type or a long **string** value. This is because a pointer value is typically only a small number of bytes in size, whereas the data that each pointer leads to may take up much more space than this. On the Raspberry Pi, a pointer to any kind of data is always 4 bytes (32 bits). It is much easier to swap two 4-byte values in an array than a pair of much larger data values, such as a pair of **string** values.

Building your own data-structures

Pointers are extremely useful for building more complex data-structures that link together items of data stored in the dynamic memory of the computer. Many well-known data-structures, including **"lists"**, **"stacks"**, **"queues"** and **"trees"** can be constructed by linking data values together through the use of pointers.

For instance, rather than storing values in an array, values can be chained together using pointers so that each item of data in the chain points to the next. This is called a **"linked-list"**. No index number is necessary to access a particular data item. All your code needs to know is where the **first** item of the list is stored in memory. The computer can access the data from this first item before following a pointer to the next item in the list. It can repeatedly examine data values and follow pointers, one item at a time, until reaching the final item in the list.

---

*Example 12.10 – **linked_list.cpp***

```cpp
#include <iostream>    // Program will be displaying some text on the screen

using namespace std;    // Will be using standard identifiers string, cout and endl

const char TAB = '\t';

// --------------------

// Create new structure. Several variables will use this later in the program.
struct person
{
    string firstName;
    string emailAddress;
    person* pNextPerson;
};

// --------------------

void displayPeopleInLinkedList( person* pPersonToStartFrom )
{
    cout << "Here are the people in the list:" << endl;

    person* pCurrentPerson = pPersonToStartFrom;

    while ( pCurrentPerson != NULL )
    {
        cout << TAB;
        cout << "Name: " << pCurrentPerson->firstName;
        cout << TAB;
        cout << "Email: " << pCurrentPerson->emailAddress << endl;

        // Follow pointer to the next node in the list
        pCurrentPerson = pCurrentPerson->pNextPerson;

    }  // end of while

    cout << "*** End of the list ***" << endl << endl << endl;
}

// --------------------
```

continues on next page...

```
int main()
{
    string newName, newEmail;

    person* pFirstPerson;
    person* pLastPerson;
    person* pCurrentPerson;

    // Mark the list as being "empty" - there are no nodes at all
    // (It will be useful to know where the list begins and where it ends)
    pFirstPerson = NULL;
    pLastPerson = NULL;

    // --------------------

    // Make a node for the first person in the list
    pCurrentPerson = new person;

    // Set values for this person
    pCurrentPerson->firstName = "Helga";
    pCurrentPerson->emailAddress = "helga@outer-space.fake.com";
    pCurrentPerson->pNextPerson = NULL;

    // Store this new person as both the start and the end of the linked list
    pFirstPerson = pCurrentPerson;
    pLastPerson = pCurrentPerson;

    // Display what is in the linked list so far
    displayPeopleInLinkedList( pFirstPerson );

    // --------------------

    // Make a second person in the list
    pCurrentPerson = new person;

    // Set values for this person
    pCurrentPerson->firstName = "Olga";
    pCurrentPerson->emailAddress = "olga@very-loud.fake.com";
    pCurrentPerson->pNextPerson = NULL;

    // Link the previous person to this new person
    pLastPerson->pNextPerson = pCurrentPerson;

    // Make the new person the last person in the list
    pLastPerson = pCurrentPerson;

    // Display what is in the linked list so far
    displayPeopleInLinkedList( pFirstPerson );

    // --------------------
```

continues on next page...

```cpp
    // Make a third person in the list
    pCurrentPerson = new person;

    // Set values for this person
    pCurrentPerson->firstName = "Florence";
    pCurrentPerson->emailAddress = "flozza@roundabout.fake.com";
    pCurrentPerson->pNextPerson = NULL;

    // Link the previous person to this new person
    pLastPerson->pNextPerson = pCurrentPerson;

    // Make the new person the last person in the list
    pLastPerson = pCurrentPerson;

    // Display what is in the linked list so far
    displayPeopleInLinkedList( pFirstPerson );

    // --------------------

    return 0;
}
```

To begin with, the linked-list is empty. The program proceeds to create three different units or **"nodes"**, linking them together to make the list. After creating each node and adding it to the list, the program displays the contents of the list so far.

The code uses three important pointers that will be used when making new nodes and to control the list. The **pFirstPerson** pointer will indicate where the first node in the list is stored in memory. The **pCurrentPerson** and **pLastPerson** pointers will be used when creating a new node and linking it to the rest of the list:

```cpp
    person* pFirstPerson;
    person* pLastPerson;
    person* pCurrentPerson;
```

Because the list is empty and does not yet contain any nodes, the pointers to the first and last nodes are given **NULL** values:

```cpp
    pFirstPerson = NULL;
    pLastPerson = NULL;
```

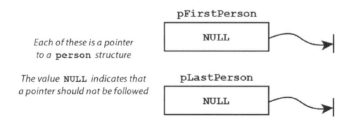

Each of these is a pointer
to a **person** structure

The value NULL indicates that
a pointer should not be followed

The **NULL** value indicates to the program that the pointer does not yet lead to any data and that it should not be followed.

The program creates the first node in memory using the **new** operator. The memory address at which the newly created node can be found is returned upon its creation and this gets stored using the **pCurrentPerson** pointer:

```
pCurrentPerson = new person;
```

The **pCurrentPerson** pointer is then followed to set values for each data member of the **person** structure:

```
pCurrentPerson->firstName = "Helga";
pCurrentPerson->emailAddress = "helga@outer-space.fake.com";
pCurrentPerson->pNextPerson = NULL;
```

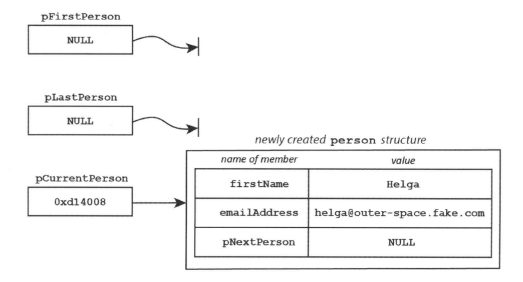

Now that the node exists and contains some useful data, the value of the **pFirstPerson** and **pLastPerson** pointers can be updated to indicate that this single node is both the first and the last node in the linked-list:

```
pFirstPerson = pCurrentPerson;
pLastPerson = pCurrentPerson;
```

The linked-list, which contains only one single node, now looks like this:

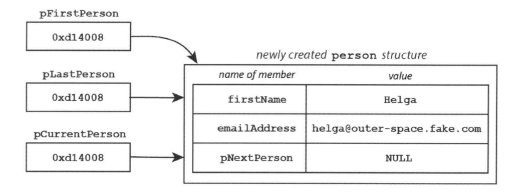

A second node is now created in memory, with the **pCurrentPointer** being used to hold the address of where it is stored. Again, the pointer is followed to set values for each data member in the **person** structure:

```
// Make a second person in the list
pCurrentPerson = new person;

// Set values for this person
pCurrentPerson->firstName = "Olga";
pCurrentPerson->emailAddress = "olga@very-loud.fake.com";
pCurrentPerson->pNextPerson = NULL;
```

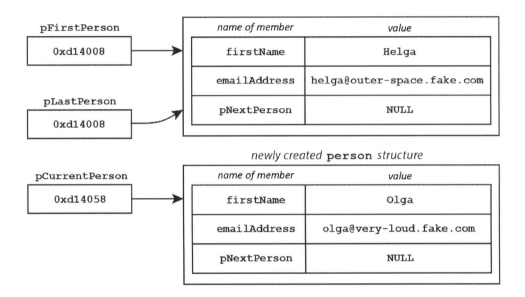

newly created **person** *structure*

The second node is now linked into the list by setting the **pNextPerson** pointer from the original node to hold the address of the second node. The **pLastPerson** pointer is also updated to hold the address of the second node:

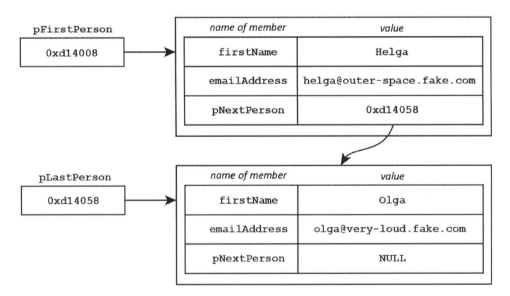

Finally, the third node is created and is linked into the list. The **pNextPerson** pointer of the second node is made to hold the address of the newly created third node. The value of the **pLastPerson** pointer is also updated to hold the address of the third node:

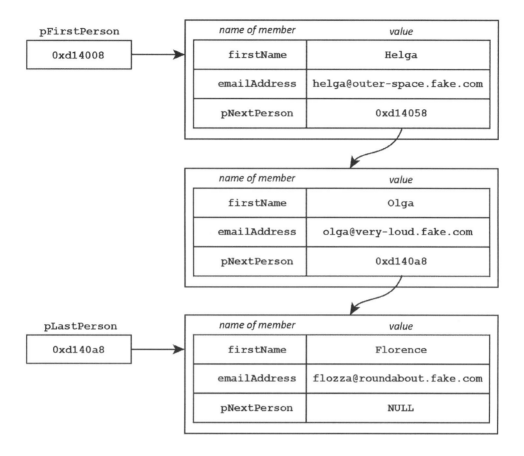

Here is what you should see when you run the program:

```
Here are the people in the list:
        Name: Helga   Email: helga@outer-space.fake.com
*** End of the list ***


Here are the people in the list:
        Name: Helga   Email: helga@outer-space.fake.com
        Name: Olga    Email: olga@very-loud.fake.com
*** End of the list ***


Here are the people in the list:
        Name: Helga   Email: helga@outer-space.fake.com
        Name: Olga    Email: olga@very-loud.fake.com
        Name: Florence       Email: flozza@roundabout.fake.com
*** End of the list ***
```

This simple example only creates nodes for three people. A more flexible program would allow you to repeatedly enter as many people as you like. See *Example 12.14 - linked_list_menu.cpp* at the end of this chapter.

To see how the pointers link the nodes together, you can modify the program code to display their values along with the name and email address of the person. Under normal circumstances, a user would not actually want to see the pointer values displayed, but the code below will show you exactly how each node is linked to the next item in the list once it executes:

*Updated code for Example 12.10 – **linked_list.cpp***

```
void displayPeopleInLinkedList( person* pPersonToStartFrom )
{
    cout << "Here are the people in the list:" << endl;

    person* pCurrentPerson = pPersonToStartFrom;

    while ( pCurrentPerson != NULL )
    {
        cout << TAB;
        cout << "Address of current node: " << pCurrentPerson << endl;
        cout << TAB;
        cout << "Name: " << pCurrentPerson->firstName;
        cout << TAB;
        cout << "Email: " << pCurrentPerson->emailAddress << endl;
        cout << TAB;

        cout << "Next node is at address: " << pCurrentPerson->pNextPerson << endl;

        cout << endl << TAB << "----------" << endl;

        // Follow pointer to the next node in the list
        pCurrentPerson = pCurrentPerson->pNextPerson;

    }  // end of while

    cout << "*** End of the list ***" << endl << endl << endl;
}
```

Now you should be able to see how one node in the linked-list holds the address to the next node.

The screenshot below shows what was displayed on my Pi once all three nodes had been added to the linked-list:

```
Here are the people in the list:
        Address of current node: 0xd14008
        Name: Helga   Email: helga@outer-space.fake.com
        Next node is at address: 0


        ----------
*** End of the list ***


Here are the people in the list:
        Address of current node: 0xd14008
        Name: Helga   Email: helga@outer-space.fake.com
        Next node is at address: 0xd14058


        ----------
        Address of current node: 0xd14058
        Name: Olga    Email: olga@very-loud.fake.com
        Next node is at address: 0


        ----------
*** End of the list ***


Here are the people in the list:
        Address of current node: 0xd14008
        Name: Helga   Email: helga@outer-space.fake.com
        Next node is at address: 0xd14058


        ----------
        Address of current node: 0xd14058
        Name: Olga    Email: olga@very-loud.fake.com
        Next node is at address: 0xd140a8


        ----------
        Address of current node: 0xd140a8
        Name: Florence      Email: flozza@roundabout.fake.com
        Next node is at address: 0


        ----------
*** End of the list ***
```

Remember that you will see different memory addresses on your own computer. The data values will not be stored in the same memory locations as on my Pi.

Recycling memory once you have finished using your dynamic data

We saw earlier in this chapter that it is possible to create a data value on the heap, storing its address in a pointer:

```
string* pHolidayDestination = new string( "Monster Island" );
```

What happens when we no longer need this data? Remember that although the heap is a very large amount of memory, this amount is still **finite**. Even the heap could eventually become completely filled up, leading to problems for programs that are running if they are unable to obtain the memory that they need in order to store their data.

It is good practice for a program to clean up after itself by destroying any dynamic data values that are no longer in use. Once you are sure that a data value is no longer needed, your program can **delete** the value. Any memory that the data value was taking up on the heap then becomes free again for other programs to make use of.

To destroy a data value that is currently stored on the heap, your program can use the **delete** operator:

```
delete pHolidayDestination;
```

This tells the computer to follow the pointer to the data on the heap and then delete it from memory. Watch-out though! Once the data has been destroyed, the pointer still holds the address of the deleted data. Your program must **not** attempt to follow this pointer. When a data item has been deleted, the pointer should be marked as unused by setting it to contain the special **NULL** value:

```
pHolidayDestination = NULL;
```

Example 12.11 – delete.cpp

```cpp
#include <iostream>      // Program will be displaying some text on the screen

using namespace std;     // Will be using standard identifiers string, cout and endl

int main()
{
    // Create a new item of data on the heap and store address of data in pointer
    string* pPerson = new string( "Miss Wendy Cheeseboard" );

    // Attempt to follow the pointer, then display the item of data
    cout << "The winner is... ";
    cout << *pPerson << endl;

    // Delete the item of data from the heap so that it does not exist anymore
    delete pPerson;

    // Attempt to follow the pointer again, now that the data has been deleted
    cout << "Is there anybody there? " << endl;
    cout << *pPerson << endl;

    return 0;
}
```

If you attempt to execute this program, you should find that it crashes with spectacular results. Try it!

```
The winner is... Miss Wendy Cheeseboard
Is there anybody there?
Segmentation fault


------------------
(program exited with code: 139)
Press return to continue
```

The crash is a result of trying to follow a pointer to a data value that no longer exists.

Here is a modified version of the program that checks whether or not the pointer is safe to use after the nodes are deleted:

Example 12.12 – *delete_safely.cpp*

```cpp
#include <iostream>     // Program will be displaying some text on the screen

using namespace std;     // Will be using standard identifiers string, cout and endl

int main()
{
    // Create a new item of data on the heap and store address of data in pointer
    string* pPerson = new string( "Miss Wendy Cheeseboard" );

    // Attempt to follow the pointer, then display the item of data
    cout << "The winner is... ";
    cout << *pPerson << endl;

    // Delete the item of data from the heap so that it does not exist anymore
    delete pPerson;     // Destroy the data on the heap
    pPerson = NULL;     // Mark the pointer as unused

    // Attempt to follow the pointer again, now that the data has been deleted
    // Checks whether the point is not NULL
    // NULL value for pointer indicates that it should not be used anymore
    cout << "Is there anybody there? " << endl;
    if ( pPerson != NULL )
        cout << *pPerson << endl;
    else
        cout << "NULL pointer - the data does not exist anymore" << endl;

    return 0;
}
```

Attempting to run this program will not result in a crash as the program will not attempt to follow the **pPerson** pointer to the deleted data on the heap. It will exit with the usual code of **0** to indicate that everything appears to be ok.

```
The winner is... Miss Wendy Cheeseboard
Is there anybody there?
NULL pointer - the data does not exist anymore
```

As already mentioned, it is good practice for a program to clean up after itself, deleting items of data from the heap that are no longer needed. Many programs include code to delete their dynamic data as a last step before they finish execution. This helps to ensure that enough heap memory is available on your Pi for other programs to use and that they continue to run smoothly.

You can imagine that a shortage of heap memory can lead to slower performance on your Pi as programs wait longer for space in memory to be made available to them. A program that finishes execution, but which leaves dynamic data in existence in heap memory, can lead to less memory being available for other programs that are currently being executed. This is called a **"memory-leak"**, where dynamic data is gradually lost.

Memory leaks are often caused by inefficient programming or sloppy code where a programmer forgets to delete some data. Gradually, such wasted space can lead to slower performance, especially if the computer is left running for a long time. This is one reason why even servers need a re-boot every now and again - to clear out any old data from memory that is not actually needed anymore.

This next program simulates the problem of a lack of heap memory. It uses a loop to repeatedly create more and more data items, using up the memory from the heap. This will lead to a large amount of memory being dynamically allocated to the program at the expense of any other programs that are running.

Example 12.13 – *heap_filler.cpp*

```cpp
#include <iostream>     // Program will be displaying some text on the screen

using namespace std;    // Will be using standard identifiers string, cout and endl

int main()
{
    // WARNING! THIS PROGRAM *WILL* AFFECT THE PERFORMANCE OF YOUR PI.
    // YOU MAY NEED TO RE-BOOT YOUR PI AFTER RUNNING THIS PROGRAM.
    // TO AVOID DATA-LOSS, MAKE SURE YOU HAVE SAVED ANY DOCUMENTS THAT ARE OPEN.
    // EXECUTE AT YOUR OWN-RISK! AFTER SEVERAL MINUTES, YOUR PI SHOULD FREEZE!

    // Single pointer that holds address of some string data on the heap
    // This will be used again and again when creating data, but never actually
    // be followed usefully!
    string* pData;

    // Inifinite loop that will never terminate
    while ( true )
    {
        // Create a new item of data on the heap, storing address of data in pointer
        pData = new string( "This string value uses up heap memory!" );

        // Display the data
        cout << *pData << endl;
        // The address of each new item will replace the old address stored in the
        // pointer variable, but the data will still remain on the heap with no
        // way to find it again using the original pointer

    }  // end of infinite while loop

    return 0;
}
```

The program enters an infinite **while** loop that creates a new copy of the same **string** value again and again on the heap. If you leave the program running for a long time, you may notice that your system begins to slow down as an increasing proportion of the heap becomes allocated to the program's **string** data. Your Pi will begin to run low on dynamic memory, resulting in slower performance. This may be particularly noticeable if you have any other programs running. They may begin to slow down or behave oddly.

From the desktop, try running the above program in one terminal window, whilst executing the **top** command in another window. You will immediately see the amount of RAM available start to decrease, eventually followed by the swap space.

This is a more useful program that allows you to build a linked list of people and their email addresses. It allows you to enter as many people as you like. Once you choose to exit the program, it destroys the nodes in the linked list one-by-one to free up the heap memory that they were previously taking up, before finishing execution.

Example 12.14 – linked_list_menu.cpp

```cpp
#include <iostream>      // Program will be displaying some text on the screen

using namespace std;     // Will be using standard identifiers string, cout and endl

const char TAB = '\t';

// --------------------

// Create new structure. Several variables will use this later in the program.
struct person
{
    string firstName;
    string emailAddress;
    person* pNextPerson;
};

// --------------------

person* addPersonToLinkedList( person* pLastPersonInList )
{
    // Make a node for the first person in the list
    person* pNewPerson = new person;

    // Input the details for the new person

    string newName, newEmail;

    cout << "Type in the name of the new person:" << endl;
    getline( cin, newName );

    cout << "Type in their email address:" << endl;
    getline( cin, newEmail );

    // Copy details into the new node
    pNewPerson->firstName = newName;
    pNewPerson->emailAddress = newEmail;
    pNewPerson->pNextPerson = NULL;

    // If the list was not previously empty then link what
    // was previously the last node in the list to the new node
    if ( pLastPersonInList != NULL )
        pLastPersonInList->pNextPerson = pNewPerson;

    // Return pointer to the new node so that it is recorded as the last node
    return pNewPerson;
}

// --------------------
```

continues on next page...

```cpp
void displayPeopleInLinkedList( person* pPersonToStartFrom )
{
    cout << "Here are the people in the list:" << endl;

    person* pCurrentPerson = pPersonToStartFrom;

    while ( pCurrentPerson != NULL )
    {
        cout << TAB << "Name: " << pCurrentPerson->firstName;
        cout << TAB << "Email: " << pCurrentPerson->emailAddress << endl;

        pCurrentPerson = pCurrentPerson->pNextPerson;
    }

    cout << "*** End of the list ***" << endl << endl << endl;
}

// --------------------

void searchForPersonInLinkedList( person* pPersonToStartFrom )
{
    string targetName;

    cout << "What name are you searching for?" << endl;
    getline( cin, targetName );

    person* pCurrentPerson = pPersonToStartFrom;

    while ( pCurrentPerson != NULL )
    {
        if ( targetName == pCurrentPerson->firstName )
        {
            cout << "Found! Their email is " << pCurrentPerson->emailAddress << endl;
            break;
        }   // end of if decision

        // Move on to the next node in the list
        pCurrentPerson = pCurrentPerson->pNextPerson;

    }   // end of while loop

    if ( pCurrentPerson == NULL )
        cout << "Person could not be found" << endl;
}

// --------------------
```

continues on next page...

```cpp
void destroyLinkedList( person* pPersonToStartFrom )
{
    // Destroy the list data that is currently stored on the heap
    person* pCurrentPerson = pPersonToStartFrom;
    person* pNextPersonToDelete;

    while ( pCurrentPerson != NULL )
    {
        pNextPersonToDelete = pCurrentPerson->pNextPerson;

        delete pCurrentPerson;

        pCurrentPerson = pNextPersonToDelete;
    }   // end of while loop

    cout << "*** List destroyed - heap memory freed ***" << endl << endl << endl;
}

// --------------------

int main()
{
    // Mark the list as being "empty" - there are no nodes at all
    // (It will be useful to know where the list begins and where it ends)
    person* pFirstPerson = NULL;
    person* pLastPerson = NULL;

    // --------------------

    person* pNewPerson;

    string choice;

    while ( true )
    {
        cout << endl << "Choose what to do: add, display, search or quit" << endl;
        getline( cin, choice );
        cout << endl;

        // Add a new person to the list
        if ( choice == "add" )
        {
            // Enter details of person and store them at the end of the list
            pNewPerson = addPersonToLinkedList( pLastPerson );

            // The new node will definitely be the last node in the list
            pLastPerson = pNewPerson;

            // If list was previously empty, mark the new node as the start of list
            if ( pFirstPerson == NULL )
                pFirstPerson = pNewPerson;
        }   // end of if decision
```

continues on next page...

continued...

```
        // Display details from each node in the list
        if ( choice == "display" )
            displayPeopleInLinkedList( pFirstPerson );

        // Search through the list for a particular name
        if ( choice == "search" )
            searchForPersonInLinkedList( pFirstPerson );

        // Destroy all data from the list once you have chosen to quit
        if ( choice == "quit" )
        {
            // Destroy all nodes in the linked list
            destroyLinkedList( pFirstPerson );

            // Mark the list as empty - final precaution!
            pFirstPerson = NULL;
            pLastPerson = NULL;

            // Break out of the menu loop so that the program can finish
            break;
        }  // end of if decision

    }  // end of infinite while loop

    cout << "End of program" << endl;

    return 0;
}
```

To begin with, the list is empty. Here is what happens if you try to display the contents of the empty list:

```
Choose what to do: add, display, search or quit
display

Here are the people in the list:
*** End of the list ***
```

The details for a person are now added and displayed on the screen:

```
Choose what to do: add, display, search or quit
add

Type in the name of the new person:
Arvo Kruse
Type in their email address:
arvo@webface.fake.com

Choose what to do: add, display, search or quit
display

Here are the people in the list:
        Name: Arvo Kruse    Email: arvo@webface.fake.com
*** End of the list ***
```

After entering the details for another person, you can see that they are added into the list:

```
Choose what to do: add, display, search or quit
add

Type in the name of the new person:
Ted Zed
Type in their email address:
tedz@potato-world.fake.com

Choose what to do: add, display, search or quit
display

Here are the people in the list:
        Name: Arvo Kruse     Email: arvo@webface.fake.com
        Name: Ted ZedEmail: tedz@potato-world.fake.com
*** End of the list ***
```

It is also possible to search through the list for a particular person:

```
Choose what to do: add, display, search or quit
search

What name are you searching for?
Ted Zed
Found! Their email is tedz@potato-world.fake.com

Choose what to do: add, display, search or quit
search

What name are you searching for?
Nobody Noname
Person could not be found
```

Finally, once you choose to quit, the program deletes all data from the list. This frees up the heap memory for other programs to use:

```
Choose what to do: add, display, search or quit
quit

*** List destroyed - heap memory freed ***


End of program
```

You may have noticed by now that our programs are beginning to get larger and more sophisticated.

The next chapter introduces some very important ideas about **"object-orientation"**. As your programs and data-structures start to get more complex, you can use object-oriented ideas and techniques to help keep your program code easy to understand and maintain.

Here's what we have covered in this chapter:

Named values can be grouped together to make a larger "**structure**" using the keyword `struct`. The new structure can be given a **name**.

Each value within a structure is called a **member** of the structure.

Individual members within a structure can be accessed using the **. membership operator**.

Values within a structure can be **assigned** inside `{ }` curly braces.

A structure that you create can also be used as a named **data-type** for other variables and constants in your code.

Static data values are stored in a fixed amount of memory space that your program has available to it.

Attempting to exceed the amount of space reserved for static data will cause your program to crash.

Data values can be stored **dynamically** in a much larger pool of memory called "**the heap**".

The amount of data stored by your program on the heap can grow and shrink as the program executes.

An **address** is used to locate **where** an item of data is stored in memory.

Memory addresses are usually displayed on the Pi using **hexadecimal** (base-16). When displayed on the screen, hexadecimal representations of addresses begin with `0x`.

It is possible to find out the address of an item using the **& reference operator**.

A memory address can be stored in a **pointer** and given a name. The name of a pointer usually begins with `p` to distinguish it from a non-pointer value.

A pointer can be followed in order to access some useful data in memory.

When **declaring** a new variable or constant, the `*` symbol indicates that the value will be a pointer.

A **null pointer** is a pointer that contains the value `NULL` rather than a memory address. This indicates that the pointer is not ready for use and that it should not be followed.

It is possible to obtain a data value from a pointer using the `*` **de-reference operator**. It is also possible to follow a pointer using the `->` **pointer-to-member operator**.

To find out how many bytes of memory an item of data takes up you can use the `sizeof()` operator.

The `new` operator can be used to create a dynamic data value that is to be stored on the heap. It returns the address of the newly created value which can be stored using a pointer for later use.

The `delete` operator can be used to destroy an item of dynamic data that is no longer needed so that the heap memory it currently takes up can be re-used.

Once data has been deleted, any pointers that were previously used to access the deleted data should be set to `NULL` so that your code does not attempt to follow those pointers.

1.	Create an array called **symbols** that holds **10** different **char** values. Create a pointer to a character called **pSymbol**. Store the address of the first item in the **symbols** array. Use **++** to increment the **pSymbol** pointer three times. Display the data that the updated pointer value now points to.
2.	Create two variables: one that uses the **float** data-type and one that uses the **int** data-type. Now create two different pointers and use them to store the address of each of the new variables. Is it possible to assign the value of one of these pointers to the other?
3.	Create an integer constant called **FIXED_PRICE** with a value of **1500**. Create a pointer to this value. Using pointer de-referencing, attempt to change the value of **FIXED_PRICE** to **1000**. What happens?
4.	Add a new function called **displayInReverse** to *Example 12.14 linked_list_menu.cpp*. It will recursively call itself to follow the links between nodes until reaching the end of the linked list. Once the end is reached, as each instance of the recursive function terminates, make it display that person's details. This should result in the contents of the list being displayed in reverse order. You will need to make the new function take a single parameter as input, called **personToStartFrom**. This will be a pointer to a **person** (similar to the existing **displayPeopleInLinkedList()** function). When called, **displayInReverse()** will use **personToStartFrom** and examine the **pNextPerson** pointer that points to the next person in the linked list. If this is not the end of the linked list and another person exists, **displayInReverse()** should recursively call itself again, passing in the pointer to the next person. After the recursive call, the function will need to display the details of the current person. You will also need to add a new option to the menu to call the **displayInReverse()** function.

Chapter 13:
Objects and classes

Packaging up related data items

So far, our programs have made use of data. Some have even made use of **struct** to create structures that package together several related data items. Our program code can make use of this data to perform useful processing.

Below an example of a **struct** that describes in general terms the data that can be known about a mountain:

Structure: `mountain`

string	name
string	range
int	elevation

The program below makes use of the new **mountain** structure to make two different variables called **highestInWorld** and **highestInUK**. The code contains a function called **displayMountainDetails()** which will display the individual data members on screen for a particular **mountain** that you have created.

Example 13.1 – struct_mountain.cpp

```cpp
#include <iostream>      // Program will be displaying some text on the screen

using namespace std;     // Will be using standard identifiers string, cout and endl

// --------------------

struct mountain
{
    string name;
    string range;
    int elevation;
};

// --------------------

void displayMountainDetails( mountain thisMountainObject )
{
    cout << thisMountainObject.name;
    cout << ", " << thisMountainObject.range;
    cout << " (" << thisMountainObject.elevation << "m)";
}

// --------------------

int main()
{
    // Create 2 different objects, each one is an instance of the mountain struct
    mountain highestInWorld;
    mountain highestInUK;
```

continues on next page...

```
    // Set values for each mountain

    highestInWorld.name = "Mt. Everest";
    highestInWorld.range = "Himalayas";
    highestInWorld.elevation = 8848;

    highestInUK.name = "Ben Nevis";
    highestInUK.range = "Grampian Mountains";
    highestInUK.elevation = 1344;


    // Display the details for each by calling the displayMountainDetails function
    // passing it the particular mountain

    cout << "You'll need oxygen to climb ";
    displayMountainDetails( highestInWorld );

    cout << endl << endl;

    cout << "The highest in the UK is ";
    displayMountainDetails( highestInUK );

    cout << endl << endl;

    return 0;
}
```

Here's what the program displays for each mountain:

```
You'll need oxygen to climb Mt. Everest, Himalayas (8848m)

The highest in the UK is Ben Nevis, Grampian Mountains (1344m)
```

Notice that your program code is free to make use or process any of the data members that the **mountain** structure contains. There are no restrictions regarding how or when your program accesses them. This means that in theory, a program could create an incomplete example of a **mountain** where only **some** of the data members are given values, the rest of them being left undefined:

```
    mountain partlyDefinedMountain;
    partlyDefineMountain.name = "K2";
```

In this example, only the **name** has been defined for the **mountain** shown above. It does not yet have meaningful values set for the **range** or **elevation** items. These are undefined and may well contain random values at run-time.

Notice also that the structure only defines the **data** that will be stored about a mountain. It does not define **how** the data can be processed or what can be done to it. The **mountain** structure does not and cannot contain any functions. The code that processes the data is separate from the structure, being part of the main program.

Packaging data and functions together in a class

C++ allows you to define your own custom data-types called "**classes**". Classes are general descriptions of things that can exist and how they behave. These general classes can be used to create "**objects**". Objects are specific examples or "**instances**" of a general class that represent things in the real world.

Classes usually contain one or more useful data items, which are known as "**data members**". Classes also define various functions that can be performed on the data members, called "**member functions**". Unlike a C++ **struct**, a class packages up all of the member data along with the member functions that operate on it. This makes it much easier to understand how and where the member data is processed in your code. It allows you to build programs in a more organised and methodical fashion.

Once a class has been defined, we can use it to create specific instances or objects. Variables can be created that make use of the new class as their data-type.

Here is a specific example: Imagine that we create a class called **human**. We could describe in general terms what details might be known about a human being, such as their **name**, **date-of-birth**, **gender**, their **nationality** and **whether they are alive or not**. We could represent each of these facts using a data member within the class. We could also define what **type** of data is used for each of these members.

The data members for the general **human** class are shown below:

Class of objects: **human**

string	name
string	dateofBirth
char	gender
string	nationality
bool	alive

We could then create an object that is an **instance** of the class **human**, giving the new object a descriptive name, such as **firstPersonInSpace**. Each of the data members for **firstPersonInSpace** can be assigned values that apply to that particular person:

firstPersonInSpace
instance of class **human**

name	Yuri Gagarin
dateofBirth	09-Mar-1934
gender	M
nationality	Soviet
alive	N

Further instances of **human** could be created, giving each of them a descriptive name, such as **oldestKnownPerson** or **inventorOfWeb**. Each instance could be assigned values to the data members that it contains.

Here is another example of a general class called **mountain**:

Class of objects: **mountain**

string	name
string	range
int	elevation

A specific instance of the **mountain** class is shown below:

highestInWorld
instance of class **mountain**

name	Mt. Everest
range	Himalayas
elevation	8848

Declaring the data and member functions that a class contains

We will now look at how a class can be defined in C++ and how instances of that class can be created.

Below I have started to define a new class which can be used to describe a mountain in general terms. Unsurprisingly, the name that I am going to give this class will be **mountain**.

Nearly all useful classes contain one or more items of data, called data members. The new **mountain** class will contain three items of data: **name**, **range** and **elevation**.

Below is the declaration for **mountain** showing the data members that it contains:

```
class mountain
{
    // These data items are members of the mountain class... member items.
    string name;
    string range;
    int elevation;
};
```

It is also usual to declare one or more functions that will allow access to the data items or process them in some way. Each function that will operate on the member data can be **declared** within the class along with the member data. Such functions are called **"member functions"**. Once the various functions have been declared in the class, the actual body of each function which contains the C++ statements to perform the processing can be **defined** elsewhere in your code.

Here is an example of the **mountain** class containing declarations for two functions that will operate on the member data:

```
class mountain
{
    // These data items are members of the mountain class... member items.
    string name;
    string range;
    int elevation;

    // These functions are also members of the mountain class... member functions.
    public:
        mountain( string newName, string newRange, int newElevation );
        void displayDetails();
};
```

The first of the functions, **mountain()**, is a special **"constructor function"**. It will be called when your program attempts to create a new **mountain** object.

Constructor functions carry out useful tasks or assign values to data members when setting up a new instance of a class. One or more constructor functions must be declared and made available for code outside the class to use, otherwise it would not be possible to create or make use of any instances of the class, hence part of the declaration is labelled as **public**.

The second of the functions in the **mountain** class is called **displayDetails()**. When called for a particular instance of the **mountain** class, this function will display the value of each item of member data that the object contains. Given a particular **mountain** object, the function will display the **name**, **range** and **elevation** values belonging to that object.

The difference between `private` and `public` members of a class

We have not yet finished defining our new **mountain** class though. It is possible to **control** which parts of the class can be accessed by other parts of the program and which parts are to not to be accessed or tampered with.

When defining a new class, we can use "**access-specifiers**" to make it clear which parts of the program are allowed to access and use the data members and functions that are associated with the class. Note that we have already seen one of these on the previous page: the **public** access-specifier that allows access to the constructor function for the **mountain** class.

There are three kinds of access that you can allow to individual data members and functions.

A **public** data member or function can be directly accessed by other parts of your program outside of the class. There are no restrictions on how and when the **public** members will be accessed. Other parts of your program will be able to examine or change these data members, or call these member functions.

A **private** data member or function cannot be accessed by parts of your program that are outside of the class. The data can only be accessed by the member functions for that class. Other parts of the program will not be able to examine the private data members, to change their values or call the private member functions.

A **protected** data member or function can only be accessed by the class that it belongs to, or by other classes that are based on that class ("*inherited* classes", which will be covered later in this chapter). Other parts of your program will not be able to examine the protected data members, to change their values or to call the protected member functions.

If you do not specify whether your member items or functions are **public**, **private** or **protected**, then by default the C++ compiler will treat them as **private**. This means that they will be restricted to prevent them from accidentally being accessed or tampered with.

The class declaration below makes all of its member data and functions **publicly** available to the rest of the program. Program code that is not part of the **mountain** class will be able to make use of the **name**, **range** and **elevation** member items. Code from any part of the program can also call the **mountain()** and **displayDetails()** functions.

This relatively uncontrolled access could lead to problems in your program. Code could mistakenly change member data or call a function, leading to an error.

```
class mountain
{
    public:
        // Data members - all of these are public. Code elsewhere in the program
        // will be able to access the directly.
        string name;
        string range;
        int elevation;

        // Member functions to create a mountain object and to display data about it
        mountain( string newName, string newRange, int newElevation );
        void displayDetails();
};
```

The example on the next page has been refined slightly. This time, the data members have been declared as **private**, whilst the **mountain()** and **displayDetails()** functions have been declared as **public**. This means that other parts of the program outside of the **mountain** class will not be able to directly use the **name**, **range** or **elevation** data members. The only way to read, write or process these values will be through the **publicly** available **mountain()** and **displayDetails()** functions. Access to the data members is now rigorously controlled to prevent their misuse.

```
class mountain
{
    // This private data is not directly accessible by other parts of program.
    // It can only be accessed through the public functions provided by this class.
    private:
         string name;
         string range;
         int elevation;

    public:
         // Member functions - these are public and can be called elsewhere by
         // code that is not part of this class.
         mountain( string newName, string newRange, int newElevation );
         void displayDetails();

         string getName();  // Allows value of name to be examined
         string getRange();
         int getElevation();

         void setName( string newName );  // Allows value of name to be modified
         void setRange( string newRange );
         void setElevation ( int newElevation );
};
```

In order to access **private** member items to read or update their values, classes often provide "**get**" and "**set**" functions. For instance, the **getName()** function above returns the value of the **name** data member to any code that calls it. The **setName()** function takes a **string** value as input and assigns it to the **name** data member. In this way, your class can define how and when data members are accessed to guard against unauthorised access or accidental modification.

Making a data member **public** allows that value to be examined and also to be modified. **Both** kinds of access are allowed, not just one or the other. This kind of unrestricted access should be used sparingly to avoid potential confusion in your code.

By making data **private** you have more control, choosing which kind of access you want to allow. If you want to make a data member read-only and prevent its value from being modified, you can provide a "**get**" function but not a "**set**" function.

```
class mountain
{
    // This data is read-only and can only be accessed through the get... functions.
    private:
         string name;
         string range;
         int elevation;

    public:
         // These public member functions can be called elsewhere.
         mountain( string newName, string newRange, int newElevation );
         void displayDetails();

         string getName();  // Allows value of name to be examined
         string getRange();
         int getElevation();
};
```

Defining the body of a member function for a class

Once you have **declared** the member functions that your new class will contain, you can **define** their bodies: the set of statements that each function carries out. You can write your function in a similar way to those from our previous programs. As we have seen though, when defining a function that belongs to a class, you must prefix the name of the function with the name of the class and the `::` *scope-resolution operator*. This tells the compiler which class the function belongs to.

A very simple example is shown below. The `displayDetails()` function displays each of the `mountain` data members, one at a time:

```
void mountain::displayDetails()
{
    // Displays each of the private data members for a mountain object
    cout << name;
    cout << ", " << range;
    cout << " (" << elevation << "m)";
}
```

Notice that the name of the function has been prefixed with the name of the **mountain** class. This clarifies which class the new function belongs to (the **scope** of the function) and avoids potential confusion with any other functions that might otherwise have the same name.

You can think of:

```
void mountain::displayDetails()
```

...as meaning:

"The function `displayDetails()` which is part of the `mountain` class and does not take or return any values."

Constructors: functions that are called when an instance of a class is created

As mentioned previously, every class needs at least one constructor function that will be called when an instance of the class is being created. The constructor function will allow values to be assigned to data items and other initial processing to be carried out for a new object.

Constructor functions do not give back a value, hence you do not need to specify a return type for them. You may however choose to define any input parameters that a constructor function will take.

Note that you can define more than one different constructor function for a class. This allows you to create instances of your class in different ways. The simplest possible constructor function does not take any arguments at all as it is often used to create a "blank" object whose member values are yet to be set. You can provide different constructor functions, taking different combinations of input values, depending on how you want to create the object.

In the case of the **mountain** class, two different constructor functions might be **declared** like this:

```
public:
    mountain();
    mountain( string newName, string newRange, int newElevation );
```

Note that both of the constructors above are made publicly available so that the rest of your program code can call them.

The **body** of each constructor function would also need to be **defined** once the `mountain` class has been declared:

```
mountain::mountain()
{
    // Constructor function that takes no arguments.
    // Assigns a blank default value to each data member.
    name = "";
    range = "";
    elevation = 0;
}

mountain::mountain( string newName, string newRange, int newElevation )
{
    // Constructor function that sets name, range and elevation for a new mountain.
    name = newName;
    range = newRange;
    elevation = newElevation;
}
```

Once you have declared a class and defined the constructor functions for it, your program code can create **instances** of that class. Your code can declare variables that take the new class as their data-type, calling the constructor functions to assign values to each of data members for that instance:

```
mountain blankMountain();
mountain highestInWorld( "Mt. Everest", "Himalayas", 8848 );
```

blankMountain *(instance of* **mountain** *class)*

name of member	value
name	(blank)
range	(blank)
elevation	0

highestInWorld *(instance of* **mountain** *class)*

name of member	value
name	Mt. Everest
range	Himalayas
elevation	8848

The first instance of **mountain**, a variable called **blankMountain**, would use the simple constructor that takes no arguments as input. This constructor simply sets each data member of **blankMountain** to contain a blank or zero value.

The second instance, a variable called **highestInWorld**, would be created using the constructor function that takes three arguments as input. This constructor might be passed the three argument values **Mt. Everest**, **Himalayas** and **8848** to set each of the data members in the class: **name**, **range** and **elevation**.

Example 13.2 – *class_mountain.cpp*

```cpp
#include <iostream>     // Program will be displaying some text on the screen

using namespace std;    // Will be using standard identifiers string, cout and endl

// --------------------

class mountain
{
    // This private data is not directly accessible by other parts of program
    private:
        string name;
        string range;
        int elevation;

    // These public functions can be called by other parts of program
    public:
        mountain( string newName, string newRange, int newElevation );
        void displayDetails();
 };

// --------------------

mountain::mountain( string newName, string newRange, int newElevation )
{
    // Constructor function that is called when creating a new instance of this class
    name = newName;
    range = newRange;
    elevation = newElevation;
}

// --------------------

void mountain::displayDetails()
{
    // Displays each of the private data members for a mountain object
    cout << name;
    cout << ", " << range;
    cout << " (" << elevation << "m)";
}

// --------------------
```

continues on next page...

continued...

```cpp
int main()
{
    // Create 4 different objects, each one is an instance of the mountain class

    mountain highestInWorld( "Mt. Everest", "Himalayas", 8848 );

    mountain highestInUK( "Ben Nevis", "Grampian Mountains", 1344 );

    mountain steepestInWorld( "The Great Trango Tower", "Karakoram", 6286 );

    mountain highestVolcano( "Mauna Kea", "Hawaiian Islands", 4207 );

    // Call the displayDetails() member function for each of the 4 objects

    cout << "You'll need oxygen to climb ";
    highestInWorld.displayDetails();

    cout << endl << endl;

    cout << "The highest in the UK is ";
    highestInUK.displayDetails();

    cout << endl << endl;

    cout << "The trickiest has got to be ";
    steepestInWorld.displayDetails();

    cout << endl << endl;

    cout << "The highest volcano in the world is ";
    highestVolcano.displayDetails();

    cout << endl << endl;

    return 0;
}
```

Here is what the program displays:

```
You'll need oxygen to climb Mt. Everest, Himalayas (8848m)

The highest in the UK is Ben Nevis, Grampian Mountains (1344m)

The trickiest has got to be The Great Trango Tower, Karakoram (6286m)

The highest volcano in the world is Mauna Kea, Hawaiian Islands (4207m)
```

Note that this program only makes use of a single constructor function, which takes three arguments as input to set the values for the data members of each new instance of the **mountain** class.

Now that you have created a class in your program-code, the *Symbols* **pane** in Geany displays the name of the **mountain** class, along with the line-number at which the class definition begins in the "*class_mountain.cpp*" file. Clicking on the name of the class takes you straight to its declaration in the text-editor window. You may find this a very convenient way to navigate through your source-code, rather than scrolling up and down with a mouse to locate the code that you want to work on.

The need for an empty constructor function

When creating an instance of a class, your program will usually want to supply it with values for some of its data members.

The statement below declares an instance of the **mountain** class, naming it as **steepestInWorld**:

```
mountain steepestInWorld( "The Great Trango Tower", "Karakoram", 6286 );
```

The constructor function used takes three arguments to supply the data members with their values:

```
"The Great Trango Tower", "Karakoram", 6286
```

There are some cases however when you might want to declare an object without explicitly assigning it any values at all.

For example:

```
mountain firstClimbed, secondClimbed, thirdClimbed;

mountain climbed[10];
```

In both of the examples above, instances of the **mountain** class could be created by your program. Although they appear not to use a constructor function, they automatically make use of the special constructor function that takes no arguments.

The constructor function would need to be declared in the **mountain** class as a **public** member:

```
public:
    mountain();
```

Without such a function, the instances cannot be created and your program will not normally compile.

This constructor function also needs to have a body defined somewhere in your code, prefixed by the name of the class:

```
mountain::mountain()
{
    // Constructor function that takes no arguments.
    // Assigns a blank default value to each data member.
    name = "";
    range = "";
    elevation = 0;
}
```

The **climbed** array of **mountain** objects allows your program to iterate through the ten instances using a loop, rather than writing repetitive code to process each object separately.

The program on the next page shows how this can be achieved. In the process of creating the **climbed** array at run-time, the **mountain()** constructor function is automatically called to create each of the ten **mountain** instances. Once created, the program iterates through the instances to display their details on the screen, calling the **displayDetails()** member function for each one.

Example 13.3 – *class_array_of_objects.cpp*

```cpp
#include <iostream>      // Program will be displaying some text on the screen

using namespace std;     // Will be using standard identifiers string, cout and endl

// --------------------

class mountain
{
    private:
        string name;
        string range;
        int elevation;

    public:
        mountain();
        void displayDetails();
        void setName( string newName );
        void setRange( string newRange );
 };

// --------------------

mountain::mountain()
{
    // Constructor function that is called when creating a new instance of this class
    name = "";
    range = "";
    elevation = 0;
}

// --------------------

void mountain::displayDetails()
{
    cout << name;
    cout << ", " << range;
    cout << " (" << elevation << "m)";
}

// --------------------

void mountain::setName( string newName )
{
    name = newName;
}

// --------------------

void mountain::setRange( string newRange )
{
    range = newRange;
}
```

continues on next page...

```cpp
// -------------------

int main()
{
    const unsigned int NUM_TO_CLIMB = 10;
    const unsigned char TAB = '\t';

    // Create 10 different mountain objects, each one with blank data member values

    mountain challenge[NUM_TO_CLIMB];


    // Display the details of the newly created mountain objects

    cout << "The details to begin with look like this:" << endl << endl;

    for ( unsigned int num = 0; num < NUM_TO_CLIMB; num++ )
    {
        cout << TAB << "Mountain number " << num << " holds this data:" << TAB;
        challenge[num].displayDetails();
        cout << endl;
    }

    cout << endl << "After setting values, they contain this data:" << endl << endl;


    // Set some data values for each mountain and redisplay them

    string generatedName;

    for ( unsigned int num = 0; num < NUM_TO_CLIMB; num++ )
    {
        generatedName = static_cast <char> ( 'A' + num );

        challenge[num].setName( "Mountain " + generatedName );

        challenge[num].setRange( "unknown range" );

        cout << TAB << "Mountain number " << num << " holds this data: " << TAB;

        challenge[num].displayDetails();

        cout << endl;
    }


    return 0;
}
```

When the program runs, you should see the following output displayed on the screen:

```
The details to begin with look like this:

        Mountain number 0 holds this data:       , (0m)
        Mountain number 1 holds this data:       , (0m)
        Mountain number 2 holds this data:       , (0m)
        Mountain number 3 holds this data:       , (0m)
        Mountain number 4 holds this data:       , (0m)
        Mountain number 5 holds this data:       , (0m)
        Mountain number 6 holds this data:       , (0m)
        Mountain number 7 holds this data:       , (0m)
        Mountain number 8 holds this data:       , (0m)
        Mountain number 9 holds this data:       , (0m)

After setting values, they contain this data:

        Mountain number 0 holds this data:       Mountain A, unknown range (0m)
        Mountain number 1 holds this data:       Mountain B, unknown range (0m)
        Mountain number 2 holds this data:       Mountain C, unknown range (0m)
        Mountain number 3 holds this data:       Mountain D, unknown range (0m)
        Mountain number 4 holds this data:       Mountain E, unknown range (0m)
        Mountain number 5 holds this data:       Mountain F, unknown range (0m)
        Mountain number 6 holds this data:       Mountain G, unknown range (0m)
        Mountain number 7 holds this data:       Mountain H, unknown range (0m)
        Mountain number 8 holds this data:       Mountain I, unknown range (0m)
        Mountain number 9 holds this data:       Mountain J, unknown range (0m)
```

Creating objects dynamically on the heap

So far, all the instances of our classes have been created in **static memory**. As with simple data-types and structures, objects based on classes can also be created **dynamically**. We can store them in heap memory and use pointers to locate and make use of them. This next program creates an instance of the **mountain** class on the heap, rather than in static memory:

Example 13.4 – *class_heap.cpp*

```cpp
#include <iostream>      // Program will be displaying some text on the screen

using namespace std;     // Will be using standard identifiers string, cout and endl

// -------------------

class mountain
{
    private:
        string name;
        string range;
        int elevation;

    public:
        mountain( string newName, string newRange, int newElevation );
        void displayDetails();
        void setName( string newName );
        string getName();
};
```

continues on next page...

```
// ------------------

mountain::mountain( string newName, string newRange, int newElevation )
{
    // Constructor function that is called when creating a new instance of this class

    name = newName;
    range = newRange;
    elevation = newElevation;
}

// ------------------

void mountain::displayDetails()
{
    cout << name;
    cout << ", " << range;
    cout << " (" << elevation << "m)";
}

// ------------------

void mountain::setName( string newName )
{
    name = newName;
}

// ------------------

string mountain::getName()
{
    return name;
}

// ------------------
```

continues on next page...

```cpp
int main()
{
    // Create a mountain object on the heap and store a pointer to it
    mountain* pMatterhorn = new mountain( "Matterhorn", "Pennine Alps", 4478 );

    cout << "This object is stored on the heap:" << endl;
    pMatterhorn->displayDetails();

    cout << endl << endl;

    // Update the name of the mountain by appending it's alternative name
    pMatterhorn->setName( pMatterhorn->getName() + "/Monte Cervino");

    // Display the member data once again
    cout << "The object has been updated:" << endl;
    pMatterhorn->displayDetails();

    cout << endl << endl;

    // Destroy the mountain object
    delete pMatterhorn;
    pMatterhorn = NULL;

    cout << "The object has been destroyed." << endl;

    cout << endl << endl;


    return 0;
}
```

Here is the program in action:

```
This object is stored on the heap:
Matterhorn, Pennine Alps (4478m)

The object has been updated:
Matterhorn/Monte Cervino, Pennine Alps (4478m)

The object has been destroyed.
```

Note that the final part of the program uses **delete** to destroy the **mountain** object. All data members that were directly contained within the object get destroyed, freeing up the memory that they had been using on the heap.

There is however a potential problem when deleting objects from the heap. If an object contains one or more **pointers** to some other dynamic data, then when the object is destroyed using the **delete** operator, those pointer values will also be destroyed as part of the object. The dynamic data that they pointed to will still exist on the heap, taking up space. To make matters worse, not only is the data taking up heap memory, but there is no longer any way to access it in order to clear it up. The data on the heap has effectively been "orphaned". Recall that this kind of wastage is called a "**memory leak**".

Fortunately, there is a solution. On attempting to destroy an object, a special "clean up" function can be called automatically. This function can clear up any data that the object was previously using, prior to the object itself being destroyed. This can then ensure that memory is not tied-up unnecessarily once the object no longer exists. Such a function is called a "**destructor function**".

A destructor function for a class always begins with ~ (*tilde*) and is followed by the name of that class.

For example, the destructor function for the **mountain** class would be declared as follows:

```
public:
    ~mountain();
```

Note that the destructor function needs to be a **public** function as it is automatically called when code elsewhere destroys the object.

Once declared, you can define the body of the destructor function elsewhere in your program code:

```
mountain::~mountain()
{
    // Use this function to destroy any data that the class has been using
    // so that it can be re-used by your Pi

}
```

As explained on the previous page, you can place statements in a destructor function to destroy any dynamic data that the object has been making use of, prior to destroying the object itself. This guarantees that the dynamic data will not be orphaned on the heap.

The following program features a modified version of the **mountain** class, making use of dynamic data. A **destructor** function has been added which will be called automatically when any instance of **mountain** gets destroyed by a **delete** operation. This destructor function will delete each item of dynamic data that the object had previously been using, freeing up the heap memory.

Example 13.5 – *class_destructor.cpp*

```
#include <iostream>     // Program will be displaying some text on the screen

using namespace std;    // Will be using standard identifiers string, cout and endl

const char TAB = '\t';

// --------------------

class mountain
{
    private:
        string* pName;
        string* pRange;
        int* pElevation;

    public:
        mountain( string newName, string newRange, int newElevation );
        ~mountain();
        void displayDetails();
};
```

continues on next page...

```
// --------------------

mountain::mountain( string newName, string newRange, int newElevation )
{
    // Constructor function that is called when creating a new instance of this class
    // Creats all data items on the heap, storing their addresses using pointers
    pName = new string( newName );
    pRange = new string ( newRange );
    pElevation = new int ( newElevation );
}

// --------------------

mountain::~mountain()
{
    // Use this function to destroy any data that the class has been using
    // so that it can be re-used by your Pi
    cout << TAB << "Destructor activated! Destroying data items.";
    cout << endl << endl;

    delete pName;
    delete pRange;
    delete pElevation;

    cout << TAB << "Data items deleted. Exiting destructor function.";
    cout << endl << endl;
}

// --------------------

void mountain::displayDetails()
{
    cout << *pName;
    cout << ", " << *pRange;
    cout << " (" << *pElevation << "m)";
}

// --------------------

int main()
{
    // Create a mountain object on the heap and store a pointer to it
    mountain* pMatterhorn = new mountain( "Matterhorn", "Pennine Alps", 4478 );

    cout << "This object is stored on the heap:" << endl;
    pMatterhorn->displayDetails();

    cout << endl << endl;
```

continues on next page...

```
    // Destroy the mountain object

    cout << "About to delete the object..." << endl << endl;

    delete pMatterhorn;
    pMatterhorn = NULL;

    cout << "The object has been destroyed." << endl << endl;

    cout << endl << endl;


    return 0;
}
```

Here is what you should see when the program runs:

```
This object is stored on the heap:
Matterhorn, Pennine Alps (4478m)

About to delete the object...

        Destructor activated! Destroying data items.

        Data items deleted. Exiting destructor function.

The object has been destroyed.
```

At the end of the program, the instance of **mountain** that was being used to represent the Matterhorn is destroyed using the **delete** operator. It follows the pointer to remove the instance from the heap, where it is stored dynamically:

```
    delete pMatterhorn;
```

The **~mountain** destructor function is automatically called as part of this process. This function uses the data members contained within the **mountain** instance to delete each individual value that was being stored dynamically:

```
    delete pName;
    delete pRange;
    delete pElevation;
```

Your Pi can now destroy the Matterhorn instance of **mountain** without leaving any orphaned dynamic data lying around.

As an extra final precaution, the pointer that was previously used to access the instance is set to **NULL** so that it cannot be used by the program:

```
    pMatterhorn = NULL;
```

(In this example, this is unlikely as the **main()** part of the simple program is just about to finish, but it is not always so.)

Overloading operators

Whilst the previous class uses the **displayDetails()** function, it is not possible to use an object a **cout** statement unless your class is shown how to make use of the **<<** redirection operator.

Under normal circumstances, it is not possible to send the contents of an object to a stream unless your code defines exactly how the data members of the object should be dealt with, such as how they should be displayed or saved to a file:

```
cout << steepestInWorld;      // This will not currently work

outputFileStream << steepestInWorld;      // This will not currently work
```

It is possible to define how a particular operator symbol works with any new class that you create. This is called "**operator overloading**". You can define exactly **how** each operator can be used to process the data members of your class. This can often make classes easier to use, as you can use familiar operator symbols such as **+** or **=** instead of calling functions.

The program below shows how to **overload** the **<<** operator so that an instance of the **mountain** class can be sent to a stream, such as to **cout** (the screen) or to an **ofstream** (output file stream). The **<<** operator can then be used with **mountain** objects in the same way as for simple data-types, rather than calling the **displayDetails()** function.

Example 13.6 – *class_overloaded_operator.cpp*

```cpp
#include <iostream>      // Program will be displaying some text on the screen

using namespace std;     // Will be using standard identifiers string, cout and endl

// --------------------

class mountain
{
    private:
        // Data members
        string name;
        string range;
        int elevation;

    public:
        // Member functions and operators
        mountain( string newName, string newCountry, int newElevation );
        void displayDetails();
        friend ostream& operator<< ( ostream &outStream, mountain &objectToDisplay );
};

// --------------------

mountain::mountain( string newName, string newRange, int newElevation )
{
    // Constructor function that is called when creating new instance of this class
    name = newName;
    range = newRange;
    elevation = newElevation;
}
```

continues on next page...

```
// -------------------

void mountain::displayDetails()
{
    // Manually displays the value of each data member on the screen
    cout << name;
    cout << ", " << range;
    cout << " (" << elevation << "m)";
}

// -------------------

ostream& operator<< ( ostream &outStream, mountain &objectToDisplay )
{
    // Overloads the << operator to allow the data members for the mountain object
    // to be sent to a stream, such as cout (the screen) or an output file stream

    outStream << objectToDisplay.name << ", " << objectToDisplay.range
            << " (" << objectToDisplay.elevation << "m)";

    return outStream;
}

// -------------------

int main()
{
    // Create an object that is an instance of the mountain class
    mountain steepestInWorld( "The Great Trango Tower", "Karakoram", 6286 );

    // Display the data members for the object

    cout << "These two methods should produce the same results on screen:" << endl;

    cout << steepestInWorld << endl;

    steepestInWorld.displayDetails();

    cout << endl;

    return 0;
}
```

Both approaches result in the same text being displayed on the screen when the program executes:

```
These two methods should produce the same results on screen:
The Great Trango Tower, Karakoram (6286m)
The Great Trango Tower, Karakoram (6286m)
```

Note that the program makes uses of the **friend** reserved word to allow the output stream to access the **name**, **range** and **elevation** data members of the **mountain** class. This is necessary because these data members have been declared as **private**, meaning they can only be accessed by member functions of **mountain**. By declaring that the operator **<<** is a **friend** of the **mountain** class, when the **<<** operator tries to access the data members, it will have permission to do so, enabling them to be displayed.

Inheritance – creating new classes that are based on other existing classes

Sometimes, your program may need to create an object that is **similar** to an existing object, but that is not quite the same. For instance, you might want to make a new kind of object that is very much like an existing object, but that also possesses one or more additional data members or functions.

In this situation, it is possible to define a new kind of class that is based upon some other existing class. You can specify additional members that the new class contains, such as new data members, additional member functions or overloaded operators that the class will make use of.

Creating a new class that is based upon another existing class is called **"inheritance"**. The new class will automatically be given any data members, operators or functions that were defined for the existing class that it is based on.

For instance, we have already created and used the `mountain` class in several of our programs. If we wanted to make a new `volcano` class, we could make a brand new class and specify every single data member, function and operator that it uses.

In addition to the `name`, `range` and `elevation` data members that the `mountain` class contains, we might want to add two additional data members to the `volcano` class: `extinct` and `lastErupted`. These indicate whether the real-life volcano is still active.

Class of objects: `mountain`

string	name
string	range
int	elevation

Class of objects: `volcano`

string	name
string	range
int	elevation
bool	extinct
string	lastErupted

Class `volcano` *contains two additional data members* `extinct` *and* `lastErupted`

We could save some effort however using inheritance. It is likely that any object that represents a real life volcano will have some **similarities** with a mountain: both a mountain and a volcano have a name, their elevation can be measured and they belong to a geographic mountain-range. Both classes will need to contain the **name**, **elevation** and **range** data members.

Whilst we could write the code for the new class entirely from scratch, we can instead base the new `volcano` class on the existing `mountain` class, using inheritance to supply some of the members. This means that when we create the new class, telling the compiler that `volcano` will be based on the `mountain` class, we will only need to specify the **additional** members that the new class needs - those that were not part of the original `mountain` class.

Class of objects: `mountain`

string	name
string	range
int	elevation

Class of objects: `volcano`
based on class `mountain`
with additional data members

bool	extinct
string	lastErupted

members `name`, `range` *and* `elevation`
are inherited from class `mountain`

Both classes will need constructor functions to create object instances. We may also want to perform similar processing on both kinds of objects, such as displaying all values for their data members on the screen. We can provide functions to allow access to their data members, such as `displayDetails()` and `setName()`.

Member functions from the existing class can be inherited by the new class. Sometimes though, rather than inheriting a member function, the new class may replace it with code which operates differently from that of the original class, especially where it needs to use the new data members.

We have already briefly considered the difference between **public**, **private** and **protected** members of a class earlier on in this chapter.

We have seen that **private** members of a particular class cannot be directly accessed by any code that does not belong to that class. Any **private** data members can only be accessed by the member functions of that class, whilst **private** member functions can only be called by functions of the same class.

What happens when one class inherits data members or member funtions from another class?

Any members that were specified as being **private** would not be directly accessible by the new inherited class. To allow access to a member for an inherited class, it is necessary to declare that member using the **protected** access-specifier. Any member of a class that is **protected** can be accessed either by that class, or by any other class that is inherited from that class.

In the next program, you will see that the data members for the **mountain** class have been made **protected** so that the inherited **volcano** class can make use of them:

```cpp
class mountain
{
    protected:
        // Protected data members can be accessed directly by this class
        // or by classes that inherit from it, such as the volcano class
        string name;
        string range;
        int elevation;
        mountain();  // Will not get used, but volcano will try to inherit this

    public:
        mountain( string newName, string newCountry, int newElevation );
        void displayDetails();
        void setName( string newName );
};
```

To specify that we are **inheriting** the **volcano** class from the existing **mountain** class, we would begin the declaration for the new class as follows:

```cpp
class volcano : public mountain
```

This is followed by the rest of the declaration, specifying the additional data members and member functions that the new **volcano** class will contain, as well as how they are able to be accessed.

The entire declaration for the new **volcano** class is shown below:

```
class volcano : public mountain
{
    private:
        bool extinct;
        string lastErupted;

    public:
        volcano();

        volcano( string newName, string newRange, int newElevation,
                bool newExtinct, string newLastErupted );

        void displayDetails();
        bool isExtinct();
        string getWhenLastErupted();
};
```

You can see that it contains the two new data members: **extinct** and **lastErupted**, which are **private**.

It also declares several member functions which are **public** so that code outside of the **volcano** class can call them.

Two of these functions are **constructors** for the new **volcano** class. These will be used to create new instances of the class:

```
        volcano();

        volcano( string newName, string newRange, int newElevation,
                bool newExtinct, string newLastErupted );
```

There is also a new version of the **displayDetails()** function:

```
        void displayDetails();
```

Although the original **mountain** class already contained a **displayDetails()** function, this new version displays **all** of the data members of the **volcano** class - both those that were inherited from **mountain**, and the new **extinct** and **lastErupted** data members. The **volcano** class needs to make an updated version of this function, rather than relying on the old one that was supplied as part of the **mountain** class that it inherits from.

Finally, two new member functions are declared that were not in the original **mountain** class:

```
        bool isExtinct();
        string getWhenLastErupted();
```

The program below defines and uses the new **volcano** class, which is inherited from the **mountain** class:

Example 13.7 – *class_inherited.cpp*

```cpp
#include <iostream>    // Program will be displaying some text on the screen

using namespace std;    // Will be using standard identifiers string, cout and endl

// -------------------

class mountain
{
    protected:
        // Protected data members can be accessed directly by this class
        // or by classes that inherit from it, such as the volcano class
        string name;
        string range;
        int elevation;
        mountain();   // volcano() constuctor will always try to call this

    public:
        mountain( string newName, string newCountry, int newElevation );
        void displayDetails();
        void setName( string newName );
 };

// -------------------

mountain::mountain()
{
    // Class must have this default constructor
    // Any class that inherits from mountain will attempt to inherit this
    name = "Not assigned yet";
    range = "Not assigned yet";
    elevation = 0;
}

// -------------------

mountain::mountain( string newName, string newRange, int newElevation )
{
    // Constructor function that is called when creating a new instance of this class
    name = newName;
    range = newRange;
    elevation = newElevation;
}

// -------------------
```

continues on next page...

```
void mountain::displayDetails()
{
    // This class WILL be inherited by the volcano class
    cout << name;
    cout << ", " << range;
    cout << " (" << elevation << "m)";
}

// -------------------

void mountain::setName( string newName )
{
    name = newName;
}

// -------------------

class volcano : public mountain
{
    private:
        bool extinct;
        string lastErupted;

    public:
        volcano();

        volcano( string newName, string newRange, int newElevation,
                bool newExtinct, string newLastErupted );

        void displayDetails();
        bool isExtinct();
        string getWhenLastErupted();
};

// -------------------

volcano::volcano()
{
    // Class must have
    // Values for name, range and elevation get assigned in mountain::mountain()
    extinct = false;
    lastErupted = "Unknown";
}

// -------------------
```

continues on next page...

```cpp
volcano::volcano( string newName, string newRange, int newElevation,
                  bool newExtinct, string newLastErupted )
{
    // Constructor function that is called when creating a new instance of this class
    name = newName;
    range = newRange;
    elevation = newElevation;
    extinct = newExtinct;
    lastErupted = newLastErupted;
}

// -------------------

void volcano::displayDetails()
{
    // This class WILL be inherited by the volcano class
    cout << name;
    cout << ", " << range;
    cout << " (" << elevation << "m), ";
    cout << ( extinct ? "Extinct" : "Active" );
    cout << ", " << lastErupted;
}

// -------------------

int main()
{
    // Create one instance of each of the mountain and the volcano classes
    mountain lastClimbed( "Mt. Roraima", "Guiana Highlands", 2810 );

    volcano nearestVolcano( "Katla", "Mid-Atlantic Ridge", 1512, false, "Oct 1918" );

    // Display the details of the newly created objects

    cout << "Here are the details of the mountain and volcano:" << endl << endl;

    lastClimbed.displayDetails();

    cout << endl;

    nearestVolcano.displayDetails();

    cout << endl << endl;

    // Update data member and redisplay details of the mountain object

    lastClimbed.setName( "Mt. Roraima (\"The Lost World\")" );

    // Update inherited data member and redisplay details of the volcano object

    nearestVolcano.setName( "Katla (\"Ketill\")" );
```

continues on next page...

```
    //Display the updated information about the objects

    cout << endl << endl;
    cout << "The objects have now been updated with extra information:";
    cout << endl << endl;

    lastClimbed.displayDetails();

    cout << endl;

    nearestVolcano.displayDetails();

    cout << endl;

    // Create blank volcano using volcano() constructor

    volcano blank;

    cout << endl << endl << endl;
    cout << "Protected member values for the blank volcano object are inherited:";
    cout << endl << endl;

    blank.displayDetails();

    cout << endl << endl;

    return 0;
}
```

Below, you can see that **Mt. Roraima** is an instance of the **mountain** class, whilst **Katla** and **blank** are instances of the **volcano** class (which both inherit data members from the **mountain** class):

```
Here are the details of the mountain and volcano:

Mt. Roraima, Guiana Highlands (2810m)
Katla, Mid-Atlantic Ridge (1512m), Active, Oct 1918



The objects have now been updated with extra information:

Mt. Roraima ("The Lost World"), Guiana Highlands (2810m)
Katla ("Ketill"), Mid-Atlantic Ridge (1512m), Active, Oct 1918



Protected member values for the blank volcano object are inherited:

Not assigned yet, Not assigned yet (0m), Active, Unknown
```

Classes can even inherit data members and functions from more than one other class. This is called **"multiple inheritance"**.

Although useful for building more complex programs, multiple inheritance is quite a tricky concept for many beginners and is beyond the scope of this book, hence it is not covered here.

Declaring your classes using .h header files

So far, when we have used classes in our programs, their member functions have been declared and defined in the same source-code file as our main program. As we have already seen in **"Chapter 4: Keyboard input and screen output"**, it is possible for a program to **include** code from separate reusable **header files** that contain declarations of constants or functions. By convention these header files are given filenames that end with the ".*h*" extension.

When declaring a new class, the details of that class can be stored in their own header file. This header file can then be included by any program that needs to make use of the new class. Typically, the filename of the header file will be taken from the name of the class, ending in ".*h*".

Below is a reusable header file that contains the declaration for the **mountain** class that we have used in our examples:

Example 13.8a – mountain.h

```
// This file declares a new class called mountain.
// You can use it again and again in many different programs.

// The source-code for each member function of mountain is saved in mountain.cpp

// The compiler will only attempt to declare the new class if identifier _mountain
// has not already been defined i.e. this mountain.h file has not been included
// already by any other file of source-code in your program.

#ifndef _mountain
#define _mountain

#include <string>      // Program uses variables of type string

using namespace std;    // Will be using standard identifiers cout and endl


// --------------------

class mountain
{
    // This private data is not directly accessible by other parts of program
    private:
        string name;
        string range;
        int elevation;

    // These public functions can be called by other parts of program
    public:
        mountain( string newName, string newRange, int newElevation );
        void displayDetails();
};

#endif
```

Note that it is **not** necessary to compile or build the above header file. All that is necessary for another file to make use of the **mountain** class is to include the name of the header file in the new file by adding the following directive:

```
#include "mountain.h"
```

The code for each member function of the new class is usually saved in a separate file. This will also be named after the class, but will end with the ".*cpp*" filename extension.

This means that we now need another file that will define the code for each member function in the **mountain** class:

Example 13.8b – *mountain.cpp*

```cpp
#include "mountain.h"     // The mountain class is declared in this file

#include <iostream>       // Program will be displaying some text on the screen

using namespace std;      // Will be using standard identifiers cout and endl

// --------------------

mountain::mountain( string newName, string newRange, int newElevation )
{
    // Constructor function that is called when creating a new instance of this class
    name = newName;
    range = newRange;
    elevation = newElevation;
}

// --------------------

void mountain::displayDetails()
{
    // Displays each of the private data members
    cout << name;
    cout << ", " << range;
    cout << " (" << elevation << "m)";
}
```

Before any other programs can make use of the **mountain** class or the members that it contains, it is necessary to **compile** the "***mountain.cpp***" class file.

From the command line, you could use the following to do this:

```
g++ -Wall -c mountain.cpp
```

The above command will compile the code, but will **not** attempt to **link** it to any other routines to make an executable file.

Alternatively, if you are using Geany then you should use the *"Compile"* button, rather than the *"Build"* button:

Once compiled, your other programs can now make use of the **mountain** class, using it to make objects.

Here is an example that creates several instances of the **mountain** class after including the reusable "***mountain.cpp***" file:

Example 13.8c – highest_mountains.cpp

```cpp
#include <iostream>      // Program will be displaying some text on the screen

#include "mountain.cpp"     // Code for the functions contained in the mountain class

using namespace std;     // Will be using standard identifiers cout and endl

int main()
{
    // Create 3 different objects, each one is an instance of the mountain class

    mountain highestInWales( "Mt. Snowdon/Yr Wyddfa", "Snowdonia", 1085 );

    mountain highestInAfrica( "Kilimanjaro", "Eastern Rift", 5895 );

    mountain highestInSouthAmerica( "Aconcagua", "Andes", 6961 );


    // Call the displayDetails() member function for each of the 3 objects

    cout << "The highest mountain in Wales is ";
    highestInWales.displayDetails();

    cout << endl << endl;

    cout << "The highest mountain in Africa is ";
    highestInAfrica.displayDetails();

    cout << endl << endl;

    cout << "The highest mountain in South America is ";
    highestInSouthAmerica.displayDetails();

    cout << endl << endl;

    return 0;
}
```

Note that the program contains a directive to include the "***mountain.cpp***" code:

```cpp
        #include "mountain.cpp"
```

This source-code file defines the code for the body of each member function in the **mountain** class.

In turn, "***mountain.cpp***" also includes the "***mountain.h***" header file, which declares the actual existence of the **mountain** class and sets out the details of each of the members that it contains.

You can now **build** the main program in the normal way. The build process will take care of the compilation of the main program, linking the object file produced to that of the object file for the `mountain` class, along with other operating system routines to make an executable program.

Bear in mind though that the build process will **not** be successful unless you have already compiled the "*mountain.cpp*" file, otherwise the object file for the `mountain` class will not exist - the linker would then fail to create a final executable.

```
The highest mountain in Wales is Mt. Snowdon/Yr Wyddfa, Snowdonia (1085m)

The highest mountain in Africa is Kilimanjaro, Eastern Rift (5895m)

The highest mountain in South America is Aconcagua, Andes (6961m)
```

Taking classes and inheritance further

There are many ways in which you can combine the basics of classes and object-orientation to produce more complex programs that model or represent real world systems and their interactions.

Using an object-orientated approach, you can either create your own classes and data-structures, or use libraries of pre-made classes, along with inheritance to help you customise them to fit the problem that you are trying to solve.

One such library is the C++ Standard Template Library. This provides ready-made classes and **"templates"** that implement many common data-structures and algorithms that can be found in computer science, particularly those for storing, sorting and searching through data in an organised and efficient way.

Using the Standard Template Library requires you to be fairly confident in the workings of classes, although once mastered, inheriting from these classes can save you a lot of work when developing your own code.

You can also begin to build up your own libraries of reusable code to make it easier to write new programs, rather than starting afresh each time.

Summary of Chapter 13: Objects and classes

Here's what we have covered in this chapter:

C++ allows you to define your own custom data-types called **classes**. These are general descriptions of things that can exist in the real world and how they behave.

Classes can be used to create **objects**. Objects are specific examples or **instances** of a general class.

Classes usually contain one or more useful data items, which are known as **data members**.

Classes also define various functions that can be performed on the data members, called **member functions**.

Use the reserved word `class` to declare a new class in your code.

When creating a new class, you may base it upon some other existing class. This technique is called **inheritance**.

A class must include one or more **constructor functions** that carry out useful tasks or assign values to data members when creating a new instance of that class.

Access-specifiers can be used to make it clear which parts of the program are allowed to access and use the data members and functions that are associated with a class. This prevents parts of your code accessing member data or functions in an uncontrolled way.

A `public` data member or function can be directly accessed by other parts of your program outside of the class.

A `private` data member or function cannot be accessed by parts of your program that are outside of the class. The data can only be accessed by the member functions for that class.

A `protected` data member or function can only be accessed by the class that it belongs to, or by other classes that are based on that class through inheritance.

By default, members are treated as `private` unless you specify otherwise.

In addition, classes can provide "**get**" and "**set**" functions to further control access to member data.

When defining a member function, the name of the function is preceded by the name of the class that it is associated with and the `::` **scope-resolution operator**.

Objects can be created as **static data** or **dynamically** on the heap.

A class may include a **destructor function**. This is a member function that is responsible for carrying out some processing when the object is about to be destroyed. The name of a destructor function is always the same as the class name and must be preceded with a ~ *tilde*.

A destructor function may be used to tidy up or destroy dynamic data that the object was using on the heap in order to avoid **memory leaks**.

New classes can **overload** operator symbols to define how those symbols should process the class data members.

A class can provide additional access to particular functions or operators by specifying that another class is a `friend` of that class.

Storing the definition of a class in a separate "*.h*" **header file** allows it to be used by other programs.

The code for the member functions of a class can also be stored in a separate "*.cpp*" file, making your source-code more organised.

1.	Create a class called **computer** which contains data members to store various properties about machines: **name** **speed_GHz** **gigabytes_RAM** **storage_device** **operating_system**
2.	Add the following member functions to **computer**, making sure that they accessible to code outside the class: A constructor function **computer()** which does not take any arguments and creates a default instance of the **computer** class. An alternative constructor function that allows you to supply values for each of the data members. A function called **displaySpec()** to display the data members on the screen for a particular instance. Make sure that you define the code for the body of each function.
3.	Overload the **<<** operator so that the data members of instances of **computer** can be directed to a stream. Write a program that creates three different instances of **computer**. Use the overloaded operator to display the details of the three instances of **computer** on the screen. Use the same overloaded operator to save their details to a simple text file.
4.	Save the declaration for the **computer** class in a separate header file, calling this "**computer.h**". Create a new **computer.cpp** file to contain the code for each member function associated with the class. Write a simple program to include and make use of the new "**computer.cpp**" file.
5.	Create new **laptop** class that inherits from **computer** adding the following additional data members: **screen_size** **weight_kg**

Appendices

Useful information

The ASCII character set and character codes

ASCII code	Symbol
0	Null
1	
2	
3	
4	
5	
6	
7	
8	
9	
10	
11	
12	
13	
14	
15	
16	
17	
18	
19	
20	
21	
22	
23	
24	
25	
26	

ASCII code	Symbol
27	
28	
29	
30	
31	
32	Space
33	!
34	"
35	#
36	$
37	%
38	&
39	'
40	(
41	)
42	*
43	+
44	,
45	-
46	.
47	/
48	0
49	1
50	2
51	3
52	4
53	5

ASCII code	Symbol
54	6
55	7
56	8
57	9
58	:
59	;
60	<
61	=
62	>
63	?
64	@
65	A
66	B
67	C
68	D
69	E
70	F
71	G
72	H
73	I
74	J
75	K
76	L
77	M
78	N
79	O
80	P

ASCII code	Symbol
81	Q
82	R
83	S
84	T
85	U
86	V
87	W
88	X
89	Y
90	Z
91	[
92	\
93	]
94	^
95	_
96	'
97	a
98	b
99	c
100	d
101	e
102	f
103	g
104	h
105	i
106	j
107	k

ASCII code	Symbol
108	l
109	m
110	n
111	o
112	p
113	q
114	r
115	s
116	t
117	u
118	v
119	w
120	x
121	y
122	z
123	{
124		
125	}
126	~
127	Delete

Shaded characters in the above table are "**non-printable**" or "**control**" characters.

C++ reserved words

These are special words that are part of the C++ language. Each one has a special use, therefore you can't use them as names for your own variables, constants, classes or functions in the program code that you write – trying to do so would give you an error when you try to compile your code.

Examples of errors caused by trying to use a reserved word might include:

```
// Indicate whether the substance floats in water…
bool float = true;      // Whoops! float is a reserved word

// Get a wholenumber and double it...
int myNum;
cin >> myNum;
int double = myNum * 2;      // Whoops! double is a reserved word
```

Here is a list of the main reserved words that you cannot use as identifiers:

and	continue	if	register	typedef
and_eq	default	inline	reinterpret_cast	typeid
asm	delete	int	return	typename
auto	do	long	short	typeof
bitand	double	mutable	signed	union
bitor	dynamic_cast	namespace	sizeof	unsigned
bool	else	new	static	using
break	enum	not	static_cast	virtual
case	explicit	not_eq	struct	void
catch	extern	operator	switch	volatile
char	false	or	template	while
class	float	or_eq	this	xor
compl	for	private	throw	xor_eq
const	friend	protected	true	
const_cast	goto	public	try	

In addition, there are other tokens used by the compiler that begin with two _ underscore characters. You should also avoid using these as names:

__alignof	__extension__	__typeof
__alignof__	__inline	__typeof__
__asm	__inline__	__volatile
__asm__	__label__	__volatile__
__attribute	__signature__	__wchar_t__
__attribute__	__signed	
__const	__signed__	
__const__		

Special symbols used in C++ and what they mean

#	Directive	Tells the compiler to do something before compiling the source-code. `#include <iostream>`
;	Semi-colon	Marks the end of a statement in a program. `cout << "Hello" << endl;`
//	Single-line comment	Used to mark the start of a comment that takes up one single line or part of a line. `// This will be ignored by the compiler` `cout << timer << endl; // Display time left`
/* */	Start of multi-line comment block — End of multi-line comment block	Used to mark the beginning and end of a block of comments that may take up more than one line of text. `/*` `secure.cpp - program to encrypt email messages` `written by J. Bloggs 22nd Sept 2015` `*/`
( )	Left bracket — Right bracket	Encloses an expression, such as an arithmetic expression or a logical expression. `( timeLeft * 10 ) + 500`
{ }	Left curly-brace — Right curly-brace	Marks the start and end of a block of program statements. `if ( isTrue )` `{` `}`
[ ]	Start of array index — End of array index	Encloses an index to an item in an array. `firstItemInArray = myArray[0];` `currentItem = myArray[pos];`
<<	Redirect to output	Sends values to an output stream of your choice, such as the screen or a file. `cout << "Hello";`
>>	Redirect to input	Obtains values from the input stream of your choice, such as the keyboard or a file. `cin >> menuChoice;`
*	Pointer-to or de-reference operator	Used when creating or de-referencing a pointer. `string* pName;` `cout << *pName;`
.	Member-of operator	Used when calling a member function or accessing data that belongs to an object. `passwordString.length()`
->	Pointer-to-member operator	Allows you to access the value of a member by following a pointer. `pFlight->destination = "Detroit";`
::	Scope resolution operator	Used to denote the owner of an identifier, such as the name of a variable that belongs to a particular namespace. `std::cout`

Operators and their precedence

Here is a list of operators that can be used in C++ expressions, listed in order of their precedence. The operators that have the highest precedence (which are performed first) are at the top of the list. The operators with the lowest precedence (which are performed last) are at the bottom.

(	**Left-bracket** (Groups together parts of an expression.)
)	**Right-bracket** (Groups together parts of an expression.)
/	**Divide** (Divides one numeric value by another.)
*	**Multiply** (Multiplies two numeric values together.)
+	**Add** (Adds two numeric values together or appends a `char` or `string` to another `string` value.)
−	**Subtract** (Takes one numeric value away from another.)
%	**Modulus** (Divides one numeric value by another to obtain the remainder.)
++	**Increment** (Increases a numeric value by `1`.)
−−	**Decrement** (Decreases a numeric value by `1`.)
==	**Equivalent to** (Determines whether two values/expressions are the same.)
!= `not_eq`	**Not equivalent to** (Determines whether two values/expressions are **not** the same.)
! `not`	**Logical NOT** (Obtains the **opposite** of a `bool` value/Boolean expression.)
&& `and`	**Logical AND** (Produces `true` if a pair of `bool` values/Boolean expressions are both found to be `true`. Produces `false` if they are **not** both `true`.)
|| `or`	**Logical OR** (Produces `true` if one or both of a pair of `bool` values/Boolean expressions are found to be `true`. Produces `false` if they are **all false**.)
^	**Logical XOR** (Produces `true` if a pair of `bool` values/Boolean expressions are found to be **different**. Produces `false` if they are the same.)
+=	**Add on to the current value / append to the current value** (Adds a numeric value to an existing numeric value. With `string` values, appends a `char` or a `string` value to an existing `string` value.)
−=	**Take away from current value** (Subtracts one numeric value from another numeric value.)
&=	**Logical AND with the current value** (Produces `true` if both the current `bool` value/Boolean expression and another `bool` value/Boolean expression are both found to be `true`. Produces `false` if they are **not** both `true`.)
|=	**Logical OR with the current value** (Produces `true` if one or both of the current `bool` value/Boolean expression and another `bool` value/Boolean expression are both found to be `true`. Produces `false` if they are **not** both `true`.)
^=	**Logical XOR with the current value** (Produces `true` if the current `bool` value/Boolean expression and another `bool` value/Boolean expression are found to be **different**. Produces `false` if they are the same.)

Data-types and ranges of values

Data-type	What it is used for
short	Small whole numbers that can be positive or negative. These can range between -32768 and 32767.
unsigned short	Small positive numbers in the range 0 to 65535.
int	Positive or negative whole number values. These can range between -2147483648 and 2147483647.
unsigned int	Positive whole numbers in the range 0 to 4294967295.
long	Larger whole numbers, positive or negative. These can range between -2,147,483,648 and 2,147,483,647.
unsigned long	Larger whole numbers, positive only. Cannot be used to represent negative values. These can range between 0 and 4,294,967,295.
long long	Even larger whole numbers, positive or negative. These can range between -9,223,372,036,854,775,808 and 9,223,372,036,854,775,807.
unsigned long long	Even larger whole numbers, positive only. Cannot be used to represent negative values. These can range between 0 and 18,446,744,073,709,551,615.
float	Floating-point decimal numbers, positive or negative. These can range between $1.17548 \times e^{-38}$ and $3.40282 \times e^{38}$.
double	Double-precision floating-point decimal numbers, positive or negative. These can range between $2.22507 \times e^{-308}$ and $1.79769 \times e^{308}$.
long double	Extended-precision floating-point decimal numbers, positive or negative. These can range between $3.36210 \times e^{-4932}$ and $1.18973 \times e^{4932}$.
bool	Boolean values that are always either true or false. No other values are allowed for variables that have the data-type bool.
char	A single-byte value, often used to represent a single character symbol in the ASCII character set. Values can range between -128 and 127. Note however that the ASCII character set begins with code 0 (the code for the NULL non-printable character), thus negative values do not directly correspond to ASCII characters.
wchar_t	A 2-byte "wide character" value that may be used to represent a UNICODE character. These can range between 0 and 65535.
unsigned char	An 8-bit whole number value that ranges between 0 and 255. Allows access to full range of ASCII character codes. All of the 8-bit patterns are used to represent only the positive numbers, none are "wasted" on negative numbers.
string	A sequence of zero or more character-symbols. Use of the string data-type in your program requires you to add #include <string> at the start of your code, unless another library that you have included has already done so.

Header files for C++ and C library functions that you can include in your programs

`<string>`	Allows you to use the `string` data-type and to carry out operations on `string` values.
`<iostream>`	The **input-output stream** library. Keyboard input and screen output.
`<iomanip>`	The **input-output manipulator** library for formatting values that are sent to a stream.
`<fstream>`	The **file-stream** library. Input/output operations to read or write files.
`<istream>`	The **input-stream** library. Input operations to read files.
`<ostream>`	The **output-stream** library. Output operations to write files.
`<sstream>`	The **stringstream** library. Performs conversions between `string` values and other data-types.
`<cstdlib>`	Allows you to use the `exit()` function to terminate the execution of your program. Also allows use of `random()` and `srandom()` functions for choosing and seeding random numbers.
`<ctime>`	Allows you to use the `time()` function, which is useful as the seed for a random number.
`<unistd.h>`	Allows you to use the `sleep()` function to delay parts of your program. Note that this is a C library which is compatible with C++. (It is not actually a standard C++ library, hence the filename ends in ".*h*".)
`<cmath>`	Allows you to use the `pow()` (*power*) and `sqrt()` (*square-root*) functions.
`<cctype>`	Allows you to use the `toupper()` and `tolower()` functions to convert the case of a `char` value. A program that uses the `string` library does not need to include this, but a program that does not would need to include it if working with single characters and converting their case.
`<climits>`	Useful when flushing unwanted characters from `cin` during keyboard input. Defines the `INT_MAX` constant.

Escape-sequences to control the colour of text on the screen

The following is a list of typical colours that your program might use when displaying text on the screen.

Each escape-sequence can be sent to channel-out, either as a literal string in its own right:

```
cout << "\e[32m";     // Change all future text to green
```

...or embedded within another literal string:

```
// Display several different colours on one line, then reset
cout << "\e[41m red alert \e[42m green grass \e[44m blue moon \e[0m" << endl;
```

Changing the foreground "ink" colour – background colour will be unaffected

\e[30m	Black text
\e[31m	Red text
\e[32m	Green text
\e[33m	Standard yellow text (may appear brown/orange on your screen)
\e[34m	Blue text
\e[35m	Magenta (purple) text
\e[36m	Cyan (light-blue) text
\e[37m	White
\e[38;5;226m	Brighter yellow! Just in case you don't like the standard yellow

Changing the background colour - foreground colour will be unaffected

\e[41m	Red background behind text
\e[42m	Green background behind text
\e[44m	Blue background behind text

Changing the weight or "thickness" of text

\e[1m	Turns bold text on
\e[21m	Turns bold text off

Reset all colours and weight of text back to normal

\e[0m	Reset to default settings - normal colours and weight (bold text off)

Finding and correcting common mistakes in your C++ source-code

Sooner or later, you will encounter an error in your code that either prevents it from compiling, or which causes it to behave in a way that you did not expect at run-time. Sometimes, the solution is extremely simple and you may well be looking straight through the real cause of the problem.

Here are some very common mistakes that people often make in their code.

Incorrect spelling of identifiers – mistakes with names of variables and constants

```
int finalScore = flagsCollected + timeLeftOver;

cout << "Game Over - you scored " << finalscore << endl;
```

Notice that the first line of code above features a variable called `finalScore`, containing a capital "S" (underlined).

The second line of code contains a typing-error, `finalscore` contains a lower-case "s" rather than a capital "S".

The compiler treats `finalscore` and `finalScore` as two **different** variables. When it encounters the line of code containing `finalscore` it decides that this variable has never been declared elsewhere in the program.

This will generate an error-message during compilation:

Undeclared identifier

Very often, a human might read the program and use their common-sense to interpret the mistake. They might recognise that the variable names are different, but that they were **meant** to be exactly the same.

The compiler does not have common-sense. It does not **know** that the two variable names are actually meant to refer to the same variable. Even if it guessed that they were the same thing, it is not guaranteed. This is why the compiler displays an error-message just in case.

A `while` loop that can never terminate

```
int timeLeft = 60;

while ( timeLeft > 0 )
{
    cout << timeLeft << " seconds left" << endl;
    sleep( 1 );
}
```

This above code mistakenly creates an infinite loop. The intention was that it should count down from **60** towards **0**, using the variable `timeLeft`.

Unfortunately, after setting the original value of `timeLeft`, the loop fails to make any change to it whatsoever. The value of `timeLeft` remains at **60**, meaning that the condition `timeLeft > 0` always evaluates as **true**. As a consequence, the loop will never terminate. Below is the corrected code:

```
while ( timeLeft > 0 )
{
    cout << timeLeft << " seconds left" << endl;
    sleep( 1 );
    timeLeft--;   // Reduce the amount of time left by 1
}
```

What does this line of code mean?

```
;
```

The semi-colon marks the **end** of a statement. So if you type a semi-colon on a blank line, then this is effectively marking the end of an **empty statement** - one that does nothing. Imagine having a conversation with the compiler. The compiler asks you "What is this line?" and you tell it "Oh, don't worry about it - it's nothing..."

Be really careful not to put a semi-colon in the middle of a statement when you don't actually need one. An unwanted extra semi-colon can cause run-time errors. Your program code might look to you as though it should work, but it will actually do something that you didn't expect it to.

Unwanted semi-colons can be quite difficult to spot, as we don't always read every single symbol in each line of code, right to the very end. In the three examples below, the unwanted semi-colons have been highlighted... **;**

Here is common example of a semi-colon that has accidentally been typed in the middle of a **for** statement, which is normally regarded as a single statement by the compiler, but which takes up more than one line of code on the screen:

```
for ( number = 1; number < 1000; number++ );
    cout << number * 10 << endl;
```

The semi-colon at the end of the first line makes the program do something completely different to what the programmer wanted it to do. It would perform an empty statement **1000** times, then display only one single message on the screen. What the programmer actually wanted to do was to display **1000** different messages on the screen.

The same problem can affect a **while** loop:

```
while ( timeLeft > 0 );
{
    cout << timeLeft << " seconds left" << endl;
    sleep( 1 );
}
```

Notice that both examples were supposed to repeatedly do something meaningful. Once an infinite loop begins execution though, your program would appear to pause or "hang" while the loop iterates around and around, executing empty statements.

Whatever was supposed to be sent to the screen in the second example does not get displayed, and this is a handy clue to what is going on: the program is not managing to reach the display statement – the execution is stuck in a loop. Once you have fallen for this kind of mistake in the past, it is quite easy to spot such an error in future.

When we write code to make decisions, an unwanted semi-colon can make our program behave in ways that we didn't expect:

```
if ( temperature >= 100 );
    cout << "The water is boiling now." << endl;
```

The **if** statement has actually decided whether or not to execute the empty-statement that has been denoted by the semi-colon. No decision will be made as to whether to execute the **cout** statement. Your Pi will always display the message **"The water is boiling now."** regardless of the value of the **temperature** variable.

This kind of run-time error can be very difficult to spot when you run your program.

It is very important not to mix-up the = **assignment** operator (which should be used to **set** the value of a variable) with the == **comparison** operator (used to **compare** whether two values are the same).

This is often a problem for programmers that have previously written programs using languages such as BASIC, which uses the same single = symbol for both kinds of operation – for assignments as well as comparisons.

Consider this `if` statement, which performs a simple comparison:

```
if ( num == 60 )
    cout << "num is the same as 60";
```

The intention of the above statement is that the computer should only ever display a message on the screen when the value of the variable **num** is found to be **60**.

When trying to test whether two values are the same, accidentally using = instead of == will produce incorrect results at run-time.

For instance:

```
if ( num = 60 )
    cout << "num is the same as 60";
```

The first thing that this code does is to execute the contents of the expression (`num = 60`), which is part of the `if` statement.

Although the original intention of the programmer was to **compare** the two values, the expression **sets** the value of the variable **num** to **60**. It performs an **assignment** rather than a **comparison**.

So what? Well, consider what happens to the contents of the brackets and how they affect the `if` statement...

The assignment takes place without causing any errors - it is successfully carried out. But here's the dangerous part: the computer treats the successful execution of the assignment statement as yielding a positive, non-zero value when it attempts to evaluate it. This non-zero value has the same effect as `true` when executing the `if` statement.

It does not matter what the value of **num** is, the success of the assignment statement always gets evaluated, effectively giving a `true` value. Thus the body of the `if` statement gets triggered every single time, rather than only when the value of **num** is **60**.

Incorrectly evaluating an expression due to different operator precedences

At first-glance, an expression may look as though it should correctly calculate a particular result. The different precedences of each operator in the expression may mean that the operations are not carried out in the order originally intended by the programmer.

Here is an expression that is supposed to subtract the value **64** away from the value of the variable **keyChar**, then subtract the result from another variable called **originalChar**:

```
decryptedChar = originalChar - keyChar - 64;
```

In the above statement, both subtraction symbols have the same operator precedence – they are equally important.

The computer works from the left of the expression, moving towards the right, performing each subtraction. This means that the statement has the same effect as:

```
decryptedChar = ( originalChar - keyChar ) - 64;
```

What was actually intended though, was this:

```
decryptedChar = originalChar - ( keyChar - 64 );
```

Imagine that the value of **originalChar** is **'P'**, which has an ASCII value of **80**, and the value of **keyChar** is **'C'**, which has an ASCII value of **67**.

The original expression would produce this result:

```
80 - 67 = 13     // originalChar - keyChar
13 - 64 = -51    // result of above with 64 subtracted from it, not ASCII code
```

But by adding a pair of brackets, the expression **originalChar - (keyChar - 64)** produces:

```
67 - 64 = 3      // ( keyChar - 64 ), gives result of 3
80 - 3 = 77      // subtract result of above from decryptedChar, 77 is code for M
```

(This is indeed the result that was intended.)

The important lesson here is that you should be very careful to make sure that an expression does **exactly** what you want it to do.

To make absolutely sure that the computer performs the different parts of the expression in the intended order to produce the correct result, you should add additional brackets to control which parts to perform first.

Accidentally changing the scope of a variable by adding too many { } braces

Unnecessary { } curly braces around statements can cause the scope or lifetime of a variable to be changed accidentally. This could cause an error during compilation.

Consider these statements that use the variable **timeLeft**:

```
int timeLeft = 100;

cout << timeLeft << endl;

timeLeft--;
```

Including unnecessary { } braces around the first two lines, would change the variable declaration. It would mean that the variable **timeLeft** is local only to the block of code within the { } braces:

```
{
    int timeLeft = 100;

    cout << timeLeft << endl;

}  // timeLeft no longer exists - it was local to the { } block above

timeLeft--;  // Compiler issues an error when trying to use timeLeft
```

Any subsequent code after the braces would not be able to access the **timeLeft** variable as it no longer exists outside of the { } block.

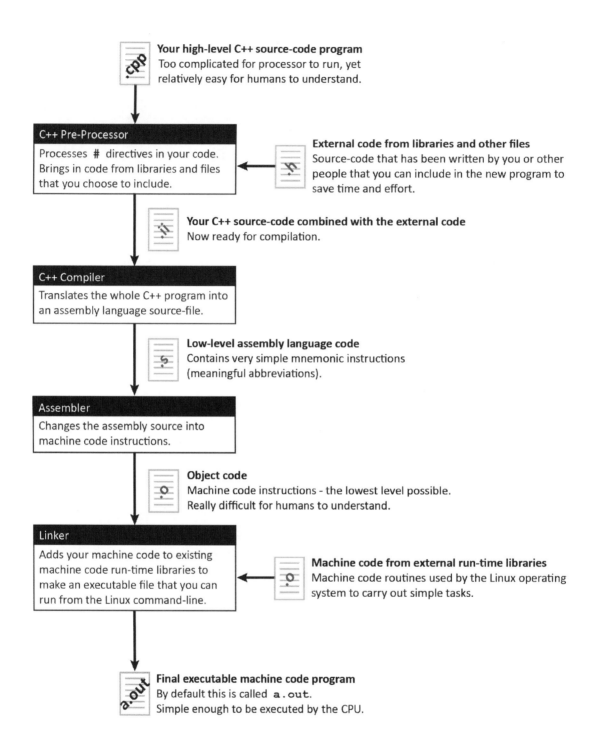

Your high-level C++ source-code program
Too complicated for processor to run, yet relatively easy for humans to understand.

C++ Pre-Processor
Processes # directives in your code. Brings in code from libraries and files that you choose to include.

External code from libraries and other files
Source-code that has been written by you or other people that you can include in the new program to save time and effort.

Your C++ source-code combined with the external code
Now ready for compilation.

C++ Compiler
Translates the whole C++ program into an assembly language source-file.

Low-level assembly language code
Contains very simple mnemonic instructions (meaningful abbreviations).

Assembler
Changes the assembly source into machine code instructions.

Object code
Machine code instructions - the lowest level possible. Really difficult for humans to understand.

Linker
Adds your machine code to existing machine code run-time libraries to make an executable file that you can run from the Linux command-line.

Machine code from external run-time libraries
Machine code routines used by the Linux operating system to carry out simple tasks.

Final executable machine code program
By default this is called `a.out`.
Simple enough to be executed by the CPU.

Useful compiler options for g++

When compiling C++ source-code from the command-line, you are able to specify one or more options to tell the compiler how to operate.

g++ -v	Displays the version information about your C++ compiler. The programs in this book were compiled with GNU g++ version 4.6.3. They should still work on any other version that you have on your Pi.
g++ *source.cpp*	Compiles a C++ source-code program, producing an executable file called "*a.out*".
g++ -o *executable source.cpp*	Compiles a C++ source-code program, producing an executable file called "*executable*", rather than calling the executable "*a.out*".
g++ -S *source.cpp*	Compiles a C++ source-code program, to produce an assembly language source-file, but then stops. No executable file will be created. (n.b. you must use *capital* **-S**)
g++ -c *source.cpp*	Compiles a C++ source-code program, to produce object-code, but then stops. Does not continue to link your object code or other files to create an executable file.
g++ -Wall *source.cpp*	Compiles a C++ source-code program, displaying all possible warnings as well as error-messages.
g++ -v *source.cpp*	Compiles in "verbose" (detailed) mode. Messages will be displayed during compilation to tell you what the compiler is doing.
g++ -fpermissive *source.cpp*	Permissive compiling mode. Some kinds of errors will be treated as non-critical, generating only warning messages at compile time.

Note that these options can be used in combination with each other when compiling from the command-line.

For example:

```
g++ -Wall -v -o my-new-executable source.cpp
```

Making it easier to run your executables at the command-line

Normally, when you ask your Pi to run an executable file, it will try to locate the executable in one of several standard Linux directories that are commonly used to contain programs. Unless you have copied your new executable file into one of these standard directories, you will need to supply a **path** to the executable file.

If you don't supply a path to the executable file, your Pi will only attempt to look in these standard directories. It will not look in any other directory that might actually contain the executable. It would then tell you that it was unable to locate your file.

For instance:

```
pi@eno ~ $ search_planets
bash: search_planets: command not found
```

This is why it is usually necessary to precede the name of the executable file with **./** when running it.
./ tells the Pi to look in the current directory for the executable file, rather than in a standard Linux directory:

```
pi@eno ~ $ ./search_planets
```

This literally means...

> *'look in the current directory for the file called "search_planets", then execute this file.'*

Removing the need to type ./ in front of the name of an executable

In your home directory there is a hidden file called "*.bashrc*" which contains various settings that are read in and used whenever you open up a new Bash terminal window. Note that "*rc*" commonly stands for "*resources*" in many Linux filenames.

It is possible to add an extra line to the `.bashrc` settings file to change where the terminal looks when trying to find an executable. Once you have done this, you will no longer need to add the **./** before the name of your executable when running it.

From your home directory, load your *.bashrc* file into a text editor, such as Nano:

```
pi@eno ~ $ cd ~
pi@eno ~ $ nano .bashrc
```

You can then add the following new line at the end of the file:

```
export PATH="/home/$USER/:$PATH"
```

PATH and **USER** are **shell variables** that are available for programs and scripts to use when they run in your Bash shell.

PATH holds a list of the paths that Linux uses when it attempts to locate an executable file.

USER holds your username, which is commonly used as the name of your starting directory within the standard Linux **/home** directory.

The new line in the file effectively takes the path of your home directory, such as **/home/pi** for the user called "*pi*", adding it to the beginning of the existing list of paths in which Linux will look for executables.

The **export** command at the start of line makes the new value of the **PATH** variable available to all programs and scripts.

Below is an example from my Pi, showing the newly added line at the end of the *.bashrc* file:

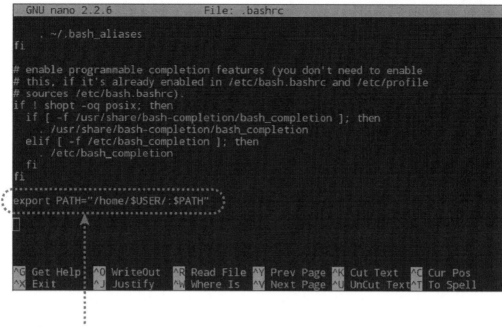

add this line at the end of the file

You can then save the changed file and exit Nano.

In order for your changes to take effect, you need to close your terminal window (if working on a graphical desktop) and open it again. The new terminal window will read in the contents of the updated *.bashrc* file, including the newly altered path.

Alternatively, you can use the **source** command to reload the *.bashrc* file:

```
pi@eno ~ $ source ~/.bashrc
```

Either method should then allow you to run an executable without the need to type **./** in front of the name of the program:

```
pi@eno ~ $ search_planets
```

This time, my program would execute without an error message.

Viewing assembly language that the compiler produces

From the command-line, type:

```
g++ -S source.cpp
```

Given a C++ program called "***source.cpp***" this will produce a file called "***source.s***". The new file will contain all of the low-level assembly source that the compiler generated after compiling your own C++ source-code.

The example below shows a program being compiled from the command-line using the −S option. Once compiled, you can use the `ls` command to confirm that the new file of assembly source has indeed been created:

```
pi@eno ~ $ g++ -S array_search_item.cpp
pi@eno ~ $ ls *.s
array_search_item.s
```

Opening this file in a text editor, such as Nano, will allow you to examine the assembly source:

```
pi@eno ~ $ nano array_search_item.s
```

You will be able to read the assembly **mnemonics ("meaningful abbreviations")** for the various operations that your program carries out.

```
  GNU nano 2.2.6              File: array_search_item.s

        str     r3, [fp, #-28]
.L6:
        ldrb    r3, [fp, #-21]
        eor     r3, r3, #1
        uxtb    r3, r3
        cmp     r3, #0
        beq     .L8
        ldr     r3, [fp, #-28]
        cmp     r3, #7
        ble     .L9
.L8:
        ldrb    r3, [fp, #-21]
        eor     r3, r3, #1
        uxtb    r3, r3
        cmp     r3, #0
        beq     .L10
        ldr     r0, .L25+32
        ldr     r1, .L25+56
        bl      _ZStlsISt11char_traitsIcEERSt13basic_ostreamIcT_ES5_PKc

^G Get Help   ^O WriteOut   ^R Read File  ^Y Prev Page  ^K Cut Text   ^C Cur Pos
^X Exit       ^J Justify    ^W Where Is   ^V Next Page  ^U UnCut Text ^T To Spell
```

Don't expect to understand much of this low-level code - it is **extremely** technical and requires a detailed knowledge of how the central processing unit in your Pi works. Just be aware that assembly-source is produced as part of the translation process that breaks down high-level C++ source-code into a machine-code executable.

Each short mnemonic corresponds to a binary "**operation-code**" and is followed by one or more items of data, or "**operands**". For instance, `cmp` stands for "***compare***", `beq` stands for "***branch if equal***", and `ldr` stands for "***load register***".

Operands that begin with "**r**", such as `r1` and `r3` are **registers** - memory locations inside the CPU of your Pi.

This assembly-source may be further translated into machine-code by the GNU Compiler Collection as part of the normal compilation process to produce a final linked machine-code executable file that you can run. Normally, you would be unaware that this process is taking place when you build your C++ programs since g++ and Geany take care of it for you.

You should easily be able to pick out some of the static data or literal text values from your original C++ source-code.

For instance, the assembly-source below contains the literal text values that will be stored in the array of planet names in my program. It also contains the error message that will be displayed on screen when a planet cannot be found:

```
 GNU nano 2.2.6              File: array_search_item.s

        .align  2
.LC7:
        .ascii  "Neptune\000"
        .align  2
.LC8:
        .ascii  "Which planet are you searching for?\000"
        .align  2
.LC9:
        .ascii  "Planet number \000"
        .align  2
.LC10:
        .ascii  " in the array is \000"
        .align  2
.LC11:
        .ascii  "No matching planet found\000"
        .text
        .align  2
        .global main
        .type   main, %function

^G Get Help   ^O WriteOut   ^R Read File  ^Y Prev Page  ^K Cut Text   ^C Cur Pos
^X Exit       ^J Justify    ^W Where Is   ^V Next Page  ^U UnCut Text ^T To Spell
```

In addition, the assembly-source also contains information about the C++ source-code file and the compiler that was used to generate it:

```
 GNU nano 2.2.6              File: array_search_item.s

        .arch armv6
        .eabi_attribute 27, 3
        .eabi_attribute 28, 1
        .fpu vfp
        .eabi_attribute 20, 1
        .eabi_attribute 21, 1
        .eabi_attribute 23, 3
        .eabi_attribute 24, 1
        .eabi_attribute 25, 1
        .eabi_attribute 26, 2
        .eabi_attribute 30, 6
        .eabi_attribute 34, 1
        .eabi_attribute 18, 4
        .file   "array_search_item.cpp"
        .section        .text._ZNSt11char_traitsIcE7compareEPKcS2_j,"axG",%prog$
        .align  2
        .weak   _ZNSt11char_traitsIcE7compareEPKcS2_j
        .type   _ZNSt11char_traitsIcE7compareEPKcS2_j, %function
_ZNSt11char_traitsIcE7compareEPKcS2_j:

^G Get Help   ^O WriteOut   ^R Read File  ^Y Prev Page  ^K Cut Text   ^C Cur Pos
^X Exit       ^J Justify    ^W Where Is   ^V Next Page  ^U UnCut Text ^T To Spell
```

From the above, you can see the name of the C++ source-file was "*array_search_item.cpp*". You can also see that assembly-source produced is for the ARM processor used in a Raspberry Pi - the **armv6** architecture.

It would not be possible to assemble this code into a machine-code executable that would run on a Windows PC or an Apple Macintosh that uses some other kind of CPU. Firstly, the mnemonics and their corresponding op-codes are different for each kind of CPU. Secondly, each operating system has its own library of low-level routines that the linker needs when creating a final executable. The run-time libraries for the Pi are very different to those used by Windows or MacOS.

In order to run the same program on a different kind of computer, it is necessary to recompile your C++ source-code files using the compiler and run-time libraries for that particular computer. This is called "**source-code portability**". The source-code may be transferred and used on more than one kind of computer, as long as you have a specific compiler that can generate and link object files for a particular processor and operating system to make a new machine-code executable.

Viewing the machine code instructions of your executable

Once an executable has been created, it is possible to view the contents of the file using a **"hex-dump"** tool.

From the command-line, you can run the **xxd** hex-dump utility, giving it the name of the executable that you want to view:

```
xxd executable
```

Below is an example of a program being compiled at the command-line to create an executable called **"search_planets"**:

```
pi@eno ~ $ g++ -o search_planets array_search_item.cpp
pi@eno ~ $ ls -l search_planets
-rwxr-xr-x 1 pi pi 10540 Feb 19 21:41 search_planets
```

Once created, the **xxd** utility is then used to display the contents of the executable:

```
pi@eno ~ $ xxd search_planets
```

By default, **xxd** will display the contents of each memory location using hexadecimal, since this is a compact way to display as much of the program as is practical on the screen.

```
0000ea0: 0030 a0e1 0500 a0e1 0410 a0e1 0320 a0e1  .0...........
0000eb0: d7ff ffeb 0030 a0e1 0000 53e3 0100 001a  .....0....S.....
0000ec0: 0130 a0e3 0000 00ea 0030 a0e3 0300 a0e1  .0.......0......
0000ed0: 0cd0 4be2 3088 bde8 f843 2de9 0070 a0e1  ..K.0....C-..p..
0000ee0: 4c60 9fe5 4c50 9fe5 0660 8fe0 0550 8fe0  L`..LP...`...P..
0000ef0: 0660 65e0 0180 a0e1 0290 a0e1 59fe ffeb  .`e.........Y...
0000f00: 4661 b0e1 f883 bd08 0450 45e2 0040 a0e3  Fa.......PE..@..
0000f10: 0140 84e2 0430 b5e5 0700 a0e1 0810 a0e1  .@...0..........
0000f20: 0920 a0e1 33ff 2fe1 0600 54e1 f7ff ff1a  . ..3./...T.....
0000f30: f883 bde8 7c01 0100 7001 0100 1eff 2fe1  ....|...p...../.
0000f40: 0840 2de9 0880 bde8 0100 0200 4d65 7263  .@-.........Merc
0000f50: 7572 7900 5665 6e75 7300 0000 4561 7274  ury.Venus...Eart
0000f60: 6800 0000 4d61 7273 0000 0000 4a75 7069  h...Mars....Jupi
0000f70: 7465 7200 5361 7475 726e 0000 5572 616e  ter.Saturn..Uran
0000f80: 7573 0000 4e65 7074 756e 6500 5768 6963  us..Neptune.Whic
0000f90: 6820 706c 616e 6574 2061 7265 2079 6f75  h planet are you
0000fa0: 2073 6561 7263 6869 6e67 2066 6f72 3f00   searching for?.
0000fb0: 506c 616e 6574 206e 756d 6265 7220 0000  Planet number ..
0000fc0: 2069 6e20 7468 6520 6172 7261 7920 6973   in the array is
0000fd0: 2000 0000 4e6f 206d 6174 6368 696e 6720   ...No matching
0000fe0: 706c 616e 6574 2066 6f75 6e64 0000 0000  planet found....
0000ff0: 0000 0000 78f9 ff7f 8443 9b01 b0b0 b087  ....x....C......
0001000: ffff 0127 2804 c804 0048 b801 8805 008c  ...'(....H......
0001010: 0280 02f8 0400 9804 0488 0500 b804 0400  ................
```

↑   ↑   ↑

hexadecimal address of   *contents of each memory location*   *contents of each memory location*
first memory location   *shown on as two hexadecimal digits* *shown as ASCII characters*
shown on each row   *e.g. $3f_{16} = (3 \times 16) + 15 = 63_{10}$* *e.g. ? (which has ASCII code 63)*

Each row displays the contents of sixteen different 8-bit memory locations. The very first item on each row is the hexadecimal memory address of the first location shown on that row. This helps you work out the memory address for an individual item if you need to. The item circled in the screenshot above is the fifteenth location in the row. To find the address of this location, add fourteen on to the address shown at the start of the row (the address of the first item **0x0000fa0**) which gives **0x0000fae**.

The contents of each memory location are shown using a pair of hexadecimal digits. Notice that **xxd** leaves a gap after every four hexadecimal digits to make it a little easier to read what is on the screen. This means that each group of four digits represents the contents of two different memory locations.

You may instead choose to display the contents of each memory location using binary, which is how each value is actually stored in the electronic circuitry of your Pi. To do this, you can add the **-b** option when running **xxd**:

```
pi@eno ~ $ xxd -b search_planets
```

By default, only eight different locations are displayed on each row. More than this would require a very wide display! Although the memory addresses on the left-hand side of the display are shown as hexadecimal to save space, the contents of each 8-bit memory location are now shown as a pattern of eight binary-digits, followed by a gap:

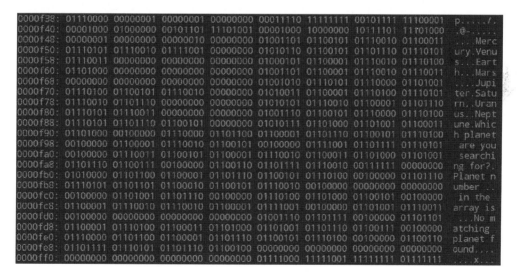

It is very difficult to interpret or understand what this binary means or what the program does, hence the column of ASCII characters becomes very useful. In the screenshot above, you may be able to pick out some of the information that the executable contains, such as the names of the Linux libraries that it uses.

Further down the display, you may also be able to pick out some of the static-data by looking at the equivalent ASCII characters on the right-hand side:

The ASCII column shows the names of the planets and other literal text that the program uses. As we saw with the assembly-source in the previous section, this text is stored as static data within the executable.

Command	Description
`clear`	Clears the screen or terminal window. You may find this useful if your screen becomes full of messages from programs or commands that you have executed.
`pwd`	Print Working Directory. Shows which directory you are currently working in.
`cd`	Change Directory. Changes the current working directory to your usual/default working directory (the directory that you normally start at when you first log-in to the computer).
`cd ..`	Changes directory, relative to whatever working directory that you are currently in, by moving up one level in the filesystem to the parent directory.
`cd` /home/pi/source	Changes directory, starting from the root / directory, following the exact or absolute path, regardless of the working directory that you are currently in.
`ls`	Displays a list of the files that are stored in the current directory.
`ls -l`	Displays a list of the files that are stored in the current directory, along with details of what can be done to each file, which user made it, how much storage space it takes up and when it was created.
`mkdir` mycode	Makes a new directory called "**mycode**".
`cat` myfile.cpp	Displays the contents of the file called "**myfile.cpp**".
`cat` myfile.cpp | `more`	Displays the contents of "**myfile.cpp**", pausing each time that the screen is completely full.
`nano` filetoedit.cpp	Opens the Nano text editor. If the file called "**filetoedit.cpp**" exists the contents will be displayed, ready for you to make changes. If no such file exists, Nano will create a new blank text document with this filename.
`sudo apt-get install` packagename	Downloads and installs a new program on your machine from a package. Requires super-user privileges, hence it is usually preceded by "**sudo**", which means "super-user do command".
`g++` source.cpp	Compiles a C++ source-code program, to produce an executable file called "**a.out**".
`mv` oldfilename newfilename	Renames (moves) the file called "**oldfilename**" to a new file with the name "**newfilename**".
`rm` filetodelete	Removes a file that you no longer want. Warning! There is no "recycle bin" so once removed, you cannot usually recover the file again if you deleted it by mistake.
`xxd` myexecutable	Displays the machine code instructions and data of an executable file as hexadecimal, using the **xxd** (hex-dump) tool.
`xxd -b -c 1` myexecutable	Displays the machine code instructions and data of an executable file as a single column of binary, using the **xxd** (hex-dump) tool.

Glossary of useful terms

AND	Logical operator that only produces a `true` result if all parts of an expression are all `true`.
argument	A value that is given to a function or program as input.
arithmetic operator	A symbol used in arithmetic, such as `+` `-` `/` `*` `%`
array	A named collection of values, all of which have the same data-type. Each item in the array can be accessed using one or more index numbers.
ASCII	American Standard Code for Information Interchange.
assembler	Program that converts assembly language into machine code instructions.
bit	A single binary digit. A bit can either hold the value `0` or `1`.
byte	A group of eight binary-digits (bits).
bool	Simple C++ data-type that represents a `true` or `false` Boolean value.
Boolean operator	A logical operator such as AND, OR, NOT, XOR etc. Often used by programs to make a decision or as part of an expression.
case statement	(see `switch` statement)
channel	A pathway along which data may flow, either in or out of the computer's memory.
char	Simple C++ data-type that represents a single character.
character	A single symbol that can be represented by the computer.
command-line	Computer interface that allows you to type a command that will be executed by the computer.
comment	A line of text that will be ignored by the compiler in a source-code file and that is useful only for a human to read. It will not be translated into machine code or executed by the computer.
compiler	A program that translates high-level source-code files into low-level object-code in one complete operation. The finished object code can usually be linked and executed.
condition	A logical or relational expression that produces the value `true` if it is satisfied, or the value `false` if it is not satisfied.
constant	A named value that cannot ever change while the program is running.
data-type	The type or "kind" of data that describes a particular value. A value might be an integer, a real value, a character, a string or a Boolean value. Alternatively, you can create your own data-types.
debug	To find and correct bugs or errors in a program.
declaration	A statement in a program that tells the compiler that a constant, variable, function, structure or class exists, prior to it being ready to use in your code.
directive	An instruction to the C++ pre-processor to do something. Not actually a C++ statement.
error message	A message displayed during compilation to alert you to a critical problem with your source-code.
escape-sequence	A special sequence of characters that directs a screen or other device to behave differently.
equivalence operator	Tests whether two values or expressions can be evaluated to the same value.
exception	A particular kind of event that occurs or a condition that is detected which requires the computer to respond in some way to deal with what has happened.
execute	Carry out one or more instructions.
executable	A file whose contents can be executed.
expression	A sequence of symbols that can be evaluated to give a result e.g. `score + 100`
file	A named collection of data that is stored on a device or storage medium.
float	Simple C++ data-type that represents a floating-point real number.
floating-point number	A number that can contain a decimal point, held in two parts: an exponent and a mantissa.
function	A named sub-routine or "chunk" of code that performs some processing, often taking one or more values as input and returning a value as output.
function call	To activate a function using its name.
GNU	Open-Source software produced by the Free Software Foundation.
header file	A separate file that contains identifiers or declarations for functions and classes. A header file can be used by a source-code file or another different header-file.
high-level	Code that is easier for a human to understand, but which must be translated into a set of simpler instructions before it can be executed by the computer.
identifier	A name that is given to a constant value, variable or function.
include	A directive that instructs the compiler to bring in and make use of some existing code.
index	A number that identifies a particular item in a data-structure, such as a particular character in a string or a particular item in an array.
input	To feed in data to be processed by a function or by a program.
int	Simple C++ data-type that represents integers (whole numbers).

integer	A whole number.
iteration	Repeatedly execute one or more statements again and again.
keyboard buffer	A small, temporary storage area for characters that are typed on the keyboard. Characters are held in the buffer until the computer is ready to receive and process them.
library	A set of ready-made sub-routines or functions that are stored in a file, for use in other programs.
linker	Software that combines existing low-level code routines with compiled object-code to make an executable program.
logical error	A problem in a program that can be compiled and executed, but which contains flawed decisions or instructions that lead to incorrect results or outcomes.
logical operator	A symbol that represents a logical operation, such as `&&` `||` `!` `and` `or` `not`
loop	Repeatedly execute one or more program statements again and again.
low-level	Program instructions that are simple enough for a computer to execute directly, or requiring very little further translation. Often difficult for humans to understand.
machine-code	Low-level numeric instructions that the computer can carry out directly, without needing to translate or simplify them further before execution. Each instruction activates hardware to perform a very simple task.
member	A data item or a function that is part of (or "belongs to") a particular object, class or structure.
modulus %	An operator that gives the remainder after one number is divided by another number.
namespace	A collection of identifiers that can be used in one or more programs.
NOT	A logical/Boolean operator that always gives an output value that is the opposite of its input value.
null pointer	A pointer whose value has not been set to any meaningful memory location. The value `NULL` indicates that the program should not attempt to follow the pointer.
object	An instance of a class. An object in a program often represents something that exists in the real world.
object-code	Code that is generated by a translator after examining a high-level program.
operand	A value that an operation will make use of.
operating system	Software that controls the most basic operations of the computer system.
operation	A task that the computer carries out e.g. adding up.
operator	A symbol that denotes an operation to be carried out by the computer, e.g. `+`
OR	Logical operator that produces a `true` result if one or more parts of an expression are `true`.
output	The result(s) of a function or process that has been carried out.
overflow	An error that arises when trying to store a value that is too large for a particular data-type, either by directly setting the value or adding another value on to it.
parameter	A value that is passed into a function as input. The function can make use of the parameter value during execution.
pointer	A data-type that indicates where in the computer's memory another data item is stored. A pointer holds the address of a data-item so that the item can be found and accessed.
post-increment	Operator that increases the value of a variable immediately after making use of its value.
pre-increment	Operator that increases the value of a variable before making use of its value.
procedure	A sequence of instructions that is given a name and which performs a specific task in a program. Procedures are similar to functions, although a procedure does not return a value or result. In C++, a procedure is effectively a `void` function.
process	A program that is being executed by the computer.
program	A sequence of instructions that can be executed by the computer.
prompt	Visual indication, usually on the screen, that tells you that the computer is ready for you to enter a command, some data or some other response.
recursion	A function that calls itself.
reference	An address that indicates where in memory a particular value is stored.
reserved word	A special word that is already used by a programming language and that you are not allowed to use as an identifier name in your own code, such as for a variable or constant.
return value	A value that is produced as the result of executing a function. The value is passed back or "returned" to the code that called the function.
run	To "run-through" or execute a program.
run-time error	Error that occurs whilst a program is being executed.
segmentation fault	An error that occurs when a program erroneously attempts to access a value in memory that it does not have permission to use.
short	Simple C++ data-type that represents an integer in the range `-32768` to `32767`.

source-code	Code written in a language that can be translated into lower-level code.
sub-routine	A named sequence of program statements or "chunk" of code that perform a particular task.
stack	A special area in memory that stores variables and addresses used by the computer during the execution of a program.
statement	An instruction that has been written in a programming language that tells the computer to do something.
stream	A path that data follows, such as into the computer from a keyboard, out from the computer to a display, or out to a file.
string	C++ data-type that represents a sequence of character symbols.
structure	A special data-type that you can define and make use of in your program. A structure often consists of one or more simple items of data.
syntax-error	An error caused by a statement in a program that does not correctly obey the rules of a particular programming language.
text	Character data, typically containing letters of the alphabet, numeric digits or other symbols.
text editor	A program that allows you to read and edit a file of text.
token	A string of characters that has some sort of meaning - usually a word or symbol that is contained within a larger body of text, such as within a program statement or a word in a sentence.
valid	Acceptable. Conforms to a set of rules.
value	Either a numeric quantity, symbol or sequence of symbols.
variable	A named item of data whose value can be changed during the execution of a program.
void function	A function that does not return any value once it has completed execution.
warning	A message that is displayed during compilation to draw your attention to a potential problem that may affect your program when it executes.

How to download the software that you need

If you don't have a Raspberry Pi, you can still create the programs using a PC with the Linux operating system installed, or use an Apple Macintosh computer with the MacOS operating system.

Debian and Ubuntu users

Before you install any additional software, you might want to **update** the list of packages that are available to you, then **upgrade** any software that you have installed on your system:

```
sudo apt-get update
sudo apt-get upgrade
```

Whether on a Pi or a PC, Linux users usually have the Nano text editor installed. If for some reason you don't have it on your system then you can download it yourself:

```
sudo apt-get install nano
```

Most PC Ubuntu Linux users will still need to install the **GNU C++ compiler**, which is part of GCC (the GNU Compiler Collection). Note that GCC is already installed as part of Debian and Raspbian on the Pi.

If you want to install **GCC**, the **GNU Compiler Collection**, which includes **g++**:

```
sudo apt-get install build-essential
```

One of the most helpful extra tools that you can install is "**Geany**". Geany is a text editor with a graphical-user interface. It lets you cut, copy and paste code, helps you navigate around your program and works alongside other tools to make it easier for you to create and test C++ programs.

Whilst Geany is included when you install Raspbian (the latest operating system for the Raspberry Pi), it was not originally included with earlier versions of the Debian operating system on the Pi.

To download and install **Geany** text editor:

```
sudo apt-get install geany
```

Apple MacOS X users

Apple MacOS X is based-on an underlying version of the UNIX® operating system called "Darwin". Although Darwin is not actually a version of Linux, you will find that GCC can be installed on a Macintosh computer and that the programs work successfully.

Originally, MacOS X included the GCC tools as part of their Xcode developer software. If your Macintosh computer came with a the Xcode DVD or if you downloaded Xcode from Apple, this would include the **g++** compiler.

More recently, due to licensing changes, Xcode now uses the **LLVM** compiler instead of GCC, although GCC is still freely available for you to download separately to use on your Macintosh computer.

You should find that the Nano text editor is already installed and can be activated from a Terminal window.

Useful web-links

Learn to Program Using C++ on the Raspberry Pi blog

https://program-using-gnu-cpp.blogspot.co.uk

The GNU project

https://www.gnu.org

The GNU Compiler Collection

http://gcc.gnu.org

Stack Overflow

http://www.stackoverflow.com

ISO C++

https://isocpp.org

The Raspberry Pi Foundation

https://www.raspberrypi.org

Raspbian Linux home

https://www.raspbian.org

Debian Linux home

https://www.debian.org

Ways to obtain or download Debian can be found at **https://www.debian.org/distrib/**

Ubuntu Linux home

http://www.ubuntu.com

Specific information about running Ubuntu on desktop computers can be found at **http://www.ubuntu.com/desktop**

Ubuntu itself can be downloaded from **http://www.ubuntu.com/download**

The Free Software Foundation home

The Free Software Foundation provides funding and the critical infrastructure for the GNU Linux project. They also hold the copyright to many GNU products, including the GNU Compiler Collection.
http://www.fsf.org

These web addresses are correct at the time of writing, August 2017, and may be subject to change.

Answers to exercises

Chapter 1: Getting things up and running

1. "High-level" code is easier for humans to understand and write. It cannot be executed directly by the computer. "Low-level" code is less easy for humans to understand. The computer can only execute low-level machine-code.
2. Compilation breaks source-code down into simpler, low-level code.
   High-level C++ code is not simple enough for a computer's processor to execute directly.
3. The filename of a C++ program should always end with "*.cpp*".
4. By default, g++ will create an executable called "*a.out*".
5. An error is an explanatory message about why your C++ code would not compile successfully to create an executable. A warning is a message that suggests why your code may not execute as you intend it to, even though the code will successfully compile and produce an executable.
6. The convention is for a C++ program to return a whole number value between **0** and **255**.
   This indicates whether or not any errors or special conditions occurred during the execution of the program.
   A value of **0** usually indicates that no errors were encountered during execution.

Chapter 2: Writing some simple code

1. **99 % 33** gives the result **0** (remainder).
2. Both statements need to end with a **;** semi-colon symbol to mark their end.
3. **string myName = "CAPTAIN SENSIBLE";**
4. The operands are **heightA**, **heightB**, **heightC** and **3**. The operators are **+ + ( ) /**.
5. **main** should be preceded by **int** to show that it returns an integer value.
   main should also be followed by **()** to indicate that it does not take any inputs.
   return should begin with a lower-case "**r**".

Chapter 3: Data-types and values

1. After "wrapping around" from negative to positive, **myVal** would hold the positive value **32765**.
2. **1stPersonToGuessCorrectly** begins with a numeric-digit.
   D.O.B. contains full-stops.
   weight Of Kyak contains spaces inbetween each word that makes up the name.
   phoneNumber@Work contains @ asquith symbol.
3. **bool onHoliday = true;**
4. The compilation will fail. You will see the message:
   error: increment of read-only variable 'NEVER_CHANGING_INT'.
5. Gender of a person: **char**. Number of people in a room: **int** (ideally **unsigned int** as it can only be zero or positive whole number). Telephone number: **string** (could contain separators such as space, hyphen or brackets). Weight of a person in kilograms: **float**.

Chapter 4: Keyboard input and screen output

1. Enter a whole number and display using different widths.

```
#include <iostream>
#include <iomanip>

using namespace std;

int main()
{
    int num;
    cin >> num;

    cout << setw( 1 ) << num << endl;
    cout << setw( 5 ) << num << endl;
    cout << setw( 10 ) << num << endl;

    return 0;
}
```

2. Enter a sentence and display it three times using different colours.

```cpp
#include <iostream>

using namespace std;

int main()
{
    cout << "Please type in a sentence: " << endl;
    string sentence;
    getline( cin, sentence );

    cout << "\e[31m" << sentence << endl;
    cout << "\e[32m" << sentence << endl;
    cout << "\e[34m" << sentence << endl;
    cout << "\e[0m";

    return 0;
}
```

3. Enter a whole number and use it to pause execution for a certain number of seconds.

```cpp
#include <iostream>
#include <unistd.h>

using namespace std;

int main()
{
    cout << "Please type in a whole number:" << endl;
    int num;
    cin >> num;

    sleep( num );

    return 0;
}
```

4. Enter three whole numbers and display their sum total.

```cpp
#include <iostream>

using namespace std;

int main()
{
    cout << "Please type in three numbers:" << endl;
    int num1, num2, num3;
    cin >> num1;
    cin >> num2;
    cin >> num3;

    cout << "Total is " << num1 + num2 + num3 << endl;

    return 0;
}
```

1. Choose six random numbers between 1 and 60.

```cpp
#include <iostream>
#include <cstdlib>
#include <ctime>

using namespace std;

int main()
{
    srandom( time( 0 ) );

    cout << 1 + random() % 60 << "\t";
    cout << 1 + random() % 60 << "\t";
    cout << 1 + random() % 60 << "\t";
    cout << 1 + random() % 60 << "\t";
    cout << 1 + random() % 60 << "\t";
    cout << 1 + random() % 60 << endl;

    return 0;
}
```

2. Type in two numbers, then raise the first to the power of the second.

```cpp
#include <iostream>
#include <cmath>

using namespace std;

int main()
{
    int num, power;
    cout << "Type in a whole number: " << endl;
    cin >> num;
    cout << "Type in power: " << endl;
    cin >> power;

    cout << num << " to the power " << power << " is " << pow( num, power );

    return 0;
}
```

3. Raising 10 to the power of a decreasing variable.

```cpp
#include <iostream>
#include <cmath>

using namespace std;

int main()
{
    int power = 0;

    cout << pow( 10, --power ) << endl;
    cout << pow( 10, --power ) << endl;
    cout << pow( 10, --power ) << endl;
    cout << pow( 10, --power ) << endl;

    return 0;
}
```

```cpp
#include <iostream>
#include <cstdlib>
#include <ctime>

using namespace std;

int main()
{
    srandom( time( 0 ) );

    int num1 = random();
    int num2 = random();

    cout << num1 << " and " << num2 << endl;
    cout << "Largest is " << max( num1, num2 ) << endl;

    return 0;
}
```

Chapter 6: Making decisions

1. Type in number of sides and display name of a shape.

```cpp
#include <iostream>

using namespace std;

int main()
{
    cout << "How many sides?" << endl;
    int num;
    cin >> num;

    cout << "You typed " << num;
    cout << " - the shape is a ";
    switch ( num )
    {
        case 3: cout << "triangle"; break;
        case 4: cout << "quadrilateral"; break;
        case 5: cout << "pentagon"; break;
        case 6: cout << "hexagon"; break;
        case 7: cout << "heptagon"; break;
        case 8: cout << "octagon"; break;
        default: cout << "unidentified"; break;
    }
    cout << endl;

    return 0;
}
```

2. Effect of a semi-colon in the middle of an `if` statement.

```cpp
int daysHoliday = 0;

if ( daysHoliday > 0 );
    cout << "You still have some holiday left";
```

The `;` semi-colon marks the end of the `if` decision, halfway through the statement. This means that if it is true that **daysHoliday > 0** then nothing will be done. Whatever the result of the expression **(daysHoliday > 0)**, the next statement **cout << "You still have some holiday left";** will always be executed, even when **daysHoliday** has the value **0** or less.

Current value of **score** is **5300** and the value of **time** is **20** before executing the statement.

```
score = ( time > 10 ) ? score + time * 100 : score + 500;
```

time has the value **20**

It is **true** that **(20 > 10)**

This means the conditional statement will evaluate **score + time * 100**
(It will not evaluate the alternative **score + 500**)

The result will be **5300 + 20 * 100 = 7300**

```cpp
#include <iostream>

using namespace std;

int main()
{
    cout << "Type in some text containing only 0s, 1s or spaces:" << endl;
    string text;
    getline( cin, text );

    int badCharPos = text.find_first_not_of( "01 " );

    if ( badCharPos > -1 )
        cout << "Contains characters that are not valid";

    return 0;
}
```

Chapter 7: Repetition using loops

```cpp
#include <iostream>

using namespace std;

int main()
{
    for ( char letter = 'Z';  letter >= 'A';  letter-- )
        cout << letter;

    cout << endl;

    return 0;
}
```

2. Repeatedly prompt for a word that contains exactly 8 characters.

```cpp
#include <iostream>

using namespace std;

int main()
{
    string word;

    do
    {
        cout << "Type in a word that contains exactly 8 characters:" << endl;
        cin >> word;
    } while ( word.length() != 8 );

    return 0;
}
```

3. Display sequence of terms starting at 50, increasing by 25, ending at 150.

```cpp
#include <iostream>

using namespace std;

int main()
{
    int term = 50;
    while ( term <= 150 )
    {
        cout << term << "\t";
        term += 25;
    }
    cout << endl;

    return 0;
}
```

4. Count the number of upper-case letters that are typed in.

```cpp
#include <iostream>

using namespace std;

int main()
{
    char typed;
    int upperLetters = 0;
    while ( true )
    {
        cout << "Type a character:" << endl;
        cin >> typed;
        if ( typed >= 'A'  and  typed <= 'Z' )
            upperLetters++;
        cout << "Upper-case letters so far: " << upperLetters << endl;
    }

    return 0;
}
```

```
while ( elapsedTime <= 10 )
{
    distance = distance + speed;

    cout << "Been falling for ";
    cout << GREEN << elapsedTime << NORMAL << " sec(s) ";

    cout << "Speed is " << GREEN << speed << NORMAL << " m/s ";

    cout << " Dist. fallen " << GREEN << distance << NORMAL << " m";

    cout << endl;

    speed = speed + ACCEL;

    if ( speed > 54 )
        speed = 54;

    elapsedTime++;

}
```

Chapter 8: Characters and text strings

1. Repeatedly type a character, appending to a `string` of all the characters that have been typed in so far.

```
#include <iostream>

using namespace std;

int main()
{
    char typed;
    string charsSoFar = "";
    while ( true )
    {
        cout << "Type in a character:" << endl;
        cin >> typed;
        charsSoFar += typed;
        cout << "Characters typed so far: " << charsSoFar << endl;
    }

    return 0;
}
```

```cpp
#include <iostream>
#include <cstdlib>
#include <ctime>

using namespace std;

int main()
{
    string word;
    cin >> word;

    int pos1, pos2, wordLen;
    char temp;

    wordLen = word.length();
    srandom( time( 0 ) );

    for ( int swaps = 0;  swaps < 10;  swaps++ )
    {
        pos1 = random() % wordLen;
        pos2 = random() % wordLen;

        temp = word.at( pos1 );
        word.at( pos1 ) = word.at( pos2 );
        word.at( pos2 ) = temp;

        cout << word << endl;
    }

    return 0;
}
```

```cpp
#include <iostream>

using namespace std;

int main()
{
    string text;
    getline( cin, text );

    unsigned int textLen = text.length();
    string newText = "";

    for ( unsigned int pos = 0;  pos < textLen;  pos++ )
    {
        switch ( text.at( pos ) )
        {
            case '1':  newText += "one";  break;
            case '2':  newText += "two";  break;
            case '3':  newText += "three";  break;
            case '4':  newText += "four";  break;
            case '5':  newText += "five";  break;  // etc. up until 9
            default:  newText += text.at( pos );  break;
        }
    }

    cout << newText << endl;

    return 0;
}
```

4. Change a word to upper-case and insert a symbol between each pair of letters.

```cpp
#include <iostream>

using namespace std;

int main()
{
    string text;
    cin >> text;

    unsigned int textLen = text.length();
    string newText = "";

    for ( unsigned int pos = 0;  pos < textLen;  pos++ )
    {
        newText += toupper( text.at( pos ) );
        if ( pos < textLen-1 )
            newText += "-";
    }

    cout << newText << endl;

    return 0;
}
```

Chapter 9: Arrays of data

1. Validating an array index.

```cpp
#include <iostream>

using namespace std;

int main()
{
    string cityName[3];

    cityName[0] = "London";
    cityName[1] = "Paris";
    cityName[2] = "New York";

    int choice;

    while ( true )
    {
        cout << "Type a number 0, 1 or 2:" << endl;
        cin >> choice;

        if ( choice < 0  or  choice > 2 )
            cout << "That number is not a valid array index" << endl;
        else
            cout << cityName[choice] << endl;
    }

    return 0;
}
```

2. Create a 10 x 10 grid of random digits and display it on screen.

```cpp
#include <iostream>
#include <cstdlib>
#include <ctime>

using namespace std;

int main()
{
    srandom( time( 0 ) );

    int grid[10][10];
    int row, col;

    for ( row = 0;   row < 10;   row++ )
        for ( col = 0;   col < 10;   col++ )
            grid[row][col] = random() % 10;

    for ( row = 0;   row < 10;   row++ )
    {
        for ( col = 0;   col < 10;   col++ )
            cout << grid[row][col] << '\t';

        cout << endl;
    }

    return 0;
}
```

3. Calculate and store the first 20 terms of the Fibonacci sequence in an array.

```cpp
#include <iostream>

using namespace std;

int main()
{
    int fibonacci[20];

    fibonacci[0] = 1;
    fibonacci[1] = 1;

    int term;
    for ( term = 2;   term < 20;   term++ )
        fibonacci[term] = fibonacci[term-1] + fibonacci[term-2];

    for ( term = 0;   term < 20;   term++ )
        cout << fibonacci[term] << endl;

    return 0;
}
```

```cpp
#include <iostream>

using namespace std;

int main()
{
    bool divisibleByFive[100];

    for ( int index = 0;  index < 100;  index++ )
        divisibleByFive[index] = ( index % 5 == 0 );

    int totalTrue = 0;
    int totalFalse = 0;

    for ( int index = 0;  index < 100;  index++ )
        if ( divisibleByFive[index] )
            totalTrue++;
        else
            totalFalse++;

    cout << "Total numbers divisible by 5: "<< totalTrue << endl;
    cout << "Total numbers not divisible by 5: "<< totalFalse << endl;

    return 0;
}
```

Chapter 10: Functions

1. Create a function called `displayColourLine` that displays a `string` value in a chosen colour.

```cpp
#include <iostream>

using namespace std;

void displayColourLine( string textToDisplay, char colour )
{
    switch ( colour )
    {
        case 'r': cout << "\e[31m"; break;
        case 'g': cout << "\e[32m"; break;
        case 'b': cout << "\e[34m"; break;
    }
    cout << textToDisplay << endl;
}

// --------------------

int main()
{
    displayColourLine( "Fire engine", 'r' );
    displayColourLine( "Rain forest", 'g' );

    return 0;
}
```

2. Write a function called `trimString` that removes spaces from the beginning and end of a `string` value.

```cpp
string trimString( string originalString )
{
    int lengthOriginal = originalString.length();
    string trimmedString;

    int leftPos = 0;
    while ( leftPos < lengthOriginal and originalString.at( leftPos ) == ' ' )
        leftPos++;

    if ( leftPos < lengthOriginal )
    {
        int rightPos = lengthOriginal - 1;
        while ( rightPos >= 0  and  originalString.at( rightPos ) == ' ' )
            rightPos--;

        trimmedString = originalString.substr( leftPos, 1 + rightPos-leftPos );
    }
    else
        trimmedString = "";

    return trimmedString;
}
```

3. Create a function that prompts for an integer and checks whether the user has typed in a valid whole number.

```cpp
#include <iostream>
#include <climits>

using namespace std;

int promptForInteger( string promptMessage )
{
    int typedIn;

    bool validIntSupplied = false;
    while ( not validIntSupplied )
    {
        cout << promptMessage << endl;
        cin >> typedIn;
        if ( cin.good() )
        {
            cout << "Thank you." << endl;
            validIntSupplied = true;
        }
        else
        {
            cout << "You did not type in a valid integer." << endl;
            cin.clear();
            cin.ignore( INT_MAX, '\n' );
        }
    }
    return typedIn;
}

// -------------------

int main()
{
    promptForInteger( "Please type in a whole number." );
    promptForInteger( "Now type in another." );

    return 0;
}
```

```
bool mirrorStrings( string firstString, string secondString )
{
    int lengthFirstString = firstString.length();
    int lengthSecondString = secondString.length();

    if ( lengthFirstString != lengthSecondString )
        return false;
    else
    {
        bool mirrorImage = true;
        int leftPos = 0;
        int lastPos = lengthSecondString - 1;
        while ( leftPos < lengthFirstString )
            if ( firstString.at( leftPos ) == secondString.at( lastPos - leftPos ) )
                leftPos++;
            else
            {
                mirrorImage = false;
                break;
            }

        return mirrorImage;
    }
}
```

Chapter 11: Files of data

1. Read in a file and display a summary of the number of blank and non-blank lines that it contains.

```
#include <iostream>
#include <fstream>

using namespace std;

int main()
{
    cout << "Please type in the filename:" << endl;
    string fileName;
    cin >> fileName;

    ifstream myFile;
    myFile.open( fileName.c_str() );

    if ( myFile.is_open() )
    {
        string lineOfText;
        int numBlankLines = 0;
        int numNonBlank = 0;
        while ( myFile.good() )
        {
            getline( myFile, lineOfText );
            if ( lineOfText.length() == 0 )
                numBlankLines++;
            else
                numNonBlank++;
        }
        myFile.close();

        cout << "Lines in file: " << numBlankLines + numNonBlank << endl;
        cout << "Blank lines: " << numBlankLines << endl;
        cout << "Lines that contain text: " << endl << numNonBlank  << endl;
    }
    else
```

```
        cout << "File not found!" << endl;

    return 0;
}
```

```
#include <iostream>
#include <fstream>

using namespace std;

int main()
{
    cout << "Please type in the filename:" << endl;
    string fileName;
    cin >> fileName;

    ifstream myFile;
    myFile.open( fileName.c_str() );

    if ( myFile.is_open() )
    {
        char charFromFile;
        int alphabetCount[26];
        int alphabetIndex;
        for ( alphabetIndex = 0;  alphabetIndex < 26;  alphabetIndex++ )
            alphabetCount[alphabetIndex] = 0;

        while ( myFile.good() )
        {
            myFile.get( charFromFile );
            if ( isalpha( charFromFile ))
            {
                charFromFile = toupper( charFromFile );
                alphabetCount[charFromFile-65]++;
            }
        }
        myFile.close();

        for ( alphabetIndex = 0;  alphabetIndex < 26;  alphabetIndex++ )
        {
            cout << "Letter " << static_cast <char> ( 'A' + alphabetIndex );
            cout << " appears " << alphabetCount[alphabetIndex] << endl;
        }
    }
    else
        cout << "File not found!" << endl;

    return 0;
}
```

3. Save copies of data to five different files that use a sequence of filenames.

```cpp
#include <iostream>
#include <fstream>

using namespace std;

int main()
{
    string startOfFileName = "data";
    ofstream myNewFile;

    for ( char digit = '1';  digit <= '5';  digit++ )
    {
        myNewFile.open( ( startOfFileName + digit ).c_str() );

        for ( int num = 1;  num <= 10;  num++ )
            myNewFile << ( "blah blah moo data " );

        myNewFile << endl;
        myNewFile.close();
    }

    return 0;
}
```

4. Read in a file and highlight all space and tab characters using different colours.

```cpp
#include <iostream>
#include <fstream>

using namespace std;

int main()
{
    cout << "Please type in the filename:" << endl;
    string fileName;
    cin >> fileName;

    ifstream myFile;
    myFile.open( fileName.c_str() );

    if ( myFile.is_open() )
    {
        char charFromFile;

        while ( myFile.good() )
        {
            myFile.get( charFromFile );
            switch ( charFromFile )
            {
                case 32:    cout << "\e[42m";    break;
                case 9:     cout << "\e[41m";    break;
                default:    cout << "\e[0m";     break;
            }
            cout << charFromFile;
        }
        cout << "\e[0m";
        myFile.close();
    }
    else
        cout << "File not found!" << endl;

    return 0;
}
```

Chapter 12: Structures, pointers and memory

1. Increment a character pointer and access the data that it points to.

```
#include <iostream>
using namespace std;

int main()
{
    char symbols[10];
    for ( int i = 0;  i < 10;  i++ )
    {
        symbols[i] = '!' + i*3;
        cout << i << " - " << symbols[i] << endl;
    }

    char* pSymbol = &symbols[0];
    pSymbol++;     pSymbol++;     pSymbol++;
    cout << *pSymbol << endl;

    return 0;
}
```

2. Attempt to assign one pointer to another of a different type.

```
#include <iostream>
using namespace std;

int main()
{
    float quarter = 0.25;
    int ten = 10;

    float* pFloat = &quarter;
    int* pInt = &ten;
    pFloat = pInt;

    return 0;
}
```

Attempting to compile the program will result in an error. It is only possible to assign the value of one pointer to another if they both point to values that share the same data-type.

3. Attempt to use a pointer to change the value of a constant.

```
#include <iostream>
using namespace std;

int main()
{
    const int FIXED_PRICE = 1500;

    int* pPrice = (int*) &FIXED_PRICE;
    *pPrice = 1000;

    cout << *pPrice << endl;
    cout << FIXED_PRICE << endl;

    return 0;
}
```

Although the de-referenced value of **pPrice** is displayed as **1000**, the original value of **FIXED_PRICE** is unchanged.

```
void displayInReverse( person* pPersonToStartFrom )
{
    if ( pPersonToStartFrom != NULL )
    {
        if ( pPersonToStartFrom->pNextPerson != NULL )
            displayInReverse( pPersonToStartFrom->pNextPerson );

        cout << "\tName: " << pPersonToStartFrom->firstName;
        cout << "\tEmail: " << pPersonToStartFrom->emailAddress << endl;
    }
}
```

Additional code for the menu:

```
if ( choice == "reverse" )
    displayInReverse( pFirstPerson );
```

Chapter 13: Objects and classes

1. Declaration of class members for class `computer`

```
class computer
{
    private:
        string name;
        float speed_MHz;
        int megabytes_RAM;
        string storage_device;
        string operating_system;
};
```

2. Member functions for class `computer`

```
class computer
{
    private:
        string name;
        float speed_MHz;
        int megabytes_RAM;
        string storage_device;
        string operating_system;
    public:
        computer();

        computer( string new_name, float new_speed, int new_RAM,
                  string new_storage, string new_OS );

        void displaySpec();
};

// --------------------

computer::computer()
{
    name = "";
    speed_MHz = 0;
    megabytes_RAM = 0;
    storage_device = "";
    operating_system = "";
}

// --------------------
```

```
computer::computer( string new_name, float new_speed, int new_RAM,
                    string new_storage, string new_OS )
{
    name = new_name;
    speed_MHz = new_speed;
    megabytes_RAM = new_RAM;
    storage_device = new_storage;
    operating_system = new_OS;
}

// --------------------

void computer::displaySpec()
{
    cout << name << ", ";

    if ( speed_MHz >= 1000 )
    {
        cout << speed_MHz / 1000;
        cout << " GHz CPU, ";
    }
    else
    {
        cout << speed_MHz;
        cout << " MHz CPU, ";
    }

    if ( megabytes_RAM >= 1000 )
    {
        cout << megabytes_RAM / 1000;
        cout << " GB RAM, ";
    }
    else
    {
        cout << megabytes_RAM;
        cout << " MB RAM, ";
    }

    cout << storage_device << " storage, ";
    cout << "running " << operating_system << endl;
}
```

3. Overloaded << operator

```
#include <iostream>
#include <fstream>

using namespace std;

class computer
{
    private:
        string name;
        float speed_MHz;
        int megabytes_RAM;
        string storage_device;
        string operating_system;

    public:
        computer();

        computer( string new_name, float new_speed, int new_RAM,
                  string new_storage, string new_OS );

    friend ostream& operator<< ( ostream &outStream, computer &objectToDisplay );
};
```

```
// -------------------

computer::computer()
{
    name = "";
    speed_MHz = 0;
    megabytes_RAM = 0;
    storage_device = "";
    operating_system = "";
}

// -------------------

computer::computer( string new_name, float new_speed, int new_RAM,
                    string new_storage, string new_OS )
{
    name = new_name;
    speed_MHz = new_speed;
    megabytes_RAM = new_RAM;
    storage_device = new_storage;
    operating_system = new_OS;
}

// -------------------

ostream& operator<< ( ostream &outStream, computer &objectToDisplay )
{
    outStream << objectToDisplay.name << ", ";

    if ( objectToDisplay.speed_MHz >= 1000 )
    {
        outStream << objectToDisplay.speed_MHz / 1000;
        outStream << " GHz CPU, ";
    }
    else
    {
        outStream << objectToDisplay.speed_MHz;
        outStream << " MHz CPU, ";
    }

    if ( objectToDisplay.megabytes_RAM >= 1000 )
    {
        outStream << objectToDisplay.megabytes_RAM / 1000;
        outStream << " GB RAM, ";
    }
    else
    {
        outStream << objectToDisplay.megabytes_RAM;
        outStream << " MB RAM, ";
    }

    outStream << endl;

    outStream << objectToDisplay.storage_device << " storage, ";

    outStream << "running " << objectToDisplay.operating_system << endl << endl;

    return outStream;
}

// -------------------
```

```
int main()
{
    computer original_Pi( "R-Pi Model A", 750, 256,
                          "8 GB SD-card", "Debian Linux" );

    computer video_stream_Pi( "R-Pi 2 Model B", 900, 1000,
                              "16 GB Micro SD-card", "LibreELEC" );

    computer latest_Pi( "R-Pi Model 3", 1200, 1000,
                        "32 GB Micro SD-card", "Raspbian" );

    cout << original_Pi << endl;
    cout << video_stream_Pi << endl;
    cout << latest_Pi << endl;

    ofstream dataFile;

    dataFile.open( "pi-data" );

    dataFile << original_Pi;
    dataFile << video_stream_Pi;
    dataFile << latest_Pi;

    dataFile.close();

    return 0;
}
```

4.a Header file for class `computer` - *computer.h*

```
#ifndef _computer
#define _computer

#include <string>

using namespace std;

class computer
{
    private:
        string name;
        float speed_MHz;
        int megabytes_RAM;
        string storage_device;
        string operating_system;

    public:
        computer();

        computer( string new_name, float new_speed, int new_RAM,
                  string new_storage, string new_OS );

        friend ostream& operator<< ( ostream &outStream, computer &objectToDisplay );
};

#endif
```

```cpp
#include "computer.h"

#include <iostream>

using namespace std;

computer::computer()
{
    name = "";
    speed_MHz = 0;
    megabytes_RAM = 0;
    storage_device = "";
    operating_system = "";
}

// -------------------

computer::computer( string new_name, float new_speed, int new_RAM,
                    string new_storage, string new_OS )
{
    name = new_name;
    speed_MHz = new_speed;
    megabytes_RAM = new_RAM;
    storage_device = new_storage;
    operating_system = new_OS;
}

// -------------------

ostream& operator<< ( ostream &outStream, computer &objectToDisplay )
{
    outStream << objectToDisplay.name << ", ";

    if ( objectToDisplay.speed_MHz >= 1000 )
    {
        outStream << objectToDisplay.speed_MHz / 1000;
        outStream << " GHz CPU, ";
    }
    else
    {
        outStream << objectToDisplay.speed_MHz;
        outStream << " MHz CPU, ";
    }

    if ( objectToDisplay.megabytes_RAM >= 1000 )
    {
        outStream << objectToDisplay.megabytes_RAM / 1000;
        outStream << " GB RAM, ";
    }
    else
    {
        outStream << objectToDisplay.megabytes_RAM;
        outStream << " MB RAM, ";
    }

    outStream << endl;

    outStream << objectToDisplay.storage_device << " storage, ";

    outStream << "running " << objectToDisplay.operating_system << endl << endl;

    return outStream;
}
```

```cpp
#include "computer.cpp"

#include <iostream>

using namespace std;

int main()
{
    computer latest_Pi( "R-Pi Model 3", 1200, 1000,
                        "32 GB Micro SD-card", "Raspbian" );

    cout << latest_Pi << endl;

    return 0;
}
```

5. Inherited class `laptop`

```cpp
#include <iostream>

using namespace std;

class computer
{
    protected:
        string name;
        float speed_MHz;
        int megabytes_RAM;
        string storage_device;
        string operating_system;

    public:
        computer();
};

// -------------------

class laptop : public computer
{
    private:
        float screen_size;
        float weight_kg;

    public:
        laptop();

        laptop( string new_name, float new_speed, int new_RAM,
                string new_storage, string new_OS,
                float new_screen, float new_weight );

        void displaySpec();
};

// -------------------

computer::computer()
{
    name = "";
    speed_MHz = 0;
    megabytes_RAM = 0;
    storage_device = "";
    operating_system = "";
}
```

```cpp
// --------------------

laptop::laptop()
{
    screen_size = 0;
    weight_kg = 0;
}

// --------------------

laptop::laptop( string new_name, float new_speed, int new_RAM,
                string new_storage, string new_OS,
                float new_screen, float new_weight )
{
    name = new_name;
    speed_MHz = new_speed;
    megabytes_RAM = new_RAM;
    storage_device = new_storage;
    operating_system = new_OS;
    screen_size = new_screen;
    weight_kg = new_weight;
}

// --------------------

void laptop::displaySpec()
{
    cout << name << ", ";

    if ( speed_MHz >= 1000 )
    {
        cout << speed_MHz / 1000;
        cout << " GHz CPU, ";
    }
    else
    {
        cout << speed_MHz;
        cout << " MHz CPU, ";
    }

    if ( megabytes_RAM >= 1000 )
    {
        cout << megabytes_RAM / 1000;
        cout << " GB RAM";
    }
    else
    {
        cout << megabytes_RAM;
        cout << " MB RAM";
    }

    cout << endl;

    cout << storage_device << " storage, ";

    cout << "running " << operating_system << endl;

    cout << screen_size << " screen size" << ", ";

    cout << weight_kg << " kg" << endl << endl;
}
```

```
// -------------------

int main()
{
    laptop homeLaptop( "Dell Inspiron(TM)", 1600, 4096,
                       "500 GB HDD", "Ubuntu 16.04", 15.6, 2.2 );

    laptop workLaptop( "Toshiba Portege(TM)", 2700, 8192,
                       "100 GB SSD", "Windows 7", 12.5, 1.1 );

    homeLaptop.displaySpec();
    workLaptop.displaySpec();

    return 0;
}
```

Index

#define directive 107
#endif directive 107
#ifndef directive 107
#include directive.................... 52, 79, 88, 96, 106, 363

.bashrc Bash resources file................................. 532, 533

<cctype> library 199, 247
<cfloat> library..65
<climits> library............................... 63, 121
<cmath> library 147, 149
<cstdlib> library............................. 143, 429
<ctime> library 137
<fstream> library................................. 390
<iomanip> library................................. 110
<iostream> library 52, 88, 89, 96, 115, 199, 390, 429
<sstream> library 426
<string> library 73, 96
<unistd.h> library 103

A

a.out executable 23, 24, 26, 27, 29. 30
absolute path 391
access-specifier 486, 504
add-amount operator +=.............................132, 262, 266
addition operator + ... 261
ANSI 13, 17, 106
append..............................261-264, 266, 268, 332
append() member function for **string** class 267
argc argument count 310
argument 309, 310, 324, 332, 344, 348, 351, 352
argv array of argument values 309, 310
arithmetic expression 48, 197, 242
arithmetic operations 244
array 290-293, 352, 353, 412, 416
ASCII...........................67, 68, 151, 154, 168, 224, 225, 409
assembly.......................................88, 534, 535
assignment................................... 47, 81, 130
assignment operator =...................................... 130, 176
at() member function for **string** class...102, 189, 246

B

backslash character \ 68, 73, 98, 100
backspace character \b.......................... 67, 98, 104
BASIC programming language 16, 77, 529
best-case scenario...................................... 383

binary search........................... 374, 375, 376, 380, 383, 384
bitand operator 157, 161
bitor operator..................................... 157, 160
bit-wise **&** AND operator 161
bit-wise **^** XOR operator..................................... 157, 162
bit-wise **|** OR operator.................................. 157, 160
bit-wise **~** NOT operator....................................157
bit-wise operators 47, 157, 160-162, 165, 168
block...42
body...323
boolalpha manipulator...113
bool data-type...58
Boolean 48, 58, 157, 160-162, 183, 193, 196
brackets **()** 150, 197
break 235
bubble-sort... 353, 355
buffer 119-121, 391
Build option in Geany 29-32
byte 67, 447, 448

C

C# programming language....................................... 16, 17
c_str() member function for **string** class............423
calling functions 148, 324, 328, 330, 332, 336, 368-370
carriage-return character 98, 104
case..201
cast..136, 154, 155, 156, 243
cat command 393, 394, 396
char............................. 58, 67, 68, 69, 225, 242, 244, 251
character 58, 67, 68, 225
character code 67, 224, 243, 244, 249, 251
character set 67
cin channel-in.............. 115, 117, 119, 120, 123, 126, 390
class 484, 485, 486, 492, 498, 503, 510
clear() function...121, 428
close() function..391, 425
comma separated values (CSV) 420
comment **//** 20, 43, 44, 53
compare() member function for **string** class 260
compilation 20, 30-33, 52, 83, 101, 445, 534
compiler 18, 19, 20, 23
compl 159
compound statement..42, 174
conditional operator **?** 180, 206
const 60, 73
constant 60, 71, 73, 74, 75
constructor function.............485, 486, 488, 489, 491, 503

control character 67, 68
cout channel-out 88, 89, 92, 390, 501
C-style null-terminated string 309, 310, 423
curly braces **{ }** 42, 229

D

data member 438, 455, 483-487
data value 58
data-type 58-62, 71, 75, 426
Debian operating system 13, 18, 21, 542, 543
declaration 71
declaring variables 83
decrement operator **--** 130, 131
default 203
delete operator 470, 497, 498, 500
de-reference operator ***** 451
destructor function **~** 497, 498, 500
detached sort 461
dictionary file 403
directive **#** 52, 88, 364
divide operator **/** 136
division by zero 138
double data-type 58
double-backslash character **** 100
do-while 213, 215
dynamic data 446, 472, 498
dynamic memory 455, 462

E

e-notation 66
empty statement 234
empty string **" "** 69
end-of-line character **endl** 90, 97
equivalence operator **==** 47, 176, 259
erase() function 278, 279
error code 31, 35, 326, 453
error messages 25, 32, 33
escape-sequence 98, 101
executable 23, 24, 27, 30
execute 31
exponentiation 147
expression 45, 48, 52, 130, 196

F

file 390
file permissions 27
file-handling 390
find() member function for **string** class 271, 273
find_first_not_of() function 283, 285
find_first_of() function 284
fixed manipulator 112
float data-type 58, 65, 426
floating point number 58, 66
flow of execution 328, 329, 330, 354
flush character 102, 103, 104
for 219, 220, 221, 228, 229
forward declaration 362
friend access-specifier 501, 502
function 46, 328, 330, 347, 351, 352, 361, 488
function prototype 362
functions 322

G

garbage collection 231
GCC 13, 17, 18, 19, 542, 543
Geany 18, 22, 28, 29, 30, 31, 32, 33, 35, 84, 348, 542
get() function 401
getline() function 117, 401, 419, 420
global variable 232
good() function ... 123, 125, 126, 398, 399, 401, 422, 425

H

header file 106, 107, 363, 510, 512
heap 446, 450, 455, 456, 470-477, 497, 500

hexadecimal 224, 449, 536, 537
hex-dump 449, 536
hidden file 401, 532
high-level code 20
history file 400-402

I

identifier .. 52, 58, 63, 71, 74, 77-79, 91, 107, 447, 519, 525
if statement 40, 126, 168, 172, 175, 194, 526
if-else statement 40, 151, 183, 188, 193, 206
ifstream input file-stream 401
ignore() function 121
increment operator **++** 130-132, 225
indentation 49, 53
index 148, 246, 253, 273, 276, 290-297, 308
indirect access 451
infinite loop 233, 234, 525, 526
inheritance 503-513
inline function 366, 367
interpreted languages 16
ifstream input file-stream 424
input redirection operator **>>** 115
insert() member function for **string** class 274
insertion sort 356
instance, object 484, 489, 491, 509
instruction 40
int data-type 58, 60, 426
INT_MAX 63, 121
integer 58
ios::app append-to-file mode 396
is_open() stream function 425
isalpha() character function 199, 247
iscntrl() character function 247
isdigit() character function 199, 247, 429
islower() character function 247
ISO 13, 17, 31, 33, 543
isprint() character function 247
ispunct() character function 247
isspace() character function 247
isupper() character function 247
iteration 212

J

Java programming language 16, 29
JavaScript scripting language 16, 29

K

keyboard buffer 119, 121

L

length() member for **string** class 249, 252, 410
library 59, 79, 88, 96, 103, 107, 324, 364, 365, 513
linear search 302, 374, 384, 414
linked list... 462-469, 473
linker..363, 513, 530, 535
literal text 45, 68-70, 423, 535, 537
literal value 45, 48, 69, 130, 138, 212, 233, 455
LLVM compiler 13, 542
local value 351
local variable... 231, 324
logical OR operator **|| or**........................ 47, 186
logical AND operator **&& and**................47, 177, 183, 374
logical expression.. 48
logical shift operators **<< >>**................................ 165
long data-type 58, 61
low-level code........................... 20, 23, 27, 30, 33, 534, 535
ls command 393
LXTerminal... 31, 108

M

machine code..................................16, 18, 20, 23, 534-536
MacOS X operating system 13, 18, 542
main() function... 20
max() function 151
member 436
member function 246, 484, 485, 486
membership operator 249, 436
memory 72, 231, 251, 297, 328, 352, 445-477
memory address 352, 446, 447, 450, 451, 453
memory leak................................. 472, 497
memory location...446, 447, 453
Microsoft Visual C++ 17
min() function... 151
MinGW 18
mnemonic....................................... 534
modulus amount operator **%=** 245
modulus operator **%** 47, 142, 145, 179, 334
multi-dimensional array................................. 312
multiple inheritance.................................. 509
multiply operator ***** 134

N

named values.................................... 45, 46, 71
namespace...79
Nano text editor............................ 18, 21, 22, 26, 538, 542
negation..47
negation operator **!** 196
nested **if** statements.......................... 194
new operator.................................. 455, 465
new-line character **\n**............................. 98, 121
noboolalpha manipulator................................. 113
node.. 464
non-equivalence operator **!=** 47, 181
non-printable character 58, 67
not_eq operator 181
NULL value..454, 464, 470, 500
null character **\0** 98, 446, 447

null-terminated strings 423

O

object 484, 503
Objective-C programming language 17
ofstream output file-stream............................391, 501
one-dimensional array 314
open() function.......................... 391, 396, 423
Open-Source 17
operating system....................................... 13, 16, 17, 540
operator......................................45, 46, 47, 52, 501
operator overloading 501
operator-precedence 146, 148
ofstream output file-stream............................391, 424
output redirection operator **<<**..............................89, 92
output stream 391
overflow 62, 94

P

path...532
pathname...391
permissive compiling...231
pointer 446, 450, 453, 461, 462, 470, 500
pointer indirection 451
pointer-to-member operator **->**..........................455, 458
post-increment **++** 131
pow() power-of function.................................149, 151
pre-increment **++**............................131
pre-processor 79
printable characters 67
private access-specifier 486, 487, 502, 504, 514
procedure.......................................347
program 40
protected access-specifier 486, 504, 514
public access-specifier 485, 486, 487, 492, 504
Python programming language 16, 29

Q

quotation marks **"** 68

R

random numbers.....................................143
random() function 143, 145
Raspbian operating-system 18
real values 58, 65, 112, 113
recursion 368, 371
reference operator **&**.....................157, 352, 354, 448, 450
relational expression 48, 193
remainder 47, 142
replace() member function for **string** class 280, 281
reserved word 51, 78
return.. 35, 36, 325
returned value................................. 45, 46, 330, 332
rfind() member function for **string** class............271
run-time error 138

S

scope...488
scope-resolution operator **::** 89, 488
seed() function...144
segmentation fault 445, 453
semi-colon **;**..41

setprecision() manipulator function 112
setw() manipulator function.............................110, 111
short data-type 58, 61
single quote ' 242
sizeof() function 448
sleep() function...102, 103
source-code...20
source-code portability 16, 535
stack 328, 354, 368
stack overflow 368
standard namespace std 59, 79, 89, 91
Standard Template Library 513
statement...14, 40-46, 50, 51
static data.......................................445, 449, 455, 535, 537
static memory 446, 450, 455, 456, 495
static_cast 136, 156, 224, 243
str() member function for stringstream class....428
stream 88, 89, 110, 112, 113, 115, 117, 121, 390-392
stream manipulator...110
string data-type 59, 69, 70, 423, 425
stringstream.................................. 426, 427, 428, 429
struct structure.................436, 437, 440, 444, 455, 482
substr() member function for string class 275
subtract-amount operator -= 132
sub-string 271, 273, 276, 277
swap() member for string class 285, 286, 355
swapping values 82
switch................................... 200, 201, 203, 256
Symbols pane in Geany...348, 491
syntax...16, 23
syntax-highlighting 29

T

tab character \t 67, 73, 99, 416, 419
text editor 16, 18, 21, 22, 28, 29, 348, 491, 542
text string 59, 423
tilde character ~ 68, 345, 498
time() function 137, 144

token 284, 519
tolower() character function.......................... 168, 257
toupper() character function........... 168, 237, 332, 373
translation 16, 534
two-dimensional array... 314- 316

U

Ubuntu operating system 13, 538, 543
underscore character _..................................... 71, 77
UNICODE characters 67
uninitialized variables 72, 83, 453
unsigned prefix..60, 61, 250
unsigned long data-type 61
unsigned long long data-type 61, 339
using... 79
usleep() function... 109

V

validation..!.............. 138, 271
variable.........................47, 60, 61, 65, 68, 70-75, 93, 332
vertical-tab character \v 98, 99
void...327, 347, 349
volatile.. 390

W

-Wall compiler option.............................30, 32, 33, 83
warning messages........................... 30, 33, 34, 35, 83, 94
wchar_t data-type 67
while... 216, 217
white-space 52, 111
wild-card.. 406, 408

X

xxd command...449, 536, 537

Z

zero-indexing 246, 253, 275, 291

Printed in Great Britain
by Amazon